Economic Theory and Marketing Practice

Angela Hatton
and
Michael Oldroyd

Published on behalf of
the Chartered Institute of Marketing

BUTTERWORTH
HEINEMANN

Butterworth-Heinemann Ltd
Linacre House, Jordan Hill, Oxford OX2 8DP

 PART OF REED INTERNATIONAL BOOKS

OXFORD   LONDON   BOSTON
MUNICH   NEW DELHI   SINGAPORE   SYDNEY
TOKYO   TORONTO   WELLINGTON

First published 1992

British Library Cataloguing in Publication Data
Hatton, Angela
  Economic theory and marketing practice.
  I. Title II. Oldroyd, Michael
  380.1

ISBN 0 7506 0241 4

Composition by Genesis Typesetting, Laser Quay, Rochester, Kent
Printed and bound in Great Britain by Thomson Litho Ltd, East Kilbride, Scotland

Contents

Preface

Economics is an immensely valuable support subject to those studying and working in the area of business and particularly marketing. As a relatively new subject, marketing has developed by borrowing heavily from the older, more established business disciplines. The contribution made by economics has been particularly significant.

This book has been designed to address the needs of those students of business and marketing who are studying economics. The prime focus of the book is students of the Chartered Institute of Marketing (CIM), but many business students will find our marketing oriented approach to economics valuable and easy to relate to their business studies.

Our experience as examiners for the Chartered Institute of Marketing has led us to the conclusion that a significant number of students do not, even at the end of their studies, appreciate the importance and relevance of economics, to their work as marketers or to the general management of business. Our objective in compiling this book was to make the value and contribution of economics clear.

In the past we have found it difficult to recommend a single economics textbook that meets the needs of marketing students throughout their economics course. Such students are often mature business professionals, with considerable experience of business and therefore national economic issues. Introductory economic texts often fail to cover macroeconomic issues in a sophisticated and descriptive enough way to allow business people to build easily on their current knowledge. Unfortunately more advanced texts provide complex analysis of the micro concepts, which in the limited study time available prove too difficult for many marketing students to appreciate completely.

In writing this text for a clearly identified student group, we have been able to address this problem by producing the material in two distinct parts:

- **Part I**, the micro section, provides a simple examination of the theory and concepts of economics. The material is presented under sections covering the marketing mix variables, and reviews the economists' contribution to each of these marketing tools.
- **Part II**, the macro section, presents a descriptive analysis of the economy and the factors that make up the macro-environment in which business operates. Issues that are of particular importance to the marketer, such as population changes, are highlighted. An understanding of the workings of the economy and an appreciation of how government policy impacts on business are provided in detail that will help readers to develop their existing knowledge and appreciate the wealth of economic information and data so readily available to business and in the media.

Summary reviews, activities and projects

Economics is not a dry, academic subject to be learnt by rote. We are all practising economists, making economic decisions daily about how to spend our limited incomes. It is also a real and dynamic dimension of business, which managers must understand and take into account when planning. To help you appreciate and build on your current economic expertise and achieve the necessary competence in the subject, you will be encouraged to play an active part in your study. You will find examples, illustrations and activities throughout the book helping you to link the theory and concepts of economics to business and marketing activities.

Glossary

Every subject has its own jargon. Your familiarity with a topic is often judged by the ease with which you use the appropriate abbreviations and language. Economics is no exception, using not only terminology with which you may not be familiar, but also commonly used terms in very specific ways. To help you cope with this 'new language', you will find that at the beginning of every chapter we have included a brief glossary of the economic terms you will meet within that chapter.

Although these terms are explained and defined fully at the appropriate point in the text, we feel it helps the student's understanding to have some sense of concepts and meanings before working through any material. We recommend that you spend a few minutes familiarizing yourself with any new terms and checking the economist's definition of more commonly used words, before starting each section.

Using this book

We have written this book to help support your study of economics; it should be used in conjunction with lectures, distance learning materials and teaching notes. Textbooks are not designed to be read like a novel, starting at page 1 and passively reading through page by page. Although we have compiled the material in a logical sequence, it can also be delved into to support the lecture order and programme devised by your tutors.

Use the material here as, when and how it can best support your studies. Reinforce your learning by reading a good newspaper or a periodical such as the *Economist* regularly, and make a note of the main economic developments that have an impact on you personally, influence the organization you work for and affect your country during the months of your course. You will find many TV and radio programmes provide excellent coverage of economic issues, and as you gain a better understanding of the basic concepts, so these will become an invaluable way of developing your economic competence still further.

More detailed advice on further reading can be found in the final section of the book.

Angela Hatton
Michael Oldroyd

Acknowledgements

Special thanks are due to Karen, Mandy, Frances and Nicky for all their work typing the manuscript and to our immediate families; Karen, Rebecca and Dave for their support and encouragement.

Angela Hatton
Michael Oldroyd

PART I
MICROECONOMICS

Section One
Introduction

The aim of this relatively short introductory section is to help you to set the scene for your study of economics and clarify the relationship between economics and marketing. Throughout your work as a marketer you will find yourself returning to many of the basic principles and concepts of economic theory, and as a manager you will be making decisions that have to be based on an informed appreciation of the wider economic environment in which you operate. By examining the links between these two subjects at the outset of your studies you will be better able to identify for yourself the value and relevance of economic theory to your activities as a marketer and to your functions in business.

Understanding the foundations and development of any subject that is new to you is an important first step. We have taken the opportunity of using this section to examine not only the basis and relevance of economics, but also the development of marketing.

There are two chapters in this first section:

- *Chapter 1 Economics and marketing*
- *Chapter 2 The economic problem*

The aims of this section are to:

- Examine the value and scope of economics.
- Identify the common ground between economics and marketing.
- Provide a framework to allow readers to assess their practical competence as economists.
- Examine the marketing approach to resolving the economic problem and the economists' view of the development of marketing.

1
Economics and marketing

- What do economics and marketing have in common?
- Why should a student of business and marketing have an understanding of economics?
- How can the theoretical models of the economist benefit those working in the real dynamic world of marketing?

Aims

These questions are typical of those commonly asked by business and marketing students faced, for the first time, with the subject of economics. Besides addressing them, the aims of this introductory chapter are to examine the common ground between these two business disciplines by:

1 Examining the links between economics and marketing.
2 Considering the contribution economics can make to marketing.
3 Examining the economist's view of the development of marketing.

Glossary

Consumption – means the using up of goods and services, but in macroeconomics it is used to describe the spending of the household sector of the economy.

Customer orientation – the company is focused on the needs of the customer.

Macroeconomics – the branch of economics that studies the economy as a whole, how it operates, and factors such as inflation and unemployment, which affect it. Macroeconomics is dealt with in depth in Part II of this book.

Marketing concept – the business philosophy and attitude of management that put the customer first and form the foundation of a marketing approach to business.

Positive economics – economic theories formulated on the basis of observed facts, which can then be rigorously tested against those facts.

Product orientation – a management approach based on primary concern with the product and the operation.

Sales orientation – goods are produced and management's main concern is the selling of that output.

Social cost – cost to society resulting from the actions of an individual or a business in pursuit of their own needs.

Economics and marketing – common and uncommon grounds

Before you start

How much common ground can you identify between economics and marketing? Take 10 minutes and draw up a list of all the similarities between them and refer to it as you work through this chapter.

At first it may seem that there are more differences than similarities between the two subjects:

- Economics is one of the oldest business disciplines, whereas marketing is one of the newest. Economics is a mature subject. The first major academic text on economics was Adam Smith's *Wealth of Nations*, published in 1776, and a great deal of study has been undertaken since. Marketing is relatively underdeveloped. It is an invention of this century, only newly recognized as a relevant business function in many sectors of economic activity.
- Economics is a science. As with the natural sciences, it deals mainly with positive statements, i.e. ones backed by fact derived from observation. Positive economic theories are formulated so as to be rigorously testable against those facts. Marketing, on the other hand, is more an art than a science. The theory of marketing has been developed by borrowing extensively from other, more established business and behavioural subjects. Its body of knowledge has not yet been adequately synthesized to enable it to be considered a science.

Creativity is a highly valued characteristic in the marketer. There are no recipes for success, only a collection of tools and techniques to be used with skill, judgement and experience. Like any practical craft, marketing cannot be learned only from a textbook, but must be practised. This characteristic is highlighted by a recent description of marketing by the American marketing guru Philip Kotler: 'Marketing takes two hours to learn and a lifetime to master'.

- Economic models are based upon assumptions that to the casual observer may appear unrealistic and theoretical. Marketing is more likely to be viewed as a highly pragmatic subject. It proposes a practical approach to business management.

Does this positioning of the two subjects reflect your perception of them?

Those whose first impressions are of two subjects, as in Figure 1.1, positioned poles apart may make the mistake of looking no further into economics. They are likely to wonder why they are required to study it, and be tempted to dismiss the subject as theoretical, impractical or irrelevant to the business person.

Such an assessment would be a mistake. Those who take the time to look more closely will find the subjects have a lot in common, and that economic theory has important contributions to make to marketing. An understanding of its concepts and principles can be of real benefit to the marketing practitioner.

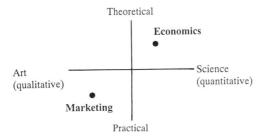

Figure 1.1 *Positioning map of economics and marketing*

Marketing's roots lie in economics. Both subjects are about people and markets and are concerned with consumer behaviour and a study of the exchange process.

Economics provides the models that demonstrate the principles of demand and supply, examining and analysing choices made by individuals, firms and communities. The theoretical models of the economist provide an invaluable insight into the workings of the market. The concepts, knowledge and skills of the economist underpin the marketer's understanding of consumer behaviour and the role of marketing activities. Marketers 'borrowed' these models and principles as the foundation for their subject, developing and managing strategies to help the business match demand and supply, thus providing them with a solid framework as a basis from which the art of marketing can be practised.

Besides the very specific contribution economics makes to marketing, it also provides an understanding of the economic environment, which is essential to all business people. Strategies are developed and implemented against the background of a rapidly changing economic environment. Forecasting and pro-active management depend on a thorough grasp of the underlying principles and dynamics of the economy. Macroeconomic theory provides the business person with an insight into the dynamics of that business environment.

Although easily criticized for its unrealistic 'assumptions' and lack of 'working in the real world', the predictions of economic theory tend to hold true in general terms, and its contribution to marketing and business cannot be ignored and should not be under-estimated. Its first real contribution can be in providing the marketer with an explanation as to why marketing is such a new function of business.

The development of marketing – the economists' view

If you do not produce what people want to buy, you will go out of business. This essence of marketing seems so obvious and fundamental that it is easy to dismiss it as nothing but common sense.

Way back in 1776, in that first major economic text *The Wealth of Nations*, Adam Smith wrote, 'The sole end purpose of production is consumption'. It seems that even the earliest economists would find nothing in the philosophy of marketing to disagree with; and yet it took nearly 200 more years before the philosophy of marketing was recognized by business. Marketers do need to understand why their function, apparently so critical and so obvious back in 1776, has only come into the arena of business so recently.

Why has marketing not been practised as long as economics?

Activity

First take the time to clarify your own knowledge and experience of the dynamics of the marketplace and how changes affect the customer. Markets are made up of buyers and sellers, and the balance of power in the market depends on how many of each there are.

1 Imagine a market where there is a sudden shortage of supply.
   How might you expect such a change to affect:
      (a) the product sold,
      (b) its price,
      (c) the level of customer service.
   Does your assessment change if the shortage is expected to last a long time rather than a few weeks?

2 What if in the same market there was a sudden glut of goods available?

See how your predictions relate to the changing attitude of business as the balance of demand and supply shifts.

The tardiness of marketing to become an accepted business function can be explained by examining the development of the marketing concept. This is best done through an economist's assessment of the changing dynamics of the marketplace, which over time have resulted in fundamental changes in the culture of business organizations. These stages can be seen by looking at the economic development of a country such as the UK from pre-Industrial Revolution (IR) times or by considering the development of an industry from its inception through to maturity.

Product orientation

The first stage of development is characteristically one where the latent demand is greater than the available supply. This was the case in pre- and early post-IR days, and it is also the situation faced by the first company to launch a new, innovative product on the market.

Such a scenario allows those producers operating in the market to take a rather sanguine view of their business. There are plenty of customers around, so there is little motivation to be overly concerned with whether or not they are satisfied with the products being made available to them.

If one customer does not like the product, its quality, colour or performance, someone else will be glad to have it. There is no customer choice and there is no need to offer one. Customers beat a path to your door, *not* because your products are necessarily good, but because they are in short supply. This is a *sellers' market*. It exists when there is more demand than supply in a marketplace. In such a situation you can expect firms to be charging high prices and making excess profits, but choice, service and customer care to be minimal or non-existent. The business is run around the needs of the operation and the staff, and scant attention is paid to the customers.

The service and professional sectors in the UK have been protected from competition until very recently, and examples of this product-oriented philosophy of management can still be seen. For example it is not many years since:

1 Banks had restricted opening hours, closing early to allow staff time to balance the books at the end of the day.
2 Hospitals woke patients up early to suit the needs of the nursing staff.
3 Colleges were shut for long periods to allow staff vacations.

Changes in all these sectors have resulted from changed levels of competition, often precipitated by changes in legislation. Increased supply and more customer choice are leading to a change of attitude and new methods of operation in these previously product-oriented sectors.

But marketers need to recognize that, while operating in a marketplace where there is more demand than supply, it is legitimate for business managers to concern themselves with the operation and product. If the firm wishes to sell more or make more profit under these conditions, it simply needs to produce more. Logically, emphasis should therefore be on production, and managers can justify a product-oriented attitude to business.

Sales orientation

However, unless there are some restrictions on new firms entering a market, organizations have seldom been able to maintain a sellers' market for long. Attracted by high profits, new firms and therefore more resources will move into the industry. On top of this there is increased output from those already in the industry who have been concentrating on improved production processes in order to take advantage of their waiting list of customers. These two trends combine to change the conditions of the market, increasing the supply of available goods.

Eventually demand and supply become more evenly balanced. Waiting lists dwindle and the queues of potential customers vanish. To survive in such an environment the firm has to ensure that its products reach the customers who are in the market. Management's attention is now diverted from production to distribution and promotion. The firm will be successful as long as it is able to push its products into the marketplace. Gradually management's approach changes to a philosophy of sales orientation.

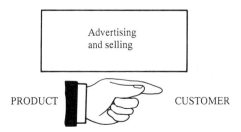

Figure 1.2 *Product- and sales-oriented business focus*

This management culture is often confused with a marketing orientation, because advertising and selling, two of the functions of marketing, are so important to the sales-oriented manager. The fundamental difference between the two is the role of the customer. At both product- and sales-oriented stages the organization decides what to make and pushes its offering to the customer. This sales-oriented attitude can be seen in the famous quotation from Henry Ford, 'They can have any colour they want, so long as it's black'. Still very little attention is paid to what the customer wants. See Figure 1.2.

Customer orientation

Conditions in the marketplace are always changing; new technology and increased competition from home and overseas means that supply has a tendency to continue to increase. As it does so, the balance of power in the market continues to shift in favour of the customer. Once supply is greater than demand, there is a *buyers' market*.

There are more goods available than customers to buy them. Survival depends on the organization's ability to ensure its products are those selected by the increasingly scarce customers. The most effective method of addressing this problem is to ask customers exactly what they need before committing resources to production. This emphasis on the customer is the management orientation that is at the core of the marketing concept. The customer now comes before the production process, not after it. See Figure 1.3.

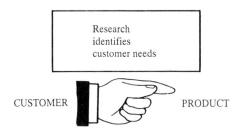

Figure 1.3   *Marketing-oriented business focus*

Once this economic situation is recognized and the marketing approach adopted, the whole culture within the organization will alter. There will be an appreciation of the truth behind Adam Smith's words. For a firm to stay in business and for employees' jobs to be safe, there have to be customers who want to buy the products being produced.

Although this view just seems common sense in a competitive environment, it is important for marketers to understand the parameters within which customer orientation is a valid philosophy for management to adopt (see Figure 1.4). When one reviews the stages of management development, the driving force for change can be clearly identified as a change in the balance of power in the marketplace. Only when supply exceeds demand is a marketing approach the best way of ensuring business survival. As these market conditions have only existed in the Western World over recent decades, it can be seen why marketing is such a relatively new addition to the manager's toolbox.

It is equally important for the marketer to recognize that customers needs and priorities continue to change. Therefore there are pressures on marketing to continue to evolve and develop in order to meet these changing demands.

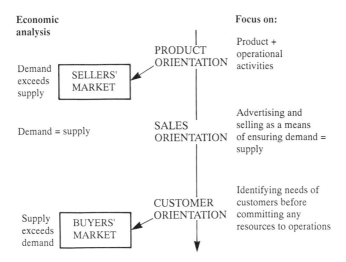

Figure 1.4 *The changing focus of management philosophy*

Growing concerns with the environment and social costs arising from the process of providing goods to satisfy individual needs and wants have caused marketers to modify their definition of marketing. The wider **Societal marketing concept** put forward by Philip Kotler demands that business provides goods and services that satisfy the individual and meet the objectives of the organization, but are not damaging in the long run to either the individual or society as a whole.

So marketing is a new business approach, still evolving and changing and with many sectors of business only just beginning to evaluate the contribution it can make to them. Economics, on the other hand, is one of the oldest business disciplines, more theoretical but dealing with many of the same issues.

Summary review

1 List the major economic changes over the last 2 years that have had a significant impact on the prosperity of a business sector you are familiar with.

2 Sit down with a quality Sunday newspaper and identify how many articles have an economic theme.

3 Consider the following products and services:
- High street banking
- Local library services
- Women's magazines
- Video cassette recorders
- Dentistry
- Children's toys
- Breakfast cereals
- Organic vegetables

For each identify what you think is the current balance of demand and supply and the prevailing philosophy of management within that sector. Make a list of evidence to support your assessment.

2
The economic problem

This chapter examines the rationale of economics as a discipline and considers the contribution that marketing has made in the quest for a solution to the economic problem.

Aims

The aims of this chapter are:

- To define the economic problem and the role of economics.
- To consider how that same economic problem is experienced by individuals, firms and countries.
- To examine alternative approaches that countries can adopt in their efforts to resolve the economic problem.
- To consider the economic problem from the marketing perspective.

Glossary

Direct taxation – a tax levied on and payable by a person or company, which cannot be passed on to a third party, e.g. income tax.

The economic problem – a universal problem, resulting from the finite and limited resources that are available to satisfy the unlimited needs and wants of people.

Market economy – a system that allows decisions to be made by the marketplace, and where resources are owned privately.

Microeconomics – the branch of economics that examines the economic behaviour of individuals and firms. These topics are covered in detail in the first part of the book.

Mixed economy – the real world compromise, combining aspects of the planned and market approach.

Normative economics – not testable against observed facts alone, but including an element of opinion and social judgement.

Planned economic system – an economy where all the resources are owned collectively, and economic decisions are made centrally.

Production possibility curve – this is a curve which represents the various combinations of two products or types of product (like weapons and food, or public and private sector output) which can be provided from the same number of resources.

Resources – this term is used to refer generally to the factors of production necessary to make goods and services: land, labour, capital and enterprise.

Defining economics

To come to understand the shared roots of marketing and economics, it is necessary to examine their foundations and to clarify exactly what each is concerned with.

Economics is a social science concerned with finding solutions to the *economic problem*. This problem is universal and exists because the needs of individuals and societies are infinite but the resources available to them are limited. Economics is concerned with how these scarce resources can and should be allocated, so that the most benefit is derived from them.

Just as in your role as a consumer you are experienced in marketing, so as an individual you may be surprised to find you are also an expert and practising economist. The word economics is derived from Greek and means the management of the household, a craft we are all experienced in.

Each of us has a mental checklist of things we need and want, perhaps a new car or a holiday in America, shoes for your children or a night out with your partner. Just how many items on your shopping list can be bought is determined by the resources available to you – your income. You may own property or shares, you make decisions about how much to spend and how much to save, and about the value of qualifications to your future career potential, and whether to let out your spare room to a lodger or not. You are constantly engaged in the process of solving your own personal economic problems: prioritizing needs, making choices and allocating your income in a way that provides you with as much satisfaction as possible.

Similar choices have to be made by firms, which only have so many machines, workers, space and managers available to them. They have to decide what goods to produce and who to produce them for. Managers have to make decisions about how best to use these available resources to get the most benefit or return for the organization.

When we are looking at the economic problem as faced by individuals or firms, we are looking at *microeconomics*. Micro being derived from the Greek word for small, this branch of economics puts parts of the economic system 'under the microscope' to gain an understanding of how they work. Another part of economics looks at how the complete system operates. It deals with aggregates or totals, and considers how the country as a whole goes about solving the economic problem – this is *macroeconomics*.

The essence of the problem facing the nation is really no different to that facing the individual – unlimited wants and needs, e.g. for improved roads, better schools, upgraded health care, more community services, but limited resources. In total the resources of the whole community are determined by the factors of production available to it: the quantity and quality of its land, labour, capital and enterprise. How best to use these available resources to provide maximum benefits for the community as a whole is the macroeconomic problem.

Alternative solutions to the national economic problem

All countries and communities are faced with this same economic problem – caused by a relative scarcity of the resources of land, labour, capital and enterprise. This combination of unlimited needs and wants and insufficient resources means that important decisions and choices have to be made.

For the country as a whole, solving the economic problem boils down to answering three basic questions:

- What to produce?
- How to produce it?
- Who gets to consume the goods and services produced?

An additional dimension of time needs to be added to these decisions. Should we produce goods for immediate consumption, or produce goods now that will lead to increased production and therefore consumption in the future?

There is a general consensus amongst all societies about the objectives we should be trying to achieve in the resolution of the first two of these questions. All countries wish to produce as many goods and services as they can, i.e. make the most efficient use of their available resources.

Figure 2.1 represents a production possibility curve. This illustrates the combination of public and private sector goods this community can produce with its given level of resources. Any combination on the curve indicates it has satisfied the first of these objectives and is producing as much as possible. Production at point Z would indicate that it is not making efficient use of its resources, and is worse off than it need be.

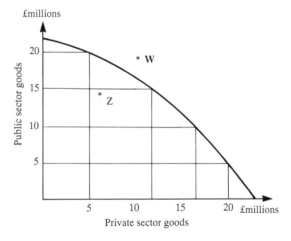

Figure 2.1   *Production possibility curve*

Point W represents a desired objective, when we can produce more output with our available resources. This requires economic growth, investment to improve the quality of our inputs, e.g. innovation to improve the technology of capital, or training the ability of our workforce.

Secondly, these goods and services should be ones that yield the maximum benefit to the people in the community. In other words, resources should not be wasted on goods that have a low priority in the country's list of needs. We do not want to produce guns if the community would derive more benefit from better health care, or more cornflakes if it would prefer baked beans. Marketing research has an important role to play in helping to identify what people's needs and priorities are and how these are changing.

It is the third of the questions that brings about wide variations of opinion and debate. Put in its most basic form, it is a question of income distribution, and views are many and varied, reflecting a wide spectrum of political opinion and social values. If the economist says how the reflecting a wide spectrum of political opinion and social values. If the economist says how the wealth of the community should be divided, he/she is making a 'normative' statement, which cannot be supported scientifically and implies that a value judgement has been made.

Statements such as 'Teachers should be paid more' are normative statements. The objective economist should try to remain outside the politics of such decisions and instead provide the decision-makers with 'positive' statements of the implications of decisions:

- If teachers' pay is increased by x per cent, direct taxation would have to go up by y pence in the £.
- If teachers' pay does not go up, fewer teachers will be attracted to the profession, and the shortage of teachers by 1995 is forecast to be 4,000.

Alternative economic systems

Although the economic problem is the same, alternative strategies or systems for its resolution have been developed. The extremes of these now represent theoretical models hardly ever found in their pure forms. In practice countries have ended up adopting aspects from both models. The combination is known as a *mixed economic system*.

An examination of the two alternative models, the *planned or command economy* and the *market economy*, allows a better understanding of the characteristics and variations of the mixed economic model.

The planned/command economy

This economic model works in much the same way as individuals go about solving their problems. The resources available are identified and assessed and the list of needs and wants compiled and prioritized.

An approach that works well for the individual is much less successful when applied to the whole country. Resources have to be owned and controlled centrally, and it is practically impossible to be able centrally to monitor and measure the changing pattern of customer needs and priorities.

Under such a system the economic questions are characteristically answered by:

- 5-year and 10-year plans, which determine *what* goods are to be produced. The plans are based on a bureaucratic assessment of what goods and services will be of most benefit to the community collectively.
- Resources are allocated to meet State objectives. Production is managed and controlled centrally. Individual choice and freedom of occupation are unlikely to exist.
- Output is allocated according to decisions made by the government. The ideal may be an equal distribution of income, but some groups, such as those with political control, may get more. There is, however, unlikely to be reward for additional effort, so there is little motivation to work harder.

The planned economy has its disadvantages. Many of these have been evident in the rationale for the Eastern bloc countries' desire to adopt a more market-based economic system, but it also has its advantages and these should not be overlooked.

Table 2.1   Planned economy

Advantages	Disadvantages
Allocation of resources can reflect some order of social priority. Welfare goods, such as health, education and defence, can be provided.	Production decisions made centrally tend to be inflexible and slow to respond to changing customer needs.
Social costs, such as combating pollution, can be reduced and accounted for.	Resources are wasted on an extensive bureaucracy. Red tape and committees slow down decision-making, and centralized marketing research and planning and control use up scarce resources.
Resources are not 'wasted' on competition and marketing.	Difficulties in central co-ordination lead to frequent bottlenecks, caused by resource or material shortages in a sector.
	Lack of profit motive and incentives result in low productivity levels.

Table 2.1 highlights the pros and cons of a planned economy.

As countries in the Eastern bloc and China, which we have traditionally labelled as operating planned economies, adopt more of the features of market economies, using them as examples becomes less and less appropriate. They also carry with them a political dimension that may distract you from the purely economic merits and demerits of the approach.

An alternative illustration of a planned system in operation is an economy at war, e.g. the UK in the Second World War:

1 Government took over the factors of production.
   Factories were taken over, and labour conscripted and allocated to roles that the government chose.
2 Decisions on what goods the country needed were made centrally according to war objectives and priorities set by the Cabinet.
3 Goods were allocated on an equal basis by rationing.

In times of national crisis it can be seen that in order to achieve an overriding national objective central orchestration of the economic process is the most valid and widely adopted approach.

The market economy

At the opposite extreme lies the economic model that is most often associated with capitalism – the market economy. Here the economic problem is not tackled centrally, but addressed by allowing individual customers and firms to make decisions in their own best interests.

Individuals choose goods that will give them the most satisfaction, and the firm makes decisions that will maximise its profitability.

Collectively this pursuance of self-interest will ensure firms use resources most economically and channel them into areas that represent the greatest profit, reflecting customer demand. Should customers' priorities change, a decrease in the amount demanded will be immediately signalled through the price mechanism. As prices and profits fall, resources will be reallocated.

In its extreme form the market system calls for a *laissez faire* economic policy of government: no involvement and no intervention. It is not surprising to find that, although this system offers merits missing in a planned approach, there are some difficulties inherent in it. See Table 2.2.

Table 2.2 Market economy

Advantages	Disadvantages
The system is flexible, channelling resources to areas of high demand and away from goods not wanted.	Unequal distribution of income means resources may be attracted to the profitable production of luxury goods for the rich, rather than necessities for the majority.
The system is automatic; no resources wasted in its operation	There will be an inadequate supply of merit goods, such as health, education and defence.
There are incentives for both the individual and the firm to increase output.	Individuals and firms seeking to maximize their own best interest may act against the interest of the community as a whole, resulting in heavy social costs, congestion, pollution, etc.
Shortages of commodities are less likely, as the gap between planned and actual consumption does not exist.	The system will only ensure automatic optimum allocation of resources if the market is perfectly competitive. Large powerful producers, such as monopolists, can prevent the market mechanism operating.
	If production is all in the hands of small competitive firms, there will be no increased efficiency from exploiting improved economies of scale.

A comparison of the two models shows how the disadvantages of one system are frequently the advantages of the other. It is therefore hardly surprising to find that in practice most governments have sought to get the best of both worlds by adopting a mixed system.

A mixed economy

In a mixed economy the planned approach is represented by the activities of the public sector and the market system by the private. The consistency of a country's mix can be determined by identifying what percentage of the country's output (wealth) is controlled by the public sector. A decade of Thatcherism, with its policies of privatization and market-based policies, saw the UK mix change dramatically, as the nationalised industry sector shrank to a third of the size it had been in 1979.

The public sector is financed through taxation and government borrowing. The amount of direct and indirect taxation taken from households and business, plus the amount that the government borrows, represent most of the purchasing power the government is going to allocate on your behalf. In other words this is how much that is available to spend on public sector goods and services.

Marketers should remember that the public sector represents the single biggest customer in the UK and in many other countries, with spending on public and merit goods like law and order, defence, health, education and social services. The common criticisms made of the public sector reflect the weaknesses of the planned system of resource allocation – bureaucratic, inefficient, unresponsive. Recent changes to the operation of the public sector, discussed in more detail in Chapter 8, have sought to address some of these shortcomings by encouraging more competition in the form of competitive tendering and a more customer-oriented approach from management.

The private sector supplies goods to the marketplace according to the decisions of individual firms. In practice they are unlikely to be profit maximizers. The risks of strategies of profit maximization do not ensure a firm's survival, and where the ownership and management of an organization is split, survival is likely to be the overriding consideration. Profits that will satisfy shareholders, and business plans which have taken into account changes in the marketplace, represent the survival goals of many managers.

Operating a mixed economic system is not without its own difficulties. The balance between the two sectors determines what difficulties the economy is likely to suffer. If there is too big a public sector, as in the UK before 1979, the problems are likely to be those of the planned economy. Too many resources in private sector control, and the country is faced with the limitations characteristic of a market economy.

Figure 2.1 indicates the production possibilities between the two sectors, and the alternative combinations of private and public sector mix possible between the two extreme systems.

Marketing's view of the economic problem

At both micro and macro level the role of economics is to examine the processes in action and look for possible solutions to the economic problem. In this respect marketing has a contribution to make to economics. In essence the marketing philosophy represents a practical solution, which attempts to solve the economic problem at a micro level. Both private and public sector organizations can be seen to be increasingly taking the marketing option.

Marketing is also about resource allocation. It is a business function, so it is concerned with the economic problem of the firm – how the organization can get the maximum benefit from its limited resources. The critical factor to ensure survival and success of the organization is to prevent resources being wasted.

The role of marketing research

Waiting for changes in demand to signal the customers' changed tastes and wants is not an acceptable option. Firms use the tool of marketing research to help them identify and anticipate customer needs, so that they can respond pro-actively in the marketplace – thus further reducing the risk of business failure. The firm needs to ensure that what it produces will be demanded. The marketing solution to the economic problem is to find out what customer needs are before committing any resources to production. See Figure 2.2.

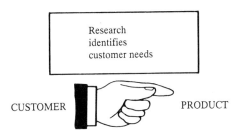

Figure 2.2   *The role of research*

   By carefully identifying a group of customers and researching their needs, the firm can use its skills and resources to provide products and services that will offer those customers benefits they will find satisfy their needs. The philosophy of marketing is simply to put the customer first.
   In doing this, both the firm and the individual will benefit from 'mutually profitable exchange'. Resources will not be wasted. The customers' needs are satisfied and the organization achieves its various objectives.
   It should be noted that although economists usually assume that the firm will make decisions to maximize its profits, this is not the only objective found among organizations. Marketing can therefore be used to help achieve any stated and quantified objective. It could be to sell x more or to increase revenue by $£y$, but it may equally well be to maximize donations if it is a charity, or to increase the utilization of its facilities by $z\%$ if it is, say, the public library. Increasingly the non-profit-making public sector is turning to a marketing solution to resolve its economic problem.
   In Section Two, we shall be taking a more detailed look at what economics says about how the individual solves the economic problem and makes his/her purchase decisions.

Summary review

1 Spend 10 minutes brainstorming a list of all the goods and services provided for you, without direct payment, by the public sector. On what basis are these allocated?

2 If you were in government and faced with more and more instances of water shortages during the summer months, what alternatives would be available to you to resolve these difficulties? What would be the advantages and disadvantages of each of your suggestions?

3 If a country decided to abolish money, what decisions would now have to be taken centrally? What difficulties might you expect to arise from such a move?

Section One: Project

The country is facing an election. One party is proposing we abandon our current mixed economic system for a planned approach, the other that we move to a totally market-based model.

Choose one of the parties and prepare a list of the key points which should be included in the manifesto to help convince the public to vote for you.

Section Two
The product

The 'P' of Product is a critical element of the marketing mix, yet it can be taken for granted. Its influence in the decision-making process can be under-estimated when considered against the more 'glamorous' 'P' of Promotion or the more dynamic issues of price and distribution. We will do something to redress that imbalance by taking the Product as the first 'P' in the economists' view of the marketing mix.

The marketers' appreciation of the dynamics of the marketplace – what demand is, and how it can be influenced – represents the essence of the marketing activity. This is a significant area where economics has a substantial contribution to make to the marketers' knowledge and understanding. In this section we will aim:

- To evaluate the economists' view of consumer behaviour and decision-making.
- To identify and consider the marketing implications arising from this view.
- To examine and understand the dynamics of the market mechanism, by which customers signal their needs to suppliers, and resources are allocated.
- To consider the strengths and practical limitations of a market-led approach.
- To examine the concept of the product life-cycle, and the rationale for new product development, from an economist's perspective.

The role of marketing is about matching demand and supply. This is the same function as the price mechanism. In this section the shared roots of economics and marketing can be seen clearly. Understanding the economic framework makes it easier to appreciate the real economic role of marketing.

There are three chapters to this section:

Chapter 3 What is a product? Examining the concepts of utility, value and choice. Identifying the basis of individual decision-making.

Chapter 4 Demand and supply and how, why and when they change. Identifying the factors influencing demand. Firms are concerned with the market demand and need an understanding of how and why that demand changes.

The response of suppliers – identifying the factors influencing supply

Examining the changing market at different stages of the product life-cycle.

Chapter 5 Elasticity – its calculation and marketing implications. Measuring the effect of changes in the demand variables. Elasticity's value to the marketer.

3
What is a product?

The first chapter in this section examines consumer behaviour and decision-making from the economists' point of view. This aspect of economics is particularly relevant to marketers whose business it is to understand and influence consumer behaviour. The economists' picture of a rational decision-maker may not hold true in the real marketplace, but it does provide a useful basis from which consumer behaviour can be analysed.

Aims

This chapter aims to:

- Help find an answer to the question 'What is a product?'
- Provide a theoretical framework for understanding the scale of benefits consumers derive from a range of products.
- Examine how customers decide what to buy.
- Consider the costs in making choices and decisions.
- Identify the contribution that this economic view of customer behaviour makes to marketing.

Glossary

Conditions of the market – Any variable other than price that affects the quantity supplied or demanded in a market.

Elasticity – is a measure of how much demand or supply changes as a result of a change in one of the variables that influences them. So price elasticity of demand measures how much the quantity demanded will change as a result of a price change, and income elasticity is the change in quantity demanded as income changes. *Elastic* denotes sensitivity to the variable, and *inelastic* insensitivity to the variable.

Law of diminishing marginal utility – states that, in any given time period, consuming more and more units of a commodity generates progressively lower additional benefit/satisfaction.

Margin – the concept of the margin recurs throughout economic theory. It is important because all business decisions are made 'at the margin'. Literally it means at the edge, or the last. So *marginal cost* is the cost of the last unit produced and *marginal utility* the benefit derived from the last unit consumed.

Opportunity cost – a broad view of cost used extensively by economists. It measures the cost of one option in terms of the foregone benefits that would have been derived from the next best alternative.

Total utility – the total benefit derived, from which customer behaviour can be analysed.
Utility – the amount of benefit or satisfaction derived from consuming a product. Units of
    satisfaction are *utiles*.

Before you start

This chapter is about consumer behaviour and decision-making. This topic is one we are
already experts in because of our own experience as customers.

Take a little time out, before you read on, to consider the following questions. This
will help you to clarify your own thoughts and experiences and relate them more easily
to the economic theory and marketing practice. Jot your answers down and refer to them
while you are working through this chapter.

1 Can you define a product?

2 What was the last product you bought?
   • Why did you want it?
   • Was there any choice?
   • What factors influenced your selection?
   • Would you buy it again?

3 Would you rather have a cup of coffee or a cup of tea?
   • Why?
   • Would you regularly have a second cup?
   • And a third?

4 If you won £1,000 tomorrow, what would you spend it on?

5 Think about making a decision to go/or not to go on holiday. Write down as many
   things that may influence your decision as you can.

The basics

The answer you get to the question 'What is a product?' will depend on who you ask.

The *accountant* may see it as an asset. The *economist* and *operations manager* will probably see
it as the bundle of resources used in its production: so much labour, machine time and space
(the economist would express these resources in terms of land, labour and capital). To the
marketer it is a package of benefits designed to satisfy the customer's needs.

The *customer's* view is that a product is simply a tool for solving a problem – a way of
satisfying a need. If you are thirsty, that is a problem. You can solve it by having a drink: tea,
lemonade, beer or water (there are a number of options). These drink products are the tools
you use to solve your problem, and you benefit from the thirst-quenching properties of the
product you choose to consume.

Marketing, with its philosophy based on satisfying customer needs, provides a toolbox
designed to help the manager identify his/her customer's needs and provide products or

services that offer benefits designed to satisfy them. But in a competitive market environment there will be a number of products that can satisfy the same need – and the consumer has a choice.

How can the marketer know which product will be perceived as the right tool to solve the customer's problem and therefore be demanded? There is not an easy answer to this question. Marketing managers spend a great deal of time and money attempting to identify and anticipate customers' needs and then putting together product and service offerings that will satisfy them – that is in fact the essence of marketing.

Economic theory provides a starting point and framework for the marketers' understanding of consumer behaviour. Economics helps us to address a list of critical questions:

- How do consumers satisfy their needs?
- How do customers make the choice between alternatives such as lemonade and tea?
- How do they decide on how much of any product to consume?
- How is this preference signalled to the firm via market demand?

We shall examine in detail one of the economist's models of consumer behaviour and the answers it can supply to these questions. More abstract approaches, such as Indifference Curve Analysis and Revealed Preference Theory, will not be dealt with here, but for interested students they are well covered in other intermediate economic textbooks.

Economic benefit

Utility

When a good or service is used up or consumed, some benefit or satisfaction is derived, and economists refer to this benefit or satisfaction as *utility*. How much satisfaction or *utility* a person gains from any particular product is peculiar to that individual at that particular moment in time. The concept of *utility* is an abstract one, so it cannot be precisely measured, but it is useful and provides a form of evaluation with which we are all familiar.

You may not be able to say, 'I gained 5 utiles (units of satisfaction) from that glass of lemonade', but you can and do make comparative statements and rankings that indicate some subjective measurement of satisfaction:

- I prefer lemonade to tea.
- I like this brand of lemonade best.
- I don't like beer.

These sorts of statement are ones we make as consumers. They express our own personal preferences and utility indices. Marketers considering launching a new brand of lemonade would need to try and assess the likely ranking of their product to forecast its potential demand and future share of the drinks and lemonade market.

As customers we also make other sorts of statements, about value for money:

- That meal was good value.
- This brand is a better buy than that.
- This choice was a real bargain.

In effect we are saying we gained more benefit (utility) for our cash and so we are attempting to quantify utility, which in turn influences our purchasing decisions.

Imagine we *can* measure utility and that you were offered a choice of two glasses of lemonade:

Choice 1 – is homemade, freshly squeezed and ice cold; its price is 80p per glass.
Choice 2 – is carbonated, not cold and very sweet; its price is 50p per bottle.

On a warm day, if you do not have a sweet tooth, your preference is Choice 1, because it will give you more satisfaction/benefit – you judge it would give you 10 units of satisfaction. By taking the amount of utility you gain from the product and dividing it by price you can calculate how much you are paying for each unit of satisfaction (utile) – literally the value for money ratio.

$$\frac{\text{Utiles}}{\text{Price}}$$

Our first choice of lemonade would give you:

$$\frac{10}{80p} \text{ utiles} = 8p \text{ per utile}$$

Your second choice you judge will give you less benefit, only 5 utiles of satisfaction:

$$\frac{5}{50p} \text{ utiles} = 10p \text{ per utile}$$

On this occasion the more expensive product provides you with added value, that is extra utility, and so is preferred and likely to be purchased.

However, on a cold day, the relative satisfaction may change. Choice 2 may be judged by you to provide the same 5 utiles of satisfaction, but the utility of choice 1 may now fall to 8 utiles

$$\text{Choice 1} \quad \frac{8 \text{ utiles}}{80p} = 10p \text{ per utile} \qquad \text{Choice 2} \quad \frac{5 \text{ utiles}}{50p} = 10p \text{ per utile}$$

Now although Choice 1 is still preferred, i.e. gives greater total utility, its higher price means that the two products provide equal value for money, and, assuming your funds are not limited, you would be indifferent as to which you purchased. You can see that if the relative ratios continue to change, because the price of choice 2 falls to 40p or the weather gets colder, the rational decision is to change your purchase decision and select choice 2. In these circumstances you would be getting better utility for money from this option.

$$\text{Choice 1} \quad \frac{8 \text{ utiles}}{80p} = 10p \text{ per utile} \qquad \text{Choice 2} \quad \frac{5 \text{ utiles}}{40p} = 8p \text{ per utile}$$

This example of utility shows how our judgement of a product's value to us is influenced by external factors, like the weather, and so is liable to change over time. This is one of the reasons why predicting demand in the marketplace is so difficult – things are always changing.

The subjectivity of an individual's assessment of utility shows how the same product will give differing amounts of satisfaction to different people. You may love tea, while I prefer coffee. The same cup of tea would therefore give me very little utility and you considerably more. This explains why different people will choose a different product to satisfy the same need – thirst. Marketing's solution is to try and identify groups of customers with similar tastes and needs – the process of market segmentation.

This personal judgement of utility/value is based on individual perceptions. It is this perception that is fundamental to the consumer's personal decision-making. Customers' perception is based on their tastes and values as well as the image they have of the product. If you believe that the homemade lemonade will be healthier, because you assume it is more natural or has less sugar content, then it will be on that basis that you judge the relative benefit you will gain from it. The fact that the homemade product actually contains more sugar is irrelevant. This factor explains why it is that companies that in fact have superior products sometimes fail. It also emphasizes the important role of marketing in informing customers of real product benefits.

Law of diminishing marginal utility

The fact that different people have different product preferences is easy to observe and understand. So is the idea that if external factors change, so individual preferences may change.

Less obvious is the effect of a concept economists call *diminishing marginal utility*. This is a law of economics which states that, within a given continuous time period *the more of a good you consume, the less additional satisfaction you will get from consuming another unit of the same product*.

If you are very thirsty, your first glass of lemonade will be very welcome and you may derive a considerable amount of utility or benefit from it. A second glass may be pleasant, but it is unlikely you 'needed' it as much, so the utility derived is less – and so on. The more of the product consumed, the less additional (marginal) satisfaction.

If we assume that it is possible to quantify the amount of utility an individual gains from consuming a particular product, we can look at the law of diminishing marginal utility on a chart, as in Figure 3.1. The more additional (marginal) units of a product you consume, the less additional satisfaction (utility) you gain.

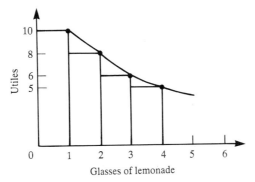

Figure 3.1 *Law of diminishing marginal utility*

It is possible to reach the point where you positively do not want more of the product and an additional unit would give *disutility* – the seventh glass of lemonade could make you sick – as can be seen in Figure 3.2.

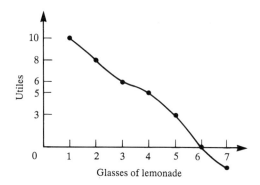

Figure 3.2   *Diminishing marginal utility, showing disutility from continued consumption*

It is important to remember that this schedule of utility would be personal, and different individuals would have different shapes and values to their utility curve for lemonade. The only common feature would be its downward slope.

If lemonade is 50p per glass, then you can see that the 'value for money' derived from the first glass of lemonade – 10 utiles/50p – represents better value than from the fourth glass, which provides 5 utiles/50p.

So how does this help us to understand and forecast how many glasses of lemonade the individual will buy?

Filling the shopping basket

Each consumer is faced with thousands of choices when making a range of purchase decisions. The economist starts with the assumption that the consumer will act rationally and will choose a basket of goods that maximizes his/her total benefit/utility within the constraints of the limited resources available – this is represented by the individual's income. You can see from Figure 3.3 that, as marginal utility diminishes, so total utility increases, but at a diminishing rate. Total utility after two glasses is 18 utiles and after three is 24 utiles.

If you were attending a friend's party and lemonade was 'free' (in other words not using up any of your scarce income resource), then the decision how much lemonade to consume is easy. You will consume lemonade until another glass gives you *no* additional satisfaction, i.e. until your marginal utility of lemonade = zero. From Figure 3.3, six glasses of lemonade would be consumed before this individual had maximized his/her total utility. This explains why some friends may seem to consume more drink at a party than when they are paying for it at the pub!

Unfortunately most of the products we consume are not 'free', and so the reality of the economic problem – unlimited needs and wants, but limited resources – forces us to make choices.

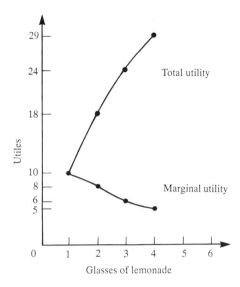

Figure 3.3 *Total and marginal utility curves*

Opportunity costs

Every decision we make has a cost. This is not just the financial cost as expressed by the price tag. Economists use a broader concept of cost – *opportunity cost* – to encompass all the costs and benefits resulting from a decision.

Opportunity cost is the cost of one option expressed in terms of the next best alternative foregone. If you choose one thing, you can't have the benefit of another. The real cost of having your house repainted this year is the benefit/utility you would have enjoyed from a week's holiday in Spain.

Financial costs of a year at college

If you were considering taking a year off work to take a master's degree, what would be the financial cost and the opportunity cost? The financial costs would be calculated by adding up the money paid out during the year for fees, books, living and travel expenses. See Table 3.1.

Table 3.1 Financial costs of a year at college

Items of expense	£
Fees	2,500
Books and materials	500
Living expenses and travel	3,250
Miscellaneous	750
Total	7,000

£7,000 is clearly not the true cost. The opportunity cost of your year at college includes the income foregone from your year off work, plus lost opportunities for promotion at work. Added to that we need to consider what the next best alternative would have been for your expenditure exclusively related to attending college, in this case fees and books + £1,000 worth of travel and miscellaneous expenses (£2,500 + 500 + £1,000 = £4,000). What else would you have done with this money? Consider the interest you could have earned by investing £4,000 for a year in your building society account or the benefits you would have gained from new double glazing or a trip across America. See Table 3.2.

Table 3.2   Opportunity costs of a year at college

Losses	£
Financial costs	4,000
Lost year's income	15,000
Lost interest on £7,000 invested	400
Total	19,400

Looking at it this way, the costs of a year at college seem to be substantial, but we must not mislead ourselves in such decisions. A year at college may be the best use of your resources, both time and money, if it leads to a better job and higher future income. You may never have called it opportunity cost, but the concept of considering the wider implications, particularly of a major purchase, will be familiar to you.

You may have used the technique of drawing up a list of advantages and disadvantages when considering buying a new car or a new house. The higher price of the hatchback is offset by the benefits of more luggage space and improved rear view visibility. The costs of moving house need to include disruption to the children's schooling and the loss of good neighbours. All these are part of the opportunity cost equation.

So in the process of filling your shopping basket you make comparisons between the utility of your chosen product divided by its price and the utility of other options divided by their prices. The one you perceive to offer the best value for money ratio is the one that will maximize your satisfaction. This will remain true while your income is unchanged and all other factors stay constant.

How much of a product to buy?

Most day to day economic decisions are made at the margin. You do not decide to have four cups of coffee. You have three and then decide whether or not to have an additional/marginal fourth cup. Therefore individuals will have maximized their total utility when the marginal utility/price ratio is equal for all the goods in their shopping basket. This can be expressed in the following way:

$$\frac{MUa}{Pa} = \frac{MUb}{Pb} = \frac{MU...x}{P...x}$$

where MU = marginal utility, P = price, and a,b. . .x represent the goods available.

If the choices you have made do not offer equal price/utility ratios, then you will be better off thinking again. If there is a product that offers more utility for the same money, you can improve your total satisfaction/economic welfare by buying this product instead of more of the first.

Assume our lemonade customer, from Figure 3.2 has the choice of sandwiches or lemonade, both at 50p per item. The first sandwich bought will give 7 utiles and the second 4 utiles. If our customer has £2.00 to spend on only sandwiches or lemonade, his/her purchases can be forecast.

- The first 50p will be spent on lemonade, giving 10 utiles of satisfaction.
- The second 50p will also buy lemonade, giving 8 utiles of satisfaction.
- The third 50p will buy a sandwich at 7 utiles.
- The fourth a lemonade at 6 utiles.

Each purchase decision causes the customer to review the alternatives available and identify the selection that offers the most utility/benefit. Although we are not consciously aware of it, our personal utility barometers are finely tuned measuring devices and very active. For the marketer, understanding the workings of that barometer is critical.

The marketing perspective

Getting to know your customers – to understand their behaviour and identify their needs – is fundamental to the success of any marketing manager's strategy. Customer behaviour is complex, influenced by a wide range of factors and variables. The economist's model of consumer behaviour is a starting point, providing some valuable insights and marketing opportunities.

Who's the competition?

The first thing that our economic model makes clear is that customers are not simply choosing between competing brands of the same product. All goods are in competition for the customer's limited income.

Companies whose marketing strategies ignore that fact may find themselves with a generic market that is shrinking. Holiday companies' biggest competition probably comes from furniture retailers and house painters. Co-operating with your competitors to increase the size of the holiday market cake may be a much more effective use of promotional resources than fighting for a bigger share of a cake that is not growing.

The marketer and the concept of utility

As customers and as marketers we may be aware of the choices the consumer has to make, but most of us are less consciously aware of the mental calculation of relative value for money options that we are actually undertaking.

Quantifying the benefits

Marketers talk about *selling benefits*, but few follow that through with an attempt to quantify what a particular product benefit or characteristic is really worth to the consumer. How many additional perceived utiles are added by the easy to open packaging or the longer product shelf life?

Competitive advantage for the company is likely to be strongest when the firm identifies and concentrates on benefits that generate high levels of customer utility.

Add value to increase sales

Equally important is the economist's clear message to his/her marketing cousin that the basis for a purchase decision is *not* price alone but the utility/price ratio. Certainly lowering the price does produce a more favourable ratio, and so will tend to increase demand and sales, but this message of *reduce price to sell more* has tended to drown out the other dimension of the equation. Economic theory clearly shows that added value/utility can also improve the ratio and lead to higher sales.

Many businesses have fallen into the trap of automatically lowering prices to increase sales. Sales staff are also accused and often guilty of assuming price reductions and discounts are the only way to secure an order. In fact experience shows that a price cut often signals lower quality and therefore value to the customers. With this changed perception of value, they end up buying less, not more, of this particular brand or product.

As a strategy for stimulating demand, a good rule for the marketer to follow is always look for ways to increase value in preference to lowering price.

Selling benefits

By understanding the range of options open to the customer and the underlying basis for choice, it is possible to help the customer's decision-making. Marketers talk about turning product features into benefits – in other words, spelling out why this product offers more satisfaction/utiles than its competitors. The phrase 'which means that' is the key to turning features into benefits. 'This washing-up liquid is more concentrated (product feature) *which means that* it will wash more dishes (consumer benefit).'

Emphasizing benefits that provide customer satisfaction is one way of changing a customer's perception of a product. Old fashioned technologies may now be promoted as environmentally friendly, and slimming products as healthy ones. Changing the positioning of the product by emphasizing different benefits is likely to attract customers with different needs, ones who will perceive it to offer a different amount of utility.

Selling extra units

The law of diminishing marginal utility does, however, provide an explanation as to why selling additional product to the same customer is often difficult. Specific marketing tactics need to be adopted to maintain the utility/price ratio as utility diminishes.

- Price reduction based on additional units bought can be a valuable approach, e.g. economy packs, bulk discounts or 'fifth one free' offers.
- Special promotional activities can be geared to increasing sales per customer, e.g. collect x tokens this month for a free gift, entry into our prize draw, etc.

Summary review

1 Identify examples of sales promotional activity that are based on the economic insight provided by:
  (a) the law of diminishing marginal utility,
  (b) the importance of the utility price ratio in making purchase decisions.

2 Conduct a 'taste test' panel with your family or friends. Provide a selection of different brands of a product and ask each person to indicate their preferences. What reasons do they give? How do they describe different brands and product benefits?

3 Imagine you had a sudden unexpected gift of £200 but it has to be spent on a single item, this month. Identify two or three alternatives and try to assess the opportunity cost of each.

4
Demand and supply and how they change

The role of marketing is to match demand to the organization's available capacity, i.e. its supply. Fundamental to the ability to do that is the marketer's grasp and thorough understanding of the dynamics of demand and supply.

Markets are made up of individual customers. The decisions of those individuals will therefore have an automatic influence on the total/market demand. This chapter examines how these individual preferences are signalled to the firm and identifies why a knowledge of demand analysis is of value to the business person.

Aims

The aims of this chapter are to:

- Examine fully the nature and meaning of demand and supply.
- Consider how information communicated in demand and supply curves can be analysed and used by the business person.
- Assess the factors that influence demand.
- Identify products that do not behave 'normally' according to the economic laws of demand.
- Find out how the economic analysis of demand can be used to inform and influence marketing strategy and tactics.

Glossary

Effective demand – the desire to buy a product backed by the necessary income to obtain it.

Elasticity – a way of measuring the extent of a change in demand or supply resulting from a change in one of the variables that influences them. *Elastic* describes sensitivity to the variable, and *inelastic* insensitivity to the variable.

Fmcg – fast-moving consumer goods.

Income effect – as prices fall, people can in effect buy the same goods for less, making them 'better off'. This has the same impact as if their incomes had risen.

Inferior goods – goods for which there is a preferred, but more expensive substitute.

Market demand – the total volume of goods being sought at a given price.

Substitution effect – when a change in price causes customers to reassess their purchase decision, substituting more of the relatively cheaper product which now represents better value for money.

Before you start

Take time to clarify your own thoughts and current level of knowledge, by working through the following questions:

1 Identify four products whose demand has changed significantly over the last few years. What reasons can you suggest to account for these changes?

2 Make a list of the factors that would influence the demand for a product/service with which you are familiar. Indicate which of these factors can be influenced by the organization and which are outside its control.

3 What makes forecasting future levels of demand difficult in your business?

The basics of demand

In business and marketing the word demand is used frequently. Before taking a detailed look at market demand, let us clarify the term and concept.

The *market demand* represents the cumulative response of all customers and potential customers to a product, and it indicates the collective quantity demanded. In this sense every customer has an impact on the total demand, but it would take similar changes from a number of individuals before there was a marked impact on the total picture.

The demand for a product or service refers to the quantity that would be bought at any particular price. Economists are only concerned with what they call *effective demand*. This means the desire to have a product supported by the resources necessary to buy it. Marketers may take a longer term view of demand, accepting that there is sometimes a considerable time gap between a customer's determination to buy and the actual point of purchase. Therefore marketing strategy in the short term may have objectives based on generating awareness and desire for products, which can over time be converted into effective demand. This would be particularly true of luxury consumer durable products.

However, the business's survival depends on cash flow not future projections, so it is effective demand today that actually determines the organisation's financial health. Therefore both the business person and the economist are happy to work with models that are based on this concept of demand as representing a commitment to buy, backed by purchasing power.

The demand curve

Economists use *demand curves* and *schedules* to communicate what quantity might be demanded at a number of price points. See Table 4.1.

This table of demand, or *demand schedule*, is sometimes referred to as an 'if' schedule. It does not tell you how many goods are being bought, and we do not know what the price of this product actually is. This schedule simply says that, given the current market conditions and attitudes to the product, then:

- *If* the price was £2.00, we would expect 25,000 units to be bought.
- *If* the price was £2.50, we would only expect sales of 15,000.

Table 4.1   Demand schedule

Price (£)	Quantity (thousands)
2.50	15
2.25	20
2.00	25
1.75	30

This same information can be communicated more effectively by means of a graph and the representation of a demand curve. See Figure 4.1.

The demand curve will normally slope downwards from left to right, indicating that at higher prices less will be demanded and at lower prices more will be demanded. This seems rational, and is a forecast of behaviour you have probably observed in your own experiences as a customer and a marketer. There are some exceptions to this rule, which we will consider later.

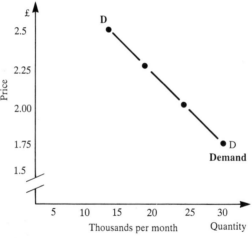

Figure 4.1   *A simple demand curve*

Two factors determine this normal pattern of demand:

1 As prices fall, so each individual can afford and will choose to buy more, as the product gives the same utility, but for less money; this is due to the *substitution effect*.
2 More people can afford to buy the product at lower prices. So those who would have bought none at higher prices can enter the market for the first time; this is referred to as the *income effect*.

The demand curve is an important tool, used by both the economist and the business person. It is not so easy to generate a demand curve for a product in the marketplace, but an appreciation of demand and its mechanics is an essential theoretical framework for the development of marketing strategies. If a marketer is to change price, increase advertising spending or open up overseas markets, it is important to know what the effect of such actions will be on the forecasted product demand.

Note:

Take care when producing or using demand curves:

- Make sure you always have price on the vertical axis and quantity demanded per period on the horizontal axis.
- Clearly label your diagram with a title. Always use a ruler and a little colour to make your work clear and effective.
- Think about the scale used – by changing the scale of one of the axes you can change the shape of your curves, making them steeper or flatter. You will see later that the curve's slope is important.

Using demand analysis

Demand curves are used to communicate information about the nature and scale of demand. To interpret and use that information you need to understand demand analysis and to think about the curves which are presented to you. When considering a demand curve for a product you need to take account of:

1 The slope of the curve.
2 The position of the curve.

The slope of the curve

The slope of the curve is determined by how the quantity demanded responds to changes in price. The slope tells you how price- sensitive demand for the product is. Products that are not sensitive to price are often illustrated by a steep curve and described by economists as price-inelastic (price-insensitive).

In Figure 4.2 you can see that as price falls quite significantly from £2.00 to £1.50, the quantity demanded only changes a little from 100,000 to 105,000 units. In effect a 25 per cent price fall has produced a mere 5 per cent increase in the quantity of goods demanded. Clearly in this case customers' purchases are not greatly influenced by the price.

A flatter curve indicates more price-sensitivity and economists would describe demand as price-elastic (price-sensitive). See Figure 4.3.

Here you can see that the same price fall of 50p (25 per cent) has brought about a significant change in the quantity demanded, from 100,000 to 140,000 units – a 40 per cent change in the demand. Customers of this product are apparently much more influenced by price.

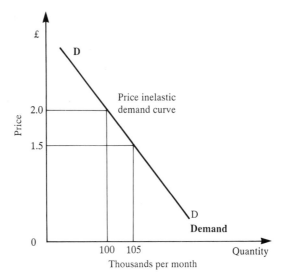

Figure 4.2   *Price-inelastic demand curve*

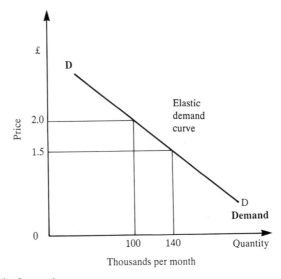

Figure 4.3   *Price-elastic demand curve*

Exercise

Spend 10 minutes brainstorming two lists of all the products you might expect to behave like those illustrated by Figures 4.2 and 4.3. Refer to these lists while you are working through the rest of this section.

Being able to identify how much demand will change as a result of a price change is obviously very important to the marketer, and a mechanism to quantify the extent of such changes is potentially very useful. So we will return to this concept of elasticity again throughout this section.

As we saw in Figures 4.2 and 4.3, changes in price are illustrated on the diagrams by movements along the existing demand curve, and economists refer to these movements as extensions and contractions in demand. See Figure 4.4.

Movements along the curve are caused by changes in price and described as extensions and contractions in demand.

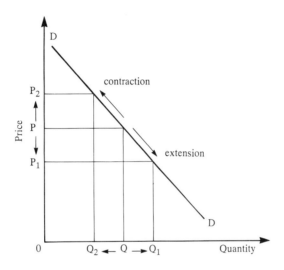

As price falls from P to P_1, so the quantity demanded extends from Q to Q_1.
As price rises from P to P_2, so there is a contraction in the quantity demanded from Q to Q_2.

Figure 4.4   *Extensions and contractions of demand*

If an organization wishes to sell more, there is a tendency to rush into lowering prices. At lower prices you will sell more. At least this is true for normal goods, i.e. those whose demand curves slope downwards from left to right. However, selling more does not necessarily mean the company is better off. The critical factor is how much more or less you sell as a result of a price change, and that is determined by the degree to which demand is sensitive to changes in price, i.e. the degree of price-elasticity. You can sell more but total revenue can fall, and you can sell less but total revenue can rise.

Activity

Go back to the two demand curves shown as Figures 4.2 and 4.3. Calculate total revenue for each at the original price of £2.00, and then see what happens when the price is reduced to £1.50.

Note that total revenue is price multiplied by quantity.

Answer
You will see that at the original price:

£2.00   100,000 units were sold = £200,000 revenue

When the price was reduced by 50p, the demand for the product with inelastic demand increased to 105,000:

£1.50 × 105,000 = £157,000

i.e. a fall in total revenue of £42,500 despite the larger volume of sales.
   The product with price-elastic demand saw the quantity demanded extend to 140,000 units:

£1.50 × 140,000 = £210,000

an increase in total revenue of £10,000
   The reverse outcomes would be true if price was to rise by 50p.

Before marketers use price to influence the quantity demanded they need to take a careful look at demand to see whether or not the nature of this product demand is sensitive to price. Where demand is inelastic:

- The marketer can raise price without losing market share significantly.
- The marketer needs to look to other variables to increase the quantity of product demanded.

A more detailed look at the measurement of elasticity is included in Chapter 5.

Exceptions to the rule

Economists make the assumption that consumers will act rationally. As long as they do, it can be argued that in most cases the demand curve will be downward sloping from left to right. This shows that people will buy less at higher prices than they do at lower.

Giffen goods

In the nineteenth century an economist, Sir Robert Giffen, observed that among the working classes the demand for bread fell as its price fell and extended as prices increased. Expressed graphically this produced a backward-sloping demand curve at complete variance with the first law of demand, which indicates the reverse behaviour should occur. This strange, seemingly irrational behaviour only occurred in markets where:

- The product was an inferior good, i.e. there were alternatives, more expensive but preferred by the customer when affordable. In the case of bread, workers would have preferred vegetables and meat, but could not afford them.
- The product was one on which the household spent most of its income. In the case Giffen observed bread was the staple diet of labourers.

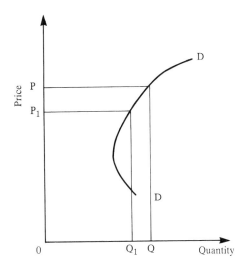

Figure 4.5 *Demand for a Veblen good*

As the price of such a product falls, the same quantity of bread can be bought for less (the income effect). Spare income could be used on alternative, preferred foods, thus reducing the quantity of bread required. The reverse happens when the price of the Giffen good rises.

Goods of ostentation or Veblen goods

Another exception to the normal law of demand also results in backward-sloping demand curves for products. The goods in question are classified as goods of ostentation or luxury goods. Products like jewellery, expensive cars and wines may actually have a particular 'snob' appeal because of their price. Price increases can make these products even more attractive, and as prices rise, so does demand. Similarly a price fall, as seen in Figure 4.5, from P to P_1 actually produces reduced sales as exclusiveness is reduced.

The marketing experience

To the economist there is little expectation that these exceptions would hold true for many products. But in the real world of the marketer the phenomenon of the backward-sloping demand curve is far from uncommon. Customers do not in fact always behave rationally. Whole ranges of products are given added value through their branding and designer labels, which serve to turn them into goods of ostentation.

In addition, there is the difficulty consumers have of making comparisons between competing goods. The economist's rational consumer is assumed to have 'perfect knowledge' of the products and markets. This is seldom the case for the real consumer. How do you judge the quality and performance of one expensive camera or TV against another? Many customers resort to using price as a guide to value: 'If it costs more, it must be better'. Not a reliable or particularly rational basis of assessment, but understandable. As a result a rise in price can change the customers' perception of the product's value, causing demand to increase. This process is known by marketers as repositioning their product, and by economists as judging quality by price.

The position of the curve

Besides the shape of the curve, the position of the curve also communicates a lot about how demand is changing. The position of the curve has to shift if any variable other than price changes.

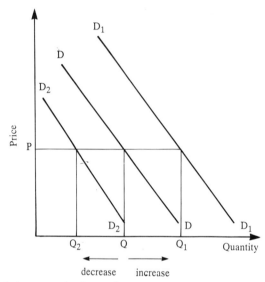

Figure 4.6   *Increases and decreases in demand*

These other variables are referred to collectively as the conditions of demand. They include income, expectation, taste and fashion, the price of other goods and the number of people in the market. As can be seen in Figure 4.6, changes in any of these would alter the total amount of a product being demanded at all prices – in effect such changes would entail a reappraisal of every individual demand schedule and priorities, causing the demand for the product to increase (shown by the curve moving to the right – D_1) or to decrease (curve moves to the left – D_2).

As the curve moves to the right, more (Q^1) is demanded at price P than previously. There are a number of possible causes for this:

1 Disposable income has increased.
2 Prices of other goods have gone up.
3 Population has risen.
4 There is an expectation of a future price rise.
5 The product has become more 'fashionable'.

If the curve moves to the left, this indicates less is demanded at all price levels, also owing to a change in the market conditions. For example:

1 Higher levels of direct tax, or inflation reducing real disposable incomes.
2 Expected future price falls.

3 Higher prices for complementary goods.
4 Lower prices for competitive goods.
5 A health scare or falling out of fashion.
6 A decline in the size of the market.

For the marketer wanting to match demand and supply a thorough appreciation of these other variables that influence demand is important. Some of them can be controlled by the marketer, and so can be used as an integral part of his/her marketing strategy. Others are beyond the individual's control, but need to be predicted and responded to in advance (pro-active management) or quickly and flexibly when changes had not been foreseen (reactive management).

The conditions of demand and marketing tactics

It is obviously important for the marketer to assess the conditions of demand from the perspective of what he or she can do to influence or control the impact of change.

Income

The customers' disposable income is outside the marketers' control, but changes in it need to be predicted and the likely impact on the level of demand can be forecast. The concept of elasticity can again be used, this time to measure how sensitive demand is to changes in income. This is *income elasticity of demand*:

- Products whose demand is not likely to change significantly when income changes are described as income-inelastic (insensitive).
- Those that respond significantly to changes in income are income-elastic (sensitive).

Normally if an individual's income goes up you would expect demand to increase. As you get wealthier, you would spend more on entertainment, holidays, food, etc. But there are some products where demand decreases as income rises. These are called *inferior goods*, for the customer perceives there to be preferable alternatives positioned in the market as more expensive, quality competitors. Bus rides may be perceived as inferior to taxi rides, tinned salmon inferior to fresh salmon, and one brand of a product inferior to a competitor's. The position of the demand curve, whether it is shifting to the right or left as a result of an increase in income, indicates whether your product is a normal or inferior product. See Figure 4.7.

It is important for the marketer to adopt a very different strategy to support his/her product if it is inferior and income levels are changing.

If the product is inferior and income levels are rising, marketers should:

- Reposition the product by adding benefits and therefore utility, e.g. margarine promoted as healthier than butter or bus journeys as more environmentally friendly than car rides.

- Look for new markets where income levels are lower. There may be different segments of the domestic market or new markets overseas.

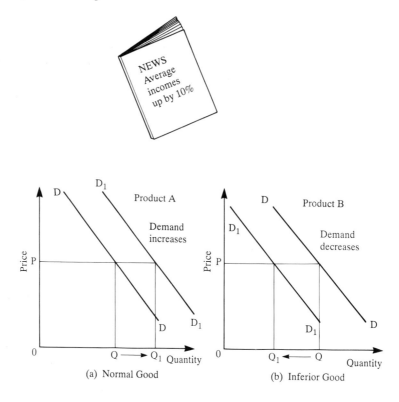

Figure 4.7 (a) & (b)   *Changes in the conditions of demand caused by a change of income*

When disposable incomes are falling in real terms, e.g. during inflation or when taxation is rising, then inferior products tend to sell well, as customers trade down to the basic model or brand.

Note that many retailer branded fmcg products are perceived by the customer to be inferior to manufacturer-branded goods.

Marketers may not be able to change income levels, but there is a great deal of published information that allows income changes to be predicted. This enables appropriate marketing and business strategies to be adopted, ensuring that the organization's supply and the level of demand remain in balance. These are examined in more detail in the macro section on national income. However, national figures can disguise significant regional and sector variations. Tight market segmentation needs matching with equally specific identification and monitoring of that segment's demand characteristics, including income levels.

Changes in the factors influencing your market segment's disposable real income are important elements in any demand forecast. During 1990–1 many companies, particularly those in retailing, such as Harris Queensway, appeared to under-estimate the true impact of high interest rates on houseowners' disposable incomes and the resulting decrease in demand for consumer durables. Forecasting the particular strength of this impact for homeowners in the South East of England, and in the 20–40 age bracket, where mortgages were particularly large, should have made the extent of the demand decrease more evident than it appears to have been.

Price of other goods

This is determined by the business strategy of competitors, and unless there is some collusion on pricing within the industry, it will be outside the organization's control. Once more it is important for the marketer to have a feel for how much of an impact competitors' activities will have on his/her market. Again the concept of elasticity can be used to provide a measurement of how sensitive demand for one product is to a change in the price of other goods. This is known as *cross elasticity of demand*:

- Where there is a significant response, demand is described as cross-elastic (sensitive to a change in the price of the other product).
- Where there is little response it is cross-inelastic.

As with changes in income, demand can increase or decrease as a result of another firm's price change (see Figure 4.8). If your demand increases as a result of another product's price being reduced, your products are complementary, bought together in some form of combination. For example, demand for industrial printing machinery is derived from demand for printed materials, and would fall into this category. Products bought together, such as compact discs and compact disc players, would also be complementary.

If demand decreases as a result of the other products' price reduction, the products are competitive. The more significant the degree of response, the closer they are perceived to be substitutes for each other. One strategy of those marketing products that have close competitors is to add distinct selling points and benefits to the product, so that customers perceive it to have no direct substitutes. This reduces the potential impact of competitors' aggressive pricing strategies on your market.

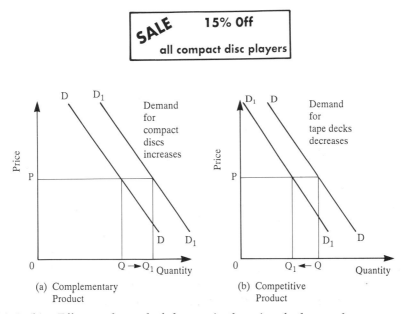

Figure 4.8 (a) & (b)   *Effect on demand of changes in the price of other goods*

Monitoring the market to identify the companies whose actions can affect your business is a regular responsibility of management. Other firms do not only pose threats; their behaviour can open up opportunities that need quick responses if commercial gains and benefits are to be made.

Taste and fashion

These are two other variables in the macro-environment that business needs to remain aware of and be ready to respond to. Categorized under the heading culture, changes in this area can represent major shifts in demand, and, if unidentified, result in the decline of not just firms but also industries. The increase in 'healthy' and 'green' products are among the most noticeable shifts in the last few years. Major trends such as these cannot be controlled by firms; neither can the dramatic shifts caused by 'scares' like salmonella in eggs and 'mad cow disease'. However, fashion and tastes can be and are influenced by marketers' use of advertising, PR and other promotional activities. Products endorsed by personalities can widen their appeal and increase demand accordingly. Marketers can shift demand by their use of the promotional variable in the marketing mix.

Expectation

The effects of expectations tend to be mainly short-term in effect. For example, before the budget demand for cigarettes and alcohol may increase as purchasers anticipate rises in indirect taxation (and therefore prices) in the budget.

The real economic significance of the variable of expectation can be best seen in the operation of the Stock Exchange. Here the expectation of share price rises and falls results in identifiable shifts in demand.

Population

Changes in the number of customers in the market are also likely to change demand. A bigger customer base is likely to increase demand. Sometimes these changes will be part of the uncontrollable macro-environment in which the firm is operating. Major demographic shifts, changes in the age profile of the population, their area of residence, birth, death and marriage rates are all beyond the organization's control, but can have a major effect on the market size. In the main these factors can be forecast a long time in advance, so there is little excuse for firms to be caught out by such changes. Major demographic trends are covered in detail in the macro section.

At a more micro level the firm's definition of its target market segment determines the size of its 'population' or market. Diversification and modification of the target market can also increase the level of demand.

Demand analysis and the marketing implications

The importance of market demand to the marketer should be evident already. The role of marketing can be seen clearly in the context of this analysis of demand.

Marketing is used to do two things:

- Change the shape of the demand curve.
- Shift the demand curve.

Marketers want to make their products insensitive to price – to give them the chance of increasing prices without losing sales or a significant percentage of their market share. Product differentiation, branding and advertising are all activities aiming to make the customers perceive the product as unique – therefore having no close substitutes and so being more price-inelastic. See Figure 4.9. However, if the marketer is successful in making the product less sensitive to price, price becomes a less useful tool in the marketer's choice of variables.

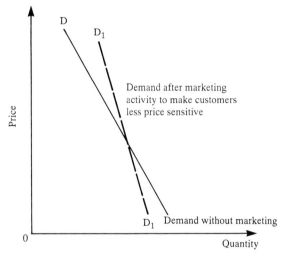

Figure 4.9 *Marketing tries to make products more price-inelastic*

Marketers also want to shift the demand curve, usually but not always to increase demand. Changing the non-price variables in the marketing mix are the methods that can be used to shift the curve:

- Changes in the product, its features or after-sales service affect the customer's assessment of utility derived from the product and therefore demand.
- Changes in promotional activity can make the product more 'fashionable'.
- Changes in the 'places' where the product is available can change the size of the market. See Figure 4.10.

Marketing's role is therefore to shift the demand curve and make it 'steeper', i.e. more price-inelastic, as can be seen in Figure 4.11.

The response of the suppliers

Students of business cannot restrict themselves to a study of demand alone. Demand only represents one half of the market equation. An equal understanding of the analysis of supply

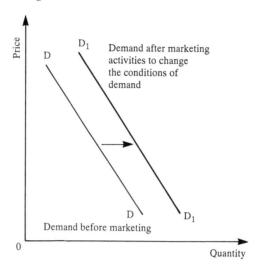

Figure 4.10   *Marketing changing the conditions of demand*

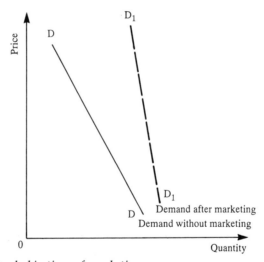

Figure 4.11   *The combined objectives of marketing*

provides managers with an insight into the nature of competition in the market and an understanding of the other dynamic half of the market mechanism.

Market supply

Represented by another 'if' schedule and curve, market supply reflects the total volume of goods the industry, i.e. all firms, are prepared to supply over a range of price points.

In this 'if' schedule (Table 4.2) you can see that if the market price was £2.50 the industry would be prepared to provide 35,000 units, whereas at the lower price of £2.00 collectively

Table 4.2   Supply schedule

Price (£)	Quantity (thousands)
2.50	35
2.25	30
2.00	25
1.75	20

firms would only be prepared to supply 25,000 units. Expressed as a curve this information demonstrates the upwards (from left to right) slope normal for supply curves (Figure 4.12).

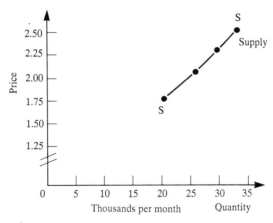

Figure 4.12   *A simple supply curve*

The reason why firms are prepared to offer more goods at higher prices can be explained by two factors:

1 At higher prices individual firms are prepared to increase their output.
2 Even less efficient firms are able to make a profit at higher prices, and so enter the market with goods for the first time as prices rise.

Supply analysis

In analysing the information contained in a supply curve there are again two aspects to consider:

1 The slope of the curve.
2 The position of the curve.

The slope of the curve

This is determined by how much the quantity supplied changes with a change in price. Supply that changes considerably with price is represented by a relatively flat supply curve and would be described as supply elastic (Figure 4.13).

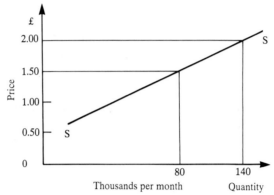

Figure 4.13   *Price-elastic supply curve*

Changes in price are represented by movements along the supply curve. As price goes up from £1.50 to £2.00 (25 per cent) supply 'extends' substantially from 80,000 to 140,000 units (75 per cent).

The position of the curve

Changes in the position of the supply curve indicate a change in the conditions of supply. These are anything other than price which influence the amount supplied.

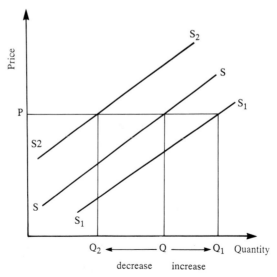

Figure 4.14   *Changes in the conditions of supply*

In Figure 4.14 curves shifting to the left (S–S₂) indicate a decrease in supply, and to the right (S–S₁) an increase in supply. These shifts represent real changes in the resources employed in this market.

Factors influencing elasticity of supply

Supply tends to be more price-sensitive/elastic over time. At any moment in time supply is fixed. In the short run the ability of supply to change with price is determined by:

- The mobility of factors of production. Where firms can increase output quickly by using part-time workers, overtime and factors that can be shifted from one use to another, then supply will be relatively more price-elastic.
- The opportunities for changing stockholdings can influence supply elasticity. Manufactured goods can be made available quickly by selling from stocks as prices rise, or withheld from the market if prices fall. Perishable output, such as services and agricultural products, do not have this option, and supply in these sectors will be more price-inelastic.
- In industries where management is prepared to take risks supply tends to be more responsive to changes in price.
- Increasing supply can also be subject to natural constraints, caused by limitations in raw material availability or the time required for production. Constraints will tend to make supply less price-sensitive.

In Figure 4.15 the steeper supply curve indicates an industry where output is not very sensitive to the change in price. Here as price falls from £2.00 to £1.50, supply contracts from 100,000 to 90,000.

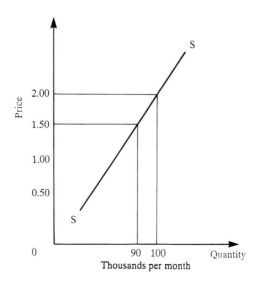

Figure 4.15   *Price-inelastic supply curve*

Conditions of supply

Costs

Output is the result of combining the factors of production. Changes in their costs increase or decrease supply. The extent of the effect of a higher wage rate on supply depends on how significant wages are as a percentage of the total costs of the business. Cost increases cause supply to decrease and the curve shifts to the left.

Technology

New technology allows increased production from the same level of resources, i.e. increased efficiency. Supply will increase and be illustrated by a movement of the curve to the right.

Price of other goods

The price of other goods represents the 'opportunity cost' for the firm. If resources are not used to produce this product how much could they earn producing another product?

Price rises in another industry may encourage firms to redeploy their resources there. This would result in a decrease in supply, and the curve moving to the left.

Alternatively price falls in other markets may encourage those firms to move their resources to this industry, causing supply to increase. The extent of this shift in resources will depend on how transferable the factors of production are. Economists tend to assume that resources can be shifted from one use to another fairly quickly and easily. In practice it may be easy for a pottery manufacturer to shift production resources from dinner services to tea services, but it is a much slower process for a farmer to replace an apple crop with pears.

Other factors

Factors outside market forces frequently affect supply. The most obvious of these is the weather, which can cause dramatic changes in the supply of crops.

Product life-cycle and new product development

So far our discussion of demand and supply has been rather like taking snapshots – considering demand at present, or if the conditions of demand change. The marketer's view of a product covers its life-cycle, during which dramatic changes occur. The role of the marketer is to manage the product over time in such a way that it satisfies its customers and makes a contribution to the achievement of the organisation's objectives.

Remember that as products mature, the market conditions and the nature of their demand will change, as will the nature and volume of competition. An appreciation of just how the conditions of the market are changing as the product moves through the life-cycle can provide a useful input to product management. See Figure 4.16.

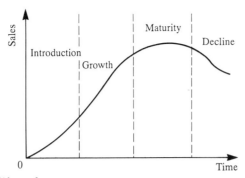

Figure 4.16   *The product life-cycle*

Introduction

Supply is limited and demand initially low, often as a result of high prices, as firms adopt policies of price skimming to maximize their short-term returns to repay new product development costs. The shortage of competitors indicates that demand is likely to be relatively price-inelastic.

Growth

The conditions of the market change as high prices and profits attract new firms and resources to the field. Supply and competition increase, making demand more price-elastic. A competitive feature of this stage of the life cycle is the emphasis on branding, used to differentiate the products and resist the tendency towards greater price-sensitivity. This increased promotional activity in the industry also changes the conditions of demand, and so results in a general increase in generic product demand as new customers increase sales volume. Costs may fall with economies of scale (see Chapter 7) and prices do fall.

Maturity

Supply and demand will settle down, and prices are no longer high enough to attract new resources to the business. Total revenue will be stable, unless managers take action to increase sales by looking for a new market, modifying the product or its marketing. Neither demand or supply is likely to be changing significantly.

Decline

With no further management action, sales will eventually begin to show a decline. This decrease in demand will usually be because a new competitive product has become more popular: it may be technologically more advanced, have a 'greener' image or a more reliable reputation. Whatever the reason for the change in customer preferences, as demand decreases, so prices and profitability will become depressed, encouraging firms to move their resources into new activities.

Good managers will in fact be in a position to forecast the changing market conditions, and pro-active firms will have new products developed for the marketplace and be ready to launch them before profits and sales begin to fall. New product development is essential to maintain continued growth and survival of the organization in the long run.

Summary review

1 How would you expect demand to change in the following scenarios:
   (a) The demand for microwave ovens following a reduction in income tax 4p in the £?
   (b) The demand for short-break holidays during a period of rapidly rising inflation?
   (c) The demand for computer software if there is a significant fall in the price of computers?
   (d) The demand for baby products in the years following a baby boom?

2 How is demand forecast in your company or your college? Try to find out and try to identify any historic trend in sales volume that can be linked to identifiable changes in the conditions of the market.

3 List the ways in which you might go about trying to forecast the demand for a new confectionery product.

5
Elasticity – its calculation and marketing implications

Throughout the last chapter we used the idea of elasticity to help us describe the responsiveness of demand and supply to changes in variables such as price, income or the price of other goods. Now we shall take a more detailed look at this concept which will actually provide decision-makers with a method of calculating the extent and impact of any such changes.

Aims

The aims of this chapter are:

1 To demonstrate how to calculate the value of elasticity.
2 To explain the implications of the various measures of elasticity and their implications for marketing tactics.
3 To examine the various classifications of elasticity.
4 To assess the contribution of the concept of elasticity to business planning and decision-making.

Glossary

Complementary goods – goods that are bought in combination, like computers and computer software.
Elastic – having a value of elasticity greater than 1, indicating a sensitivity to the variable that is changing.
Inelastic – having a value of elasticity less than 1, and indicating that there is relatively little change in quantity demanded or supplied as a result of the changing variable.
Unitary elastic – the value of elasticity is equal to 1 and any percentage change in the variable brings about an equal percentage change in the quantity demanded or supplied.

Elasticity – measurement and scale

The concept of elasticity is one of the most valuable that economics has brought to marketing and business practitioners. It is all very well knowing that as price is reduced, you can expect to sell more because your demand curve is downward-sloping. What business people need to know is how much more will they sell? What will be the change in total revenue? Similar questions need answering when incomes in your target market change or competitors alter their pricing.

The concept of elasticity provides a way of quantifying these effects, measuring the changes that are likely to occur and providing a useful contribution to the difficult area of forecasting. So far we have only used elasticity very loosely to describe a response as either sensitive to the changing variable or insensitive – elastic and inelastic. By calculating the mathematical value of elasticity we can provide a much more precise picture of the degree of sensitivity to the changing variable.

Measuring the value of elasticity

Measuring the mathematical value of elasticity, correctly referred to as the 'coefficient of elasticity' is done by comparing the percentage change in quantity with the percentage change in the variable. Note that the quantity can be quantity demanded or supplied.

For example if we were measuring price elasticity of demand, we would be evaluating how much quantity demanded would change as a result of change in price.

We would calculate it:

$$Ed = \frac{\% \; \Delta \; \text{in Qd}}{\% \; \Delta \; \text{in P}}$$

where Ed = coefficient of elasticity, Qd = quantity demanded, Δ = change, and P = price.

If the price changed by 10 per cent, and as a result the quantity demanded changed by a greater percentage, e.g. 15 per cent:

$$\frac{\% \; \Delta \; \text{in Qd}}{\% \; \Delta \; \text{in P}} = \frac{15}{10} = \frac{3}{2} = 1.5$$

The value of elasticity is greater than 1 and we would describe it as price-elastic.

It would be illustrated by a relatively flat demand curve. See Figure 5.1.

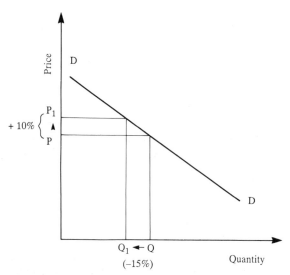

Figure 5.1   *Price-elastic demand*

If you refer back to the calculation of elasticity you will see that it tells you that for a product with a price elasticity of demand of 1.5, every 2 per cent change in price will result in a 3 per cent change in the quantity demanded. Try working out the following:

- Faced with a surplus of stock of such a product, what percentage change would be necessary for a retailer to increase sales by 33 per cent?
- If a sales tax of 6 per cent was added directly to the price of a product with a price elasticity of 1.5, what effect would you expect it to have on sales?

The scale of elasticity

Whenever the value of elasticity is greater than 1, the product is described as elastic, sensitive to the variable that is changing. If the value of elasticity is less than 1, that indicates an inelastic response. The percentage change in quantity is less than the percentage change in the variable. Demand for such a product would be classified as inelastic. So the value of elasticity provides a scale that ranges from 0 to infinity (α) and acts as a barometer to indicate the degree of responsiveness. See Figure 5.2.

We have selected a few key points of this scale, and consider what they imply for values of price elasticity of demand.

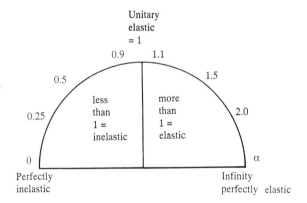

Figure 5.2   *The elasticity scale*

Perfectly inelastic demand

Products in this category have a value of elasticity of 0. No matter how significant the change in price, the quantity demanded has remained the same (see Figure 5.3). At Q despite a 20 per cent fall in price:

$$\frac{\% \; \Delta \; in \; Q}{\% \; \Delta \; in \; P} = \frac{O}{20} = O$$

Practical examples of this are not common. A very cheap product such as salt may behave like this, as would demand for a lifesaving drug that you had to take daily. No matter what happened to its price, you would always require the same dosage.

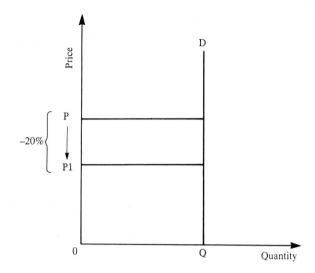

Figure 5.3   *Perfectly inelastic demand*

Price-inelastic demand

Products in this category have a value of elasticity of less than 1. As price falls from P to P_1, quantity demanded only extends from Q to Q_1. It takes a 4 per cent change in price to bring about a 1 per cent change in quantity:

$$\frac{\% \, \Delta \text{ in Q}}{\% \, \Delta \text{ in P}} = \frac{3}{12} = \frac{1}{4} = 0.25$$

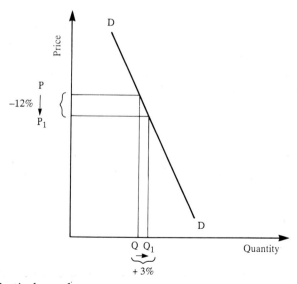

Figure 5.4   *Price-inelastic demand*

As price increases total revenue increases, and as price decreases total revenue decreases. Price-inelastic products may share the same characteristics. They are:

- Necessities.
- Without substitutes.
- Addictive.
- Representative of a small percentage of total income.

The marketers' role

Marketers will use promotional strategies and branding to position their products as unique, with no close substitutes, and to encourage brand loyalty, or addiction. In this way the marketer attempts to change the shape of the demand curve, making the product less and less sensitive to price change. The nearer to zero marketers are able to push their product's coefficient of elasticity, the more successful they have been.

A marketer wishing to sell more of a price-inelastic product should *not* reduce price to increase sales. Although more will be bought at lower prices, it will not be many more, and total revenue will fall as sales increase. For this category of product the marketers would have to use the non-price variables of the marketing mix, and develop strategies to increase sales by means of promotions, advertising or increased distribution.

A postscript for the Chancellor

When the Chancellor of the Exchequer seeks to raise indirect taxation, i.e. tax on spending, it must be focused on goods that are insensitive to price changes. Otherwise raising tax and therefore price will result in a significant reduction in sales and tax revenue.

It would not be politically acceptable to raise large amounts of fiscal revenue from necessities such as food or energy, so the Chancellor is traditionally left with products like alcohol, cigarettes, gambling and petrol, which all share the characteristics of inelasticity. As trends towards healthier living reduce the total spending on cigarettes and possibly alcohol, Chancellors will need to reassess what products are perceived to be essential and addictive today. In the 1991 Budget Norman Lamont placed a £200 tax liability on mobile telephones; in the future summer holidays abroad, video cassettes and compact discs may fall under the 'added tax burden' hammer, as increasingly consumers perceive these once luxury items as necessities for which there are no close substitutes.

Unitary elasticity

When the change in variable is exactly matched by the change in quantity, the value of elasticity is 1, unitary elasticity (Figure 5.5). Total revenue will remain constant, whether the variable, in this case price, moves up or down:

$$Ed = \frac{\% \,\Delta \text{ in Q}}{\% \,\Delta \text{ in P}} = \frac{10}{10} = \frac{1}{1} = 1$$

The curve is a rectangular hyperbola. Any rectangle drawn under the curve has a constant area. This area represents total revenue.

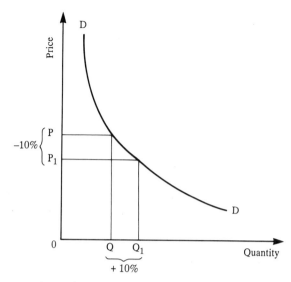

Figure 5.5 *Unitary elastic demand*

Price-elastic demand

When the value of elasticity is greater than 1, the product is sensitive to the variable. In this example every 1 per cent change in price brings about a 2 per cent change in quantity demanded.

$$Ed = \frac{\% \, \Delta \text{ in Q}}{\% \, \Delta \text{ in P}} = \frac{30}{15} = \frac{2}{1} = 2$$

- As price goes up total revenue falls.
- As price goes down total revenue increases.

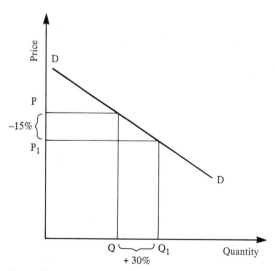

Figure 5.6 *Price-elastic demand*

Products which are price-elastic tend to:

1 Be luxuries.
2 Have close substitutes.
3 Not be addictive.
4 Represent a large proportion of total income.

The marketing lesson

The most significant lesson for the marketer to learn is how this different set of characteristics alters the impact of a price change on total revenue completely. Unlike the position with an inelastic product, lower prices *will* increase sales and total revenue. Money-off offers and special deals are likely to have considerable impact in such a market. Price rises, however, are a problem. Their impact on market share can be minimized by ensuring price rises are in line with competitors' price changes.

Identifying the true nature of your product and assessing its elasticity is an important step in the preparation of any marketing plan.

Infinitely/perfectly elastic demand

The value of elasticity of products in this category = α:

$$Ed = \frac{\% \, \Delta \text{ in Q}}{\% \, \Delta \text{ in P}} = \frac{\alpha}{O} = \alpha$$

This demand curve is represented by a horizontal line, completely flat, as in Figure 5.7. It demonstrates that customers will buy as much as they can get at price P, but if price was to change by any amount, there would be none bought at all.

This situation does not often occur in a marketplace, but it will be important later when we examine the demand curve facing the firm under conditions of perfect competition.

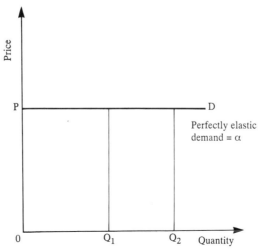

Figure 5.7 *Infinitely elastic demand*

Real Demand Curves

So far we have considered stylized curves, describing the whole curve as elastic or inelastic. In reality when we measure the value of elasticity, we are calculating it at a particular point on the demand curve. The effect of changing the price of a product from £1 to £1.50 may be very different to changing the price of the same product from £2 to £3 (although both represent 50 per cent changes in price). When you examine a real demand curve, you will find that the value of elasticity can change throughout its length. See Figure 5.8.

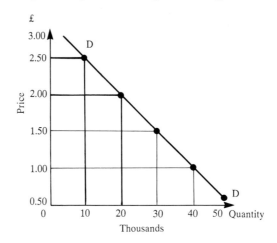

Figure 5.8   *Elasticity along the demand curve*

This means that marketers need to take great care when changing price, because a product that has always been considered inelastic can be pushed up into a more price-elastic part of the curve, and respond uncharacteristically to a change in price. In the past this has caught out the Chancellor, who one year raised the duty on cigarettes, only to find that as a result sales and tax revenue actually fell as the product demonstrated its capacity to be price-elastic.

For the marketer wishing to draw up the demand curve for his/her own product, the process is far from simple. In the real world conditions in the marketplace are constantly changing, and customers do not always respond in predictable ways.

Researching the effect of a price change does not provide reliable results. A customer asked how many units s/he would buy at a price of £x and £y is not in a position to give answers that would necessarily hold true in the marketplace. However, test marketing does allow the opportunity of varying one element of the marketing mix and comparing how much demand in two test areas varies. Observation of the market's behaviour when prices are changed, either by you or your competitors, also provides a background of data from which managers can develop a feel for the shape of their demand curve.

The increased sophistication of management information systems through improved applications of technology, particularly at the point of sale, is increasing the accuracy and reliability of the available data. Remaining aware that the customer's response to the next price change may be different from his/her response to this one is important for the practising marketer. Techniques for demand forecasting are improving, but using the economists' analysis of demand is a still a good basis for the marketers' understanding of the true nature of demand.

Measuring other types of elasticity

We have already seen that other variables besides price can also change the level of demand. Income, the price of other goods and changes in marketing expenditure can all be quantified, and therefore their impact measured by the elasticity concept.

As with price elasticity, the calculation is based on the same formula, and the resulting coefficient of elasticity will be a value between 0 and infinity:

- With values of less than 1 but greater than zero indicating an insensitivity of demand to changes in the variable described as inelastic.
- Values of more than 1 and less than infinity indicating demand sensitivity to the variable classified as elastic. See Table 5.1.

Table 5.1   Calculating other types of elasticity

Type of elasticity	Definition	Calculation
Income elasticity of demand	How much demand changes as a result of a change in income (Y).	$\dfrac{\%\ \Delta\ \text{in Q d}}{\%\ \Delta\ \text{in Y}}$
Cross-elasticity of demand	How much quantity demanded of Product A changes as a result of a change in the price of Product B.	$\dfrac{\%\ \Delta\ \text{in Q d A}}{\%\ \Delta\ \text{in PB}}$
Promotional elasticity of demand	How much quantity demanded changes as a result of a change in promotional expenditure (£ pr).	$\dfrac{\%\ \Delta\ \text{in Q d}}{\%\ \Delta\ \text{in £pr}}$
Price elasticity of supply	How much the quantity supplied changes as a result of a change in price.	$\dfrac{\%\ \Delta\ \text{in Q s}}{\%\ \Delta\ \text{in P}}$

Income elasticity of demand

If as a result of a 10 per cent rise in income, demand for a product changes by 15 per cent, the value of income elasticity is greater than 1. Demand is sensitive to income. If the marketing manager for this product is aware that average incomes for these customers are forecast to rise in real terms by 20 per cent over the next 5 years, what action should he/she take?

You will find that you cannot answer this question because you are still missing a vital piece of information. You know that for every 2 per cent rise in income there will be a 3 per cent change in quantity demanded. In this case you would be forecasting the need to change output by 30 per cent over the next 5 years. What you do not know is in which direction. Are you expecting demand to rise or to fall over this time? See Figure 5.9.

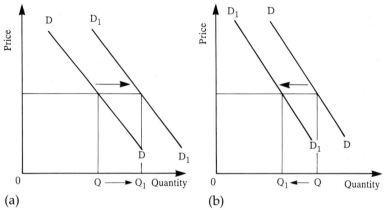

Figure 5.9   *Effect of a change in income on demand for* (a) *normal and* (b) *inferior goods*

Both the graphs in Figure 5.9 represent products whose demand is equally sensitive to changes in income:

(a) represents a normal good where demand rises with income,
(b) an inferior good, where demand decreases as income rises, e.g. a product such as white bread, which customers may perceive to be inferior to brown bread, or sausages *vis-à-vis* steak, and so on.

The direction of the change

In order to identify the direction of the change it is necessary to add positive (+) and minus (−) signs to our elasticity calculation. It is accepted that it is not necessary to do this when calculating price elasticity of demand, because it is assumed that the demand curve will be a normal downward-sloping curve, so as price goes up (+), quantity demanded goes down (−),

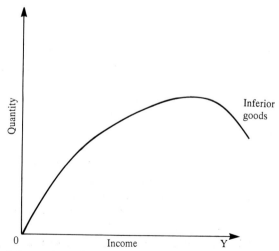

Figure 5.10   *Income and demand – inferior good*

and *vice versa*. When you calculate this, it gives you a minus sign before the value of elasticity. When quantity and variable move in opposite directions the value of elasticity will be a minus sign (−).

In Figure 5.9a income elasticity shows you that demand falls as income rises, and rises as income falls. Negative income elasticity indicates an inferior good. See Figure 5.10.

When the variable and demand move in the same direction, the value of elasticity is positive. See Figure 5.11. In this instance it can be seen that quantity demanded is rising and falling with changes in Y, giving a positive (+) value of income elasticity and representing a normal good.

The direction of the change is also important when measuring cross-elasticity of demand.

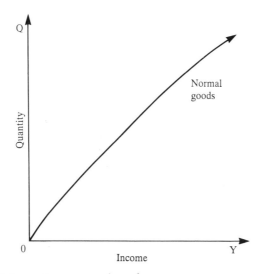

Figure 5.11   *Income and demand – a normal good*

Cross-elasticity of demand

All products are in competition with each other for the consumer's scarce income. Marketers know that sometimes quite unrelated products are in surprisingly close competition with each other. A seat at the cinema will not only be competing with the theatre, TV and video, but with the entertainment at the local pub and the value of a new pair of shoes.

Identifying which products are most closely in competition with each other is an important aspect of management planning. Competitive strategy needs to be clearly thought through and planned.

A coefficient of cross-elasticity greater than 1 indicates that a product's demand is sensitive to price changes in this other product – the two are cross-elastic. The nearer to zero the value of elasticity, the less the impact price changes in this product will have on the demand for yours, e.g. the price of bread is unlikely to affect the demand for cars significantly.

Having established the extent or significance of the relation between two products, you must consider the direction of any resulting change in demand. Again the value of the coefficient of cross-elasticity is important. See Figure 5.12.

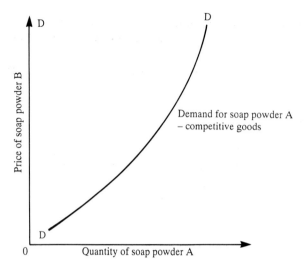

Figure 5.12   *Cross-elasticity of competitive goods*

Where the quantity and variable move in the same direction, there will be a (+) value of cross-elasticity. These products are in competition with each other. As the price of product B goes up (+), you sell more of A (+), because people turn to your product as a cheaper substitute. In markets where products have both positive (+) and high values of cross-elasticities, managers are likely to:

- Adopt strategies that make their products seem unique, in the hope that other products will be perceived as less acceptable substitutes.
- Work closely with competitive producers to ensure price changes are carried out in concert.

When the demand for A and the price of B in Figure 5.13 are moving in opposite directions, the value of cross elasticity will be a (−). Such goods are complementary; they are being

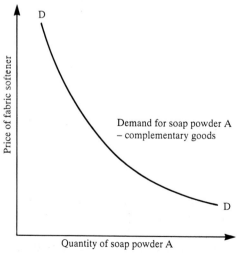

Figure 5.13   *Cross-elasticity of complementary goods*

bought together in some way, like computers and their software and manufactured goods and the machinery used to produce them. An awareness of the behaviour, forecasts and future strategies of these companies would be important. As there is no competition between them, a co-operative approach to business planning could be mutually beneficial.

A note on price elasticity

Because economists assume that in most cases the value of price elasticity of demand will be negative (−), indicating quantity and price moving in opposite directions, it is accepted practice to ignore the minus sign. If you find a positive (+) value of price elasticity there are two possibilities:

- It is a backward-sloping demand curve, i.e. one of the exceptions, where price and quantity demanded move in the same direction.
- It is in fact a value of price elasticity of *supply*.

Here firms are prepared to sell more as prices rise, so price and quantity move together. See Figure 5.14.

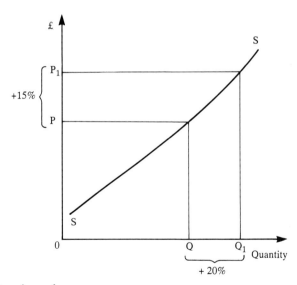

Figure 5.14   *Elasticity of supply*

A note on promotional elasticity

You would expect this to have a positive value – sales increasing with promotional effort. Unless you wish to de-market the product, you should reassess your promotional strategy if you sell less as a result of an increase in advertising spending. This measure of elasticity is far from precise. If your product proves to be promotionally inelastic – a coefficient less than 1 – it does not indicate demand will never respond to promotion. It may show that the current treatment or strategy is inappropriate. See whether other products in this generic market are more responsive before giving up on this element of your marketing mix.

Remember to deal only with changes in real expenditure, i.e. corrected for inflation, and do not forget to allow time for the sales effect to feed through. However, this measure, despite its limitations, can provide marketers with a yardstick by which the promotional marketing effort can be evaluated.

Comparisons of price and promotional elasticity may help determine whether reduced price or increased promotion is the most cost-effective method of achieving a X % sales increase.

The value of the elasticity concept

Real forecasting of demand is a complex process, because it is likely that a number of variables will be changing at any time. But business and marketing staff need to be comfortable with the concept of elasticity. An understanding of it allows:

- Improved forecasting and planning and a better understanding of the changing nature of customer demand.
- A basis for measuring change in demand resulting from changes in both price and non-price variables.

Summary review

1 A firm currently has an operating capacity of 500,000 units per annum. It has the opportunity of increasing this capacity by 100,000 units over the next year. The income of the target market for this product is forecast to rise by 10 per cent over the next 2 years. The product's income elasticity of demand has been calculated a + 1.5. How would you assess the opportunity?

2 A product has a value of price elasticity of demand of 1.2 and a promotional elasticity of 1.5. Currently the product is priced at £10 per unit and sales are 100,000 with a promotional budget of £5,000. Compare the cost and benefit to the company of a 10 per cent price reduction and a 10 per cent increase in promotional expenditure.

3 At the end of Chapter 4 we considered how demand and supply might change throughout a product's life-cycle. Now consider how you might expect price elasticity of demand to change throughout the life stages of the following products:
   (a) Satellite TV dishes.
   (b) A new traditional recipe range of tinned soups.
   (c) An environmentally friendly alternative to tinfoil.

Section Two: Projects

1 Select six items that you have bought recently. Choose as wide a variety as possible, from a new pair of trainers to your daily newspaper or a box of your favourite breakfast cereal.

Take a long hard look at these products, make a list of all their features and add to this their corresponding benefits. Now place these benefits in order to reflect your own needs and priorities. Try and quantify the utility you derive from the various features provided:

- Have these manufacturers got their marketing to you right?
- What are the major product feature differences between these products and the major competitors?

2 Design a market research project that would allow you to assess the likely demand for a new facility, e.g. a vending machine in your common room or office. Try and identify how demand would change over a number of price points:

- What are the limitations of your results?
- What is the apparent price elasticity of demand for this service at two different price points on your demand curve?

3 How would you describe the functions of *Which?* magazine in economic terms? How could the information it provides be improved to help the customer better assess the 'utility' of the various models.

If markets are customer-oriented, why is the service of a consumer organization necessary? See the information extracted from a 'Which' guide on electrical circuit breakers RCDs and report.

BUYING GUIDE

None of the portable RCDs we tested was beyond criticism. Our choices: the **B&R Powerbreaker H02** £18 (Tel 0279 434561), the **Deltasafe** £17 (serial numbers above 34836; Tel: 061–652 1111), or the **Smiths Type CB002** £19 (numbered 9030 onwards; Tel: 081–450 8944), did best in our tests.

PORTABLE RCDs: FACTS AND FIGURES AND TEST RESULTS

We tested all the different models we found in the shops. All the RCDs were made in the UK.

1 Price
The price we give is based on a survey of 100 shops in February. For those models not widely available in d-i-y sheds and electrical stores we have given the manufacturers' guide prices in *italics* and their telephone numbers below so that you can find a local supplier.

It pays to shop around – the MK Safeguard, for example, cost around £20 in some shops, £32 in others – a difference of 60 per cent. **Contactum** Tel: 081–452 6366; **Crabtree** Tel: 0922 721202; **Marbo** Tel: 0429 234611.

2 Features

All the RCDs except the Flymo Protector Plug had a test button and a mechanical indicator 'flag' to show when the RCD had tripped. All were fitted with a reset button, again with the exception of the Flymo Protector Plug which automatically reset when a plug was inserted into its socket.

M = mains 'on' indicator light

N = neon mains indicator integral with indicator. Flashes to show RCD has tripped, remains
on to show mains ON

R = reset button awkwardly sited underneath main body

T = tests itself automatically when plugged in to mains socket

3 Size

This shows the relative size of the RCD: the more ▶▶▶s, the larger. ▶ represents an RCD about the size of a 3-way mains adaptor; ▶▶ is about twice as large. A large one may not fit into a mains socket which is recessed or under a shelf, for instance.

PERFORMANCE TESTS

Our tests were based on the British Standard for portable RCDs – BS 7071. Capital letters in the Table refer to the problems described below. A small letter means the manufacturer has made a modification to cope with that problem since we bought our samples. This means that newer, modified versions of the RCD on sale in the shops shouldn't have the problem. But if you already have one of the older RCDs you should be aware of these faults, and make sure you unplug it when not in use, and test it every time you use it.

Table 5.2   Test results

	Price £	Features	Size	Electrical Safety	Durability
1 Archer RCD adaptor[1]	20	–	▶▶▶	A	F
* 2 B & R Powerbreaker H02	18	R	▶▶	Ebc	√
3 Contactum Pluguard	16	–	▶	ad[3]	Gf[3]
4 Crabtree Safetydaptor	24	M	▶▶	A	F
* 5 Deltasafe	17	–	▶	Eb	f[2]
6 Flymo Protector Plug[1]	17	NT	▶▶	ABC	FG
7 Homebase Safety Adaptor	20	M	▶▶	A	F
8 Micromark Powercutter	15	–	▶	ad	Gf
9 Marbo Safety Adaptor	23	M	▶▶	A	F
10 MK Safeguard	20	–	▶▶▶	A	F
11 Qualcast Power Safe	23	M	▶▶	A	F
*12 Smiths Type CB002	19	R	▶▶	Ebc	√

[1] Discontinued but still in shops
[2] Current production modified. Check for serial number above 34836
[3] Criticisms apply to models marked BS 4293. Newer models marked BS 7071 include modifications

4 Electrical safety
Tripping current We measured the residual current that caused the RCD to trip. All were satisfactory.
Insulation We checked that the RCD worked safely in high humidity conditions like those you might find in an outbuilding or greenhouse. All were satisfactory. We also checked that the socket met the standards required of an ordinary fixed mains socket – some failed this test because a stray wire or screwdriver could make contact with live parts through the earth pin socket (A). Some devices weren't tamperproof (D), and we have a design criticism of those with a letter E.
Wiring faults These tests check that the RCD still works safely if connected to an outlet which is incorrectly wired, or if a cable in the fixed wiring to the socket becomes disconnected. All worked safely in these tests.
Earthing Many, but not all, garden tools are double-insulated and so do not use the earth conductor. We checked the effectiveness of the earth connection of the RCD to see how it would withstand a serious fault condition. Unsatisfactory ones are shown in the Table by the letter B.
Circuit fault We checked to see if the RCD could cope with a high current which an appliance would draw if it had a serious fault. The letter C indicates it couldn't.
    The Flymo Protector Plug's indicator is a neon light which BS 7071 doesn't allow.

5 Durability
Portable RCDs are small and light and prone to be dropped and knocked, perhaps being stored in a drawer along with other gardening paraphernalia. The Standard requires them to be able to withstand such treatment and still perform safely. Our tests show some don't (F). The circuitry inside the RCD should withstand repeated use. We tripped the RCD 2,000 times and checked that it still worked correctly afterwards. Those marked G didn't.
$\sqrt{}$ = satisfactory in our tests

The prices in our Tables are based on prices we found in shops before the VAT increase announced in the Budget came into force. Any increases due to VAT won't affect our Buying Guide.

Section Three
Price

Price plays a central role in economics. It is the driving force behind the dynamic market mechanism as well as being one of the four marketing mix variables. We have already seen in Section 2 how price influences the level of demand. In this section we shall take a closer look at the contribution economic theory can make to the business person's understanding of pricing models, options and tactics.

Without doubt, pricing is one of the most difficult decision areas for any organization. The price set ultimately determines the total revenue earned, and so plays a critical part in ensuring the survival and the financial health of the operation. There are no simple solutions or formulas that can satisfactorily be used to set prices; there are too many variables and considerations for that. The marketer knows that price-setting is more of an art than a science, but an understanding of the economic elements of the pricing conundrum provides a useful and valid starting point for every student of business and marketing.

The aims of this chapter are to provide a clear appreciation of the function of price in the market mechanism and an understanding of costs and competition as key elements in any pricing decision by:

- Examining the key factors influencing pricing decisions – demand, costs and competitive activity.
- Identifying how these factors can be used to inform pricing decisions.
- Examining how costs can be classified and how they change over time and with different scales of operation.
- Examining the behaviour of firms and how decisions on price and output are made in different industrial structures.

This section is composed of three chapters:

Chapter 6 The function of price – the economist's view.
Chapter 7 Costs – the price floor.
Chapter 8 Competition – how firms make their pricing decisions.

6
The function of price – the economist's view

Aims

The aims of this chapter are to:

- Provide a framework for understanding and appreciating the impact of price changes on the market.
- Examine how price acts as the 'invisible hand', ensuring the automatic reallocation of resources in a free market.
- Identify why price often fails to ensure the best use of resources in the real world.
- Consider how government actions can influence price.
- Compare the marketers' and economists' views on price.

Glossary

Ceteris paribus – predictions of how markets respond can only be made if it is assumed that only one variable at a time is changing. The phrase is used to infer that all other things will remain constant.

Equilibrium – the price at which the quantity demanded is exactly equal to the quantity supplied.

Externalities – the term used to describe the difference between private and social costs.

Fiscal policy – the activities of government that relate to taxation and government spending.

Incidence of tax – indicates the person who is legally responsible for paying the tax.

Invisible hand – a description given to price, reflecting the way price can influence the market and ensure an equilibrium is established.

The market mechanism in operation

The function of the marketplace is to provide a system that automatically ensures the best or 'optimum allocation of resources'. To fulfil this role as the economic problem-solver, the marketer needs to be sensitive to changes in customer needs and wants, and responsive to any changes in the conditions of the market, demand or supply. Price is the critical variable in this mechanism.

Changes in customer demand cause price to change. Price changes signal changing profitability to suppliers, causing them to reassess their output decisions. This central and dynamic role of price causes economists to describe price as the *invisible hand,* which works to bring demand and supply together.

Interaction between demand and supply

In the previous section we examined demand and supply separately, we now need to consider the interaction between them. See Table 6.1.

Table 6.1   Demand and supply schedule

Price (£)	Quantity demanded (thousands)	Quantity supplied (thousands)
2.50	15	35
2.25	20	30
2.00	25	25
1.75	30	20

By plotting the information in Table 6.1. on a single graph (Figure 6.1), it is apparent that while the normal demand curve falls from left to right and the supply curve goes up from left to right, there will be a point of interaction. This point is the *equilibrium point.* It indicates the price at which the quantity demanded is equal to the quantity supplied. At the price of £2.00 25,000 units are being demanded and supplied, and the market is in equilibrium or balance. There will be no motivation on the part of either suppliers or consumers to change the market.

However, at the higher price of £2.25 there is *excess supply* in the market (indicated by shaded area on Figure 6.1). At this price firms are prepared to supply 30,000 units, but customers will only buy 20,000 units. This represents an excess of supply of 10,000 units. In order to get rid of surplus stocks, suppliers will tend to bid the price down, causing supply to contract and demand to extend, until the equilibrium price of £2.00 is reached.

Similarly at the lower price of £1.75 it can be seen that the quantity supplied has contracted to 20,000 units, but demand has extended to 30,000 units. This difference of 10,000 units represents the excess demand (cross hatched area on Figure 6.1). Suppliers will recognize that they are able to increase their profits by bidding the price up; as prices rise, demand will contract and supply will extend until again the equilibrium price of £2.00 is reached.

Remember

Movements along the demand and supply curve are caused by changes in price and referred to as extensions and contractions.

In general it can be observed that at any price above the equilibrium there will be an excess of supply and a tendency for price to fall to the equilibrium price. At prices lower than the equilibrium prices will tend to rise until the equilibrium is established. In this way price can be seen as the variable that ensures a balance between demand and supply.

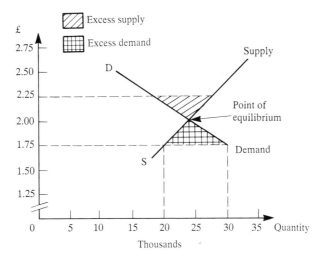

Figure 6.1 *Illustrating the equilibrium point*

The market when conditions of demand and supply change

We have seen in Chapter 4 that a change in any variable other than price is referred to as a condition of the market, and illustrated by a new demand or supply curve. We are assuming here that only one market variable is changing at any time. Economists usually indicate this by prefacing their analysis with the statement *ceteris paribus*, a Latin phrase that means all other things remain equal or unchanged.

In effect there are only four possible changes in the marketplace.

Changes in the conditions of demand

1. When demand increases

Demand may increase for the following reasons:

- An increase in income.
- A fall in the price of a competitive product.
- An increase in advertising expenditure.

See Figure 6.2.

Short-term

This increase in demand causes price to rise to P_1 and a resulting extension in supply.

Longer-term

Over a period of time the high price and therefore relatively higher profits that can be earned in this market will encourage new firms to enter the industry, increasing supply and the resources allocated to the production of this product. The new equilibrium price of P will be

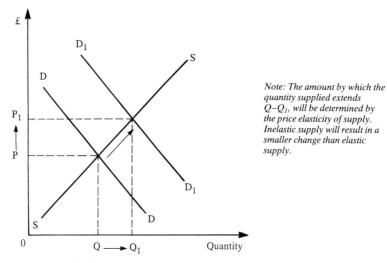

Note: The amount by which the quantity supplied extends Q–Q₁, will be determined by the price elasticity of supply. Inelastic supply will result in a smaller change than elastic supply.

Figure 6.2   *An increase in demand causes an extension of supply from Q to Q₁*

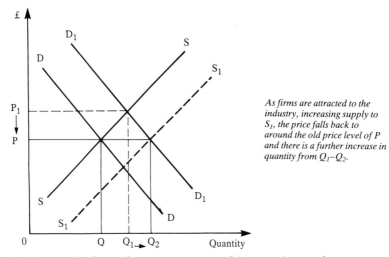

As firms are attracted to the industry, increasing supply to S₁, the price falls back to around the old price level of P and there is a further increase in quantity from Q₁–Q₂.

Figure 6.3   *An increase in demand causes an eventual increase in supply*

close to the old equilibrium, as this is the price level at which firms are making normal profits. The industry will continue to attract new entrants whenever excess profits are being earned, because firms that are seeking to maximize their profits are better off in this industry. See Figure 6.3.

2. When demand decreases

Demand may decrease as result of:

● A fall in income.
● A reduction in the price of competitive goods.
● In anticipation of future price reductions.

See Figure 6.4.

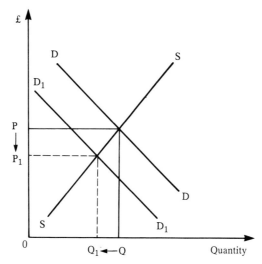

Figure 6.4   *A decrease in demand*

Short-term

The decrease in demand causes price to fall to P_1 and a resulting contraction of supply from Q to Q_1.

Long-term

Eventually the lower price of P_1 will cause some firms to leave the market. At P_1 the least efficient firms will be making a loss and will actively seek a more profitable use for their resources. See Figure 6.5.

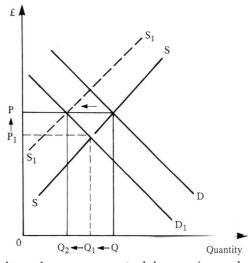

Figure 6.5   *A decrease in demand causes an eventual decrease in supply*

The new equilibrium point at the intersection of D_1 and S_1 will be at a price level of P. This is the price necessary to provide those firms remaining in the industry with normal levels of profit.

In both Figures 6.4 and 6.5 you can see how changes in the conditions of demand cause a movement in price. Price signals the change in consumer priorities, and the impact of price on profitability encourages firms to re-evaluate the alternative uses of their resources.

Price is therefore a guiding hand which helps reallocate resources between industries, in response to changing customer demands.

3. When supply increases

Such increases indicate that the relative costs of production have fallen. This may be due to:

- A bumper harvest.
- The introduction of new technology.
- Reduced costs of the factors of production.

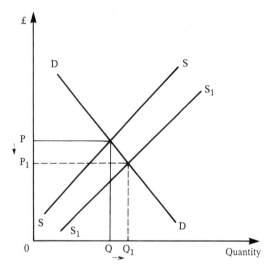

Figure 6.6   *An increase in supply*

Short-term

As supply shifts to the right, from S to S_1, the price falls to P_1, causing an extension of demand from Q to Q_1. How much demand extends will be determined by the price elasticity of demand. The more price-inelastic, the smaller the increase from Q to Q_1.

Long-term

In the longer term the relatively low price of P_1 will change the conditions of demand. Purchasers of competing goods will re-evaluate their purchase decisions, and over time demand may increase, causing prices to move back towards the original price P and normal profit levels. See Figure 6.7.

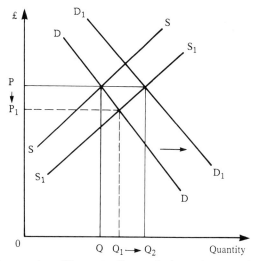

Figure 6.7   *An increase in supply will eventually result in an increase in demand*

Because of the more efficient use of resources in this sector, it is economically rational to increase the resources committed to this product, to Q_2.

4. A decrease in supply

This indicates that resources are being allocated away from this industry, and that individual firms are finding it more profitable to use their resources elsewhere, perhaps because:

- Costs have increased.
- Prices of other goods have increased, changing the opportunity cost options.

See Figure 6.8.

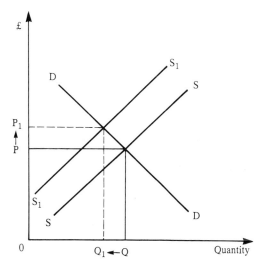

Figure 6.8   *A decrease in supply*

Short-term

As supply shifts to the left from S to S_1, prices go up from P to P_1 and the quantity demanded contracts from Q to Q_1.

Long-term

Over time the higher price of P_1 will cause customers to reassess their purchase decisions. They are likely to replace this product with relatively cheaper alternatives. As demand decreases, a price level of P will be re-established, ensuring that remaining firms make normal profits. Less resources will be used up by this industry.

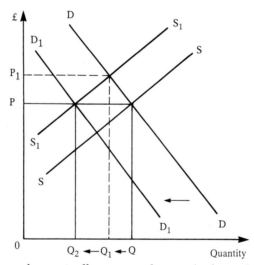

Figure 6.9   *A decrease in supply eventually causes a decrease in demand*

Benefits of the market mechanism

These alternative scenarios show how changes in the market conditions are interpreted through the market mechanism to lead eventually to the reallocation of resources. One of the main advantages of the mechanism is that it works automatically, without the expensive, often inflexible bureaucracies of a planned approach. The dynamic nature of the mechanism allows rapid readjustments in response to a variety of market changes.

By consumers making decisions that will maximize their utility and producers pursuing their goal of profit maximization, resources are used in the most efficient way. The years of Thatcherism in the UK were characterized by advocates of the benefits of the free market.

Market supporters argue for:

- Greater competition between suppliers.
- Deregulation of markets.
- Privatization of publicly owned industry.

Problems with the market mechanism

The ability of the mechanism to work effectively and produce an optimum allocation of resources is dependent on a number of conditions being satisfied. In reality these conditions often do not exist. Markets are frequently not competitive, decisions made by both producers and consumers are often inadequately informed, firms may not be seeking to maximize profits, consumers do not always act rationally, and switching resources from one industry to another is neither easy nor cheap.

Besides these constraints limiting the market mechanism's ability to do its job, other problems arise. One of the most significant of these is the result of the unequal distribution of income. The market has a tendency to favour the better off. Willingness and ability to pay influence the allocation of resources more than need. It is therefore not surprising that a side-effect of the Thatcher years was the growth in disparity between the 'haves' and the 'have nots'.

Further difficulties with the mechanism arise because of time lags that occur between the change in price and the reallocation of resources. This can be seen very clearly in the agricultural sector, where it may take years before additional fruit trees, for example, are able to yield the desired crop.

The behaviour of the agricultural market is often explained by means of the *Cobweb theorem*. Planting decisions are based on the prevailing market price in Spring, but if this is not an equilibrium price and by harvest time demand has increased, there will be an excess of demand, $Q–Q_1$, and prices will rise to P_1. See Figure 6.10.

The higher price will influence planting decisions in the second year. The extension of supply to Q_1 will cause prices to fall to P_2, and so in year 3 less, Q_2, will be sown.

If the price changes in this market become smaller each year, the market will eventually adjust to an equilibrium level. If they become greater, the market will continually swing from excess demand to excess supply. The resulting fluctuations in price can be particularly problematic in countries dependent on agricultural exports.

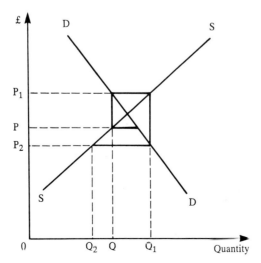

Figure 6.10   *The cobweb theorem*

Why price fails to ensure optimum resource allocation

When the market mechanism fails to produce a satisfactory allocation of resources, the cause is likely to be one of the following and result in government intervention of one sort or another.

Imperfections in the market

Imperfect competition exists wherever the number of buyers or suppliers is limited, as in the case of monopoly (one supplier) and monopsony (one buyer). In situations of imperfect competition barriers prevent new entrants to the marketplace. Lack of market information and the impact of time lags, as discussed above, are all examples of market imperfections.

Public goods

The provision of goods that benefit the whole community is not adequately covered by a market mechanism. Although in areas such as health and education some provision by the private sector may be made, it is usually necessary for governments to 'top up' the resources allocated to ensure adequate provision for all. In areas such as defence and law and order individuals would be unlikely to place enough priority on these goods without government intervention.

Social costs

Individuals and firms make decisions that can either benefit or harm others. The marketing objective is about firms seeking to 'satisfy the needs of the individual', but what if this is not either in the individual's best long-term interest or harms others?

An individual may want to drive home from the pub, but is prevented from doing so if she/he has had too much to drink, in order to protect themselves and others from accidents. An individual smoking may satisfy a personal need, but injure others who object to 'passive smoking'. Likewise firms may make production decisions that fail to take account of the true social costs caused by the pollution from their processes.

The differences between private and social costs or benefits are known as *externalities*. Because the market mechanism fails to account for these externalities adequately, resources can be misallocated. Governments intervene to protect social interests with laws, taxes and regulations.

Marketing and social costs

Marketers are steadily coming to realize that the goal of 'satisfying individual needs' without consideration of wider implications for the community will not be a recipe for business success in the twenty-first century. Increasingly consumers are themselves demanding more environmentally friendly products, produced by equally sound production methods. Marketing writer Philip Kotler developed the Societal Marketing Concept, which says that in future firms will not only have to find business solutions that:

- satisfy individual consumer needs, and
- satisfy the company's objectives,

but such solutions will also have to:

- be in the best long-term interests of the individual, and
- not be harmful to society.

The gradual extension of the simple marketing concept to the more demanding, broader-based societal marketing concept reflects the marketers' realization that in future firms will need to take social costs as well as private ones into account. It seems that, albeit slowly, the market mechanism is itself beginning to account for externalities, and only limited government intervention may be necessary in the future to ensure social costs are not disregarded. For companies like Body Shop, which have responded to the call to become greener, the reward has been profitable growth.

Market interference

The market mechanism can only work if it is allowed to. Restrictions on output or price will prevent the mechanism from achieving an optimum allocation of resources.

Governments may set price ceilings to prevent the cost of essentials such as basic foods and housing rising above a certain level. While this ceiling is above the equilibrium price, it will have no effect on the workings of the market. Figure 6.11 shows what happens if the maximum price, Pm, is lower than the equilibrium price.

At this price quantity B is demanded, but firms are only prepared to supply quantity A. The difference between A and B represents the excess demand in the market. If price cannot

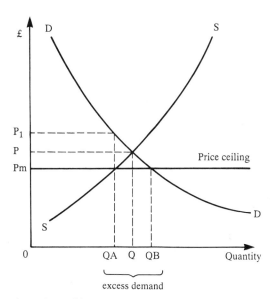

Figure 6.11   *The impact of a price ceiling*

change, then this position will not alter. Government is now faced with the problem of ensuring that the available quantity A is distributed fairly, possibly by some form of rationing.

If government interferes with price, it will also have to make decisions on output; the marketplace cannot be expected to do a satisfactory job.

The Common Agricultural Policy of the EC is well known for its market intervention. By setting a minimum price, to ensure the interests of farmers are protected, without adequate controls on the output decisions of those farmers, CAP has created excess supply. Europe now has developed some unusual features: wine lakes, and butter, grain and beef mountains. See Figure 6.12.

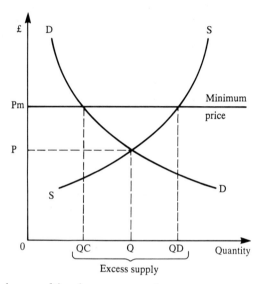

Figure 6.12   *Minimum prices resulting in excess supply*

At any price above the equilibrium, supply will extend and demand contract. The cumulative difference between C and D represents the size of the stockpile.

Reducing these surpluses is not easy. Europe found a market in the Eastern bloc, where, though they were sold at prices well below the domestic price, there was no impact on the internal market. OPEC has found that to make minimum price agreements work, agreements also have to be reached on production quotas – not easy to negotiate.

Governments' influence on price

An alternative to preventing the mechanism from working by restrictions on price and quotas is for the government to use the mechanism to achieve its objectives. This is done through fiscal policy, using indirect taxes and subsidies to influence price and costs and therefore the decisions of suppliers and buyers.

The impact of such intervention will fall on both the producer and the customer, according to the relative elasticities of supply and demand. If there is an increase in indirect taxation, the incidence of the tax will be shared:

$$\frac{\text{Customers' share of tax}}{\text{Producers' share of tax}} = \frac{\text{Price elasticity of supply}}{\text{Price elasticity of demand}}$$

For a product with a price elasticity of supply of 1.4 and a price elasticity of demand of 0.6, a 20p increase in tax would be shared in the ratio:

$$\frac{1.4}{.6} \quad \text{that is} \quad \begin{array}{l} \text{14p paid by the customer} \\ \text{6p paid by the producer} \end{array}$$

A 10p tax on the same product would have resulted in the consumer paying an extra 7p and the producer 3p.

Who pays the tax imposed is subject to the *incidence of taxation*. The legal incidence of taxation is upon the person who is responsible for paying it, in the case of indirect taxation the producer or supplier. But some or all of the burden of tax can, as we have seen, be shifted to the consumer, so the actual incidence and burden of taxation is shared. The sharing of benefits from a subsidy are also determined by the relative price elasticities.

The more price-inelastic demand is, the greater the proportion of tax that will be borne by the consumer, another reason why marketers would prefer the demand for their products to be more price-inelastic.

The effect of an indirect tax

Producers and suppliers may hesitate to hand the whole burden of a tax over to the consumer. To the customer it represents a price rise, and so will result in some contraction of demand. How significant this fall will be is of course determined by the price sensitivity of that particular product. With retail demand, particularly for consumer durables, depressed in 1991, Marks & Spencer announced that it would not be raising its prices by 2½ per cent, despite the Chancellor's VAT increase to 17½ per cent in the March 1991 Budget.

An increase in indirect taxation is illustrated by the supply curve shifting to the left (Figure 6.13). For the firm the new tax is the same as an increase in wage or raw material costs: it's

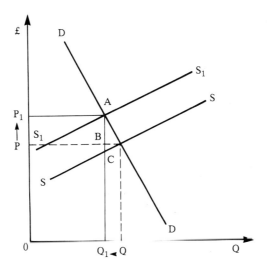

Figure 6.13   *The effect of an indirect tax. A subsidy would cause the S1 curve to shift to the right*

another bill that must be paid. The new tax shifts the curve to the left to S_1 and price increases to P_1. The incidence of tax falls largely on the consumer, as demand for this product is fairly inelastic. The consumer will pay AB of the tax and the producer BC. The effect of the tax is to reduce the quantity of goods purchased to Q_1.

A subsidy is the equivalent of a reduction in costs. The supply curve therefore shifts to the right, resulting in an increase in goods bought.

The marketer's view of taxation and subsidy

Government decisions on taxation and subsidies have a direct impact upon the marketing strategy for that product. Fiscal changes can be unexpected and sudden, leaving the company to handle a significant rise in price. Governments will try to restrict themselves to raising revenues from products that have price-inelastic demand, but, even so, there will be an impact on sales. If marketers are successful in changing the shape of their demand curves, making them more price-inelastic, they should also be aware that they are at the same time increasing the range of goods the Chancellor can target for higher indirect taxes.

Competitors will also be faced with the need for similar price rises, but customers may now reassess their demand for the generic product and switch their spending elsewhere. Marketers cannot ignore the possible intervention of government. Monitoring the political climate is an important part of business activity, particularly for manufacturers of products that may catch the Chancellor's eye around budget time.

Using marketing skills to lobby and influence political decision-makers in order to win subsidies or minimize the severity of tax burdens is a real and increasingly important aspect of the marketing activity. The political public, like the general public and financial community, are important audiences of the organization. Their attitudes and actions can and do influence the fortunes of the organization, and clear marketing and communication strategies need to be developed for each of them.

Price from the marketing perspective

To the marketer price is less significant than it is to the economist. The marketer has another three variables to influence demand, whereas the economist's rational consumer will be making purchase decisions primarily on the basis of price.

As we have already seen, the marketers' objective is in fact to reduce the value of price as a variable for influencing demand by developing strategies designed to make products less price sensitive. Yet marketers cannot afford to ignore price or leave it up to finance departments to make pricing decisions.

Price is critical because of its influence on total revenue and ultimately profitability. The pricing decision will inevitably be critical to the success of any business strategy. Marketers who fail to appreciate the real complexities of the art of pricing can make the mistake of adopting a 'pile 'em high, sell 'em cheap' approach, with little or no consideration of the effect on operations, finance or image of the organization.

So far we have been concentrating our attention on the role of price in the marketplace, how and why it changes and the effect of these changes on the resources allocated to production. Now we can turn our attention to how firms set prices and decide how many goods they will offer on the market.

Deciding on price

Demand indicates the price that the market will bear – the price ceiling. Costs represent the price floor. At the end of the day the organization will have to cover its costs if it is going to survive, and decide on a price that takes into account competitors' pricing and the influence of price on demand. In between these two lies the band of price point options within which the competition will be operating and the product has to be positioned. See Figure 6.14.

Figure 6.14   *The pricing dilemma*

Price comes in many guises – subscriptions, donations, rent, wages, fees, fares – but, whatever it is called, complex and important decisions have to be made. Seeking simple solutions, managers may be tempted to adopt a mechanistic approach to pricing, but marketers know that there is no simple and easy model or formula that can satisfactorily take all the necessary variables and considerations into account. Models need to be used as a base from which management judgements can be made. The range of strategic and tactical roles for price are immense. For example:

- Should a new product be priced high, by adopting a price skimming strategy, to maximize the revenue while there is limited competition, or priced low, a penetration strategy, to maximize market share as quickly as possible?
- Should prices be in line with established competitors when entering a new market, or should they undercut them?

We have already considered how the market conditions will change throughout a product's life-cycle; competitors will be influenced by your pricing decisions and customers may well judge product quality or value from the price set. At tactical levels price can be used as a promotion to increase sales, buy three for the price of two, or, as in the case of psychological pricing, the use of prices such as £9.99, because customers are known to perceive £9.99 as much cheaper than £10.

Creative marketers will use price to develop market opportunities and to reinforce the positioning of their products and company. To do this they need to control or strongly influence the pricing decisions of the organization. An issue as fundamental as pricing cuts across many functions and levels of management, particularly finance. Marketing managers will be unable to play their full role in developing pricing strategy unless they have a sound grasp of the theoretical concepts of pricing, a grasp that can be provided by economics.

Summary review

1 Use demand and supply analysis to illustrate the following:
   (a) The stages of management philosophy from product > sales > customer orientation, as described in Chapter 1.
   (b) The stages of the product life-cycle.

2 After the VAT increase in the 1991 budget, from 15 to 17½ per cent, a number of high street retailers, including Marks & Spencer, announced that they would not immediately be handing this rise on to their customers. Can you provide an economic and a marketing explanation for this decision?

3 Why is it that price might not ensure the optimum allocation of resources in a market economy?

7
Costs – the price floor

Aims

Appreciating that changes in price have an impact upon demand is only part of the picture; we now must turn our attention to the other part. Demand determines volume, which influences costs. Costs in their turn go on to influence price, and so there is a continuing cyclical link between costs, volume and price. See Figure 7.1.

Figure 7.1 *The vicious circle of costs/price/volume*

The aims of this chapter are as follows:

- To provide an understanding of the various costs faced by an organization.
- To demonstrate how these costs vary over time.
- To consider the advantages and disadvantages resulting from the size of the business.
- To identify how the dimension of cost can be included in practical pricing approaches and models.

Glossary

Breakeven point – the sales level at which total revenue would equal total costs.
Diseconomies of scale – where average costs are rising or no longer falling as capacity is increased.
Economies of scale – a situation where average costs are falling as the production capacity (fixed costs) is increased.
Fixed costs – costs that do not change with output, in the short run.
Law of diminishing marginal returns if you vary one of the factor inputs employed and keep the others constant, the additional output you obtain from employing successive units of this factor at first increases but eventually diminishes.

Long run – a time period when all factors can be varied and it is possible to change the scale of the operation.

Profit – to an economist profit is not just the difference between total revenue and total costs. Economists include an element of *normal profit* in their calculation of costs. This normal profit is the reward required to keep those resources operating in the marketplace. Any difference between costs, including normal profit, and revenue is *excess, super* or *abnormal profit*.

Profit-maximizing output – for all firms the output level indicated by the point where marginal costs equal marginal revenue will be the profit-maximizing production level.

Short run – a time period when at least one of the factor inputs cannot be changed.

Variable costs – costs that do increase with output, e.g. raw material costs.

Types of cost

A firm's total costs represent the value of the factors of production used in making a given volume of output. The scarce resources used in the production process can all be broken down into the following four factors: Land, labour, capital and enterprise. Although the firm may also have costs for raw materials and components, these are really indirect purchases of the same factors – a payment made for a supplier's land, labour, capital and enterprise.

Understanding costs means gaining an appreciation of how these costs will alter over time and at different levels of production.

The long run and the short

In business it is normal practice to give a specific duration to the short and long run. The short run (SR) is usually 1–3 years and the long run (LR) anything from 5+ years. Economists are not that specific, because the length of time it will take to increase or decrease productive capacity will vary from business to business.

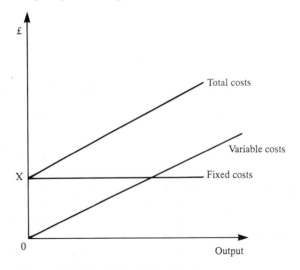

Figure 7.2 (a)   *Calculating total costs*

To calculate total costs (TC) you need to add fixed costs (FC) to variable costs (VC).

Breakeven analysis

This framework of costs can be extended to provide a picture of the breakeven position. By adding a total revenue curve for a proposed price, it is possible to see the quantity that would have to be sold to cover all the costs, i.e. break even. A second total revenue curve indicates how the sales target would change if a different price was to be charged.

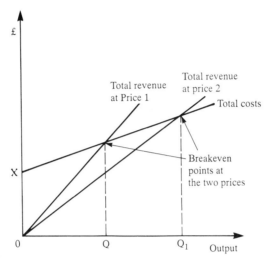

Figure 7.2 (b)   *Breakeven analysis*

Fixed and variable costs

Not all costs can be changed quickly. Some costs are *fixed* and others *variable*.

Some costs can be varied and will change as output changes. These costs include the costs of labour and raw materials. The more you produce, the more you use, and the higher the costs.

However, there are certain payments that have to be met, whether or not you are open this week. You have to pay rent on the buildings and interest on any capital invested in machinery. In all probability you will also have a number of staff on salaries, who will also need paying. These costs are incurred whether you produce something or nothing, but they do not change if you operate at full capacity – they are fixed in the *short run*.

Fixed costs can be changed. You can build an extension on your factory, buy new machinery, employ new managers, but that will take time. Today your operation is constrained by these fixed factors, which will determine the maximum volume you can produce in this time period.

Economists use this concept of fixed costs to define time periods.

- Any period during which fixed costs cannot be changed is the short run. If it takes a printer 9 months to get a new press operational, then the short run for the printer is 9 months.
- Any period when fixed costs can be varied – in other words, the capacity of the operation can be changed – is described as the long run.

Average costs

Business is interested in calculating other types of costs besides fixed and variable. The most obvious is average costs. How much has each item, on average, cost to produce? *Cost plus pricing* is a simple pricing method, and it is used by some managers, particularly where it is quite easy to assess the average cost, e.g. in retail. It is based on the average cost plus an element of profit.

$$\frac{\text{Total costs}}{\text{Output}} = \text{Average costs} \qquad \frac{\text{TC}}{\text{Q}} = \text{AC}$$

If you calculate the average costs over various outputs in the short run and plot them on a graph (Figure 7.3), you find that they form a U-shaped curve. As output starts to increase, average costs fall sharply, then level off; and if output continues, they eventually start to rise.

This U-shaped average cost curve is the same for every firm, irrespective of the business it is in or the number of competitors it has. The variation of costs with output makes it clear why, for most firms, cost plus pricing can be a very hit or miss operation. If output and sales are not fixed and guaranteed, it is hard to see which average cost the firm should use. Too few sales, and average costs may be higher; more demand than expected, and they may start to rise again.

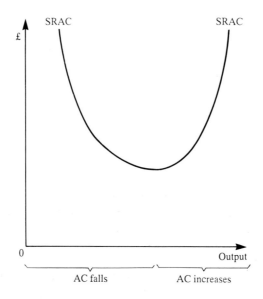

Figure 7.3 *The U-shaped short-run average cost curve*

The characteristic shape of the SRAC curve can be explained by taking a more detailed look at how both fixed and variable costs change as output increases.

Average fixed costs

$$\frac{\text{Total fixed costs}}{\text{Output}} = \text{Average fixed costs} \qquad \frac{FC}{Q} = AFC$$

Fixed costs do not change at all, so as output goes up, the same fixed cost is being divided by a larger and larger element. Therefore average fixed cost falls.

You can see from Table 7.1 that as output rises, average fixed costs fall. Initially the fall is very significant – when output increases from 1 to 2 units average costs fall by £50. At higher levels of output the average cost reduction is much less significant – when output increases from 100 to 101 units, average costs fall by only 1p.

Table 7.1 AFC movements

Output	Fixed cost (£)	Average fixed cost (£)
1	100	100
2	100	50
3	100	33.3
4	100	25
5	100	20
100	100	1
101	100	0.99p

Average variable costs

$$\frac{\text{Total variable costs}}{\text{Output}} = \text{Average variable costs} \qquad \frac{TVC}{Q} = AFC$$

Variable costs are those that vary with the volume of output, but it is unlikely that they will in fact increase in direct proportion to output. If it takes 1 man hour and £15 worth of raw materials to produce one office chair, it will not necessarily take 20 man hours and 20 × £15 worth of materials to produce twenty chairs.

The reason for this is explained by the economists in the *Law of Diminishing Marginal Returns* which states that if you keep the factors of production constant and vary just one, the additional or marginal output will at first increase as you apply more of that variable factor, but eventually it will level off and begin to diminish. This law holds true when you vary the amount of land or capital, but in the case of our analysis of SRAC labour is variable, while land, capital and enterprise are by definition fixed.

Division of labour

Many hands make light work

At first this may seem odd, but it is a phenomenon that you almost certainly have experienced yourself. It is because labour is often much more productive or efficient when it works in pairs or teams. Changing duvet covers is an excellent example of a task that can be completed by two people in less than half the time it takes one to do the same job.

The principles of the *division of labour*, first observed by Adam Smith watching production in a match factory, explain the possible variations in average output per worker. It is not that some employees work harder than others, but that by splitting the process of production into small, simple steps, you allow individuals to become very skilled at their own job, and there is less disruption and wasted time from changing activities and equipment during production.

Too many cooks spoil the broth

But you cannot keep increasing the number of workers for an operation that is fixed in its capacity and expect average output and therefore unit labour costs to keep falling. You have probably also experienced the difficulty of trying to complete a job when there are simply too many people engaged on it, each getting in one another's way. There is inadequate space, equipment or organization for any real benefit to be gained from more helpers. This is the point of diminishing marginal returns. Although the total output may go up, it starts to increase by smaller and smaller amounts. It is possible to keep on hiring workers so that total output actually falls – negative returns.

Consider Table 7.2. Up to employee 4, marginal output increased. The operation was experiencing increasing returns. During this time average production increased, so the

Table 7.2 Total output changes

No. of employees	Total output units	Average output	Marginal output
1	10	10	10
2	30	15	20
3	60	20	30
4	100	25	40
5	125	25	25
6	144	24	19
7	147	21	3
8	144	18	−3

amount of labour resource used in producing a unit fell. Total output does increase with employee 5, but the marginal increase is diminishing, i.e. is less than the previous increase. This means that the average output is no longer rising, and by the time we have employed a sixth and seventh worker the amount of labour used up in the production of a unit is increasing.

The law of diminishing marginal returns accounts for the fact that in the short run average labour costs are likely to fall initially, but eventually they will start to increase.

How many workers would you employ, given the information in Table 7.2?

Actually you need more information before you can make that decision. Assuming you wish to maximize your profits, the labour rate is £49 per worker and your products sell for £2.00 each, how many would you employ then?

By comparing the added value against the additional costs of each worker, you can make this decision. The marginal cost (MC) of an employee is £49, and the marginal revenue (MR), i.e. the additional value of employing that worker is the addition to total output × the product's market price.

The fifth worker increases costs by £49 and raises output by 25 units × selling price of £2.00 = a marginal revenue of £50. The MR is greater than the MC. You would increase profits by £1.00 if you employ a fifth worker.

The sixth worker also costs £49, and increases output by 19 units at £2.00 = a marginal revenue of £38. In this instance MC is greater than MR, and you would be worse off by £11 if you employed a sixth worker.

If the price of labour is increased to £51, you will be better off without the fifth worker; and if the price of the product is increased to £2.60 or productivity is improved, you will improve profitability by hiring the sixth worker. It is the law of DMR that demonstrates why workers who are awarded pay rises without corresponding increases in productivity often are seen to 'price their colleagues out of the market'.

Profit maximization

In economics the point of profit maximization is where MC = MR. If ever the marginal cost exceeds the marginal revenue, you can increase profitability by cutting out the last unit. If marginal revenue exceeds marginal cost, you can improve profitability by producing that unit.

ATC = AFC + AVC

The U shape of our average cost curve can now be explained by combining the impact of changes in AFC and AVC as output increases:

Why the curve falls
Initially as output increases, average fixed costs fall significantly, and average variable costs fall because of increasing returns.

These two combine to create the downward slope of the average cost curve.

Why the curve rises
Although average fixed costs continue to fall, their impact is much less significant and no longer generates any real downward pressure on costs. Average variable costs start to rise as marginal output diminishes.

While costs are falling in the short run we describe the situation as increasing returns. When costs start to rise there are diminishing returns. See Figure 7.4.

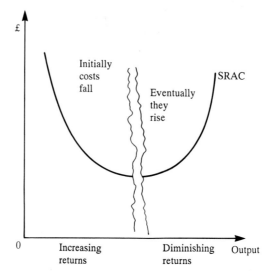

Figure 7.4   *Increasing and decreasing returns*

Expansion and its effects on costs

It is the constraints of a fixed capacity that cause costs in the short run eventually to increase. Additional employees cannot improve productivity because there are not enough machines or space to let them maximize their potential contribution to the operation.

Firms will tend towards operating at the minimum cost point, where resources are working at their most efficient. But if price changes, it may be possible to maximize profits by operating at points above or below this optimum level.

In situations where the firm believes that it will be able to sell additional output profitably, and that this demand will be sustained in the future, it will seek to produce more at the lowest possible level of costs. This will inevitably entail an expansion of capacity, adding to fixed costs. Once the operation has expanded, the firm is faced with a new SRAC curve, calculated from the revised level of fixed costs and the new possibilities of higher output.

No matter how large or small an organization is, its business decisions have to be made in the short run, against the background of constraints imposed by today's operating capacity. The scale of the operation can always be changed tomorrow – in the long run – but currently it is only possible to work with the fixed resources that are available now, i.e. within the short-run time frame.

What is the long run?

The long run represents the time frame when the fixed costs – in other words, the capacity of the business – can be changed. It is derived from a series of SRAC curves, each of which illustrates the likely costs at a different operating capacity. See Figure 7.5.

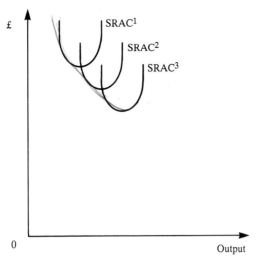

Figure 7.5 *Deriving the long-run average cost curve*

In a sense the long-run average cost curve (LRAC) does not exist. It is simply the result of joining up the minimum points of all the short-run options. The curve is therefore often referred to as an 'envelope' curve because it envelops all the short-run curves. See Figure 7.6.

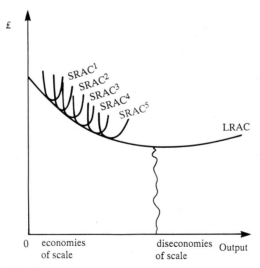

Figure 7.6 *The LRAC 'envelope' curve*

The long-run curve indicates the lowest possible cost at which it would be possible to produce any level of output.

The *very long run* is a time period when technology has changed. It indicates that new production options exist, and can only be illustrated by producing new short- and long-run cost curves.

Interpreting long-run average cost curves

There is no standard, universal shape for a long-run average cost curve. Some are L-shaped and others a flattened U, some are steep and others relatively flat. The actual shape is determined by the nature of the business, and being able to interpret the information conveyed by the LRAC will provide you with an insight into the likely structure of the industry.

A flat LRAC curve, as shown in Figure 7a, indicates that there are few cost advantages to be gained from expansion. There are few or insignificant *economies of scale*. With no obvious advantages in growth, firms operating within such an industry are likely to remain small, and competition will be fragmented. Companies such as those operating in the service sector, where labour represents a high proportion of the total costs, are among those likely to gain least cost savings from growth.

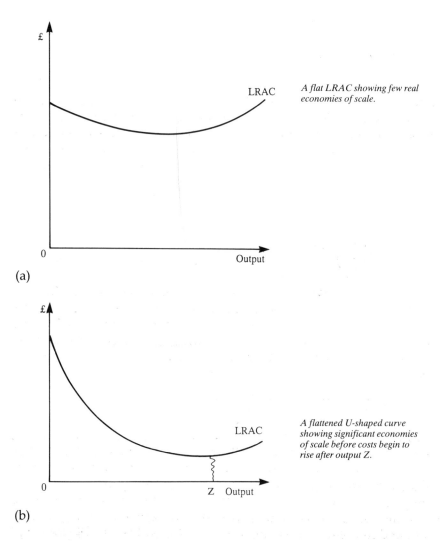

Figure 7.7 *The shapes of LRAC*

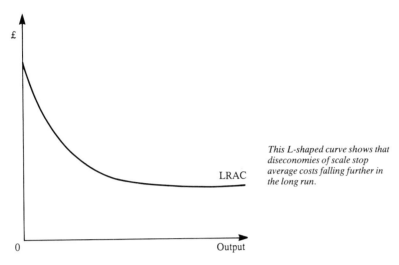

£

This L-shaped curve shows that
diseconomies of scale stop
LRAC   *average costs falling further in
the long run.*

0   Output

Figure 7.7   *The shapes of LRAC*

Figures 7.7b and c illustrate the position in a very different industry. Here substantial cost savings can be made from an increased scale of operation. Faced with such a cost structure there will be considerable incentives for firms to increase their output through expansion, merger and acquisition. A mature industry facing similar long-run average costs is likely to be dominated by a small number of large-scale operators. Firms that employ a high percentage of capital, so that fixed costs are high, as in manufacturing, are most likely to demonstrate this type of cost structure.

Economies of scale

Firms whose costs are falling as their capacity increases are enjoying economies of scale – in other words, the advantages of getting bigger.

There are a number of factors that allow average costs to fall with expansion, and these are detailed below. In simple terms, however, average costs fall when it is possible to double output without doubling all your fixed costs. You may need twice as many machines, but not a new factory or a second managing director. Internal economies of scale occur because of specialization and a more efficient use of the available resources.

Economies of linked process

Most manufacturing output requires the use of more than one machine or process. It is unlikely that the hourly output will be the same for the different machines needed. A small operation will have one of each of the machines, but the output of the operation will be dictated by the speed of the slowest.

In Table 7.3 the slowest machine B means that the factory can only turn out 5 completed units per hour. Increasing fixed costs by buying a second machine B allows output to double. To run all the machines to their maximum utilization, you would need to have an output of 60 units at each process, the capacity of the most efficient machine D.

Table 7.3   Machine outputs for one operation

| | Machines | | | |
	A	B	C	D
Output per hour	10	5	20	60

Division and specialization of labour

The larger the operation, the more scope there is for both division of labour, where tasks are split into smaller processes, and specialization, where workers no longer have to be 'jacks of all trades'. Large firms can employ specialist mechanics, administrators, marketers and financiers.

Indivisibilities

Capital equipment is frequently very expensive, and beyond the reach of small firms. This gives large organizations considerable advantages, and can actually preclude small firms entering a market because the set-up costs are so high.

Dimensional economies

Doubling the size of a tanker or storage unit increases its capacity by a factor of 8. For example, a box 2 ft × 2 ft × 2 ft has a capacity (length × breadth × height) of 8 cubic feet. Doubling the size of the box to 4 ft × 4 ft × 4 ft increases its capacity to 64 cubic feet.

Managerial economies

Not only can a large firm afford to employ specialist managers, it can often attract the best calibre of staff, and the number of operating staff to managers is likely to be higher.

Buying economies

Bulk discounts and preferential service levels can be negotiated by the large-scale producer.

Marketing advantages

The high cost of some marketing activities, such as national advertising, make it only economic for large firms.

Risk-bearing economies

The larger firms are able to diversify. They are less likely to be dependent on one product in one market than smaller firms, so risks are spread. Large firms are more likely to get cheaper insurance rates and be considered to be a better risk for borrowing from financial institutions.

Diseconomies of scale

Despite this catalogue of advantages from growth, there are also some disadvantages – the diseconomies of scale. They can result in long-run average costs rising, as in Figure 7.7b, or at least prevent them from falling further as in the L-shaped curve of Figure 7.7c.

Managerial difficulties

Organization, administration, planning and control are all more complex in a large operation. Decision-making is often slower, being spread over more than one tier of management, and such organizations can be slow to respond to changing market conditions.

Staff problems

Low morale is more likely in large organizations than small, for employees see themselves as only a small cog in a large wheel. There is less loyalty, staff turnover may be higher and industrial relations difficulties more likely.

Higher input costs

Greater demand for raw materials may force prices up, and employees may be able to negotiate higher wage rates in large firms.

Marketing diseconomies

Larger firms are further away from their customer base than small firms. Additional marketing expenditure is necessary to bridge the gap between the customer and the supplier. Market research needs to be conducted, communication costs may increase if it is less easy to identify the target audience, and distribution costs are likely to be greater. At higher levels of market share the marketing costs to gain further sales will be higher.

How much expansion is likely?

A firm's growth is not determined by the pattern of its long-run costs alone. How large any firm will become is also influenced by the corporate objectives, which may not be to maximize profits.

Growth inevitably means longer hours and more to worry about. Owners may want to keep the business small in order to maintain control or to ensure an adequate quality of social life for themselves. Large firms are most likely to have divorced the tasks of ownership and control of the business, and managers make the strategic and tactical decisions on behalf of shareholders. Security, market share and stable growth are likely to be overriding considerations for large companies. Profit is a reward associated with risk-taking; big companies are likely to be risk-adverse and may not necessarily take up cost-reducing opportunities from expansion.

Market potential can also be a very real constraint on growth. It is only advisable to increase output if there is a corresponding demand for the higher volume produced. In markets where there is insufficient demand firms can gain some economies of scale through diversification – production of other products – but with some shared operational, resource, marketing or management characteristics which can still reduce average costs.

In other sectors the nature of the product is such that it needs to be produced close to the customer base. Perishable products and services are examples of this. It may cut costs to have all your hairdressers in one central location, but it is unlikely to generate much business. Products that have a low value to weight ratio, such as bricks, also need to be produced close to the major markets to keep distribution costs down.

Industry and markets are dynamic, and new firms are always being established. All firms started off small, and growth is dependent on the success of their management decision-making and performance, and the availability of finance. Small firms find it difficult to borrow money for expansion. Growth is restricted to what can be borrowed from the high street banks and profits or capital ploughed into the business by the owners. Financial constraints are often behind the lack of expansion in small to middle-sized companies.

Is small beautiful?

Advocates of the market mechanism put a strong case for the merits of competition. The reduced numbers of firms in an industry dominated by large-scale producers does provide the potential for collusion and a lack of responsiveness to customer needs, but that does not necessarily mean that customers are better off in the hands of the small producer.

Small firms are better able to get close to their markets, and may well be niche market operators, providing products made specifically to meet the needs of a small segment of the market. Customers may feel there is more choice and more personal service, but they are also more likely to be paying a much higher price. With higher average costs than if production was expanded, prices will also be high. Some individuals would have no choice at all if output was restricted to small-scale operators, because they would not be able to afford the prices charged.

Larger-scale operators may be making higher levels of profit because of their ability to influence price levels, but the price may still be lower than a small firm would have to charge. See Figure 7.8.

Bigger companies also have the resources to spend on research and development. They are therefore more likely to offer customer benefits of modification and innovation, improving product performance.

Larger producers can and do provide customer benefits, and small is not necessarily best; customer interests can be protected if governments police the activities of large producers to make certain they do not abuse their market power. With global organizations that have

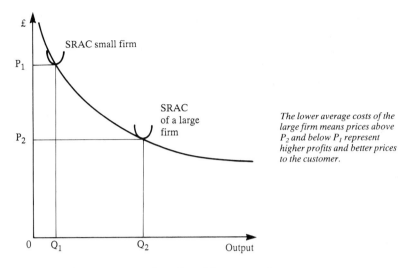

The lower average costs of the large firm means prices above P_2 and below P_1 represent higher profits and better prices to the customer.

Figure 7.8 *Comparing costs of small and large operators*

grown to a really enormous size, their political influence is probably more of a concern than their potential to abuse market power.

Marginal cost pricing

So far we have been considering average costs and how they change with output. We need to turn our attention briefly to marginal costs, because they too can be used as a basis for pricing and must be understood by the marketer.

Marginal cost is the cost of producing one more unit, and is therefore an entirely variable cost in the short run, as the fixed cost element cannot be changed. The marginal cost curve cuts the average cost curve at the lowest point. See Figure 7.9.

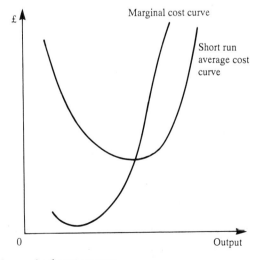

Figure 7.9 *SRAC and marginal cost curves*

Whenever the cost of producing an extra unit is less than the average cost, the average will fall. Once the cost of producing more is above the average cost, the marginal cost pulls the average up.

It is helpful for managers to know their marginal costs, and it can be tempting to use them as a basis for price negotiation. The printer who knows that a print run of 1,000 brochures will only add £300 to his/her costs, for the paper, ink and a couple of hours overtime, may be happy to accept a price of £400 for the job. The difference of £100 is *not* profit, it is a contribution to fixed costs and profits.

The printer is better off having taken the job, but the danger of setting prices on the basis of marginal costs is that, at the end of the month, the total contributions may be insufficient to cover all the fixed costs. In markets that are highly competitive on price it is easy to forget that, although covering marginal costs is fine in the short term, great for cash flow and winning

---

Summary review

1 What would you say were the main advantages and disadvantages of setting prices by using:
  (a) a cost plus formula,
  (b) marginal pricing.

2 Given the possible cost advantages from large-scale production, why are there so many small firms operating in the UK and why does the government adopt policies to encourage even more of them?

3 What do you think would be the major effect on costs if your organization or college was to double its capacity?

4 How many charity dance tickets at £15 and £20 would you have to sell to break even, given the following costs? Present your calculations diagrammatically to show the charity committee.

	£
Supper costs per person	6.00
Hire of the hall	450.00
Entertainment	350.00
Marketing costs (fixed)	125.00
Marketing costs (variable)	1.00 per ticket sold

5 A hotel manager has forty empty rooms at 9 pm one evening. A party of ten business people turn up and offer £20 a head for bed and breakfast. The normal room rate is £70 per head: what should she do? (Cost of breakfast, cleaning a room, fresh linen, etc. £8.50 per room)
  What would be the effect of this decision on the hotel's finances?
  What other advice would you offer if the hotel intended to adopt this flexible approach to its pricing on a regular basis?

new business, it will not be a basis for business survival unless all the costs can eventually be covered.

Despite the warning about marginal cost pricing, if it is used with care, it can provide managers with a pricing flexibility that can significantly improve the profitability of the business. Hotels let rooms during the off-peak periods and at weekends at rates lower than average cost but above marginal cost. If the alternative is to have the room empty, then this policy improves profitability. The key to whether or not you should accept a price below the average cost lies in the concept of opportunity cost. If you do not accept this business at this price, how else would the resources be used and what would they earn?

Faced with a sales negotiation that might be lost on the basis of price, it is understandable that marketers and sales staff put pressure on management to take a flexible approach to pricing. They need to remember that:

- Low prices today may be a precedent for low prices tomorrow, and for matching the same deal for other clients.
- That someone has to take the responsibility of checking that in the end all costs are met.

Costs represent the price floor, and for the firm to survive, they have to be covered. That is as much the responsibility of the firm's marketers as it is of its accountants.

8
Competition – how firms make their pricing decisions

Aims

The strength of competition and the behaviour of competitors are very important considerations in most pricing decisions.

The aims of this chapter are:

- To examine the economic models that predict the behaviour of firms.
- To understand the price and output decisions made by firms operating in a variety of industrial structures.
- To identify the circumstances and ways in which competitive reaction might significantly affect a firm's pricing decisions.

Glossary

Cartel – when a number of oligopolistic firms get together in order to behave like a monopolist. This allows them to earn abnormal profits by restricting output and raising prices.

Homogeneous – all the same, used normally in the context of undifferentiated products.

Imperfect competition – any market where the conditions necessary for perfect competition do not exist. There are degrees of imperfection, with a monopoly being the most imperfect.

Monopoly – where one firm controls all the industry's output; therefore there are no competitors.

Oligopoly – where the industry is dominated by a small number of large firms. Usually the numbers range from two firms (*duopoly*) to about ten.

Perfect competition – a market situation that satisfies a number of criteria, so that the market mechanism is free to operate effectively in it.

Price discrimination – where two or more prices are charged to different consumers for exactly the same product or service.

The influence of competitors

Demand determines the maximum price that can be charged for a product, and costs the minimum. Between these two extremes there will be a range of competitors' prices. Most firms would want to take the competitors' prices into account before making their pricing decisions, but how much influence the competitors will have depends on the structure of the industry the firm is operating in.

Economics provides a series of models that allow us to examine how firms in different markets, with different kinds of competition, will make decisions on price and the volume of goods they will offer the market.

Perfect competition

The difference between the various models lies in the nature of the competition facing the firms. Economists distinguish between *perfect competition* and *imperfect competition*. For competition to be perfect, a number of conditions have to exist:

- There must be a large number of buyers and sellers in the market, which means that no one person or organization can influence the price. Price is set by the market – the interaction of demand and supply – and everyone is a *price taker*, i.e. they accept the market price.
- There must be freedom of entry into and exit from the market. Firms and customers can come and go unhindered by costs or constraints.
- There must be perfect knowledge in the market. Customers will never buy a product at one price only to find it on sale more cheaply elsewhere.
- Goods are *homogeneous*, i.e. all the same – so there is no preference for one product over another.
- Customers and firms act rationally, seeking to maximize utility and profits.
- Transport costs are the same for all firms.

These conditions are very specific, and a market can only be considered perfectly competitive if they are all met. Markets that do not share these characteristics are by definition imperfect. How imperfect is the degree to which the conditions do not exist.

You can see that many of these conditions do not seem to be very realistic, and therefore real examples of perfectly competitive markets do not occur often. The closest example is probably the share market, where many of the conditions can be satisfied on the Stock Exchange floor.

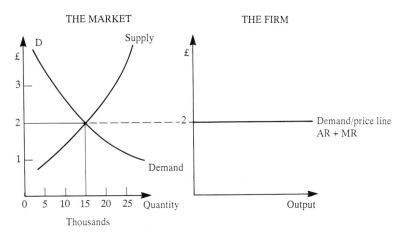

Figure 8.1   *Prices in a perfectly competitive market and firm*

But despite its practical limitations, the economist's model does provide a starting point for understanding how competition influences the behaviour of firms.

In a perfectly competitive market prices are set by the interaction of demand and supply. Firms have no option but to accept the market price. They cannot charge more, because there are many competitors, and customers have perfect knowledge of the market and are indifferent as to whose goods they buy. There is no reason to charge less, because they can sell as many as they want to at the higher market price. So the demand curve that faces the perfectly competitive firm is a straight line – it is perfectly elastic. This price line shows that firms can sell as much as they choose to at price £2.00, and nothing at any other price. See Figure 8.1.

The firm's demand curve also represents the average revenue (AR) curve. As all goods will be sold at the same price – £2.00 – then average revenue must be £2.00.

In the case of a perfectly competitive firm this curve also represents marginal revenue (MR), because the additional revenue earned by selling one more unit will always be the same as the price – £2.00. So in a perfectly competitive market the firm has little choice about price, which is determined by the market. There is a choice in how many units the firm wishes to sell. To calculate this, we need to introduce the cost curves the firm is facing. See Figure 8.2.

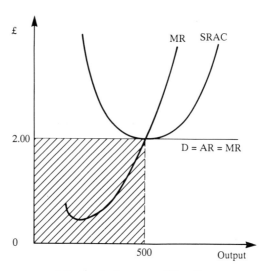

Figure 8.2   *Costs and revenue of the perfectly competitive firm*

We have already seen that the short run average cost curve facing the firm is U-shaped and that the marginal cost curve is a √- shaped curve crossing the average cost curve at its lowest point. The profit maximizing output is determined by the point where the marginal costs are equal to the marginal revenue – in this case an output of 500 units. The average revenue and average cost curves multiplied by the output allows you to assess the firm's profitability at that level of operation.

At output 500 average cost is £2.00 and total costs therefore £1,000. Average revenue is £2.00 × 500 = total revenue of £1,000. Both of these are represented by the shaded area under the curves.

Normal profit

It may seem that this firm is making no profit, but economists have a slightly different definition of costs than that used by accountants. The economists' average costs include an element of profit called *normal profit*, the amount of reward necessary if the factor of enterprise is going to keep managing the resources in this business.

A person who used to be employed at a wage of £600 per week may consider opening his own shop. In making the decision he may say that the forecast has to indicate a weekly income of £750 to make the extra effort and risk worthwhile – in this case £750 would represent the normal profit of £150 plus the £600 opportunity cost of his income.

Whenever average costs are equal to average revenue, the firm is covering its costs, including normal profit. Normal profits are enough to keep the firm operating in this industry, but insufficient to attract new firms and additional resources to it.

In the long run, when the market is in equilibrium, this will be the position facing the perfectly competitive firm. Output will be at the point where MR, MC, AR and AC meet.

How do firms respond to a change in market conditions?

We saw in Section 2 how conditions in the marketplace can change. When they do, firms will need to reassess their output decisions.

In Figure 8.3a you can see that there has been an increase in demand caused by a change in one of the conditions of demand – a change in incomes, market size or the popularity of the product. As a result price has gone up to £2.50, and the firm is now faced by a new price line at this higher level.

The increase in price has caused an extension of supply in the industry. Collectively firms are now supplying 17,000 units.

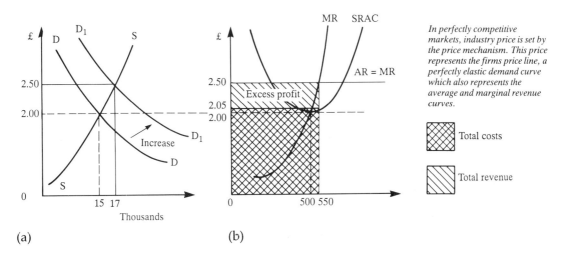

In perfectly competitive markets, industry price is set by the price mechanism. This price represents the firms price line, a perfectly elastic demand curve which also represents the average and marginal revenue curves.

(a)   (b)

Figure 8.3 (a) *The market after an increase in demand* (b) *The effect on the firm*

Nothing has happened to change the firm's costs, so those curves remain unchanged, with MC crossing the SRAC curve at the minimum point of £2.00. Demand has changed, there is a new AR and MR curve at £2.50. The firm's profit maximizing output will be where MR = MC at a new output level of 550 units. Average costs at this level of output are beginning to rise, but the higher costs are more than offset by the higher revenue. See Figure 8.3a.

Comparing total costs with total revenue we can see that:

   Average costs of est. £2.05 × quantity of 550 = £1127.50 total costs
   Price/AR of £2.50 × quantity of 550 = £1375 total revenue
   Total revenue (£1375) − total costs (£1127.50) = excess profit (£247.50)

This *excess* or *super profit* will attract new firms to the industry in the long run, so that eventually supply will increase and the price will fall to the point where average cost = average revenue and all firms are making just normal profit.

Perfectly competitive firms can also make a loss in the short run. If demand decreases, price falls and the firm's average revenue will now be below average costs. The firm will cut back output, but firms will eventually leave the industry, seeking more profitable uses for their resources. As supply decreases, so once more price will rise, until those firms left in the market are making normal profits and average costs are therefore equal to average revenue, as in Figure 8.4.

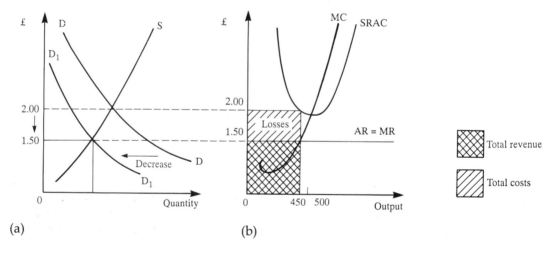

Figure 8.4 (a)   *The market after a decrease in demand* (b)   *The effect on the firm*

Decisions in imperfect markets

Although the perfect market gives us a basis for analysing the way markets work, marketers need to be particularly aware of imperfect markets as these more truly reflect situations in the real world.

Monopoly

The most imperfect competition possible, opposite of perfect competition, is monopoly – a market where there is no competition but just one firm, which therefore is the industry.

Barriers to entry will exist, preventing new firms moving into the industry. Monopolists may control an essential raw material, or profit from legal barriers, as in the case of patents or technical matters.

Note that economists use the term monopoly very specifically, when there is only one firm in the industry. The term tends to be used rather more loosely in general business.

The demand curve facing the firm is the same as the demand curve for the industry, downward sloping from left to right. Again the demand curve or price line is the firm's average revenue curve. The marginal revenue curve is different, positioned to the left of the AR and falling more steeply. See Figure 8.5.

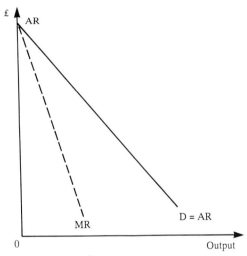

Figure 8.5 *The revenue curves of a monopolist*

The relation between AR and MR

The shape and position of the marginal revenue curve is due to the downward slope of the AR curve. If the firm wants to sell more, it has to reduce the price. The price is reduced for all sales, so although total revenue may increase, the addition to total revenue, i.e. marginal revenue, is less than the average revenue and falls more quickly. This can be seen from Table 8.1.

Table 8.1 Monopolists' revenue

Quantity	Price/average revenue (£)	Total revenue (£)	Marginal revenue (£)
10	10	100	–
11	9.50	104.50	4.50
12	9	108	3.50
13	8.50	110.50	2.50

The profit maximizing output for the firm is again at the point where MC = MR. The cost curves facing the monopolist are exactly the same shape as those facing the perfectly competitive firm. See Figure 8.6.

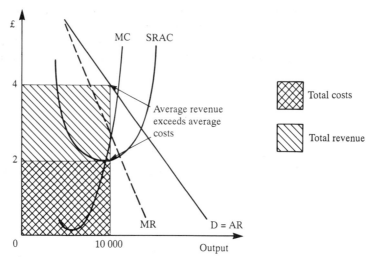

Figure 8.6   *Price and output decisions of the monopolist*

A monopolist can restrict supply in order to keep price high. Average revenue will be above average costs, indicating that the firm will be making supernormal profits. Unless the barriers to entry are breached, nothing will happen to change this position; so the monopolist can make excess profits in both the short and long run.

Where demand is price-inelastic and an industry is a natural monopoly, e.g. power, water and transport, the government may choose to run or control the industry in order to prevent supply being restricted. In these cases the operating objective will not be to maximize profits

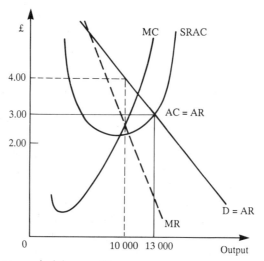

Figure 8.7   *A monopoly* not *maximizing profit*

but to cover costs. Output will therefore be at the point where AC = AR. As you can see in Figure 8.7, at this point supply is greater than under profit maximization, but average costs have started to rise steeply.

People tend to say that government-run monopolies are less efficient and cost more than if the industry was run by the private sector. In Figure 8.7 this can be seen to be true, but the higher average costs can be justified. They are the result of services being provided to customers who are not 'economic'. The marginal costs, for example, of providing water and power to small rural villages is far greater than the marginal revenue earned from these market segments, but it is viewed as an important service that must be provided.

Price discrimination

Controlling the supply of a product provides the monopolist with the opportunity to charge different prices for the same product – *price discrimination*. This pricing strategy is only worthwhile if, as a result, the firm gains more total revenue and greater profits.

For price discrimination to work the firm has to be able to identify two or more market segments, and these have to be both identifiable and capable of being kept separate. This is to prevent products leaking from the low-price to the high-price market.

Markets can be kept separate in a number of ways:

- *By space*. For example, selling a product in an overseas market at a different price than in the home market. In this case the customs service will help to keep the two markets separate.
- *By time*. For example, British Telecom charges less for phone calls made after 6.00 pm.
- *By customer*. For example, the electricity board categorizes its clients and meters, so that industrial users can be charged a different tariff from the domestic market.

Non-discrimination

To be classified as price discrimination, the product or service has to be identical. First- and second-class tickets on British Rail are not therefore an example of discrimination, as you are paying more for an enhanced quality of service.

The market segments must have different price elasticities of demand and the cost of policing the system must not outweigh the additional revenue generated from it.

In Figure 8.8 you can see that at a common price of £3.00 sales would be 50,000 units in each market, A and B. Total revenue would therefore be £300,000. Market A has price-elastic demand. To these customers the product is a luxury or there are other alternatives. Lowering the price will significantly increase demand. At £2.00 sales to this segment increase to 85,000 units, a total revenue from A of £170,000.

Demand in segment B is price-inelastic. Here the product is a necessity, with no real alternatives, and sales will not fall significantly if prices rise. Increasing price to £4.00 would only cause 5,000 sales lost. Total revenue from segment B is now £180,000.

By discriminating between customers the monopolist is able to increase revenue from £300,000 to £350,000.

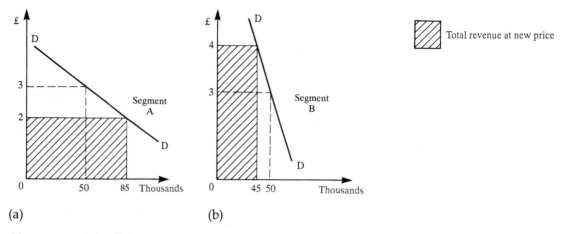

Figure 8.8   *Price discrimination by a monopolist. (a) Price-elastic demand in Segment A. (b) Price-inelastic demand in Segment B.*

Customers who realize that price discrimination is taking place can become very dissatisfied, particularly if the standards of service are not adequate. The example of British Rail commuter services is a good illustration of this. Rush-hour commuters know they pay the highest prices and in terms of service also get the worst part of the deal, with overcrowded trains and few seats available.

Marketing the idea of price discrimination needs to be done with care to minimize this customer disillusionment.

Other forms of imperfect competition

Within the extremes of perfect competition and monopoly there are other models of imperfect competition.

As you move further away from the model of perfect competition the number of firms in the market decreases and the barriers to entry increase. See Figure 8.9.

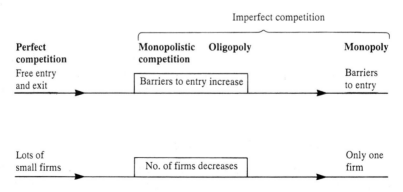

Figure 8.9   *Structure of industry – comparative chart*

Monopolistic competition

As you might realize from its name, this model examines the behaviour of firms that share some characteristics with monopoly and some with perfect competition.

This model looks at industries where there are still a large number of firms competing with each other, but where the products they sell are not perceived to be homogeneous. Suppliers use product differentiation, branding, packaging and advertising to make their products seem different to the customers. This may be the position among a group of hairdressers competing for business in a town.

The short-run position of the monopolistically competitive firm

In the short run the ability of each firm to establish a unique identity and claim for his/her product gives the firm the advantages of a monopolist. While the product is perceived to be different and positioned apart from the competitors, the firm will be able to earn excess profits.

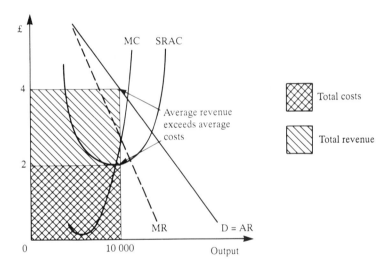

Figure 8.10   *Short-run position of a monopolistically competitive firm*

However, in the long run new firms will enter with similar products, attracted by the excess profit, and customers will realize the intrinsically homogeneous nature of the product on offer. Demand for this firm's output will decrease, the curve shifting to the left. Note this does not indicate less demand for the generic product, only for the brand offered by this firm.

The long-run position of the monopolistically competitive firm

In the long run the monopolistically competitive firm will maximize its profits where MR = MC and where AR = AC. This firm will make normal profits in the long run, just as in the case of firms under conditions of perfect competition. See Figure 8.11.

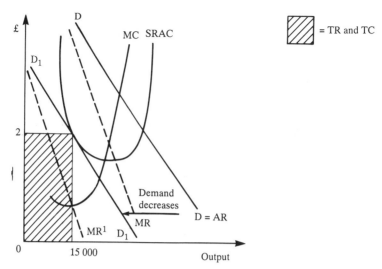

Figure 8.11   *The long-run position of a monopolistically competitive firm*

Oligopoly

The remaining model of imperfect competition is the one that in practice many marketers are familiar with. The model of oligopoly examines how firms behave when competition is limited to a small number of very influential players. An oligopolistic market is made up of anything from two (duopoly) to about 10 firms, each with a significant share of sales and the ability to influence market price.

This is the market model that covers financial institutions, car manufacturers, soap powders, beer, breakfast cereals and baked beans. In fact most of the retail sector and manufacturers of fast-moving consumer-good products can be classified as oligopolists. The products they offer are strongly branded and differentiated, but fundamentally they are very similar.

The overriding concern in the strategic decisions of these firms is the competitors. What are they doing? How will they react to our decisions? Pricing and marketing strategy is strongly influenced by these competitive concerns. It gives rise to the most unusual characteristic of these firms: the demand curve that faces them is 'kinked', though the demand for the generic product will still appear as a normal downward-sloping demand curve. See Figure 8.12.

Within an oligopolistic market there will be a band of prices within which firms operate. Some brands may be positioned at the top end of the price band, others at the lower end – there is an accepted range and pecking order around the kink in the curve.

If a firm was to raise its price above the accepted £4.00, the demand curve it would face would prove to be highly price-elastic. Competitors would do nothing. Customers would quickly switch to the relatively cheaper alternatives, so sales and market share would fall.

If the firm was to lower price to less than £4.00, competitors would have to react, otherwise they would lose customers to this now cheaper rival product. Prices across the industry would fall, and this firm would gain very few additional sales. A price war benefits the customer but not the firms.

Most organizations in an oligopolistic market want to avoid damaging price wars, so they compete through the non-price variables of the marketing mix and by treating price very

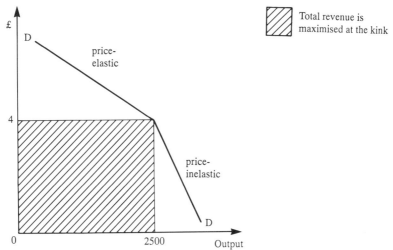

Figure 8.12   *The kinked demand curve of the oligopolist*

sensitively. Often there are tacit agreements about price, with price leaders who establish any necessary price changes, which are quickly copied by all other firms. This behaviour is most noticeable amongst financial institutions and oil companies, because price changes here are usually reported in the press.

Oligopolistic firms would argue that the relative stability of prices and lack of price competition are not signs of collusion but of highly competitive pricing. When these firms do get together to agree price or control output, they can behave collectively as a monopoly. These alliances are called *cartels*. Some cartels are well known and accepted internationally. OPEC is one. Domestically cartels are less acceptable, and any suspicious behaviour is likely to bring about an investigation from the Monopolies and Mergers Commission, which will seek to ensure that oligopolies are working in the best interests of the consumer.

The nature of competition in an oligopoly

Skilful marketing and product positioning are at the heart of a successful organization working in an oligopolistic market. With price competition unavailable to them, managers will look to find other ways of competing. These alternatives are techniques most marketers will be familiar with.

Branding and advertising are strong features of these industries, although it should be noted that there is likely to be an industry norm for advertising expenditure. Companies undertaking 'excessive' promotional activities can spark off promotion wars, which are just as damaging to company profitability as price wars.

Real product differences, features and improvements are a key element in competitive strategy. These firms are large enough to support major research and development initiatives, and customers are likely to benefit from constantly improving products.

The Marketer's Approach to Price Setting

Marketers need to take account of costs, demand and competition when setting prices, but they also need to consider the corporate objectives and image, the stage of the life-cycle the product is going through, and the image of the product.

The marketing mix elements need to be consistent and work together. Luxury products with sophisticated promotion are not served well by bargain basement prices. There are no simple answers to the pricing problem, and a wide range of alternatives. Pricing is an art the marketer will get better at with practice and improved information on the effect of previous pricing decisions. Today there are sophisticated computer programmes which help the manager forecast the impact of prices on the company profits, and which predict reactions.

The simple pricing models, such as breakeven analysis, can be used as a way of considering more than one influence at a time. Plotting different revenues generated by different price levels on to a cost graph will show the volume that would need to be sold to breakeven. By relating this information to a forecast demand curve, you can compare the likely level of demand at the various prices with the minimum volumes the firm would need to sell. See Figure 8.13.

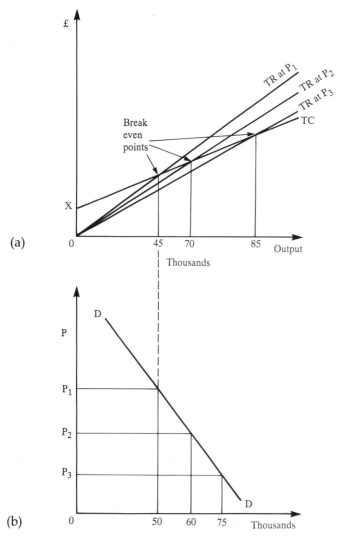

At price 1, 45,000 need to be sold to break even and the forecast demand curve shows we can expect to sell 50,000 units at this price. Demand at the lower prices is insufficient to cover costs.

Figure 8.13 *Using breakeven analysis to compare price options. (a) Breakeven chart. (b) The forecast demand for this product*

This and the various pricing models examined in this section represent useful starting points from which the marketer can build up a pricing strategy flexibly and creatively, but not blindly.

Summary review

1 Is a lack of price rivalry between firms a sign of perfect or imperfect competition?

2 How does the concept of price elasticity of demand help the oligopolist and the monopolist in their price setting?

3 Take the four product categories given in the table below and choose four competitive brands within that market – A, B, C, and D. Proceed as follows:
  (a) Make a note of the price of each.
  (b) Try and monitor any price rises over the next 6 months. Is there a pattern or an identifiable price leader?
  (c) How easy is it to compare value for money between these brands?
  (d) What structure of industry do you think is operating?

Table 8.2 Competitive products

Product/category	A	B	C	D
Petrol				
Mortgage rates				
Soap powders				
Shampoo and cut at the local hairdressers				

Section 3: Projects

1 Select a business – your own, the college bookshop or your local social club – and find out how it sets prices. Who makes the decisions, and how often are prices reviewed? What are the key influences in determining the price levels and what is the policy on discounting? How important does price seem to be to the customers?

2 Give yourself an imaginary £1,000 to spend on shares, and purchase shares in up to ten companies from a range of different business sectors. Draw up a chart that will allow you to monitor your share portfolio over 3 months. During that time you cannot buy or sell other shares, but you should record price fluctuations and use demand and supply analysis to explain the reason for fluctuations. Keep a file of relevant cuttings about the company or

industry. You may find it interesting to get a copy of the company reports. Remember that corporate marketing to the financial community is an important aspect of companies' marketing strategy.
Then ask yourself:

- Did your portfolio gain in value?
- Would you go about making your selection of shares differently in the future?

3 What are the factors a marketing person should consider when setting prices? Produce a schematic to illustrate the process you would recommend when setting the price of a new product.
4 Consider the following information from Iceland, a high street retailer of refrigeration appliances:

In recent years the whole process of refrigeration has become the centre of public environmental concern. As a leading high street retailer of freezers and refrigerators and a major user of refrigeration processes, Iceland felt that it had a responsibility to take action to limit potential harmful effects of CFC gas on the ozone layer.

Iceland was aware that an alternative gas would not be available until the mid 1990s and felt that the recycling of gases for re- use would be the most advantageous method of solving the problem. In the first year of this operation 100,000 appliances were disposed of safely and several metric tonnes of gas returned to ICI for recycling.

The Company also takes responsible citizenship to heart in a number of other major areas:

- Iceland provided all employees with the opportunity to adapt their personal vehicles to accommodate lead-free petrol, the cost was borne by the company. Iceland's own fleet of cars has been converted to lead free use.
- Iceland launched a strong carrier bag which can be used at least five times, thereby saving plastic wastage, litter and vital energy.
- Iceland is committed to allocating a minimum percentage of its profits to charitable concerns. The company is a member of the 'Per Cent Club' and donates not less than half a per cent of its pre-tax profits in each year for charitable purposes.

In 1989 Iceland became the first retailer to extract CFC gas from old fridges and freezers prior to disposal. Which groups and individuals benefit from such activity? Explain how each group and individual benefits.

What are the economic reasons for companies taking account of environmental issues?

Section Four
Promotion and Place

This final section of the microeconomic part of the text will be fairly brief. It covers the two remaining elements of the marketing mix which are the non-price variables of promotion and place.

The availability of a product, the customer's awareness and perception of it, are key aspects of delivering satisfaction to the customer. Both these variables provide added value and both are extensively covered in marketing texts, but economics makes less contribution to them. The P of promotion in particular is covered by economists not as a detailed examination of the elements of the communication mix, but as the collective 'P'. We will examine each of these marketing mix activities from the economic perspective.

The aims of this section are to:

- Examine the economists view of promotional activities, their role and value.
- Assess the importance of availability and the changing structure of the distribution sector.

There are 2 chapters in this sector:

Chapter 9 Promotion
Chapter 10 Place

9
Promotion

At various points in the early chapters of this text we have come across the concept of promotion and the economists' treatment of it. This chapter will draw together these elements and provide an economic assessment of the role, and value of this element of the marketing mix.

Aims

The aims of this chapter are to:

- Identify the economic functions of promotional activity.
- Assess the relative costs and benefits of promotional spending.
- Consider whether or not promotional activity is a waste of resources.

Glossary

Promotion – used by marketers to include all elements of the communications mix.
Publics – a term used to identify groups interested in the activities of a firm, e.g. the financial public made up of shareholders and brokers, or the 'green movement' interested in the environmental consequences of a firm's activity.

The meaning of promotion

Before considering the economists' view of the P of Promotion as a demand variable, it is necessary to clarify the marketers' understanding and use of the promotional tool.

Marketers view promotional activity in the widest sense as communication with their markets, potential markets and publics. Communication is an essential aspect of business and management, and a variety of techniques and media are available to help the marketer achieve identified communication objectives. These objectives may be long-term or short-term, may seek to generate awareness, change attitudes or encourage action.

As consumers we are well aware of the wide range of promotional tools available to the marketer. Advertising, personal selling, public relations and direct mail are just some of the options available, and are likely to be used in combination to achieve the customer's transition through the stages known as the decision-making process.

The economist views promotion much more simplistically, and tends to treat the wide range of tactical promotional tools and variations as one activity and a single influence on demand. But economic theory does provide marketers with a clear picture of what promotion is trying to achieve in a general sense, as well as an insight into the impact it has on the costs of the operation. Both of these are useful starting points for a manager who may be responsible for allocating spending for this very expensive element of the marketing budget.

Functions of promotion

It is possible to identify a number of fundamental functions of promotional activity which have an economic significance.

To inform

Promotional activity may be geared to providing information about products, the business, its operations or performance. This function is particularly important during the early stages of the product life-cycle and when developing a corporate promotional campaign.

Perfect knowledge is one of the criteria necessary for perfect competition to exist. Without information about product features, benefits and prices, the customer will not be in a position to make an informed, 'rational' choice, and the market will therefore be more imperfect.

The informative role of promotion can therefore be seen to perform an important economic function. In the complexity of the real world's marketplace, where customers are faced with making decisions between a wide range of competing products, improved awareness and knowledge should help them to choose the goods that will offer them the maximum value for money.

Informative value of PR

Public relations activities can be used to help reduce the impact of bad publicity, providing the marketplace with information to counteract stories about, for example, health scares, and so slowing down the decrease in demand.

To change the conditions of demand

We saw in Chapter 4 that one of the conditions of demand is the role of taste and fashion, and that promotional activity can influence the customer's view of what is 'fashionable'. Promotional activity is designed to add to or enhance the value/utility derived from a product, therefore giving it a higher priority in the customer's shopping list. Marketing strategy can be used to increase total demand, shifting the demand curve to the right.

As all goods are in competition with each other for the purchasers' scarce income, any increase in demand for one product implies a decrease in demand for another product or service. In a highly competitive environment when there is plenty of customer choice buyers will rationally choose the products they perceive will provide them personally with the most utility for their income.

A marketing-oriented company enjoying increased demand is therefore clearly meeting identified customer needs more effectively than other businesses. Being pro-active in the market place, identifying and anticipating customer needs, including future trends and fashions, ensures the most economic use of a firm's resources, and is a strategy for competitive advantage.

The alternative is to wait until customers' needs change and then to try and react quickly with new products and services. Forecasting changes reduces the short-run disequilibrium caused when demand changes ahead of supply. By reducing or eliminating the time lag that is inevitable if suppliers have to 'catch up' with the changed customer preferences, the operation reduces the chance of producing goods that the customer no longer wants or values as highly.

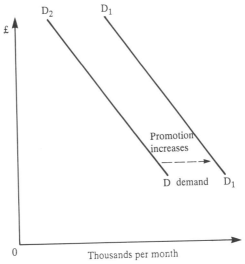

Figure 9.1 *Using promotional activity to change the conditions of demand*

Increasing demand through promotional activity (Figure 9.1) also has the potential advantage of enabling the firm to take advantage of economies of scale. Faced by higher market demand, the firm may be able to reduce average costs and possibly price, despite the additional costs of promotional activity. Again the net result would be a more efficient use of resources.

Adding value

The economist tends to take a narrow view of the product, considering mainly its functional features and benefits. There is an assumption that the customer will act rationally, which in a narrow sense may be taken to mean that he or she will buy the cheapest product able to do the job. This is clearly not how customers in fact behave. All watches perform the same basic task of telling the time, but the price tag may vary between £15 and £15,000. Does the economist imply that anyone paying over £15 is behaving irrationally?

Those who take a narrow view of the product as a functional tool are ignoring its other important dimensions. The customer sees the product in a much wider sense as offering a number of benefits, not all of which are functional. This watch may be a status symbol, or an investment, it may be a fashion accessory or have sentimental value because of the occasion on which it was bought. In recognition of the physical and symbolic or psychological benefits provided, the marketer considers the product or service offering as a bundle of benefits that can be classified by the product △ (Figure 9.2). Each of these benefits provides utility to the customer and so increases the amount the purchaser is prepared to pay for it.

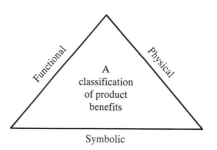

Figure 9.2   *The product △*

The symbolic values of products and services are created through branding and advertising – this brand of chocolates is a romantic gift, another is a thank-you present, and a third is served after dinner. The utility derived from them is enhanced by matching the right image with the right occasion.

Promotional strategies and activities are responsible for establishing the symbolic benefits that will appeal to the targeted market segment. In this way utility is added and the same product or 'bundle of resources' generates increased customer satisfaction.

Changing wants to needs

This aspect of promotional activity is often seen to be controversial, as it is seen to make the market more, not less, imperfect. This function is performed by persuasive promotion, designed to differentiate products, and it is used extensively during the growth stage of the product life-cycle and in the fast-moving consumer-good markets.

Developing strong branding has led to marketing being accused of manipulation and making people buy things they do not need.

We have already seen that one objective of marketing activity is to change the slope of the demand curve, making it less price-elastic. This process allows the marketer to influence demand levels through the non-price variables of the marketing mix, and reduces the influence that price has on demand.

Without this type of marketing activity, companies producing luxury goods and products with close substitutes would be very vulnerable to price changes and price competition. Aggressive pricing from another company would reduce market share, and external factors, such as higher costs, government taxation or exchange rates fluctuations, could lead to higher prices and lower sales. If done successfully, differentiation enables products that in functional terms have very close substitutes to position themselves as unique, giving them some advantages of the monopolist and freedom from the influence of price on market share.

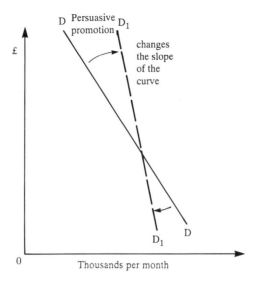

Figure 9.3   *Promotional activity used to make demand more price-inelastic*

Products which are price inelastic have no close competitors, are necessities or may be addictive. To change the shape of the demand curve, marketing has to endow the product with these characteristics (Figure 9.3).

This is done through promotional activities. Branding, packaging and advertising are used in order to differentiate products in the customers' minds. See Figure 9.4.

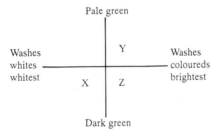

Figure 9.4   *Positioning map for soap powders*

Sales promotion techniques in particular are used to establish brand loyalty and repeat purchases, which is the marketing equivalent of addiction, and advertising can be accused of sometimes creating the illusion of necessity, implying that without this product your life will be less happy, less fulfilled or less successful. Certainly media images and role models can be accused of raising the level of aspirations among households – increasing the demand for video cameras, satellite TVs, holidays abroad and so on. As these products are seen more and more commonly, they do gradually shift from being seen as wants and luxuries to being perceived as needs and necessities.

Is persuasion a bad thing?

Economic analysis demonstrates to the marketer what needs to be done in order to make a product less sensitive to price, but there is no moral assessment of whether or not this is a bad thing. It is unlikely that such a judgement can in reality be made simply on economic grounds.

There is no doubt that the marketers' tools of persuasion are very powerful and are capable of misuse, but to assess whether or not the process of making products more price-inelastic is bad in an economic sense is best assessed by considering the process from a number of perspectives.

From the firm's point of view

If output is less sensitive to price, revenues and output requirements will be easier to predict, even in times of inflation or when faced by new impositions of tax, etc. Price insensitivity also reduces the threat of being undercut, and means that higher prices can be charged without loss of market share. This does not necessarily imply that the firm will not be sensitive to customers' needs or not responsive to changing demands. Customers in the market may be more sensitive to availability, product quality or reputation than price. Neither does it mean that customers are being 'ripped off'; the firm is simply providing additional non-price benefits that the customer values.

From the customer's point of view

Economics is based on the belief that needs and wants are unlimited, and it seems unlikely that marketing could in some way run counter to that belief. If promotion changes a customer's want into a need, in effect all that is taking place is a re-ordering of the individual's own purchasing preferences and priorities. He or she will still be faced with the same limited resources from which to make those purchases, and so total consumption cannot increase without an increase in income. There can be little damage to the economic welfare of the economy.

Customers are free to choose, and they will choose products they perceive to offer the best use of their purchasing power, based on the whole benefit package being offered.

Buyers are increasingly sophisticated in their judgement of promotional campaigns, and in reality are less likely to be 'manipulated' than may be feared. In the long run customers will only make repeat purchases if the product lives up to its promotional claims and satisfies their needs, and there is little real benefit in the marketer raising expectations that are unlikely to be satisfied. Nor is it likely that target customers will be influenced by the promise of benefits for which they have no perceived need.

From the economist's viewpoint

Turning wants to needs does not help to solve the macroeconomic problem. Persuasive promotion does not really contribute to ensuring the best use of resources. As an activity its benefits accrue only at the micro level to the firm that uses it, to which it gives increased stability and competitive advantage. Set against this there would need to be a consideration of the social costs that might arise by increasing the aspirations of market segments that do not have the resources to satisfy those needs.

The impact of promotional activities on costs

Promotional activities undoubtedly use up resources and add to the total cost of providing goods to the market place, but:

- Are these wasted resources?
- Do they lead to higher prices?

Is promotion a waste of resources?

We have seen that there are different functions of promotional activity. That used to inform or add customer benefit is clearly not a waste of resources. Customers can only buy goods if they know they are available and are aware of their functions, so informing the market is as essential a part of the manufacturing process as production is, while adding psychological benefits is as valid a way of using resources as adding more functional ones.

The question is about persuasive advertising, which is seen to create imperfections in the market through product differentiation. But in the real world of marketing it is often difficult to divorce one function of promotion from another, and to distinguish informative from persuasive campaigns.

Persuasive campaigns may not bring economic benefit to society as a whole, but it is important to the survival and success of the firm in a highly competitive environment. It could be argued that more resources would be lost if companies were unable to protect themselves to some extent from intense price competition and fluctuations.

The safeguard in the marketplace remains the customers' freedom to choose. If a lack of promotional spending and corresponding lower price levels were attractive to the customer, then the market would provide these benefits. Past experience indicates that, given the choice, customers will often prefer branded alternatives to, for example, the retailers' plain and simple own-brands.

To judge that this consumer behaviour therefore proves the economic irrationality of the customer is too simplistic. It fails to take into account the symbolic and psychological utility and benefits provided by the promotional activities of firms.

Does promotion lead to higher prices?

Promotional costs can be and often are substantial, and professional marketers have to be alert to ensure that promotional activities are undertaken to meet clearly identified objectives and to ensure that resources are not wasted. Like all business activities, promotional spending needs to be carefully controlled and monitored to avoid waste and to allow effectiveness of campaigns to be evaluated.

While this element of the marketing budget obviously adds to the total costs, it does not necessarily lead to increased prices for the customer. Promotional expenditure, by increasing demand, can allow the firm to take advantage of the economies of scale – reducing the average costs and possibly prices. See Figure 9.5.

However, it is important to note that although promotional activities can help generate economies of scale, they can also lead to diseconomies of scale. Once the firm has a significant share of the market, increased sales can become increasingly costly to win. Marketing managers need to watch their promotional costs as products move through their life-cycles to

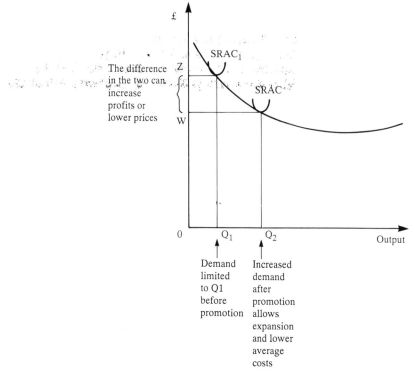

Figure 9.5   *Economies of scale through an increase in market share*

Note: Marketing costs have been included in the calculated average costs at SRAC.

ensure that across the product portfolio the budget is being allocated in the most effective way.

Summary review

1 Would you classify promotional expenditure as a fixed or variable cost and why?

2 What are the arguments for and against the proposition that advertising is a waste of resources?

3 For each of the following list what you think would be their use for promotional activities and the kind of promotional objectives they may have:
  • A company launching a new brand of ladies' perfume.
  • A national telephone company, e.g. BT.
  • A firm in a perfectly competitive market.
  • An oligopolist supplier of breakfast cereals.
  • A public health department.
  • A charity.

10
Place

Our final element of the marketing mix is the P of Place.

Aims

The aims of this chapter are to:

- Examine the influence of 'availability' on customer demand, and the elements of an effective customer service strategy.
- Identify the impact of distribution costs on profitability.
- Trace the major changes within the distribution channels and assess their significance.

Glossary

GNP – This is a measure of the total value of output produced by the country including net property income from abroad.
'Just in time' – a production system refined by Japanese manufacturers to allow minimum stockholding by precisely scheduling parts delivery at just the moment they are required.
Logistics – the process of strategically managing the movement and storage of materials, parts and finished inventory, from suppliers through firms to final customers.
Middlemen – intermediaries who come between the firm and its customers, performing some of the distribution functions on their behalf.
Minimum total transactions – the lowest number of transactions necessary to get products through the distribution channel.

The importance of place

Marketing has been defined as providing customers with the right product at the right price at the *right place and the right time*. Certainly products and services are of no value to the individual unless they are available for consumption, yet this aspect of the marketing process often receives relatively little attention from the marketing student. It seems that many are tempted to think that providing a well-promoted and neatly packaged product at the factory gates is the end of the marketing responsibility.

However, this final stage in the delivery of consumer utility is every bit as important as the earlier stages of researching and producing the product. The degree of control the marketer has in the way the product is presented to the end user will be determined by the channel decisions made, and a very significant part of the product's final selling price will be taken up by the distribution costs. Nearly one-third of GNP in a developed economy can be accounted for by the activities of distribution, so business people should not make the mistake of under-estimating its marketing role or economic significance.

The meaning of place

The exact meaning of the P of Place in the marketing mix often causes students unnecessary confusion. The marketing mix is the combination of controllable variables that influences and determines the level of demand. The P of Place provides the benefits of availability referred to by the economist as time and place utility.

When and where a product is available provides specific value to the consumer. In some instances the convenience of an easily available product will influence the decision to buy and may justify a higher price, while in others the scarcity of a product will add to the exclusive positioning, which will in itself add value to the consumers' perception of the item. The higher price of bread at the corner shop is willingly paid on a Sunday when the supermarket is shut, and the highly priced designer-label clothes products are only available at specialist outlets.

Assessment of the significance of availability in the purchasing decision should not be confined to the consumer product markets. This element is just as critical in industrial markets, where the reliability of raw material deliveries, the growing demand for *just in time* servicing, and the reliability in meeting project deadlines can all be significant factors in winning contracts.

Place is an equally important dimension in the development of a marketing mix for services, but the task is complicated by the intangibility of services. Differences between when and where a product is produced and when and where it is demanded are reconciled by the holding of stocks. This option is not available to the service sector, where decisions about the level of service provision require flexibility and close co-operation between marketing and operations.

Within the services some modifications to the variable of place may be restricted, because of a fixed location, but there are still variations possible in terms of opening hours, staffing levels and the ease with which reservations can be made. The length of time you have to wait to be served in a restaurant, the opportunity to visit a store on a Sunday or late at night, and the chance to buy your phone card at the corner shop are all service industry aspects of the place variable, which can and do influence demand.

The growing distribution challenge

Whichever sector of business a firm is operating in, the challenge of distribution is growing. Industrial and domestic consumers expect improved levels of service, and the *logistics* of moving goods around becomes more complex as firms grow and concentrate their productive capacities.

Early firms were located close to their markets, and managers needed no formal marketing activities to tell them what their customers needed, to help them communicate with their market or to ensure the distribution of their output. Their sheer physical proximity with the marketplace was enough to ensure they responded to changing customer needs and demands, with many products and services probably tailored to meet specific customer requirements. Such businesses were in effect highly marketing-oriented without the need for the highly developed tools of marketing.

As the process of industrialization took place, firms expanded and concentrated their productive resources in locations where there was a cost advantage. This may have been where there was a good supply of labour, easy access to a basic raw material or close to channels of distribution or markets. Once established in a location, new firms in the same industry gain the added advantage of *external economies of scale*, and so are also likely to locate close by.

This concentration of production took firms further away from their customer base, and so increasingly management needed to take positive steps to bridge the physical and communication gap between them and their customers. See Figure 10.1.

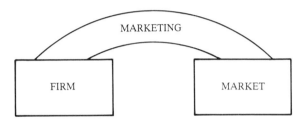

Figure 10.1   *The role of marketing*

The role of marketing is to bridge this gap. To be economically worthwhile, the savings resulting from the economies of scale of centralized production have to be greater than the additional marketing and distribution costs necessary to bridge the gap. In many industries this is clearly the case. The growth of large-scale oligopolistic firms in a number of sectors is compounded by the prospect of an increasing number of pan-European companies and increased globalization of multinational operators, particularly in such sectors as electronics and telecommunications. As customer demands increase and the distance between firms and their clients grows, it seems likely that managers in the future can expect distribution issues to take up an increasing proportion of their time and attention.

Costs v control

No physical distribution system can maximize customer service and minimize costs. The customer's needs in terms of availability merit the same careful research and analysis as his/her functional needs from the product, if resources are to be used effectively and not wasted. Delivering within 24 hours would require substantial support, would not win market share unless it is valuable to the customer, and would certainly not represent the best use of scarce resources.

The task facing the manager is not an easy one, because different market segments are likely to have different availability priorities and requirements. The existence of first- and second-class postal services, and the wide range of special delivery services provided by the Post Office, provide one example of how these various service levels can be used to segment the market. Choosing the customer service package that keeps costs to a minimum but gives the maximum competitive advantage is not an easy decision.

Marketer Philip Kotler has identified eight key areas that need to be considered when a firm is planning its policy on customer service:

- The time to fill and deliver normal orders.
- The need to fill 'emergency' orders.
- Quality of goods on delivery.
- Policy on returned/defective goods.
- Provision of after-sales service support, e.g. repairs or installation.
- Choice of shipment size or carriers.
- The willingness to carry inventory for the customer.
- Any additional service charges to be made.

Only after a thorough analysis of customer needs can a cost-effective distribution system be developed, and an informed judgement of the options available be made.

Fundamentally the firm is faced with only two alternatives – either to take the responsibility for distributing the product direct to the customer or to entrust these responsibilities to others. The dilemma faced by the manager is that direct distribution gives the firm total control of the product's presentation to the customers but is very expensive. See Figure 10.2.

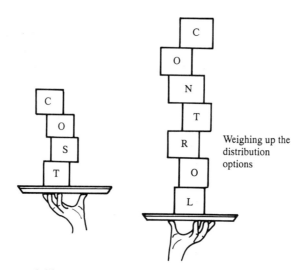

Weighing up the distribution options

Figure 10.2   *Cost v control dilemma*

Development of middlemen

Using *marketing intermediaries* to perform some of the functions of distribution can reduce the costs, but it also reduces the supplier's control over the product's marketing. The range of options – retailers, wholesalers, agents, brokers, etc. – all have different implications for costs, control, image and the type and quality of distribution services provided.

Using a middleman can only be justified on the grounds of costs. Using the services of an intermediary to break bulk and to reduce the total number of transactions can substantially reduce the total distribution costs, as can be seen in Figure 10.3.

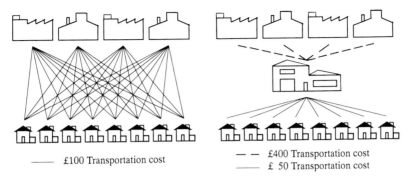
Principle of minimum total transactions

——— £100 Transportation cost

— — £400 Transportation cost
——— £ 50 Transportation cost

Figure 10.3   *Total transactions have been reduced from thirty-two to twelve by using an intermediary*

Implications for marketing strategies

Impact of reducing distribution costs

It is important that marketers bear in mind the relative impact of cost reduction on profits. In Figure 10.4 it can be seen that a 5 per cent reduction in distribution costs increases profits by 50 per cent, from £10 per £100 of revenue to £15. To earn the same additional profit from increased turnover, it would be necessary to increase sales by 50 per cent.

Selling price £100

| 10 | Profit | 15 |
| 90 Costs | | 85 |

Old   New

Figure 10.4   *Profit leverage through cost reduction*

The Pareto principle

Most firms that start out with one successful product will consider extending their range to attract additional or marginal customers. Product variations may be based on adding value to create a deluxe model or providing a basic economy version to attract lower-income customer groups. It is easy for marketers to recommend a proliferation of product lines as a strategy for increasing sales. It is, however, important that in doing so they are fully aware of the additional distribution costs that will arise. For example more product lines increase the complexity of the distribution requirement, for more stock needs to be carried, more shelf space is used up, and a more extensive provision of spare parts is necessary.

Analysis of the sales figures by product and market will indicate that the 80:20 Pareto principle is in operation. This means that 80 per cent of sales will be coming from 20 per cent of customers. Put another way, 80 per cent of distribution costs are incurred to earn 20 per cent of the revenue. When that information is considered alongside the way lower costs can increase profits, as shown above, the critical importance of marketers' carefully analysing their activities becomes obvious. The increased application of information technology to computerize distribution systems will mean that marketers will in the future have much more information available to help them analyse the cost-effectiveness of their distribution activities. The Pareto principle is illustrated in Figure 10.5.

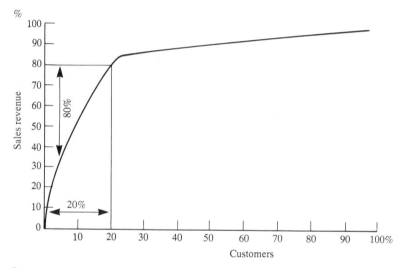

Figure 10.5   *Pareto principle in distribution*

The changing pattern of distribution

The distribution sector has undergone a number of changes over the years, resulting in a shifting balance of power throughout the channels. These changes have had significant consequences and need to be considered when developing distribution strategy.

In the earliest days the balance of power was held by wholesalers, who instructed suppliers what to produce and often had products patented themselves. As firms increasingly needed to access national markets to take advantage of the economies of scale, so gradually the power shifted to the manufacturer. Products were branded and priced by the producer. The ending of resale price maintenance brought in a period of radical change. Free to hand on cost savings in the form of lower prices, the supermarket began to flourish.

Economies of scale were substantial, and multiple retailers grew, extending the range and selection of goods offered, and by the mid-1980s expanding into large out of town sites. At the same time mergers and acquisitions gave them increased purchasing power; they could no longer benefit from the cost savings of using a wholesaler, and so the channel shortened and the retailers' power grew. Retailers' power reflects their control of the essential access to the customer. If manufacturers cannot get their brand stocked, they cannot hope to sell it.

The battle for shelf space is intense, and retailers will assess products' performance in terms of earnings per square foot. The retailer now can demand what is to be produced, and many have used their power to develop their own retail brands. These are frequently cheaper than the manufacturers', as they do not have to carry the major promotional costs of a premium brand. Similar changes have been seen across the retail sector, as now most of the high street is dominated by multiple retailers, and a similar trend can be seen gathering momentum in brewing, as the retail outlets for beer come increasingly under the control of a few major companies.

Summary review

1 Why is it that distribution decisions are so important to the marketing person?

2 What makes distributing a service more costly than distributing a product?

3 Choose an industry with which you are familiar and identify the distribution options that are available to it. What benefits from availability do the customers want, and how are these being delivered to provide competitive advantage?

4 What economic arguments could you employ for and against doorstep deliveries of milk?

Section Four: Projects

1 Over the next week create for yourself two portfolios of promotional materials, collected from the media, direct mail and packaging. One portfolio should contain examples that feature price as a main benefit, and the other where non-price variables feature.
What conclusions can you draw from your examples?

2 Identify an example of a product or service for each stage of the product life-cycle. Describe the marketing mix for each. What benefits are the customers being offered? How would you expect the marketing mix to change at the various stages of the life cycle? Would you expect any similar changes in the customers needs as products mature?

PART II
MACROECONOMICS

Section Five
The macro-environment of business

The aims of Section 5 are as follows:

- To study all significant economic factors that may make an impact on the ability of management to conduct its business successfully.
- To recognize that no organization can survive in a vacuum, but is interdependent with its environment.
- To stress the critical importance of understanding the nature of the economic and wider business environment and changes within it.
- To develop the marketers' skill in the analysis of often complex and dynamic environments.

An understanding of the economic processes will be of more concern than the current state of the economy in this section. Nothing is more certain than that the state of the economy will alter, but precisely when, how and with what impact on business is frequently uncertain.

Students of economics often feel dismayed by the apparent complexity of the subject. Complicated diagrams and mathematical formulae may make even the most committed feel confused and overwhelmed.

It is our intention in this part of the book to overcome such negative feeling by drawing on the everyday experience of the reader. In all the following chapters you will already have a bedrock of economic knowledge to draw on, acquired through your experience of business and life in general. Most of us read a paper, listen to the news and tune in to the budget as a matter of course. Similarly we will ponder and debate the causes of unemployment or inflation, and why our living standards have not improved as fast as we would have wished. We will also be aware of balance of payments problems, along with the value of the pound and, we are unlikely to have overlooked the significance of 1992.

The chapters that follow will therefore seek to deepen and organize your already considerable knowledge into a framework for fuller understanding that will inform your business decisions. It will also enhance your awareness of current events and their political and economic significance. It is said that the most powerful ideas are essentially simple and so it is with important economic concepts. The analysis and diagrams used are only devices to assist you in the appreciation of these vital concepts. If you are able to grasp their meaning and significance from the descriptive text provided, then this alone will suffice. While a full understanding of macroeconomics will require you to work through the whole book, each section and chapter is also designed to stand alone. You are not expected to work through material in the order provided – use the contents page or index to tailor your study of the text to your immediate requirements, be it coursework, a work-based application or examination revision.

Success in meeting the opportunities posed by macroeconomic change will require all the marketer's skills and abilities in:

1 *Monitoring* – audit environmental influences, plus needs of target markets.
2 *Identifying* – opportunities and threats from critical influences on the business.
3 *Anticipating* – significant changes and the need for change.
4 *Assessing* – the nature of the environment and the degree of uncertainty and change.
5 *Understanding* – interrelationships: economic models and interdependencies.
6 *Evaluating* – potential impacts and their implications for the business and competitors.
7 *Planning* – short, medium and long-term, as well as contingency plans.
8 *Adapting* – crucial to survival and success in a changing environment.
9 *Measuring* – effectiveness of plans to cope with change.

No organization, whether large or small, public or private, can be independent of its environment. Large firms may be able to exert greater influence over their business situation, but small firms may have the flexibility and scope for rapid decision to adapt more quickly.

All business faces change, often rapid change. Organizations have traditionally been concerned with change in:

- Competitor behaviour.
- Customer tastes.
- Technology.
- Macroeconomic policy.

They have, however, increasingly been forced to monitor social and political change. Public concern with pollution, conservation and health and safety, for example, requires business to modify its economic objectives or face a potential backlash from the marketplace, or punitive legislation from governments.

There are four chapters in this section:

Chapter 11 *An overview of the environment*
Chapter 12 *Business and its environments*
Chapter 13 *The human environment*
Chapter 14 *The information needs of the organization*

Summary review

1 Suggest a business that is able to survive and prosper yet ignores its environments. How is this possible?

2 List aspects of your work requiring monitoring of the wider environment.

11
An overview of the environment

Aims

- To underline the importance to the marketer of taking account of the macro-environment.
- To provide a historical context for the study of macroeconomics.
- To appreciate the significance of the Thatcher era.

Glossary

- *Balance of payments constraint* – the tendency for imports of finished goods/services to be sucked into the economy as it expands too rapidly, causing a rising trade deficit and downward pressure on the value of the pound.
- *Balanced budget* – where total government spending is balanced by revenue raised from taxation, with no need for borrowing.
- *Billion pounds* – £1000 million pounds.
- *Corporatism* – policies determined and controlled by collaboration of big business, big unions and the state.
- *Deficit financing* – where government spending is partly financed by net borrowing from the public and banking system.
- *Fiscal policies* – taxation and spending measures used by the government to control aggregate spending in the economy.
- *Gross domestic product (GDP) and national income* – GDP measures the output in any one year arising from activity in the UK. It is not adjusted for taxes, subsidies or capital used up in the process. Were these accounted for, we should be left with national income.
- *Keynesian economics* – based on the work of John Maynard Keynes (the general theory) and underpinning macroeconomic policy after World War 2. It required governments to control aggregate spending to achieve full employment by adjusting taxes and state expenditure.
- *Monetarism* – a school of economic thought that views the quantity of money and control of inflation as of primary importance in macroeconomic policy. Measures target and seek to control the main money aggregates.
- *Per capita* – means per head of the population.
- *Recession* – officially defined as arising when output falls in two consecutive quarters.
- *Stop–Go* – the tendency for the British economy to alternate between 'go' periods of growth and 'stop' periods when spending is reined back by the government to correct inflation and balance of payments problems.
- *Supply-side economics* – concern for microeconomic efficiency and policies to achieve it rather than attempting to influence business by manipulating total spending in the economy.

Setting the scene

An understanding of the workings of the economy is crucial to the assessment of the macroeconomic environment. It allows informed analysis of economic trends and indicators, and an evaluation of their implications for the business.

As the framework for their forecasts and market or industry assessments, firms invariably make assumptions about the state of the economy, movement in real disposable incomes, the rate of inflation, interests rates and so forth. Political factors, especially the outcome of elections, also need considering, as well as demographic changes affecting the market in question.

Immediate interest will focus on the year ahead, with seasonal and short-term economic influences to the fore. However, important perspective can only be achieved by establishing a long, 5- or even 10-year, view, according to the nature of the industry.

The marketer has a variety of marketing tools and techniques to help achieve profitable growth in sales. But if the general economic climate is cold and depressing, it is much less likely that sales expectations will come to fruition.

Foundation exercise

At the outset of your macroeconomic studies turn to Appendix 1 (p. 379) and complete part A of the exercise – to discover the current values for all the indices listed. Refer to the information sources (p. 194) to assist you gather the data.

An overview of the economy

This approach is not based on complicated economic models. The objective is to interpret the real-world behaviour of the macro economy, gain understanding and so contribute to more effective decision-making in business. An understanding of the economy and government policies cannot, however, be separated from an appreciation of context, so we shall briefly consider, in mainly historical and political terms, the background to the macro economy of the 1990s.

Any informed view of the present must take into account the influence and consequences of over a decade of Thatcherism. As will be seen, these years represented a distinct break from the economic and political values that dominated policy-making after World War 2.

In both macroeconomic and microeconomic senses the election of Margaret Thatcher in 1979 represented a watershed, even though the seeds of change had been sown earlier. Despite her fall from power in late 1990, many of her values will continue to shape and influence the political economy of this decade.

Thatcherism

Background

The economic history of Britain up to 1979 was of a 100-year decline from unrivalled dominance. Even in 1900 Britain ruled a quarter of the world's population and accounted for a third of total manufactured exports. The decline has been the most analysed of modern times, and assumed a central preoccupation with politicians. It combined an absolute decline in political power with a relative decline in economic status.

The persistence of the decline prompted speculation about a 'British Disease'. Certainly the diagnosis of the economic problems of the 1960s and 1970s had an uncanny resemblance to those being offered in 1900. Among others, these included:

- Over-powerful trade unions.
- Amateurish management.
- Inadequate technical training.
- Small-scale industry.
- Technological backwardness.
- Poor working attitudes.

Britain paradoxically achieved its fastest annual growth in the long boom from 1945 to 1975, but slipped relatively as other industrial economies grew faster still. Conservative and Labour governments alike believed they could realize their commitment to full employment while controlling the side-effect of inflation with incomes policies. They also jointly supported the NHS and the concept of the welfare state.

However, by the 1970s there was a growing recognition of the scale of Britain's economic problem and the depth of political failure to address it. Successive governments were viewed like the Russian harvest – 'Worse than last year's but better than the next!'

Attempts to 'dash for growth' failed in a surge of inflation and balance of payments deficits, as the economy came up against supply-side bottlenecks. Import penetration rose, while Britain's share of world manufacturing fell almost continuously in a process termed deindustrialization.

What was required was nothing short of a miracle if the process of decline was to be reversed. The potential architect of that miracle was elected to office in 1979.

Achievements

Margaret Thatcher was a dominant, determined and decisive figure, the first woman to lead a major western nation. Her determination brought an era of unprecedented change to Britain, although it also led to her downfall over Europe, the community charge and the state of the economy.

The values she promoted were Victorian in origin and may be summarized as follows:

- Hard work.
- Thrift.
- Freedom.
- Family responsibility.
- Ownership.
- Opportunity.

Self-reliance was encouraged and wealth creation rewarded to help foster an 'enterprise culture'. Personal taxation was dramatically reduced to reinforce incentives to work and save. The frontiers of the state were rolled back and reformed, with privatization central to her vision of Britain as a property-owning democracy of popular capitalism. Fifty big businesses were sold during this period, accounting for two-thirds of the nationalized sector. The role of the market was legitimized both in Britain and the world, and the seemingly invincible march of socialism was shown to be a myth. Exchange controls were abolished and financial markets progressively deregulated.

The role of law was brought increasingly to bear on chaotic labour relations as a succession of Acts of Parliament ended legal support for the closed shop, and banned political strikes and secondary action. Workers could only strike and picket their own employer, direct suppliers and customers, and this only after a secret ballot.

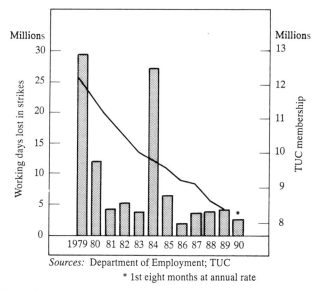

Sources: Department of Employment; TUC

* 1st eight months at annual rate

Figure 11.1   *Declining union power*

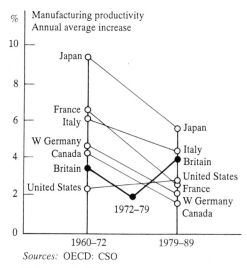

Sources: OECD: CSO

Figure 11.2   *Reversing the 100-year decline*

Union leaders were forced to face direct elections, and any breach of the law led to sequestrated funds. Donations to political parties also had to be made through a special fund approved by membership ballot.

The government abolished prices and incomes controls, reduced subsidies and confronted union power directly, culminating in the miners' strike of 1984. The success of these initiatives may be gauged by the fall of the number of strikes and rising productivity, as management reasserted its 'right to manage'.

Margaret Thatcher perhaps created the environment that allowed Britain to regain its pride and status in the world. It could also be shown, however, that the gap between rich and poor widened, with the plight of the have-nots being epitomized in 'cardboard cities' and ever tighter rules on social security entitlement. The decade paradoxically saw a record number of both homeowners and homeless! The record also shows, however, that spending on health and pensions, social security and welfare rose both in nominal and real terms, and managerial efficiency increased.

Other achievements of the era would include addressing the problem of farm surpluses and the renegotiation of Britain's European community contribution – saving Britain £10 bn by 1990. The government also initiated and embraced the Single European Market principle, although entry into the exchange rate mechanism proved a difficult step.

It was Margaret Thatcher's resistance to further progress towards European monetary union that precipitated her fall. Her fundamental vulnerability, however, arose not out of divisions over Europe or even the hated poll tax, but rather the revival of inflationary pressures. Elected after a winter of discontent with stagnating growth and rising inflation, she reversed both but at the expense of the deepest slump in 50 years. By 1990 both had returned once again, with Britain facing 11 per cent inflation and a second deep recession.

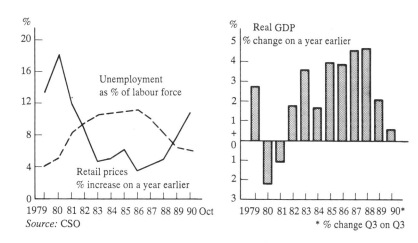

Figure 11.3 *From recession to recession*

This was primarily a failure of macroeconomics, arising out of excessive expansion over the period 1986–8. It undermined the credibility earned at the expense of over 3 million unemployed and may have set back the cause of price stability for many years.

Focus

The contrast between the Thatcher era and what had gone before has already been referred to. The main shifts in focus may be summarized as follows:

- A *focus* on real jobs rather than artificially subsidized ones.
- A *focus* on balanced budgets in place of deficit financing.
- A *focus* on wealth creation and efficiency rather than redistribution and equity.
- A *focus* on individual responsibility and a move away from welfare-state dependence.
- A *focus* on wider share ownership and homeownership by a reduction of state interference.
- A *focus* on the market, and the removal of obstacles to its effective operation, rather than corporatism.

The emphasis on inflation in macroeconomic policy was a reaction to rising price levels, as well as the belief that other important economic objectives, such as employment and growth, could best be stimulated in a non-inflationary environment. Attempts to stimulate employment and growth directly by tax cuts or increased government spending were now viewed as either self-defeating, because they crowded out private sector activities, or as a recipe for accelerating inflation.

Monetarist policies sought to gear money supply growth to real output growth, with fiscal policies subordinated to balancing the budget and keeping public spending under tight control. This enabled taxes to be cut, allowing more freedom for individuals in their spending decisions. On the supply side this would encourage work, enterprise and savings, generating growth and eventually employment. These jobs would be based on real consumer choices, not generated and maintained by generous government supports and subsidies to uncompetitive industry.

In microeconomic terms this meant individuals and business had to learn to stand on their own feet. They would succeed or fail according to the dictates of the market. It was up to business to decide what best to produce and how to produce it, and for workers to retrain or move should circumstances demand it. This represented a significant shift in the trade-off between efficiency and equity. Thatcher transformed the social acceptability of wealth and profit, but correspondingly raised the spectre of relative poverty among an underclass unable to respond to its challenge.

The break with the past was most evident in the role of state sector, as the public interest gave way increasingly to self-interest and a profit orientation. No branch of the state has been immune, with state enterprises privatized and the civil service pruned. Local authorities have

---

Summary review

1 Produce a balance sheet listing the benefits you have personally realized as a result of Thatcherism and also the costs or drawbacks.

2 Produce a similar balance sheet but this time for your organization. Do not restrict yourself to purely economic factors.

3 Compare the two and try to explain any divergence between them.

been required to put service provision out to tender, while health and education have been restructured to promote greater efficiency and a marketing-orientated concern for customer needs. The corporatist power of state, unions and major companies to decide the destiny of the nation through jointly agreed economic programmes and incomes policies was demolished, and free rein given to market forces.

Foundations of Thatcherism

The degree of discontinuity of her policies with established trends was only possible by virtue of the electoral and parliamentary system that prevails in Britain today. Constituencies are represented by whoever is first-past-the-post with the majority of votes, whether 2 or 20,000. Accordingly, when more than two parties contest an election, an overall majority seldom results. Margaret Thatcher, for example, was returned at her last two elections with less than 44 per cent of the popular vote, yet achieved an overwhelming majority in the Commons. Indeed no post-war government has been elected on over 50 per cent of the vote, and on two occasions the party capturing most votes nationally did not get elected. The Alliance party realised over 25 per cent of the popular vote in 1983 yet took only 3.5 per cent of the seats.

Once an election is won, the degree of electoral support is no longer an issue, since the disciplined 'whip system' ensures that the government always wins crucial divisions. For an MP to ignore a three-line whip to support the government in a division vote would jeopardise their future within both party and parliament.

There is no ultimate check or veto from the Crown or House of Lords on the government and its power is concentrated still further into the hands of the Cabinet and Prime Minister. The Prime Minister, with the right of appointment and dismissal over ministers, combined with election by MPs themselves, has exceptional power to exert if so inclined. Cabinet decisions are based on collective Cabinet responsibility. This built-in unfairness and concentration of power in our political system does, however, allow for 'strong government'. It provides the ability to push through often unpopular but necessary policies for the medium term without fear of a vote of no confidence or pressure for a U-turn from its own supporters. This may not be possible where a fairer, coalition government, elected, say, by proportional representation, is in power. PR can lead to compromise, and often small parties holding the balance of political power.

The first-past-the-post method then is a virtue when the country is in crisis, as it was in 1979, and what is required is strong, stable and effective government. The method, however, has its faults, if power is abused to enact, say, a community charge, despite widespread popular opposition. It can also lead to a fatal lack of continuity in policy, where governments alternate in power.

In this respect opposition parties will seek to distance and differentiate themselves from the policies of the party in power. During the 1960s and 1970s Britain experienced alternating governments and alternating policies. The period was also characterized by what was known as 'stop–go'. The economy would be expanded at the approach of an election to buy votes but then, with inflation rising and balance of payments deficits increasing, the newly elected government would be forced to apply the brakes.

The first year or two of any new government that had spent 5 years or more in opposition often produced a fatal lack of continuity. Policies would be reversed, legislation amended and institutions abolished. New and often divisive schemes, dreamt up in opposition, would be introduced, often with unexpected or undesired consequences.

The damage would be contained to the extent that the external constraints limited state power. The City's reaction and market forces often forced policies to be modified, as did international opinion and the media. In this way governments would tend to settle down to more moderate and reasonable policies, only to be voted out of office at the next election, allowing the sequence to be repeated.

The opposition's role was to appear to oppose everything, to cash in on unpopular, if necessary, measures, and to promise to reverse many initiatives if returned to office. This in turn fostered a belief in an easy alternative, which nurtured expectations in the minds of the electorate that subsequent performance could seldom match. Little wonder there was an increasing political credibility gap. For business, where stability, policy continuity, and a predictable framework of laws are all important to confidence and competitiveness, this was not a desirable state of affairs!

It should be recognized, however, that much of adversarial politics is more apparent than real. Certain priorities are often supported across party lines, if only in private. An incoming Labour Party would be unlikely, for example, to reverse union legislation or incur the heavy cost of renationalization. It is also the case that parties redefine their position to secure electoral appeal. Labour, through its leadership, policy review process and the very success of Thatcherism, has become a belated convert to the European community and market economics. Similarly the replacement of Margaret Thatcher with John Major has provided an opportunity to undermine the electoral appeal of Labour. A new classless image, a commitment to revise the poll tax while confidently restoring the economy, may be sufficient to win the 1992 election for the Conservatives.

There is a saying that 'happy is the land that needs no strong leader'. This was certainly not Britain in 1979, but if the Thatcher rejuvenation has worked, perhaps it is today!

Assessment of Thatcherism

History will always be the judge. However, the tenor of your evaluation will depend to a large degree on the answers to the following questions:

- Did you live in the North or the South?
- Were you employed in manufacturing or services?
- Did you leave school at 16 or undertake higher education?
- Did you live in the inner cities or the shires?
- Did you work in the public or the private sector?
- Did you earn a high income or depend on social security?
- Did you own your own house or rent a flat?

In microeconomic terms the period in office began with the worst recession in 50 years and finished with the next worse. The durability of the British economic miracle Mrs Thatcher delivered was brought into question with the following indicators as she departed from office:

- 11 per cent inflation.
- Balance of payments deficit of 4 per cent of GNP.
- Base rates of 13.5 per cent.
- Record business failures.
- Business confidence at a 50-year low.

The balance of payments constraint has returned with a vengeance, and is itself a symptom of repressed inflationary pressure. There is some doubt as to the government's resolve to reduce inflation to zero or even internationally competitive levels. Following the shock levels of unemployment that accompanied earlier efforts, the policy preference seemed to favour economic growth in the later part of the 1980s. Furthermore the economy must be judged not only on its impressive performance in periods of expansion, with associated productivity rates of 5 per cent per annum, but also on its ability to adjust to recession and other shocks.

The Japanese economy, for example, was a model of flexible adjustment in response to its oil shocks and a sharply rising value of the yen. It is by no means fully proven that Britain has achieved equivalent flexibility and dynamism, not to mention a lean, hungry and highly competitive management.

There is a school of thought that suggests Britain's manufacturing base was critically weakened in the early 1980s. Despite impressive productivity gains, it has been unable to supply sufficient goods to maintain growth and investment without a worsening trade account of imports needed to fill the demand gap. Taking the period 1979–88 as a whole, gross domestic fixed capital formation rose by a third in real terms yet was unchanged in the manufacturing sector. Stronger investment performance up to 1990 in this sector was then counteracted by developing recession.

As throughout the 100-year decline, the fundamental problem was in the area of pay and performance. Real earnings rose nearly a third between 1979 and 1989, double the rate in Japan, West Germany and France, while in America they actually fell! Management salaries rose even faster, especially at the senior level. They showed little signs of moderating, at an annual rate of 15 per cent, as Britain moved sharply into deep recession and Margaret Thatcher fell from power.

Any final assessment of her macroeconomic impact must therefore await the outcome of this contraction. With developing global recession, unrest in the Gulf, and the uncertainties surrounding *perestroika*, it may constitute a very real test of national character.

Summary review

1 List the characteristics of what you consider would be a strong but fair electoral system.

2 Why did those to the South of the North–South divide prosper relative to those in the North?

3 Has the 100-year decline ended? Consider progress made under Thatcherism in remedying the causes of the decline.

12
Business and its environments

Aims

The aims of this chapter are to enable the marketer to:

- Distinguish the intra-firm, micro and macro environments of the organization.
- Understand the concept of the environmental set.
- Underline the critical need to monitor environmental change.
- Identify the information needs of business.
- Recognize the diversity of sources and how to access them effectively.

Glossary

CAD/CAM – computer-aided design and computer-aided manufacture.

EDI – electronic data interchange between companies using compatible computer programs. When fully applied, it will eliminate many paper-based transactions, improving service and accuracy.

EPOS – electronic point of sale cash registers provide stock-control and sales-analysis information.

ERM – a fixed exchange rate system where member governments must intervene to maintain within narrow limits the value of their currency relative to others in the mechanism.

Global economy – a term referring to competition and marketing on an integrated, worldwide basis by multinationals supplying goods and services with global appeal.

Highly geared – a high ratio of fixed interest debt relative to equity. Meeting such payments is difficult in times of rising interest rates and falling revenue.

Just in time – a production system refined by Japanese manufacturers to allow minimum stockholding by precisely scheduling parts deliveries at just the moment they are required for assembly.

Operations – Refers to the production and delivery of the product or service, which, in manufacturing operations, would embrace production planning and control, along with distributing; and a service situation might cover processing financial transactions on behalf of clients.

Resource Converter – the process of transforming factor inputs into needed outputs of goods and services.

Single European Market – correct term for 1992, when all barriers should be removed to allow a truly free market within the European Community.

The intra-firm environment

As the microeconomic chapters make clear, the basic economic problem is that of scarce resources relative to expanding needs and wants. This scarcity requires that choices be made in allocating limited resources between competing uses. Which products and services should be produced in what quantities, and using what methods of manufacture and distribution, are the key strategic questions for society in general and the individual business entity in particular. Such choices are critical to the affluence and growth of the economy and the survival and profitability of the firm.

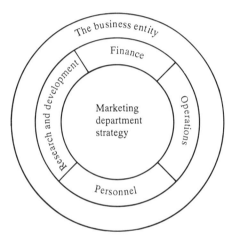

Figure 12.1   *The marketing strategy*

Despite the central importance of the marketing strategy (Figure 12.1), it must compete for resources within the organization. Claims to greater shares of revenue and capital budgets alike will be made by other functional departments. Upgrading the computer system, replacing the ageing transport fleet, robotizing the production lines, or enhancing training programmes will jostle for the attention of the board of directors. This limitation on the resources that the marketing department can deploy at any point in time underlines:

1 The importance of allocating resources to maximize customer satisfaction.
2 The interdependence of organizational activities.

The success of marketing initiatives depends on the co-operation of other departments. Marketing cannot and must not work in isolation. Relations between marketing and finance or marketing and operations are often fraught with tensions, communication problems and so forth. Unless the organization can successfully co-operate here, it is unlikely to succeed in its relations with the wider environment. With change occurring extensively, the stress on these relations is increasing. Internal bonds must therefore be both strong and flexible if the business is to succeed.

Interdepartmental rivalries, then, can and do arise, but are to an extent manageable, being within the control of the organization. Now we will consider the much less controllable forces in the external macro-environment. It is here that the business obtains its resources, creates its marketing opportunities and meets its threats. It also encounters a framework of rules, regulations, laws and customs that at once both limit and define its freedom of action.

Summary review

Identify two possible sources of conflict arising between marketing staff and counterparts in:
  1 Production planning.
  2 Stock control.
  3 Management information systems.
Explain why such conflict may arise.

The business as a resource converter

A useful way of viewing business in its relations beyond departmental boundaries is as a resource converter (Figure 12.2). Peter Drucker, author of numerous books on management, defined business as the process of making resources productive. All organizations managing scarce resources have this common goal, irrespective of profit-making. Inputs are drawn from the environment and transformed in time, place or form to create value, service and satisfaction for the final consumer.

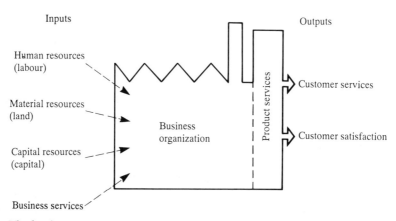

Figure 12.2   *The business as a resource convertor*

In modern business, inputs are diverse and often complex, drawn from an increasingly global economy. The traditional classification of land, labour and capital understates the complexities and interdependencies that exist. The human resource input, for example, may include numerous skills, enterprise, creative ideas and designs. Capital resources embrace not only buildings, equipment and vehicles, but also financial input to lubricate the process of resource conversion in advance of actual sales.

Business services are an increasingly important input for small and large businesses alike. Outside caterers, leased transport and marketing consultants are just a few examples of the move towards contracted-out services, as firms focus all their resources on their core conversion activities.

The resource providers may also be seen as stakeholders in an enterprise. Indeed, some writers argue that an organization is best seen as a coalition, with management's task being to maintain a workable balance between the claims of the directly interested groups, namely shareholders, employees, suppliers, customers, distributors and the community at large.

Decisions will reflect not only adaptations to the changing environment but also bargaining, negotiation and conflict between stakeholders, whose attitudes and behaviour are powerfully influenced by it. The potential for conflict is, as between departments, considerable:

- Suppliers would prefer long delivery dates, while customers demand short ones.
- Employees press for higher earnings, which may conflict with shareholder dividends and stable prices.
- The local community's wish for reduced pollution may adversely affect profits and employment levels.

Success in balancing or resolving these conflicting demands, while achieving corporate objectives of growth and market share, is not easily achieved in times of rapid change.

Internal marketing is now widely recognized as an essential part of the manager's task. Successful implementation of business strategies requires managers to identify groups of internal stakeholders and market their plans to them.

Summary review

1 Select a resource and explain the process of making it productive.

2 Distinguish between a stakeholder and a shareholder.

The micro-firm environment

The business has been viewed above as competing for scarce resources available in the macroeconomy. This is an oversimplification, in the sense that many firms also create or develop their own resources through retraining, product development, market research and so on. Information is also a valuable resource, whose quantity and quality can be improved through investment.

The fact remains that the business depends on external suppliers for most of its requirements. This idea can be extended to the other dimensions of what might be called the microenvironment. This is the immediate external environment of the firm and should be distinguished from the wider economic, technological and sociopolitical forces discussed below.

As seen in Figure 12.3, this environment consists of households, organizations and forces having significant economic effects on the marketing organization.

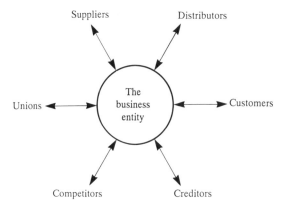

Figure 12.3   *The micro-firm environment*

Suppliers

Suppliers are normally other firms providing parts, phone lines, power and a host of business services. A vehicle manufacturer may have hundreds of suppliers, but as the arrows in Figure 12.3 show, it is a two-way dependence. Firms such as Rover and Ford are progressively reducing the number of suppliers but demanding, in return for long-term supply contracts, total quality, just in time delivery and research and development support. Both parties seek stability and security in their relations, but this must be combined with continuous investment in product design, improved performance and cost-effectiveness.

Dependence on one or two suppliers, however, has its risks, just as it is risky for the smaller firm with one or two major customers. Both parties may seek to secure advantage from close co-operation, but change in the environment can undermine it. Industrial disputes may disrupt just in time deliveries, and crises, as in the Gulf, upset costings of the price of fuel oil. Similarly sharp economic downturns, as in 1990–2, may force even substantial suppliers out of business. The demise of Coloroll in the home-furnishings market, for example, disrupted supplies of woodchip wall coverings to painting and decorating firms.

The prudent firm must be aware of the potential impact of such developments on its commercial operations. The marketing department will have an intelligence-gathering network. It will continuously scan the micro-environment to monitor and anticipate change and have contingency plans prepared.

Competitors

Competitors are the reality for the majority of businesses today. Even those companies with national monopolies generally face real competition from abroad, or the threat of it. Failing this, there is always the prospect of technical substitution occurring. Witness the fate of the Swiss watch industry and mechanical cash registers, with the onset of microprocessor-based technology.

As seen in earlier chapters, competition may come in the form of hundreds of potential rivals, as in catering and personal services, or a handful of global multinationals, as in vehicles and mainframe computers. Here again the relationship is two-way, with the marketing department able to shape and influence its competitive environment.

As seen below, market-based economies and free enterprise allow businesses discretion to adjust their marketing mix in pursuit of profit through customer satisfaction. They are free to choose and decide; to succeed or fail; within the rules of the marketplace. In a truly marketing-orientated company this philosophy will inform the entire operations, from purchasing to after-sales service. Strategies, plans, tactics and responses are not decided in a vacuum, but with careful reference to the environment and its changing threats and opportunities. See Figure 12.4.

In practice businesses may vary considerably in their responsiveness to competitive change.

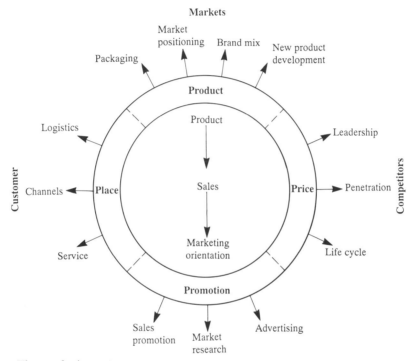

Figure 12.4   *The marketing set*

Inaction

A high-risk non-response, implying either ignorance of what is happening or a misunderstanding. Many long established small and medium-sized firms often behave in this manner, perhaps because of a production orientation or a failure to gather market intelligence. Alternatively, they may be living in the past and not accept that lasting change is in progress, or wishfully believe it will reverse. Such business dinosaurs are unlikely to survive a change in economic climate.

Reaction

The majority of firms prefer to be followers rather than leaders in the market, often failing to adapt either early or quickly enough. When change is finally forced upon them, it is likely to be unplanned and defensive. Such businesses are captives of environmental change, taking no opportunity to influence the outcome.

Pro-action

This characterises the firms that make things happen! By virtue of their marketing orientation they are aware of the dynamism of markets and the wide variety of environmental variables that can affect them. They closely monitor the competitive environment and can identify and understand the conditions of change. They adjust the marketing mix in order to lead the change, being innovative and creative within the financial constraints they are under. Such firms would be price leaders not followers, and would continually invest in new product developments and marketing initiatives to secure first-mover advantages.

It is the adaptable pro-active firm that is most likely to survive and prosper in a turbulent and fast-changing environment. Indeed such firms will influence and partly determine the rate and direction of the change. Just as IBM has set the standards for mainframe computers in the last quarter century, so the Japanese are controlling and accelerating development in consumer electronics and vehicle design.

Trade unions

Other groups in the micro environment include *national unions*, which represent sections of the workforce in most businesses. While membership has been in serious decline in recent years, unions still remain powerful if in dispute with a particular firm.

Creditors

Creditors include shareholders, suppliers, banks and other financial institutions. The terms and availability of credit are crucial to those companies that are highly geared with borrowings. Commercial banks take a particular interest in the overdrafts and capital repayments' position of small or growing firms in times of credit squeeze. As already discussed, inability to raise capital on reasonable terms has often been the major constraint on growth of small companies.

Shareholders

Shareholders are not prone to interfere in the activities of management, although weak performance will lead to share sales, a falling share price and the possibility of unwelcome takeover. There has, however, been a tendency in recent times for institutional shareholders, such as pension funds and insurance companies, to occasionally exercise voting power to block 'golden handshakes' to retiring directors.

Distributors

Distributors form, along with final customers, the last grouping for us to consider. Distributors include multiple retailers as the final link in the product chain, and the power of such distributors has been increasing relative to manufacturers in the last decade or two, not least with the expansion of retailer brands. Accounting for a high proportion of total retail sales, and in a position to promote own brands aggressively, they have posed a challenge to producers.

However, as with suppliers, the tendency of retailers today is to form closer and closer links with distributors, often through a maze of alternative channels. Tying in distributors provides the business with a competitive edge over rivals. Enabling data on stocks, prices and order status to be interrogated electronically through compatible information systems (EDI) is one such development currently being pursued by pro-active firms.

Summary review

1 Taking a business with which you familiar, identify and rank its five most important suppliers, distributors, competitors, customers and creditors.

2 What mix does it employ to:
   (a) retain and motivate its main distributors,
   (b) secure an edge over its main rivals?

3 How can a reactive business be transformed into a pro-active one?

Environmental horizons

Four different horizons may be distinguished in Figure 12.5, although the boundaries between them may be difficult to define precisely. Large numbers of small firms in building, retailing and the service sectors compete wholly in *local* markets. Logistics, the nature of the product service or limited size of the market may explain this fact.

Figure 12.5 *The four horizons*

While the health of the local economy may largely depend on circumstances in the national economy, it must be noted that variations occur. Thus Aberdeen booms in time of oil shortage. Similarly, at the *regional* level, Scottish tourism suffers in a poor summer while south Kent thrives with the Channel tunnel. The number of births may be falling nationally but Bradford's ethnic mix ensures a rising demand for schools and equipment. The marketer therefore must carefully consider the environmental influences affecting the particular market being investigated.

While the *national* market is of primary significance to domestic producers, the openness of the British economy, combined with the implications of the Single European Market, are forcing such firms to reconsider their market position. Those inactive businesses that are reluctant to search out the opportunities of this development may soon find their protected national markets exposed to new competition. If the removal of internal barriers to trade within the European Community is accomplished, and common standards established across the market, then this will become in effect Britain's domestic market. At well over 300m affluent consumers, it will be six times the size of the national market. The opportunities are clearly tremendous, but equally so are the threats from other Community firms, who will treat the British market as their own.

The International horizons for many industries in the 1990s are global rather than European. Indeed, it may yet be American and Japanese businesses that take greatest advantage of the single market in Europe. The fragmentation of national markets has protected domestic companies from severe international competition. However, as barriers are removed and regulations standardized, the entry of global competitors, and the expansion of their influence, seems inevitable.

Multinationals already characterize the major participants in industries competing for the global market. Vehicle research, production and distribution are already organized in this manner. Multinationals increasingly produce global products, using common parts sourced across frontiers to secure maximum economies of scale. This in turn forces component suppliers to operate on a global scale. Thus it is no longer sufficient for companies such as Lucas or GKN to have subsidiaries located in Europe, they must supply their customers worldwide wherever their plants are located.

Summary review

1 List one commodity, manufactured product and service supplied on the following bases:
    1 Local.
    2 Regional.
    3 National.
    4 Global.

2 Summarize the forces you feel are making it imperative for businesses to consider competing on a global scale.

The macro-environment

As we have seen, the structure of the economy is undergoing considerable change, to which business must adapt. Economic activity must be continuously analysed and interpreted. In this way business and marketing strategies may be adjusted in good time, allowing objectives to be realized.

A recent survey[1] of leading British companies found their use of external information for strategic management very limited – especially information on macroeconomic matters, demography and impending EC legislation, with two-thirds or more using little or none at all. The management consultants for whom the report was produced commented that failure to take account of these variables when formulating strategy suggests many companies are operating in a vacuum. Such organizations can only react to events when they are forced to do so, instead of pro-actively planning to allow for likely contingencies and a rapid response to emerging opportunities.

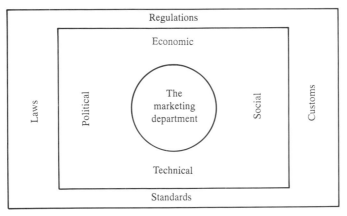

Figure 12.6 *PEST factors and the regulatory framework*

The wider business environment is often referred to be the acronym PEST (Figure 12.6). The acronym is made up from the following:

Political variables.
Economic variables.
Social variables.
Technical variables.

Changes in this wider environment are largely uncontrollable by firms, and represent the emerging opportunities and threats they need to respond to. This set of influences affects all organizations and their various stakeholders, and should not be viewed as independent of one another but rather interlinked. A shift in social values and expectations may bring about a change of government at the next election, for example. This in turn will cause adjustment of economic priorities and policies. Should the changing values embrace increased concern for the environment, then many businesses may be forced into technical change.

It must also be recognized that business operates within a framework of law. This can be expanded, as Figure 12.6 indicates, to include:

Standards – prescribed qualities and performances to which products must conform, e.g. British Standards Institute BS5750.

[1]*Information for Strategic Management, a survey of leading companies*, 1990, the Harris Research Centre for MPMG Peat Marwick Management Consultants.

Regulations – rules or orders governing various business operations and procedures, e.g. Health and Safety, Building Regulations.

Customs – long-established business practices and modes of customer behaviour, e.g. half-day closing.

Laws – established by government authority, e.g. company law.

The regulatory framework is a key role of government. On the one hand, the objective is to prevent malpractice, exploitation and injustice, but, on the other, it is hoped to avoid strangulation of business initiative in a mountain of red tape. Striking a balance between these often conflicting aims in a changing environment ensures an increasing stream of new and amending legislation reaching the statute book each year. Neglect or belated recognition of such changes may have serious consequences for businesses. It should be recognized that European Community law and directives must also be closely monitored in this regard.

Political environment

The political environment embraces this increasingly complex legal framework, which seeks both to contain and encourage business activity. The role of the state and its impact on business, however, extends far beyond the law. The philosophy of the government in office sets the climate for business. The Conservatives have sought to encourage entrepreneurship and small business through a multitude of measures, ranging from grants to advice centres, and raising finance to the structure of tax incentives.

Policies on deregulation, privatization, and the requirement on local authorities progressively to put out to open tender the majority of their services have transformed the competitive environment in many industries. Similar initiatives to devolve decision-making power to individual schools and hospitals are generating threats and opportunities for stakeholders in these sectors.

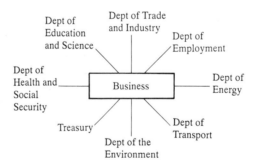

Figure 12.7   *Business–government relations*

As Figure 12.7 shows, most businesses will be affected by a number of government ministries that have a direct interest in their activities. No government adopts a passive stance towards the economic system. It is recognized that free enterprise does not operate perfectly, and some intervention is required to make markets work better.

The Department of the Environment is concerned with social costs, and has acted to limit discharges into the North Sea, for example. The DES, on the other hand, is concerned with what is in effect a merit good. The DTI will be interested in the degree of competition in markets, whether in making merger references or applying legislation to protect the consumer.

In each case business must monitor any changes in attitude or policy that may affect their activities. Reliance may be placed on the industry or trade associations to undertake this task. Marketing techniques are increasingly being used to influence politicians and ministers, to amend proposed legislation, or to lobby for action over issues of concern to members.

Macroeconomic environment

The macroeconomic environment is closely linked with the political, and will be explored in detail. Concern lies with those variables that impact on the costs, prices and competitiveness of business. The business pages of the quality press are required reading for the serious marketer; an understanding of the key economic indicators is as important to achieving success in tomorrow's marketplace as the weather forecast is to the ocean navigator.

The scope for economic turbulence appears considerable, with the new decade once again forming a watershed, marked by:

- The collapse of communism in Eastern Europe.
- The 1992 single market and 1993 Channel tunnel opening.
- Gulf crisis instability.
- Recession with the end of an 8–9 year boom.
- Rising environmental concern.

All these developments translate into potential threats and opportunities for business today. Government economic policy aims to provide a stable economic background against which business may meet these challenges. However, as recent performance in key indicators such as retail prices, balance of payments, interest rates, and unemployment underline, this is not easily achieved.

The government may have numerous economic policy levers to influence the business environment, but their use remains an art as much as a science. Similarly the fact that Britain is a very open, trade-dependent economy means we are exposed to international economic change that is beyond the control of the government. Global crises which destabilize primary product prices for example, forces oil-dependent developing countries to curtail purchases from British exporters. The net result is a move into recession that any government will find hard to resist.

Social environment

The social environment is perhaps the most difficult one to identify, evaluate and respond to. Social change is influenced by many factors, and will be reflected for the marketer in changing tastes and purchasing behaviour. The way we live and behave is a product of years of cultural conditioning by family, friends, school, work and the media. However, many of our attitudes, e.g. towards business, homeownership and credit, carry serious implications for many companies. As we examine in more detail later, the structure of the population is changing, with longer life expectancy and smaller family sizes producing an ageing population. Falling school rolls and rising participation in higher education are altering the economics of provision and foreshadowing shortfalls of young entrants into the labour force. Pro-active organizations among the large retailers and banks are already turning to married women to fill the ranks. Such a change, however, will alter the structure of many markets, putting a premium on convenience. Opportunities to better serve the needs of working mothers should now be exercising the mind of the alert marketer.

Technical environment

The technical environment is the one most readily associated with change and challenge. It is after all the dominant characteristic of an industrial society and appears to be accelerating in its pace of development and application. The lead time between an invention and its introduction to the marketplace used to be measured in decades rather than years. The diffusion of new ideas has now accelerated, owing to information technology, multinationals and increased competitive pressure, with the effect of shortening the length of the average product life-cycle.

CAD/CAM techniques now allow the Japanese to design and manufacture a vehicle in under 4 years, while western companies still take 7 or 8. Alongside the opportunities that new technologies offer in terms of new materials, new products, new markets and new services, must be set the cost. While the smaller firm and niche markets may still offer a creative context for developing new ideas, it is only larger firms that can finance their innovation and diffusion. The cost of a stake in so-called sunrise industries, such as biotechnology, satellite communications and other information technologies, is beyond all but the larger multinational companies.

It should be noted that all marketing departments have the chance to take advantage of new technology. Applications may range from automated warehousing to computer-aided interviewing. State of the art examples would include sales forecasts using EPOS systems, and electronic data interchange with suppliers and distributors. Whatever the degree of technical sophistication, the one certainty is that businesses ignore it at their peril.

Summary review

1 Suggest two examples of customs and regulations applying in the retail industry.

2 What benefits arise out of a framework of law for business?

3 Which ministries would a small firm have to contact and why when it first sets up in business?

4 Provide a summary of the main events and developments affecting a chosen business over the past week.

The environmental set

'The firm is a creature of its environment. Its resources; its income; its problems; its opportunities and its very survival are generated and conditioned by the environment' (H. I. Ansoff).

Every organization faces a 'set' of forces that may be influenced but not directly controlled. Their identification is a key input into formulating corporate strategy. In effect they form the more significant opportunities and threats currently faced, and will be specific to the organization. It is crucial that the organization identifies its environmental set and continually scans for change in its composition.

Figure 12.8 represents an environmental set for a typical manufacturer exporting extensively into Europe. The elements have been ranked, with the high cost of borrowing taking number one position:

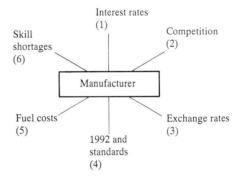

Figure 12.8   *Environmental set for a manufacturer*

- Competition is always significant in such a set, although the degree of concern will vary over time.
- While historically high money and real interest rates may ensure a top ranking, their subsequent fall will clearly reduce the intensity of this influence on the company. Conversely, a deepening recession may trigger more aggressive marketing from the competition, causing this element to assume first ranking.
- The exchange rate is of significance for any exporter, since an adverse movement can quickly eliminate the profit margin on a deal negotiated and agreed on the assumption of a more favourable rate. While exchange rate risks can be hedged, this may add unacceptably to costs and reduce competitiveness. Entry into the exchange rate mechanism (ERM) may be expected to reduce this risk, and therefore the ranking of the factor.
- The coming of the open market in 1992 and the issue of European standards also feature strongly, not least because meeting these will be a precondition to competing at all in many community markets.
- Fuel prices reflect instability in the oil market, and the importance of fuel in manufacture and transportation of products. This cost feeds direct into final prices and competitiveness, threatening loss of sales and possible cutbacks.
- Skill shortages are also identified; they have arisen out of the substantial boom in the late 1980s and a corresponding shortfall in training activity. The intensity of this factor is likely to wane for most skill areas as recession develops, to be replaced by, say, ecological regulations or new technological developments according to changing circumstances.

An environmental set for a local authority (Figure 12.9) suggests different managerial concerns. Finance assumes a similar importance but is specifically concerned with non-payment and the prospect of charge capping by central government. The importance of

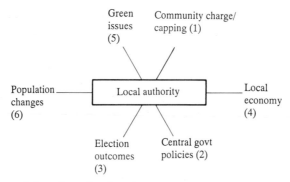

Figure 12.9   *Environmental set for a local authority*

central government is underlined by the pressure of electoral concerns, which will clearly help determine the direction and impact of council policies in future. Similarly conservative policies to encourage the sale of council housing and to put out to tender a wide variety of services fundamentally affects the role of authorities. In effect they are being encouraged to transform from being 'providers' of services to 'facilitators', seeking to obtain provision from the most cost-effective source available in order to realize best value for money for their customers.

The state of the local economy is of continuous concern, while focus on green issues through the activities of such departments as environmental health is more recent. Population change also features as an important input into forecasting requirements in areas such as housing and education.

Further sets could be developed to represent the major influences to be taken into account by businesses in financial services, retailing, education, construction and so forth. Whatever the set of influences affecting a particular business, the following should be noted.

Environmental sets will:

- Vary from organization to organization.
- Vary in intensity over time.
- Vary in their degree of complexity.
- Vary in their degree of uncertainty.
- Vary in their degree of impact on the organization.
- Vary in their rate of change over time.

They will also vary in significance according to the functional department being considered. Marketing will be most exposed to environmental influences, in marked contrast to the after-sales function. Research and development will be intermediate, being affected by technical changes, competitor moves and the possibilities of substitution and regulation. Companies researching new cosmetics or pharmaceutical products, for example, will certainly be concerned with animal-rights activities.

The elements in the set may push or pull the organization in different directions, and must not therefore be treated in isolation. Influence is in some cases two-way, where large organizations with considerable market power may seek to influence their set.

They can use their power to advertise or to lobby MPs and ministers. They can effectively operate as a pressure group in their own right. Alternatively, they may redeploy resources to manufacture in less polluting ways, and redesign products to be more acceptable to the environment. However, short of complete relocation overseas, no firm, no matter what its size, can insulate itself completely.

All organizations, whatever their form, must be responsive to the environment and aim to be efficient and productive within the constraints imposed. The more predictable managerial environment of earlier decades has been replaced by complex and dynamic change in the 1980s and 1990s. Few sectors, not even the previously sheltered professions, now face static conditions. Any organized endeavours wishing to be consistently successful must therefore:

- Scan their operating environment
- Identify the set of forces relevant to their industry.
- Respond by developing and implementing contingency plans.
- Monitor the effects of their strategic actions.
- Continue to scan regularly.

Organizations with the ability to sense environmental change tend to perform better than those who do not have that ability. It signals the need for a change in the marketing strategy, but is no guarantee of the capacity to respond. This crucially depends on the quality of management's understanding of the changes occurring in the external environment, and the flexibility of the organisation's culture and structure. Subsequent chapters will explore the economic environment with a view to providing a framework for such analysis.

Summary review

Produce an environmental set for your current organization. Rank the elements identified and consider their significance:
    (a) 12 months ago,
    (b) in 12 months time.

13
The human environment

The last chapter explored the various environments of business and concluded that all organizations face a set of forces they may seek to influence but are unlikely ever to fully control. This is especially true of the PEST factors, which made up the macroenvironment.

One important component of this environment is population. This chapter will explore various dimensions of demographic change that are of particular importance to the marketer. It also considers significant trends in employment patterns and their impact on the business organization.

Aims

The aims of this chapter are as follows:

- To emphasize the fundamental importance of population to market analysis.
- To provide insight into important demographic change, both nationally and globally.
- To consider in detail the changing structure of British population.
- To review the shifting patterns of employment and identify those with particular significance to the marketer.
- To consider the trend towards flexibility and its implications for effective marketing.
- To examine the emerging role of women in employment.

Glossary

ACAS – Advisory Conciliation and Arbitration Service.

Census – carried out every 10 years since 1801, it provides an opportunity to amass a wealth of information on demographic, social and economic change. The full census of 1991 will be the last this century.

Contractual employment – the execution of specified work at an agreed rate or fixed price.

Demographic time bomb – refers to the inevitable consequences of the sharp decline in births of the mid- to late 1970s. It is often combined with the impending sharp rise in dependents as the post-war babies retire at the turn of the century.

Multiskilling – a worker who possesses a range of relevant skills, so that he/she can complete tasks as a whole without assistance.

Norm – a pattern of behaviour that is standard. Full-time work, for example, is accepted as the rule rather than the exception.

Nuclear family – composed of mother, father and normally two children in a single household. It may be distinguished from extended families, which include other relatives within the household unit.

Part-time – workers who voluntarily work 30 hours or less per week are part-timers.
Telebanking – financial transactions by means of a phone link between the customer and the
   bank's computer.

Trends in population

A knowledge of demography is important to the marketer. Market segmentation and
assessment of market potential must start with analysis of the size and structure of the target
population now and in the future. The Office of Population Censuses and Surveys (OPCS)
publishes population data that come from a full census every 10 years and updating sample
surveys every 5 years.

Where business seeks to segment the market profitably, it must identify new customer
bases. A retailer such as Burton may focus on the rising number of over-45-year-olds and
establish a new chain of outlets dedicated to their needs. Brake friction manufacturers might
identify the characteristics of the segment who drive high performance cars, and supply a
range of specially formulated competition pads. Alternatively, the progression might be from
'yuppies' to 'swells', (i.e. 'smart women earning lots in London') in that one building society
identified this latter group as accounting for 25 per cent of its new mortgage business, twice
the figure of 10 years ago.

The structure of the population may be broken down by age, sex, marital status, region and
employment status. However, while it is clearly important for the pram or toy manufacturer
to know the number, age, sex and location of its target population, this is only one factor in its
forecasts. It will also be concerned with expenditure per child, tastes and the price of
substitutes. For a premium pram producer such as 'Silver Cross', the parents' decision to have
smaller families may actually promote sales as they decide to afford 'the best' for their only
child.

Local authorities see demographic data as crucial to planning the provision of their services.
Records of births corrected for net migration indicate the client population for education and
social services. As the number of births fell sharply in the late 1970s and early 1980s, so less
schools and teachers were required, causing rationalization to take place. Similarly data is
required on family sizes to plan council-house provision and a variety of other services.
Authorities must also identify birth-rate variations across their localities, especially where the
ethnic mix is reflected in family size variations. In Bradford, for example, a high Asian
population has resulted in rising births. This is the opposite of the national pattern, implying
very different demands and resource implications.

Population trends are also important to provide forewarning of labour shortages. The term
'demographic time bomb' has been coined to represent the sharp fall in school-leavers due to
occur in the late 1990s. A combination of falling births and rising participation rates in higher
education will conspire to produce shortages in the 1990s. Of less direct importance to
business, but of major significance to the general economic climate, are the following factors:

- A rising dependency ratio.
- Global population pressures.
- Environmental consequences of population.

Dependency ratio

The dependency ratio is the number of dependents in the population relative to those of
working age. The greater the proportion of those over retirement and under school leaving

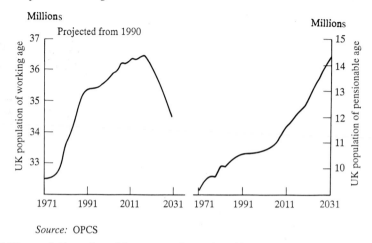

Source: OPCS

Figure 13.1   *UK population of working age and pensionable age in millions (projected from 1990)*

age, the larger the ratio. The ratio may be adjusted to account for those in full-time education, early retirement, full-time house persons, the disabled and the unemployed.

As Figure 13.1 infers, the dependency ratio is currently falling, owing to lower births and fewer retirements. This arises from the fact that birth rates were falling in the 1930s and early 1940s, owing to economic depression and war. The ratio will, however, rise sharply after 2007, when members of the post-war baby bulge begin to retire.

Pressure of global population

The pressure of global population is represented in Figure 13.2 below, and shows its exponential growth to date.

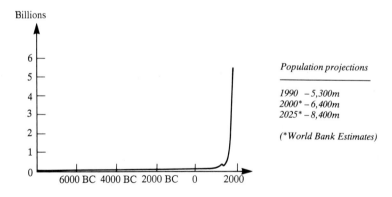

Figure 13.2   *World population growth*

The projected expansion in numbers will occur, despite the sharply falling population growth rates expected across the globe, because of the extremely high proportion of young people in the less developed countries' populations. Such countries will account for a steadily increasing proportion of world population. If developed countries, as defined in 1980, are

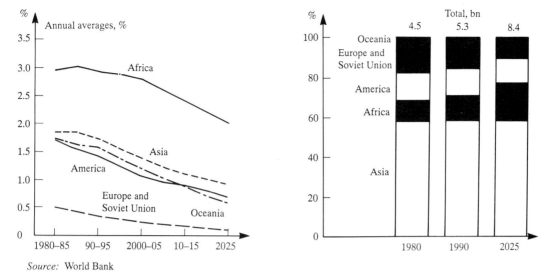

Source: World Bank

Figure 13.3   *Estimates of world population by continent*

taken, their share of world population is projected to fall from 25 per cent in 1980 to under 17 per cent in 2025. As can be seen in Figure 13.3, it is in Africa that growth rates remain significant. Africa has seen falling per capita incomes since 1960 as population has outpaced economic growth. Unlike the industrialized nations, poor countries, as in Africa, face:

- Third World debts arising out of oil dependence.
- Strict immigration laws limiting emigration possibilities.
- Ecological implications of deforestation and chemical fertilizers.

Environmental consequences

The environmental consequences of population are currently more pressing than the need to feed the rising numbers, since large food surpluses exist in Europe and America. Their equitable redistribution is the only problem. However, it is the compounded effect of population growth and expectations of rising per capita consumption that focuses attention on potential resource and environmental impacts.

These impacts however are far greater for the newborn in rich countries, as the following quote from Reinow suggests:

> Every 8 seconds a new American is born, he is a disarming little thing, but begins to scream loudly in a voice that can be heard for 70 years. He is screaming for 56 million gallons of water, 21,000 gallons of petrol, 10,150 lbs of meat, 28,000 pints of milk, 9000 lbs of wheat and great storehouses of other foods, drinks and tobacco. These are the lifetime demands on his country and his economy.

With 80 per cent of the world's population in less developed countries, any aspiration to achieve American material standards will clearly increase the pressures. On the other hand, these countries also represent potential massive new emerging markets if economic development can be achieved and sustained.

Cannon developed the concept of an optimum population. Population may be too small if society is unable to take full advantage of its resources and technology. Growing population can bring larger markets and greater mobility. A younger age structure can revitalize. However, excessive population reduces well-being through pressure on physical and biological resources. It inhibits the ability to provide public services and limits freedom of choice. As can be seen in various parts of Latin America, Africa and South East Asia, it unbalances the ecology. Overgrazing and deforestation threaten global security by destroying species and seed strains, as well as altering the climate.

Figure 13.4 indicates the combined effects of population growth and energy-intensive living standards. The global warming effects of these accumulations augur potential disaster in the next century.

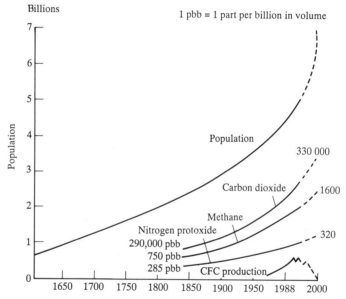

Figure 13.4   *Comparative evolution of population and greenhouse gases*

Summary review

1 What will be the effects of the demographic time bomb on:
    (a) a multiple retailer,
    (b) a medium-sized painting and decorating company,
    (c) the armed forces?

2 Taking a company like Saga Holidays (specializing in holidays for the over-60s) or McCarthy & Stone Retirement Homes, suggest how and why their marketing mix may have to be modified to meet the needs of those retiring at the beginning of the next century.

3 List all the consequences that might arise out of rapid population growth in a relatively poor country.

4 Using your knowledge of population and income elasticity, assess the market potential of the following new product ideas in the areas shown in Figure 13.5:

   (a) Area L – a new variety of savoury sausages.
   (b) Area A – a range of cordon bleu microwave meals.
   (c) Area D – oven-ready traditional recipes from bygone days.

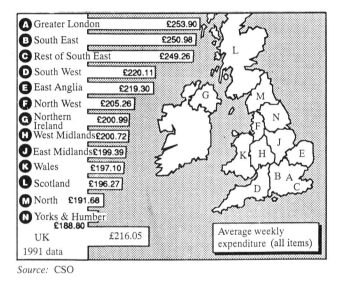

	Average weekly expenditure (all items)
A Greater London	£253.90
B South East	£250.98
C Rest of South East	£249.26
D South West	£220.11
E East Anglia	£219.30
F North West	£205.26
G Northern Ireland	£200.99
H West Midlands	£200.72
J East Midlands	£199.39
K Wales	£197.10
L Scotland	£196.27
M North	£191.68
N Yorks & Humber	£188.80
UK	£216.05

1991 data

Source: CSO

Figure 13.5 *Household spending by UK region, 1988–9*

Aggregate population

The record in population forecasting has been remarkably inaccurate. The OPCS publishes a central projection but also low and high variants, based on assumptions regarding births. The main problem currently lies in predicting births rather than deaths. As Figure 13.6 shows, the fluctuation in live births have been considerable. The projected rise follows on from the peak on births about 27 years earlier.

Population growth = birth rate − death rate + net migration

The birth rate is determined primarily by the number of women of child-bearing age officially defined as 15–44 years. The key factor is the average family size of those who marry adjusted for the incidence of remarriage and number of children born outside wedlock.

The rise in illegitimacy from 8.4 per cent in 1971 to 12.5 per cent in 1981 and 25 per cent in 1988 gives some indication of the decline in the popularity of formal marriage. This and the family size decision are influenced by a range of social and economic factors.

ECONOMIC   SOCIAL
Real income   Cultural values
Cost of housing   Religious attitudes
Opportunity cost of children   Media influence
Employment opportunities   Birth control practices

Birth rates were high in the late 1950s and early 1960s but depressed in the 1970s and early 1980s. The earlier period was characterized by low unemployment, rising living standards and relatively cheap housing. The welfare state offered free health care and education, which combined with family allowances to make child-rearing attractive. The pill was not yet developed, but more liberal parental values were bringing the freedom to marry earlier. The media image was centred around the nuclear family, implying a minimum of two children.

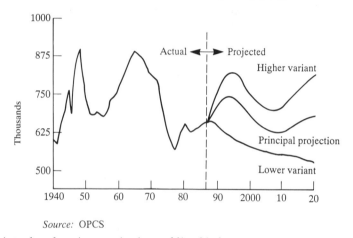

Source: OPCS

Figure 13.6   *Actual and variant projections of live births, 1940–2027*

The 1970s, in contrast, brought economic uncertainty, rising property prices and a stagnating economy. The role and expectations of women were changing with increasing education and employment. Equal pay legislation raised the opportunity cost of having children in terms of earnings and career advancement forgone. Marketing activity intensified, with travel, consumer durables, vehicles and property competing alongside children for limited income. Attitudes towards birth control were changing, with the pill, while there were rising worries over the high rate of divorce, especially among those marrying early. Even such diverse concerns as those over slimming, population explosion and the possibility of nuclear war will have had their effect.

The 'marginal' decision to have one more or one less child per family is an individual one but has compounded effects if repeated consistently across the child-bearing age group. The implications of an ability to determine sex at conception, for example, might be far-reaching for the number and sex of future births.

Death rates are much more predictable than birth rates. Indeed the life insurance industry is built upon such reliable considerations. Actuaries use these statistics to establish probabilities and determine risk premiums, which may then be marketed to various segments of the population. Death rates do change, however, in that life expectancy has been rising gradually. On the other hand, the effect of new illnesses such as AIDS or those associated with a deteriorating environment may reverse the pattern in future.

Infant mortality has fallen sharply, halving since 1971 to just 9 per 1,000, largely due to improving medical practice. Improvements in medicine, diet, medical technology and attitudes to health and fitness will all have an effect in this respect.

Net migration is the final element in the population size equation. Since UK immigration laws have been tightened, this has tended to stabilize. Figure 13.7 shows the expected pattern for the UK by age group.

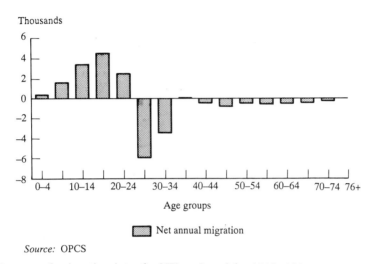

Source: OPCS

Figure 13.7   *Net annual migration into the UK projected for 1989–2027*

There has been a small net inflow since the early 1980s. As can be seen, however, it is in the younger age groups under 25 where the inflow arises, with older groups providing outflow, especially towards retirement age. The outflow of the 25–34 group represents families starting a new life, often in Canada or Australia, while the inflow is largely from the New Commonwealth.

Population structure

The demographic segmentation of the population may be undertaken in the following ways.

- By age
- By region
- By sex
- By ethnic groups
- By marital status
- By employment

By age and sex distribution

As can be seen in Figure 13.8, the distribution is complicated by a fluctuating pattern of births over the last 90 years.

The implications are very significant for the economy in general and specific markets in particular. It may be noted that there is a slight biological birth imbalance (106 male to 100 female), which is corrected by the age of 50. At the age of 75 there are twice as many females

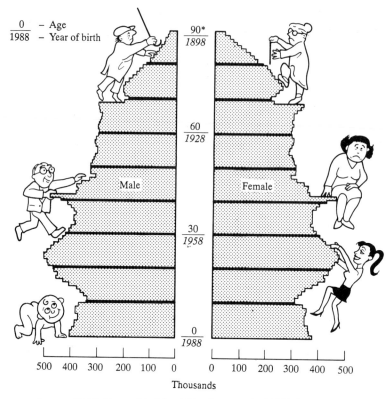

Source: OPCS, *Economist* *Aged 90 and over; male 42,000; female 174,000

Figure 13.8 *Britain's population structure, 1988 estimate*

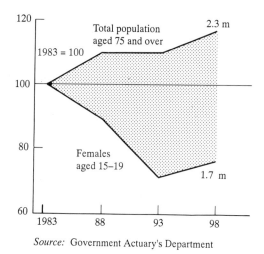

Source: Government Actuary's Department

Figure 13.9 *Population impacts on the NHS*

as males. The chart highlights actual and projected changes in various age groups into the next century. This forms vital input into formulating marketing strategy.

It also has importance from the supply side, in that Britain's population is ageing rapidly. Over the period to 1995 the number of school-leavers will shrink by 23 per cent, which is serious for those organizations that rely on recruitment from this age group. Banks, retailers, the health service and the armed forces are particularly vulnerable. Figure 13.9 highlights these impacts for the NHS: the rising population of over-75s means much increased demand for health services, whereas the fall in female school-leavers implies staff shortages.

Employers are reacting to these impending shortages in a number of ways including:

- Building links with educational institutions.
- Increased spending on recruitment.
- Improving training for the less qualified.
- Substituting less qualified staff, e.g. nursing auxiliaries.
- Improving pay and incentives.
- Tapping alternative workforces.
- More flexible employment patterns.
- Retention, retraining and promotion policies.

As can be seen in Figure 13.10, however, the shortages in the under-25s is more than made up by increased numbers in older age groups. It is anticipated that encouraging more married women in the 25–44 group to return to work and increased use of older workers will bridge the gap for many businesses.

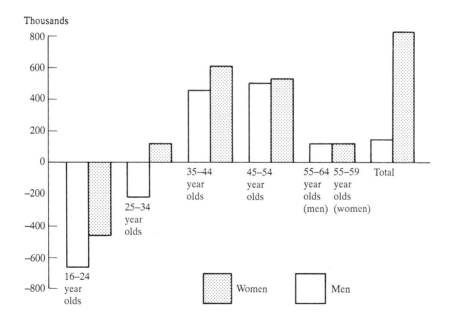

Source: Employment Department

Figure 13.10 *Projected change in GB civilian labour force of working age, 1989–2027*

The changing patterns of population in Britain are reflected in Europe, where labour force projections suggest contraction from the year 2000 (Figure 13.11). Germany, Denmark and Italy face this situation already, and may be expected to recruit across national boundaries to fill skill shortages. The UK, with poor levels of investment in training, may be particularly vulnerable to such poaching.

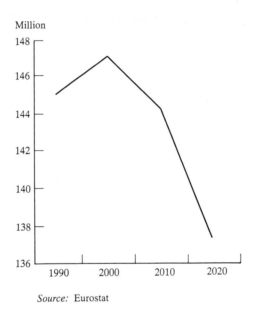

Source: Eurostat

Figure 13.11   *EC labour force projections*

Spending patterns in Europe will increasingly reflect middle-aged preferences as the proportion of over-45s rises from 37 per cent to nearly 50 per cent between 1990 and 2020. Increased expenditure on leisure, travel, tourism and transport are therefore to be expected.

One segment of this boom area is the retired. In 1970 there were 290m over-60s in the world and 26m over 80. By the year 2000 this is estimated to rise to 600m and 58m respectively. By 1990 around 15 per cent of the UK population was 65 or over, compared to only 10 per cent in Japan and 12 per cent in the USA.

However, owing to low birth rates in the 1940s, the UK proportion will actually fall up to the early years of the next century, while European countries and Japan will overtake us. The retirement of the post-war babies, however, will see the proportion rise sharply to over 26 per cent. By 2001 the over-75s will account for nearly half of all pensioners, as life expectancy increases to 80 for women and 74 for men. The expenditure implications and market opportunities of these figures are considerable. Health and social security expenditure, for example, is four times the average for the over-65s and six times for the over-75s. The pension projections are dramatic, since not only will increased numbers be retiring early next century, but they will also have earnings-related pensions and expectations of enhanced quality of life.

The government is already responding by encouraging private pension provision. It is also likely that the rules on pension calculation will be made less generous, and greater incentives provided to encourage people to work longer, or on a part-time basis. However, as the old become more numerous, their economic and political power is likely to grow. Two-thirds of personal savings are already held by the over 55s, which, combined with inheritance and homeownership, gives them a rising proportion of total wealth.

Their propensity to vote is also greater, as is their conservatism. Financially well-endowed, they may be expected to exert more pressure on governments as well as constituting important but discerning consumer markets. It must also be recognized however, that this age group also includes some of the poorest in society, with nearly 2m receiving supplementary benefit and a further 1m qualifying but not taking it up.

By marital status

This is undergoing considerable change, owing to the declining popularity of marriage and rising divorce rates. The number of teenage brides, for example, has fallen by a third over the last decade. Non-traditional households already account for over a third, with single parents representing a growing share. Cohabitation is increasing sharply, along with illegitimate births. Over 16 per cent of single, separated and divorced persons are estimated to be cohabiting in the South East, while under 11 per cent do so in Scotland and Wales.

While 25 per cent of births are to unmarried parents in Britain, the rate is nearer 50 per cent in Scandinavia. Both UK marriage and divorce rates are the highest in Western Europe. Those marrying at 17 years are ten times as likely to divorce within 10 years as those marrying at 25. Remarriages already account for a third of all marriages, and often produce composite family units, bringing together children from previous unions. This clearly forms a more complicated pattern for marketing analysis, but also richer scope for segmentation.

By region

The distribution of population across regions is changing under the influence of differential economic growth rates and net migration. The metropolitan areas of Greater London, Clydeside, Greater Manchester, Tyne and Wear and the West Midlands, for example, have been losing over ½ per cent per annum on average in the period since 1971. Industrial decline and increasing preference for suburban locations are expected to continue this pattern. East Anglia, in contrast, has been registering growth of over 1 per cent per annum; a relatively youthful age structure has contributed, along with considerable net inward migration. Speedier road and rail links to London have assisted the latter trend.

The projection for the 1990s is one of broadly static population in the North, Wales and Scotland, with growth up to ½ per cent per annum in the South and Midlands. The marketer must take care, however, to examine aggregate data for local variations that might significantly affect targeting of customer populations.

By ethnic groups

The UK population has historically had a diverse mix, with a succession of inflows from Eire, Europe and latterly the New Commonwealth. Of the 7 per cent currently born outside the UK, over half are white. The last census registered 4.4 per cent of the population classifying themselves as non-white, of which two fifths were born in the UK.

The non-whites' age structure is, however, very different, most notably with only 4 per cent aged over 60 compared to 21 per cent for the white population. The younger age structure implies a very different pattern of needs, which must be accounted for in areas such as West Yorkshire, the Midlands and parts of London where ethnic concentrations occur.

Nearly 12 per cent of births are to women born outside the UK. It may be noted that the West Indian population, the oldest of the New Commonwealth immigrant groups, now have birth rates little different from the average for the population as a whole. As the percentages of UK born rise among other ethnic groups, a similar pattern may be expected to emerge.

Summary review

1 Account for the rising number of births outside formal marriage, and consider the marketing implications of this trend.

2 In the light of the points made in this chapter, brainstorm possible opportunities and threats arising out of current population trends for your organization or college.

3 Provide examples to suggest why the marketing approach of smaller businesses might be more successful than nationally based organizations in meeting the needs of local populations.

By employment

This is the final dimension of population structure to consider, and probably the one of greatest importance to the marketer, not least because employment equates with purchasing power. Figure 13.12 provides an interesting contrast of the employment status of adults between the great depression year of 1931 and the 1981 census. The impression is of a better

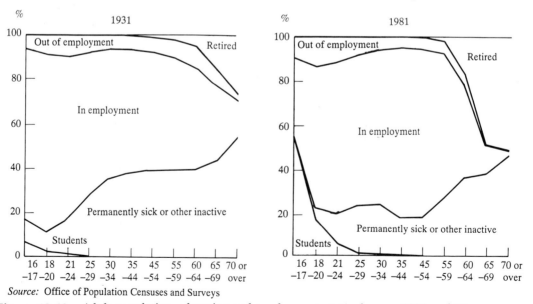

Source: Office of Population Censuses and Surveys

Figure 13.12   *Adult population–education and employment status by age, 1931 and 81*

educated, healthier, more active, earlier retiring but more fully employed society in 1981 than 1931.

A number of important employment trends may be distinguished within this pattern of change:

- From industrial to service employment.
- From manual to knowledge-based work.
- From full-time to flexitime employment.
- From paid employment to self-employment.
- From male-dominated career structures to unisex.

Distribution of employment

Two centuries ago 60 per cent or more of the employed population were engaged in the primary sectors of agriculture, forestry, fishing, mining and quarrying. By a century ago 60 per cent were employed in the secondary sector of manufacturing, construction, and utilities such as electricity and water, as industrialization was accomplished. By 1980 a further transformation had occurred, with 60 per cent now employed in the tertiary sector, including transport, distribution, finance and personal services. In the meantime the primary sector had shrunk to less than 4 per cent, a trend continued through the 1990s as Community spending on agriculture was capped and British Coal's employees fell from 230,000 to less than 70,000.

Manufacturing has also shrunk rapidly in employment terms, from a peak of 8.5 million in the mid 1960s to under 5 million today. With this sector now accounting for just 20 per cent of the employed labour force, predictions of academics such as Professor Stonier, in his book *The Wealth of Information*, that the production of manufactured wealth would require just 10 per cent of the workforce by the year 2000 may yet be realized.

Workforce in employment

As can be seen in Figure 13.13, the workforce in employment has been relatively stable over the past three decades at around 25m. The deep depression of the early 1980s and

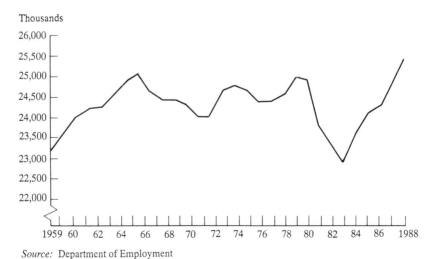

Source: Department of Employment

Figure 13.13 *Workforce in employment (GB), 1959–88 (June)*

corresponding rise in unemployment to over 3 million interrupted this picture, although the equally dramatic expansion in employment during the late 1980s more than restored the position. This unexpected rise from the third quarter of 1985 to the first quarter of 1990 was of the order of 3 million net new employees. The unemployment rate fell to around 6 per cent, with the female rate falling below 4 per cent, giving an indication of the strength of the boom conditions which prevailed during this period. However, it represented growth in part- and full-time female employment rather than in male employment, as Figure 13.14 shows.

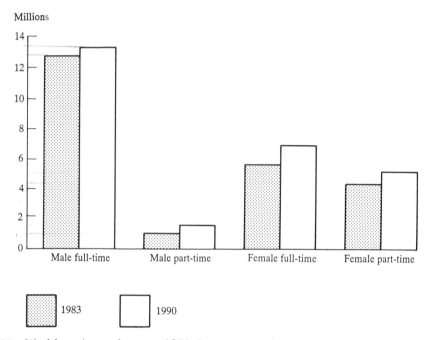

Figure 13.14   *Workforce in employment (GB), June 1983 and June 1990*

Employment growth was concentrated in the areas of financial and miscellaneous services. Distribution, hotels and catering also featured strongly.

The projected growth in the civilian workforce up to the year 2000 suggests a rise of just 100,000 males as against 900,000 extra females, the latter primarily women in the age group 35–44 years returning to work.

The rise of part-time employment

In 1988 full-time paid employment was the norm and accounted for two-thirds of all employment. Should current trends continue, this pattern may be broken. Part-timers quadrupled from 4 per cent of all employment in the decade to 1971, levelled out, then moved up sharply to 24 per cent by 1987, and are forecast to reach 28 per cent by 1995, according to the Institute of Employment Research at Warwick University. The breakdown for male and females can be seen in Figure 13.15.

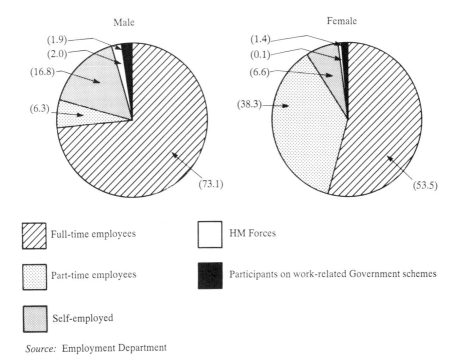

Male

Female

Full-time employees

HM Forces

Part-time employees

Participants on work-related Government schemes

Self-employed

Source: Employment Department

Figure 13.15 *Components of the workforce in employment (GB), December 1989, seasonally adjusted, per cent*

With only 6.3 per cent of males working part-time, compared to nearly 40 per cent of women, the impact of widespread redundancies in male-dominated manufacturing over the 1980s has significantly reduced full-time employment.

The female data is somewhat misleading, since it combines single women, whose employment pattern is similar to the male, and married women, for whom part-time employment is even higher. In terms of weekly hours worked the Department of Employment labour force survey reveals that while just 20 per cent of females work 40–49 hours per week, 45 per cent of males do. Indeed over 25 per cent of males work over 50 hours, against just 5 per cent of females.

The marketer must seek to adjust the marketing mix in recognition of these changing work patterns. More working women means less hours available for shopping, putting a premium on convenience. It also suggests increased purchasing power for women and more influence over household buying patterns.

Self-employment

Self-employment also rose sharply during this period, due partly to a dearth of paid employment opportunities, on the one hand, and government incentives, on the other. Self-employment in the late 1970s had fallen to an historically low level of around 6–7 per cent of the total. This was lower than most of our competitors and significantly below Japan, Italy and Germany.

Contractual employment

As can be seen in Figure 13.15, self-employment has risen to around 12 per cent of the workforce. This growth has been assisted by the increasing use by organizations of *contractual employment*.

A more competitive environment has forced many organizations to economize in the use of labour by contracting for skills only when and if they are required. The convenience of a directly employed labour force has become a luxury even big businesses can no longer afford.

Cleaning and catering services may be contracted out, as may transport and distribution to third-party operators. A marketing agency might be hired to advise on the advertising and packaging of a new product range, and a firm of consultants for financial reorganization. An ACAS survey found that 70 per cent of companies had increased their use of contractors since 1980.

Charles Handy in his book *The Age of Unreason* refers to such businesses as 'shamrock organizations'. They employ a *core* of full-time scientific, technical and managerial personnel with company specific skills who co-ordinate and facilitate the activities of the business. To undertake these activities, the organization employs a *flexible* workforce, including:

- Full-time semi-skilled clerical, process and supervisory employees who lack career prospects and tend to exhibit high turnover. Flexibility is therefore achieved by not replacing those who leave when activity slows.
- Part-time and temporary workers, job-sharers, staff on short-term contracts and those on industrial placement and government training schemes. Flexibility is even greater with these groups, and the organization has the opportunity to evaluate the employee before making a full-time commitment. The use of temporary workers from employment agencies has increased even faster than the use of part-time workers in the 1980s.

The contractual workforce is employed on the basis of payment for work done and is therefore extremely attractive, given labour is plentiful and competition prevails. The organization is, however, dependent on homeworkers and sub-contractors supplying their services on time and to standards agreed.

Customers

Customers form the final leaf of Handy's shamrock, reflecting the increasingly self-service nature of our economy. Business has been able to transfer some of the work of supplying a product or services on to the customer. Self-service and self-fitting already prevail in most of the high street, and home shopping via computer and video may further extend buyer participation. New technology in the form of expert systems will allow a degree of self-diagnosis to displace health services, and self- or distance learning become a partial substitute for classroom education. Financial services are also being similarly transacted by the customer, with telebanking set to expand rapidly.

The rise of the knowledge worker

The classification of employees into primary, secondary and tertiary sectors gives a misleading impression of the work they actually undertake. As few as a third of those employed in a manufacturing plant may be actually on the shop floor, with the balance working in design, research and development, finance, personnel, sales and marketing.

Knowledge workers would include the following:

- *Information infrastructure* – telecommunications workers, computer operators.
- *Information producers* – researchers, scientific and technical.
- *Information processors* – management, administrative, clerical.
- *Information distributors* – Educators, professions, medical.

Over half of the workforce in Britain today are estimated to be knowledge workers, although most jobs will require brains rather than brawn by the next century. Britain therefore will require a rising proportion with higher education qualifications. Despite falling births, rising participation rates and improved educational productivity, Britain currently educates less than a fifth to this level. Unless further substantial resources are deployed, critical skill shortages will surely develop, resulting in a national failure to grasp the potential opportunities of the new age.

When over 55 per cent of the unemployed are without qualifications of any kind, and two-thirds of the unemployed are under 35, Britain already faces a crisis in education and skills provision. With the Japanese pattern of educating virtually all 18-year-olds being followed by the other emerging dragons of SE Asia, they are much better placed to effect the transition to knowledge-based work than the UK is.

Flexible working lives

Many references have already been made to the theme of flexibility. An industrial economy based on standardization and the division of labour needed a disciplined workforce that clocked on and off together. The work norm was, until recently, full-time work plus overtime, and identical 2 to 3 weeks' holiday plus statutory days, over a working life from leaving school to retirement at 60 or 65. Those starting work today may look forward to a much more varied working life and a far shorter one.

Management's need for flexibility has already produced a kaleidoscope of patterns, including:

- Flexitime and staggered hours.
- Averaging of hours over longer periods.
- Flexible work years to match work peaks and troughs.
- Flexible rostering and shifts.
- Longer days and shorter weeks.
- 2–12 hour shifts at weekends.
- Lifetime tapering of hours towards retirement.

These non-standard patterns of work imply non-standard patterns of leisure, to which the marketer must respond. The above flexibility underpins changing demands for leisure services. Short break holidays; all-night entertainment and late night or Sunday opening all characterize strengthening consumer demands for flexibility and choice.

In summary then it can be seen that flexibility has been a major theme of the 1980s, as employers have sought to maintain their profitability and meet the challenge of increasingly uncertain and competitive markets. Union pressures on hours and the need to secure technical change and new skills have motivated many businesses to pursue the following forms of flexibility:

- *Numerical flexibility* – the ability to rapidly adjust employees' hours and numbers to changes in demand.
- *Functional flexibility* – the ability to effect rapid job completion and transfer through multiskilling.
- *Time flexibility* – the ability to match work time to business demand.
- *Pay flexibility* – the ability to reward work actually performed in undertaking the task, and skills acquired.

The changing role of women

Women already account for two-fifths of the labour force, a share expected to rise to 44 per cent by the end of the century as their employment prospects brighten with the fall in school-leavers. Child-bearing in the mid-20s normally interrupts a woman's career pattern, with initial return to work frequently being on a part-time basis.

The level of economic activity among married women is inversely related to the presence of children, although women are increasingly taking maternity leave and then returning to their old jobs. Most employers, however, are reluctant for this to be on a part-time basis.

The increasing role of women in employment may be explained by a number of factors:

- *Financial pressures* – arising from the cost of housing and life-style, couples' expectations force them to work longer before starting a family, enabling women to progress further in career development before family formation. In a recent survey 70 per cent of women questioned indicated it was either definitely or at least partly true that they could not manage unless earning.
- *Rising educational attainment* – with around 45 per cent of the higher education intake now female, women's horizons are widening, while their attractiveness to employers is enhanced.
- *Parental attitudes and expectations* – these are changing. Smaller family sizes and more liberal views, derived from parental experience of the liberated 1960s, is translating into more equal opportunities and treatment between the sexes.

Legislation to help women   EWD

Legislation in the form of the equal pay and sex discrimination legislation of the 1970s had a mounting impact on the views of employers as case law built up. Although disparities in earnings still exist, those for different sexes doing broadly the same job or equal value have been progressively reduced. The onus of proof where variations occur is on the employer.

Hourly earnings improved from just 63 per cent of the male rate to nearer 75 per cent by the latte 1980s. Women's low pay reflects the fact that they are normally found lower down the incremental scale, do not occupy top positions and tend to be concentrated in low pay sectors. Weak unionization and the cost and difficulty of fighting a case against entrenched discrimination also contribute, especially when jobs are scarce.

The Equal Opportunities Commission is responsible for eliminating discrimination. It conducts investigations, and brings cases against employers to the tribunal, where damages can be awarded and declarations on employee rights made. Protection is offered in all aspects of employment – interview, selection, training, promotion and remuneration.

Media and social values

Role models, whether on soap operas or in real life, affect society's perception of the female role. The success of entrepreneurs such as Anita Roddick of the Body Shop, Sophie Mirman of Sock Shop, and Laura Ashley provided evidence of what could be achieved in career terms. The appointment of a female Prime Minister in the UK provided a similar 'demonstration effect'.

A note of caution must, however, be sounded. The penetration of women into the higher echelons of business, government and the professions is very limited. Attitudes among senior executives remain very anti-women, and it may require another generation before women achieve more equal ranking in these areas.

Women continue to be concentrated in 'caring and serving' occupations, such as nursing, teaching, secretarial, retail, cleaning and personal services, but even here the senior posts are occupied by men. DES statistics on primary schools show that over 50 per cent of men employed are deputy heads or heads, compared to only 16 per cent of women, yet males account for only just over 20 per cent of total primary school staff.

In management women account for under a quarter, with personnel and administration figuring highly. Women account for less than 1 per cent of directors, and in unions they are massively under-represented. The demonstration effect is clearly still very negative, but as Table 13.1 indicates, the picture does appear to be changing.

Table 13.1   Women as a percentage of all new members of examination passes

	1975	1984
Institute of Chartered Accountants	7	23
Institute of Bankers	4	21
Law Society – Solicitors	19	54
Law Society – Bar	21	32

It may be concluded that the role of women in business and the marketplace will continue to increase and at a quickening pace. The marketer must monitor the changing role and attitudes carefully, and adapt the marketing mix accordingly. It must no longer be assumed that the car owner or the purchasing manager is male or has identical needs and requirements. Businesses that exhibit sensitivity to the changes in the human environment and respond creatively will enjoy success in comparison to those with their perceptions firmly rooted in the prejudices of the past.

Summary review

1 In the light of rising part-time employment what are the economic attractions of such a pattern to:
   (a) The business?
   (b) The employee?
   Think about labour requirements, legislation, flexibility, productivity and cost.

2 What do you understand by the *core* workforce? Why will the marketing team of a medium-sized manufacturer be part of the core but also employ contractual assistance?

3 What changes in the advertising and promotion of new motor cars have taken place as women have become more important customers? What further changes would you recommend and why?

14
The Information needs of the organization

Aims

The aims of this chapter are as follows:

- To emphasize the need for quality information to assess the environment of business.
- To underline the need to understand forecasts and their intrinsic limitations.
- To introduce the concept of a scenario.
- To detail the various information needs of business in economic terms.
- To identify the sources of available information on business.
- To highlight the developing potential of on-line sources.

Glossary

Capacity utilization – the degree to which the business is using its productive resources to the full.

Discontinuities – occur when an established trend or pattern unexpectedly ceases to exist.

Scenario – a credible and consistent view of the future. Alternative scenarios are intended to concentrate management's mind on the reality that different futures are possible and must be planned for.

Shakeout – colloquial term applied to the least productive firms in an industry being forced into bankruptcy or takeover by severe economic conditions, which expose their inefficiency.

Treasury model – a sophisticated computer-based model on the workings of the economy.

The need to forecast

'But tomorrow always arrives, it is always different and then even the mightiest company is in trouble if it has not worked on the future' (P.F. Drucker).

The previous chapters in Section Five have made clear the need to scan the environment to identify opportunities and threats. Even in simple *static market* conditions there is a need for information to enable understanding of the environment. Here analysis of past influences and their effect on the organization is the methodology required, since forecasting based on historical trends and influences should suffice. However, unexpected or discontinuous change is always a threat in such circumstances, where familiarity with established conditions is likely to have bred complacency. The market for spectacles is a case in point, as relative predictability gave way to uncertainty and change with deregulation.

In more dynamic and *complex market* environments the aim must be to understand the future rather than rely on patterns of the past. Managers must be sensitive to change and seek to break down the complexity into understandable elements. It requires that change is evolutionary rather than revolutionary in nature, implying that the seeds of tomorrow's world exist for us today if only we were sensitive enough to recognize them.

Since the shape of the future market may be different from the past, most forecasting techniques that rely on historic information and the projection of present trends will be misleading guides. Even highly sophisticated forecasts, such as those drawn up from the Treasury model of the British economy, are prone to considerable error.

For example, the rate of inflation in late 1990 was predicted to be 6 ½ per cent by this model but turned out to be 11 per cent. The consequences of such errors may be far-reaching, not least for the Treasury itself, which had to fund an extra £2bn to top up pensions and social security payments indexed to the level of retail price.

The key problems

- Which are the 'right' forecasts?
- How significant are the different trends identified?
- How long is it before a pattern of events becomes a definite trend?
- Where are the turning points?
- Which are the discontinuities?
- What is the pace of change?

As the following limerick by the economist and statistician Alec Cairncross suggests, the problems are considerable:

> A trend is a trend is a trend
> but the question is will it bend?
> Will it alter its course
> through some unforeseen force
> and come to a premature end?

Many of the distinctive trends apparent up to the 1980s have since reversed themselves or disappeared altogether. The increasing role of the state, rising membership and power of trade unions, and the decline in the importance of self- employment and small firms, are all dramatic examples of this trend reversal.

Economists unfortunately have a tendency to be right in their predictions but generally a good deal out on the dates. Disagreements over these questions have produced very different views of the future. The problem for management, however, is that the right decision must be made at the right time.

A battery of possible quantitative and qualitative approaches might include the following:

- Improve the quality of conventional forecasts.
- Combined view of experts or delphi techniques.
- Scenario formulation.

Scenarios describe possible futures that may confront the business, while quantitative forecasts seek to account for all relevant data and expert opinion in order to predict what is most likely to happen. All too often, however, a central forecast tends to dictate to management what decisions it should take and so provides it with an excuse if things go wrong.

Scenarios are not based on the idea that the future can be measured or controlled but rather that the future is uncertain. Many alternative futures are possible, and scenarios are a tool to assist in their understanding. They form the backcloth to the decision-making process, with responsibility firmly remaining with the decision-taker.

Shell UK is one of the foremost exponents in the use of scenarios. It warns all planners that the forecasts they know and love are based on a fallacy, namely that the future can be measured and controlled. It likens decisions based on them to pursuing a straight line through a minefield, and views much economic and business theory as a 'pretend world' in which people act as if they had knowledge where it cannot exist. Planners seek firm answers and optimum solutions, as if uncertainty can be eliminated.

However it is not easy for managers to put aside the misleading certainty that quantified forecasts foretell and face up to the constantly shifting features of reality.

Summary review

1 Why must business forecast?

2 What are the dangers in relying on quantitative forecasts?

3 Identify three strong trends you feel will reverse in the 1990s and explain why.

4 What is a scenario? Map out two alternative economic futures for the 1990s.

5 Use the factors you identified in your environmental set to produce a scenario for your organization.

Information needs of the business

'To manage a business well is to manage its future, and to manage its future is to manage information' (M. Harper, Jr).

Management information systems gather data both internal and external to the organization. Internal information arises out of operational activity, employment of resources, sales and the financing of transactions. Analysis of this information will inform a variety of decisions from pricing to stock control. Our concern in this book, however, is with externally generated information and its interpretation. Examples of the many types of information needed are as follows.

Competitors

- Prices, discounts, credit terms.
- Sales volumes by segment, product, region, distribution channel.
- Market shares.
- Promotional activity, catalogues, distributor incentives.
- New product development; expansion plans; personnel changes.
- Financial reserves, balance sheet position, profit and loss, change in relations with suppliers and distributors.

Economy

- Economic indicators, e.g. inflation, unemployment, vacancies, interest rates.
- Business confidence indicators, e.g. retail sales, capacity utilization, investment rates.
- Population and labour market data.
- Income, output and expenditure patterns.

Industry

- Sales volumes by product, segment, region.
- Sales growth, cyclical patterns.
- Forecasts and projections.
- Production levels and stock positions.
- Production capacities and investment plans.

Similar lists could be made for headings such as government policy, legislation, technological developments, social trends and customer tastes. Clearly the need for information is wide-ranging. In an environment of rapid change, where time and delay cost money, the ability to obtain a clear and accurate picture of the situation can provide the firm with a distinct competitive advantage. To obtain such an edge requires not only a knowledge of the key sources of information but also how to access them quickly and cost effectively.

Information sources for business

Information on business and its environment has traditionally originated from two sources: published material and trade sources.

Published material

Such sources (Figure 14.1) are seldom used regularly or systematically by business decision-makers. Collection, classification and distribution to interested managers are

Figure 14.1   *Business information needs*

expensive and time-consuming. Organizations such as Extel grew by providing specific information on typed cards or microfiche. Similarly McCarthy cards summarize press cuttings on particular firms. However, while the value of such information in informing decisions has always been recognized by the more perceptive marketing executives and planners, the use of such sources by the majority of businesses has been haphazard. It is the complex and time-consuming methods of retrieving this information that are the main deterrents to its effective use.

Trade sources

The traditional technique for keeping informed in business is the 'grapevine'. A network of information sources is cultivated, ranging from daily conversations with colleagues, customers and industry contacts to more formal mechanisms, such as the analysis of sales records and consultancy reports. Much of this primary or source material will be sifted and supplemented by day to day reading of published or secondary data. See Figure 14.2.

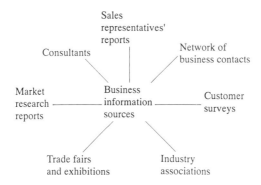

Figure 14.2   *Business information sources*

Keeping a business ear to the ground, however, may not always be effective. The information may come too late or not become relevant until later, when it may be crucial to securing a contract or diversifying into a new market. Furthermore the volume of potentially useful data in one form or another is almost boundless. With the environment becoming ever more complex and with government economic and legislative change impacting daily on decisions, the need to manage information effectively becomes paramount. The shakeout in British industry that occurred in the early 1980s, combined with continued competitive pressure in deregulated markets, have produced streamlined organizations who must work more smartly to survive. This has increased demand for better quality information to support management decisions. A changing industrial structure in favour of heavy information-using sectors such as financial services and retailing, add to this demand, as does an expanding small-firm sector requiring value added information services that provide advice and consultancy.

Mass markets are in many cases fragmenting into specialist niches, again requiring more sophisticated marketing information if businesses are to take advantage of the opportunities they present.

The above trends, combined with a transformed climate for business during the Thatcher era, have yielded a flood of new business-focused information. Sources range from new national newspapers, such as the *Independent* and *European*, to more than 3,500 business to business magazines. The quality and status of these have improved significantly, earning them the title 'business press'.

An efficient information system must be able to programme information gathered into the 'corporate memory'. This must then be accessible in usable form as and when needed. The advent of new technology now offers alternative and complementary support to the traditional methods outlined above.

On-line business information

Databases are revolutionizing the use of business information. A database is simply a file of information but computerized for ease and speed of access and manipulation. On-line means the database is stored on a remote computer but is accessible directly by business users via communication networks. The rapid take-up of fax and mobile communications, combined with desk-top micros, is expanding the potential of this source. The types of database currently available may be seen in Figure 14.3.

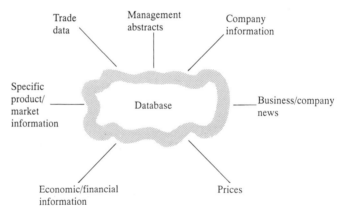

Figure 14.3   *Database*

Computer technology is providing a wealth of business information. Electronic communications allows the information to be transmitted easily and cheaply around the world. Business databases are at the heart of fundamental change, allowing continuous search and delivery of new data on any subject to the relevant user. Instead of investing large amounts in buying and organizing collections of information in the hope of future use, businesses may now access relevant external information as the need arises.

On-line searching is already well-established among larger companies and in the financial service sector. The ability to transfer centrally available information to desk-top micros will greatly expand the number of users.

With information crucial to the marketing function, areas of applications should include:

- Market planning.
- Market research and analysis.
- Marketing presentations – use of computer graphics.
- Customer and sales force communications.

The benefits of on-line searching compared to traditional methods may be summarized as follows:

On-line features		*Benefits*
Speed in searching	=	Time-saving
Selectivity in searching	=	Quality data
Flexibility in searching	=	Comparative data
Interactive searching	=	Flexible scope
Data manipulation	=	Usable statistics
Up to date	=	Best available data
User-friendly	=	Will be used
Charge on actual use	=	Economic access
Professional methodology	=	Competitive edge

The above benefits would seem to suggest that on-line information is the solution to all the marketer's problems. However, some problems remain, not least the learning curve to be surmounted on the use of such systems, and the cost of search that can be sustained.

Summary review

1 What information should be gathered on technical developments and social trends by a clearing bank? Give your reasons.

2 How should an organization ensure that the right information is collected at the right time for the right person?

3 Discover two examples of on-line database and examine what information they contain.

Section Five: Projects

1 Compile an *information sources booklet* either for general use or for specific application to an organization. The objective is to identify key information sources under relevant headings and summarize in a short statement their location, ease of access, content, ease of use, applications and star rating evaluation. Headings might include *company information* – i.e. on competitors, suppliers, distributors, financial institutions – *industry data, economic indicators, overseas markets, trade media, technology, organizations and methods, business texts and journals* and so forth.
Reading: *Online Business Source Book* by A. Foster and G. Smith, and *Business Information Yearbook* (Headland Press).

2 Prepare a *competitor analysis study*. First select a company and a market segment it competes in, and then identify competitors, using directories, e.g. *Kompass*. The competitors may be UK-based or foreign exporters. Information on these companies can be internal, e.g. annual reports, CRO information, and external, e.g. Datastream, Key British Enterprises, Extel. The analysis should include such information as parent companies, key directors, financial position, sectors competing in, turnover, rates of return and industry rankings.

Trade sources should be used to assist assessment of competitor strengths and weaknesses. This might include marketing mix, evaluation of pricing, promotional capabilities, delivery, product quality, etc.

3 Obtain the last 3 years' annual reports of a UK plc of your choice by writing to the company secretary or visiting a main reference or college library. Paying particular attention to the chairman's and chief executive's reports, identify the main opportunities and threats for the company. Report on any change in the importance attached to them over the three years covered.

4 *Plan for demographic change.* A national retailer is extremely worried about its ability to recruit staff in sufficient numbers over the coming decade. You have been commissioned to prepare a marketing plan to overcome the problem. The retailer is prepared to adopt any cost-effective proposals you may suggest, but requires full justification with supporting data where appropriate.

Section Six
The economy as a whole

The aim of this section is to understand the crucial concept of *national income*. This term may be best understood as the flow of output or wealth produced each year. It embraces more than goods and services consumed, since those would exclude net new investment. It acts as a barometer of economic activity, and full understanding will involve a consideration of:

- Its measurement.
- Its fluctuation.
- Its level.
- Its growth.
- Its determination.
- Its importance.

Discussion of these dimensions will provide important insights into the working of the economy. It will supply a framework for analysing the process of inflation and how and why it so damagingly affects the marketing climate. Similarly unemployment may be examined as an adverse economic situation arising out of inadequate income growth, again depressing market conditions when it occurs.

The aims of this section are:

1 To understand how national income is measured and to distinguish activity in the formal and informal economy.
2 To understand what determines the level of national income in order to forecast change in economic activity.
3 To identify and assess sources of fluctuation in national income and to relate this to decision-making over the economic cycle.
4 To explore the causes and consequences of the twin evils of inflation and unemployment.

The section is divided into four chapters:

Chapter 15 *The concept of national income*
Chapter 16 *The level of national income*
Chapter 17 *The problem of unemployment*
Chapter 18 *The problem of inflation*

15
The concept of national income

Aims

The aims of this chapter are:

- To distinguish between the formal and informal economy.
- To help the marketer understand the variety of national income concepts and the difference between them.
- To discuss three methods of measuring national income and review its composition and growth.
- To underline the uses of national income statistics, while providing cautions on their interpretation for business purposes.

Glossary

Collective goods – a good or service that is difficult to price and cannot be efficiently provided through markets, by private enterprise. If the good is supplied to one consumer, it can be supplied to others at no extra cost. Individuals cannot be excluded even if they refuse to pay, but equally they cannot refrain from consumption even if they want to, e.g. nuclear defence provision.

Grey products – often of equivalent or similar standard to branded products but sold at discounted prices, owing to their doubtful origin or status.

Marketable output – output that is traded and generates revenue or foreign exchange. It does not include 'free goods' such as health and defence.

Merit goods – such goods can be provided by private enterprise, but concern as to whether the market would provide sufficient quantities leads governments to make provision. Such goods tend to produce social benefits above and beyond the return obtained by the individual alone.

Transfer payment – a payment made by one organization or individual to another. Old age pensions are transfer payments made by government authority.

Structure of the economy

Several separate economies may be distinguished: the state, the market, the household, the voluntary and the black. How the economies may be divided is shown in Figure 15.1.

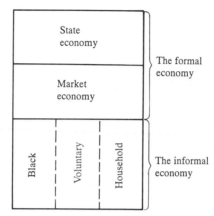

Figure 15.1   *The three economies*

State economy

The state economy is responsible for providing public goods and services, often referred to as collective goods or merit goods. Collective goods are difficult to obtain payment for directly and must therefore be financed through general taxation. Examples would include defence, the police, parks and gardens. Merit goods include health and education, which society believes should be made available to all irrespective of purchasing power.

Market economy

The market economy embraces businesses whose goods and services are marketed, and would therefore include the nationalized industries. It is marketable output that accounts for the majority of investment, exports and household disposable income. Taxes levied on incomes, output and expenditure generated in this part of the economy largely finance the activity of the state economy. Together they comprise the measured or *formal economy*, and generate the national income that future chapters will focus on.

However, it must also be recognized that an *informal economy* exists, one upon which taxes are either not levied or successfully collected, and on whose activity very few official statistics are collected. Surprisingly this is not a small economy but a very large one, which may vary in size and significance according to economic circumstances.

Household economy

The household economy includes all work undertaken for domestic purposes, such as cooking, cleaning, and care of infants and the elderly. It is said to be the country's largest industry, representing as much as 35 per cent of gross domestic product. Do-it-yourself activities, ranging from car maintenance to property renovation, also clearly add value and consumer satisfaction. None of the above are treated as wealth creation by the government statisticians. Some insurance companies do offer policies to cover domestic activities, should the person responsible for undertaking them be incapacitated. They calculate that over £200 per week would be required to buy equivalent domestic services.

Expanding DIY activities suggests a change from a manufacturing to a self-service rather than to a service economy. With the price of services rising twice as fast as the price for manufactured goods, households are opting to buy relatively cheap tools and equipment to provide their own services. TV and video are substituted for the cinema and concert visits, while automatic washers are substituted for expensive domestic help. As long as productivity growth is more difficult to achieve in services than in manufacturing, the incentive for such substitution will continue.

Voluntary economy

The voluntary economy refers to services undertaken without remuneration by both individuals and organizations. The activities of church, charities and a multitude of other organizations would come under this umbrella, as would assistance to elderly or handicapped neighbours. The activities of various charities retailing secondhand clothing to raise funds blurs the distinction between market and voluntary economies.

Black economy

The black or shadow economy is both visible and invisible. Activities include moonlighting, where a worker employed in the market economy applies the same skills outside working hours to realize legally earned but undeclared income. It also includes illegal income arising, say, out of drugs, or smuggling, and income in kind from pilfering at factory, dock or warehouse. White collar 'fiddles' are particularly widespread, with small businesses providing considerable scope. Tax evaders are often referred to as 'ghosts' because their earnings remain invisible. The unemployed may have the greatest motive to participate, yet it is the self-employed, whose numbers climbed from 2m to over 3.4m between 1980 to 1990, who have the greatest opportunity.

The black economy appears to be thriving, accounting for an estimated 10 per cent of gross domestic product (see Figure 15.2). This is in excess of £50bn, implying a tax loss to the Exchequer of considerable proportions. Indeed the black economy appears to be a world growth industry, not least in Italy, where it is reported to account for 30 per cent of GDP, and the USSR, where shortages of even the most basic products abound in the formal economy, yet those products can be found 'at a price' in the informal.

This economy can constitute serious competition for law-abiding businesses, in that so called 'grey' products or services may undermine prices and margins. Many companies in the personnel service sector must contend with such competition. As unemployment rose in the early 1980s, so did shadow economy activity, as the registered unemployed turned to cab driving, painting and decorating or no questions asked labouring under assumed names. This helped to account for buoyant retail sales in otherwise depressed regions. Recent falls in income-tax rates and the rise in economic activity may have dented its growth, but this may be expected to resume as recession bites deeper.

Clearly the marketer must not ignore the shadow economy, either in terms of its hidden spending power or potential competition. Many businesses originate in the shadow or household economies; then, as turnover grows, they graduate into the formal economy.

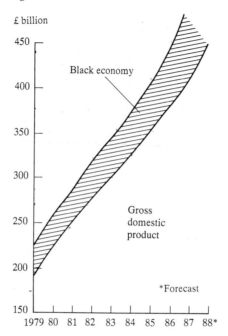

Figure 15.2   *GDP and the black economy*

There is a grey area between the black and formal economy undertaken by small businesses operating below the VAT registration limit and declaring just a proportion of their earnings. A buoyant economy may cause them to migrate into the formal economy and *vice versa*.

Summary review

1 List all the government goods and services, and categorize them under merit or collective goods. Are there any which do not fit neatly under one heading?

2 Why have the prices of services risen so much faster than manufactured goods? Can you think of any technological developments that might help to reverse this tendency?

3 The shadow economy is very difficult to estimate. Suggest possible measures or approaches you might use to improve the accuracy of these estimates.

Measurement of national income

Economic activity has been depicted as a process producing a vast river of output, a ceaseless flow of goods and services emerging from a variety of enterprises. National income measures this flow of products in money terms on an annual basis, and the data recorded is central to any meaningful analysis of the economic situation.

The value of national income is of prime importance to all business people, as it represents the total amount available for spending on goods and services. Changes over time will indicate to businesses the additional purchasing power for which they are competing.

The countless economic transactions occurring daily must be classified in a systematic fashion to enable rational analysis of how national income is determined. An explanatory theory is also required, and indeed the format and rapid development of national accounting statistics stems from the application of Keynesian analysis and successive governments' concern with national income determination and its growth.

There is an understandable confusion over the variety of terms used to define national income and expenditure. What is the difference for example, between gross national product (GNP) and gross domestic product (GDP)? Why are some figures expressed at market prices and others at factor cost?

This chapter explains how these concepts are defined and the meaning of the various price bases in which national income statistics are expressed. A clear understanding of the variety of terms is important if business people are to interpret economic reports in the media correctly.

The main source of information on national income statistics is the *Blue Book*, published annually in September by the Central Statistical Office (CSO). Marketers may also wish to consult *Economic Trends* for more up to date estimates, and the *Monthly Digest of Statistics*, which provides data in summary form. International comparisons are available in the *UN year book of national accounts statistics*, *OECD National Accounts* and the *National Accounts Yearbook* of the European Commission Statistical Office.

Gross domestic product (GDP)

The most important macroeconomic variable for policy purposes is gross domestic product (GDP). This is the measure of total annual output of goods and services, and must be clearly distinguished from total sales in the economy. One cannot simply add up the value of production and sales of every industry, since a proportion of the output would be double-counted. GDP therefore measures the value of final output, and to avoid duplication, ignores intermediate transactions. The value of oil feed stock in producing plastic sheeting, for example, would not be counted, since it would be included already in the market price of the final packaging product.

GDP then should either be viewed as the value of final output or more accurately the sum of the value added at each stage of the production process. This is easier to grasp for the marketer, since it equals the value of sales made by each and every producer, less the cost of all inputs bought from foreign and domestic suppliers. This in turn must represent the sum of wage costs plus trading profits of each business:

GDP = sales output value − input cost values = wages + profits

As mentioned above, great care must be taken by the business person in the use of national income statistics, since they can be expressed in different forms.

GDP at market prices

Here final output is measured, using the prices at which it is sold. In many cases this includes value added tax (VAT) levied at the current rate, as well as excises on such items as drink, tobacco and motor vehicles. Understatement may also occur where state subsidies reduce market prices below the actual costs of production.

GDP at nominal prices

GDP may rise (or even fall), due to a change in the general level of prices irrespective of any real increase in production. Inflation will therefore tend to mislead the unwary unless the figures can be adjusted to remove its distorting effects.

GDP at constant prices

GDP may be expressed in 'real terms' by making an inflation adjustment. A base year is taken, currently 1990 (rebased every 5 years), and GDP for all other years is valued in terms of the average prices ruling at this time. Year by year comparisons may then be made to provide a less ambiguous picture of real changes in the economy. GDP nominally rose by 16 per cent in 1979–80, for example, but at constant prices actually fell by 1.6 per cent.

GDP at factor cost (FC)

This measures final output in terms of the cost of its production. It is a truer valuation of aggregate output produced, since indirect taxes net of any subsidies are deducted from the market price valuation of GDP. While from the point of view of expenditure it is appropriate to value final output at the market prices paid, this would not tally with the sum of factor incomes generated during its production.

Gross national product (GNP)

This term can easily be confused with GDP. The UK is an open economy – indeed since 1980 it has had no exchange controls on overseas investment. UK companies and households have made various investments abroad over the years, from which they receive income in the form of rents, interest, dividend and profit. Corresponding though currently smaller remittances are made to foreign holders of UK assets, leaving *net property income from abroad* to be added to GDP to equate it with GNP. In practical terms this is a relatively small addition equal to around 1.5 per cent of GDP at factor cost.

Net National Product (NNP) and Net Domestic Product (NDP)

All the measures discussed so far overstate the value of final output. No allowance has been made for the wear and tear on plant and equipment during production. Some fixed capital will wear out, other factors may become obsolete, so, as with companies, the national accounts must be adjusted for depreciation. Capital consumption in the process of wealth creation must be fully made good out of current output if future production capacity is not to be impaired.

In practice marketers will find it is GDP and GNP that are most frequently quoted in analyses, reports and international comparisons. This is because estimates of capital consumption are very approximate, often being made on the basis of convention or some arbitrary principle of calculation.

National Income (NI)

Net national product at factor cost that remains after adjustment for depreciation is normally termed national income, since it represents the amount available for consumption and net addition to capital stock through investment.

National Disposable Income (NDI)

It may be noted that national income is not precisely what is available for expenditure. Overseas aid payments, gifts or transfers such as European community contributions will reduce NI. Net current transfers paid abroad must therefore be deducted to correct for this factor. Figure 15.3 summarizes NI measures.

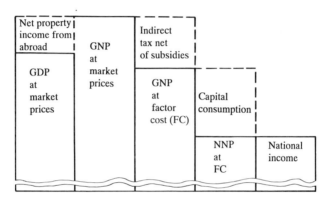

Figure 15.3 *Summary of national income measures*

As with company accounting standards and practices, so national accounting conventions can be subjected to criticism. It has already been noted that non-market transactions in the informal economy are not counted as part of the final output. The accounts only include goods and services recorded as exchanged for money, thus avoiding the problem of placing a value on activities such as DIY, household services, vegetable gardens and so on. This can, however, produce a paradoxical situation, as first outlined by the economist A.C. Pigou. He pointed out that if a person married his housekeeper, national income would fall. Similarly, when prohibition ceased to be illegal in America, its national income rose.

Consumer durables also provide classification problems, since they yield a flow of services over more than 1 year. Owing to valuation difficulties, they are included at market value when bought. The only exception is housing, where a yearly imputed rent value is included for owner-occupied houses. If this was not done, national income would fall as the degree of owner-occupation rose.

The main point to note is that no accounting classification can address all the questions that may arise. The classification adopted by the CSO is constructed in reference to a desired objective, mainly determination of national income and its breakdown into component parts that can be influenced by government policy. The extent the classification is appropriate to answer specific questions will be a matter of judgement. However, once selected, it must be applied logically and consistently. In this way the direction of change will be clear, even if the correctness of the initial magnitudes are suspect. There is nothing 'final' about the accounts as they evolve over time in response to changing needs and requirements.

Measuring GDP

There are three ways of measuring GDP:

1 *The expenditure measure or GDP (E)* – this is the value of all final expenditure on goods and services produced, less the cost of imports.
2 *The income measure or GDP (I)* – this is the sum total of all incomes earned by people living in the UK that derive from the production of goods and services.
3 *The output measure or GDP (O)* – this is the final output or sum of value added of each industry producing goods and services.

Aggregate income, output and expenditure are defined to be equivalent, since they are measuring the same thing, namely GDP as represented by the circular flow of income.

The expenditure measure

Estimates of expenditure are drawn mainly from a wide range of industrial enquiries and household surveys, such as the Family Expenditure Survey and central and local government accounting data. On the expenditure side, GDP is the total paid by purchasers for goods and services, either for final consumption or for capital investment. Final consumption (C) is taken to include all kinds of day to day spending on goods and services, whether by private consumers (consumer expenditure) or by government departments and local authorities (government final consumption (G)). Investment (I) may be in the form of fixed assets such as factories, machinery, houses and other buildings (gross domestic fixed capital formation) or stocks of raw materials and finished goods or work in progress.

National expenditure excludes intermediate transactions. *Total domestic expenditure (TDE)* is therefore obtained by totalling final purchases, and represents the sum of all expenditures by UK nationals as consumers, and of all gross investment in fixed assets and stocks within the economy:

$$TDE = C + G + I$$

However, in an open economy, finished goods and services sold in Britain will include imports and imported materials. These contribute to the national income of overseas countries. To arrive at the figure for expenditure on GDP, exports of goods and services (X) are first added to TDE, providing an aggregate called *total final expenditure (TFE)*. Imports of goods and services (M) are then deducted from TFE to give expenditure on GDP, or GDP (E) at market prices.

$$TDE + X = TFE - M = GDP \text{ (E) at market prices}$$

By far its largest component is consumer expenditure, accounting for almost half the total. Gross fixed investment accounts for another 15 per cent.

The income measure

Incomes of UK residents, whether individual or corporate, derived from the current production of goods and services are known as 'factor incomes', because they are received by the factors of production of land, labour and capital. They include the wages and salaries of employees, the income of the self-employed, the gross trading profit of companies, the gross trading surplus of the public corporations and other public enterprises, rent and other imputed incomes.

Some types of income are, however, excluded. State benefits, such as family allowances, child benefit and retirement pensions, are paid from national insurance contributions and taxation, and therefore represent *redistribution of existing income* rather than new income generated by economic activity. To avoid double-counting, such 'transfer payments' are therefore excluded from calculations of total domestic income.

The resulting figure is GDP valued at factor cost, which must then be adjusted for stock appreciation. In business accounting any increase in the money value of stocks or materials and finished goods during the period would enter into profit. If this approach was adopted in national accounting, the rise in the money value of stocks would be treated as an addition to wealth, even though the physical value had remained constant or declined. To be consistent, only real additions to stock arising from economic activity are included. After allowance for errors and omissions in collecting the data, known as statistical discrepancy, the income and expenditure measures give identical measures of GDP. The following figures show the various components of the income and expenditure measures discussed above: Table 15.1. Figure 15.4 shows how GDP and national income have grown in real and money terms since 1985.

Table 15.1   Gross domestic product by expenditure and income 1990 (£billion, current prices rounded)

(C) Consumer expenditure +	350	Income from employment	318
(G) Government expenditure +	110	Gross trading profits	60
(I) Investment expenditure	105	Government trade surplus	4
= (TDE) Total domestic expenditure	565	Rent etc.	96
+ (X) exports	130	Total domestic income	478
− (M) imports	−150	− stock appreciation	−6
= Gross domestic product at market prices	545	GDP at factor costs	472
− Factor cost adjustment	−73		
= GDP at factor cost	472		

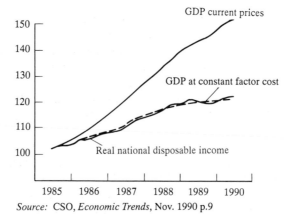

Source: CSO, *Economic Trends*, Nov. 1990 p.9

Figure 15.4   *Growth of GDP and NI in money and real terms, 1985–90*

The output measure

This is based on survey data from producers. The production estimates are available far sooner than income and expenditure figures, and therefore provide the best indication of economic activity in the short term. Such estimates are provisional, but are published quarterly after only a few weeks' time lag.

In measuring national output the economy is split into a number of different sectors according to the nature of output produced:

1 Agriculture.
2 Energy and water supply, including mining and North Sea oil and gas.
3 Construction.
4 Manufacturing, broken down into its major groups.
5 Services.

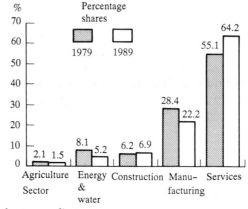

Note: Shares may not sum to 100 due to rounding
Sources: United Kingdom National Accounts 1990 (*CSO Blue Book*) *Economic Briefing*, Dec. 1990, HM Treasury.

Figure 15.5   *Share of manufacturing and services*

Figure 15.5 confirms the contraction in the relative share of manufacturing and the corresponding growth in services to three times the size in GDP terms. Energy and water have shrunk, reflecting the declining contribution of North Sea oil and a sharp contraction in coal mining. There can, however, be little doubt in the conclusion that Britain is now a predominantly *service economy* rather than a manufacturer.

Figure 15.6 shows the share of manufacturing output accounted for by different industrial sectors in 1988. Each sector is then given a 'weight' proportional to the distribution of net output in 1985.

Figure 15.7 shows how services have grown at the expense of most other sectors over the last decade. Discussion of relative shares should not, however, disguise the fact that real output rose strongly through much of the period. Between 1985 and 1988, for example, manufacturing rose 14 per cent, construction 17 per cent and services 15 per cent. Only agriculture and energy were static, as GDP advanced by 13 per cent overall.

Figure 15.7 also provides a breakdown of the wide-ranging service sector. Financial services alone account for two-thirds the share of manufacturing as does distribution. The fall in the relative share of manufacturing should not, however, be viewed in isolation, since other advanced industrial economies have experienced similar contractions, as Table 15.2 shows. It may be viewed as the inevitable consequence of rising affluence reflected in an increasing proportion of household expenditure on services.

Table 15.2   Manufacturing output as a share of GDP (per cent)

	UK	US	Japan	Germany	France	Italy	Canada
1960	32	28	35	40	29	29	na
1979	25	23	29	34	26	28	19
1988*	21	19	29	31	21	23	17

There are some differences in the definition of series between countries.
* Figures for UK and US are for 1987, and for 1986 for Canada.
Source: OECD Historical Statistics.

Others view it as a process of 'deindustrialization' where Britain's industrial base has eroded too rapidly, making it unable to generate sufficient marketable output to satisfy domestic needs for manufactured goods, exports and investment. A widening deficit on trade is the result. Service exports find it difficult to compensate for this, since a 1 per cent fall in manufacturing export value would require a rise of 2.5 per cent in service export value to offset it.

Summary of the uses of national income statistics

As an indicator of living standards

National income as a flow of output in the form of goods and services has been expressed in a number of ways to provide an indication of welfare. However, the figures cannot be accepted

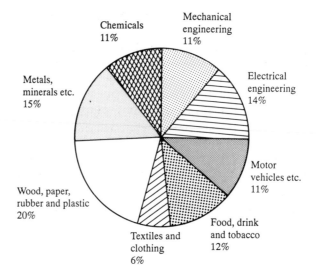

Note: Shares may not sum to 100 due to rounding.
Source: United Kingdom National Accounts 1990 (*CSO Blue Book*).

Figure 15.6   *Share of manufacturing output of industrial groups, 1988*

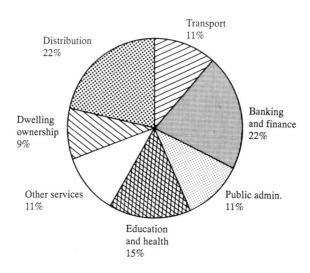

Note: Shares may not sum to 100 due to rounding. The 'Adjustment for Financial Services' has been removed from the output of the Banking and Finance Sector. See *CSO Sources & Methods* for more detail.
Source: United Kingdom National Accounts 1990 (*CSO Blue Book*).

Figure 15.7   *The growth of services*

without reservation, and allowance must be made for the following:

1 Changes in the general level of prices need allowing for, to reflect 'real income'.
2 Changes in population need accounting for, to determine per capita income.
3 Increases in military or investment goods will not be reflected in real consumer living standards.
4 Increased GNP arising from export surpluses does not improve current living standards.
5 Average per capita income does not account for the distribution of income.
6 No valuation is placed on leisure.
7 Increased GNP may arise from longer hours or increased female participation rates, which may lead to unaccounted costs in terms of child care and domestic stress.
8 Government spending is valued at cost; if resources were redistributed from, say, social services to defence, there would be no apparent change shown in GNP.
9 GNP is swollen if people pay for services previously performed by themselves in the household economy.
10 No account is taken of the social costs and benefits of increased GNP, e.g. air, water or noise pollution.
11 Activity necessary to rectify environmental damage is included in the calculation of GNP.
12 Change in the design and quality of goods over time may not be reflected in their market price.
13 Non-marketed output is not accounted for.

To compare different countries' standards of living

Such comparisons must be treated with considerable caution since they are subject to many qualifications.

1 GNP figures expressed in different currencies need a common denominator for comparison. Exchange rates may not reflect accurately the internal purchasing power of currencies.
2 Different tastes and needs must be allowed for e.g. heating requirements for Canadians are much greater than for Africans.
3 The proportion spent on defence varies.
4 Variance in the working week, participation rates, DIY (subsistence) and black economy sectors.
5 Varying efficiency of data collection agencies.

To calculate the rate at which a nation's income is growing

National income statistics may be used as a rule of thumb in this case.

To assist the 'management' and 'planning' of the economy by government

This requires accurate figures on the sizes of the various components of national income to form the basis for decisions. Data provided by the central statistics office (CSO) are of vital importance, as will be seen in the next chapter.

Summary review

1 Scan quickly through the quality newspapers and the *Economist* for articles on economic activity and growth. Look for references to national income and try to find references for all the measures mentioned in this chapter.

2 Draw a flow diagram linking expenditure made between individuals, firms, governments and overseas countries. Trace the effects of:
   - An increase in government spending on the infrastructure.
   - An increase in demand for British exports.

3 Britain's GDP grew by 8.5 per cent between 1989 and 1990. Does this mean we were substantially better off? Was it good news for marketers?

4 What is Britain's GDP in £m?

16
The level of national income

The measurement of national income and its components provides the information that may allow the government to understand and then influence the level of economic activity. This first requires, however, an understanding of the workings of the macroeconomy upon which its actions may be based.

Aims

The aims of this chapter are as follows:

- To understand the circular flow concept and its contribution to economic stability.
- To relate the analysis to developments in the British economy over the past decade.
- To explain the workings of the multiplier and accelerator.
- To examine in detail the determinants of consumer and investment spending and the insight they provide to buyer behaviour.
- To provide a formal analysis of income determination and the idea of deflationary and inflationary gaps.

Glossary

Closed economy – a domestic economy where no trade with other countries is assumed to take place.

Hyper inflation – defined as prices rising in excess of 50 per cent per month.

Money illusion – failure to realize that rising prices reduce the value of anything measured in monetary terms, e.g. wages and savings.

Precautionary savings – savings take place for a variety of reasons; for old age, a target purchase or 'for a rainy day'. The desire for security in the event of unexpected circumstances causes precautionary savings to be made.

Short run – a variable time period when at least one factor of production is fixed.

Sustained growth – continuous growth uninhibited by shortages or bottlenecks. Investment, productivity and exports ensure that the growth of demand does not produce inflation or balance of payments problems.

Wealth effect – a rise in the value of owned assets that causes individuals to spend more and save less.

The circular flow

Earlier chapters focused on the microeconomic decisions of millions of individuals and firms. Scarcity forced choices to be made in allocating resources and incomes in an attempt to satisfy needs and objectives. Choices were expressed through the medium of markets, with prices signalling comparative value for money to individuals, factor incomes to resource owners, and potential profitability of alternative inputs and outputs to firms.

Factor payments, made by firms to those who own resources, provides the income to satisfy wants through the purchase of goods and services. As the simplified Figure 16.1 shows, private ownership of resources generates factor payments from firms in the form of wages, salaries, interest, rent and dividends for services provided. Individuals then use this income to finance spending on goods and services. In so doing, we come 'full circle'. It is the study of the flows of income, output and expenditure that is the central concern of macroeconomics.

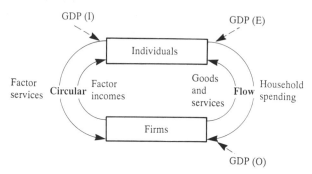

Figure 16.1   *Simple circular flow*

Determination of the level of national income in a mature economy is a complex matter, and it is therefore necessary to simplify initially in order to build understanding. In the simple closed economy represented above there is no mention of trade or government, or of saving and investment. However, by viewing the above as circular flows of liquid wealth in the form of incomes, output and expenditure, we can relate it to the three measures of GDP. Each one is measuring the same depth of flow but at different points of the circuit.

Since World War 2, economies such as Britain's have been characterized by a long-run upward trend in real national income but with short-run fluctuations in activity levels. Income has not grown steadily but has alternated between spurts of relatively rapid growth and periods of stagnation or even recession. Successive governments have therefore pursued the objective of *sustained growth,* combined with high employment and stable prices. As Chapter 17 will show, these objectives have proved to be elusive in practice. The following analysis of the circular flow will, however, be set against these objectives. See Figure 16.2.

In the simplest case let us assume that all income (Y) received by individuals is immediately and completely spent consuming (C) the output of the firms. In such a case there is no

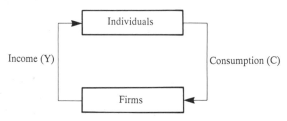

Figure 16.2   *Equilibrium in the circular flow*

tendency for change in the level of national income. Incomes paid to individuals arising from production are just sufficient to buy the entire output of the firms. With sufficient cash flow and incentives, the firm will produce at the same activity level over the next period of time.

The only possible problems would be microeconomic, in that some product- and sales-oriented firms might produce output that individuals were not fully prepared to buy. This would be resolved by relative price changes, which would then signal the correct allocation to producers for the next period. In this case demand and prices would fall, depressing profits for the affected firms and forcing them to contract output. Firms that got their product and marketing right would experience increasing sales.

While the activity level in Figure 16.2 is stable, there is no guarantee that it is sufficient to ensure high employment. If not, then one solution would be for a government to intervene to raise the level of spending in order to encourage firms to produce more. This might work, but equally firms might respond by raising their prices. Instead of creating jobs for unemployed resources, this would only lead to inflated prices and profits.

Alternatively, market economists would claim that a free and competitive labour market would ensure high employment. Flexible wages would adjust to the level where those wanting employment just equalled vacancies. The only unemployment possible in this situation would be *voluntary*, among those not prepared to work at the going wage rate. The reality of the labour market is rather different, with a variety of frictions preventing its efficient operation. Notable among these are the unions, which may use their power to prevent the labour market clearing at the full employment level.

This explanation of high unemployment lay behind the government policies of the early 1920s. Efforts to force down wages across the economy were successful, despite the General Strike of 1926. The policy, however, did not reduce unemployment, since it failed to recognize the corresponding fall in individual income that occurred. This reduced consumer spending, and would have actually depressed activity levels and employment further, had not prices also fallen to reflect lower wage costs.

The effect of savings

Let us make the simple economy more realistic by introducing the virtue of thrift. If individuals decide to save, say, 10 per cent of their income and hoard it for safekeeping, then 10 per cent of expenditure will in effect 'leak out' of the circular flow. Firms will find consumer spending sufficient to purchase only 90 per cent by value of what they have produced. An unintended rise in stocks of finished goods takes place, and sales revenue will be insufficient to finance factor payments at the previous activity levels. Less resources would therefore be employed as production plans were scaled back and less income paid out. Should individuals persist in net savings out of their shrinking aggregate income, the process of declining activity levels would continue, in theory at least, until zero activity prevailed. This is termed the *paradox of thrift*, whereby normally virtuous savings behaviour, in which we are all encouraged from birth to indulge in, may produce a highly negative outcome in terms of income and employment. See Figure 16.3.

It might be expected that as unemployment rose, affected individuals would be forced to spend their accumulated savings, so reinjecting purchasing power back into the flow. Unfortunately, while this may be the case, it is also likely that as employment prospects deteriorate, those still in jobs will tend to save more for precautionary purposes. This was seen during the historically high levels of unemployment during the 1979–81 recession, when

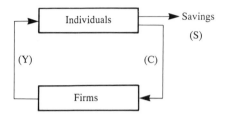

Figure 16.3   *The effect of savings*

consumption was deferred until the outlook improved. Then as the economy boomed, total domestic savings as a percentage of GDP at factor cost fell from over 8 per cent to nearly zero, before recovering as recession approached again.

The effect of investment

The other factor so far neglected is investment (I) spending, which may form a compensating injection of spending into the circular flow. In a modern economy savings are seldom hoarded but are placed for security and interest in a variety of financial institutions. Financial deregulation over the past decade has invigorated competition among the banks, and lately the building societies. A variety of savings accounts offering combinations of convenience, flexibility and return are actively marketed. They compete with those marketing alternative uses of such funds, e.g. the purchase of home improvements, cars and leisure goods as much as with other savings vehicles.

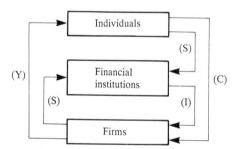

Figure 16.4   *The effect of investment*

If the savings (S) leakage can be fully offset by an investment (I) injection into the circular flow, then national income will once more be stabilized where S = I (Figure 16.4). Achievement of this condition for stability, however, is not straightforward. Since saving decisions are often made by individuals while investment decisions are made by firms, is there any certainty that their wishes will coincide?

In practice firms also save, retaining earnings for investment at a later time. Many companies, such as Hanson plc, have a mountain of funds (estimated in 1992 at around £6bn) available to finance possible acquisitions. There is still no guarantee, however, that sufficient borrowers will be available to channel these funds back into the circular flow. See Figure 16.5.

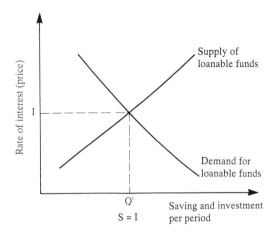

Figure 16.5 *The rate of interest mechanism*

Market economists again maintain that a mechanism does exist in the form of the *rate of interest* on loanable funds. Free adjustment of supply and demand should establish the rate to clear the market and ensure a stable circular flow, where savings = investment. While this again sounds a persuasive theory, in practice it may not prove to be fully effective.

Savings are not very responsive to small changes in interest rates and it may require a relatively large and potentially destabilizing change in rates to affect behaviour quickly. A 0.5 per cent cut in mortgage lending rates may have little effect, whereas a 4 per cent change will bring a flood of applications.

The ability to save as determined by changes in *disposable income* may often have much greater influence. Savings are also affected by changing *attitudes and expectations*. The growing social acceptability and convenience of credit, and a growing desire among the young to live now and pay later, are both part of the process. The offer of instant and easy credit has become an integral element in marketing a widening spectrum of goods and services. Credit and charge cards are now offered without a hint of social stigma, and may often be an important consideration in the decision to purchase.

Savings behaviour will also be affected by *expectations of inflation*. Concern over rising prices might be expected to lead to sharply increased spending, as consumers seek to avoid erosion in the value of their savings. While such behaviour is found with hyper inflation, Britain's prices have increased at a much slower rate, and sharp rises in personal savings have been associated with quickening inflation, especially in the late 1970s. This is thought to have arisen out of uncertainty regarding the future, combined with an erosion of personal wealth that individuals sought to restore by extra savings.

During times of inflation the distinction needs to be drawn between real and nominal savings and interest rates. At relatively low rates of inflation, or when it is unexpected, savers may be subject to *money illusion*, believing nominal rates are also real rates. Inflation-adjusted real rates of interest were actually negative in the 1970s, yet savings were high; whereas in the 1980s they were historically high in real terms, yet personal savings slumped. Clearly there is no simple relation between savings behaviour and the interest rate.

The savings behaviour of companies and the government also fluctuate. Increased company savings during the 1980s owed more to buoyant profits than rising interest rates. The turn-round in public sector savings is more complicated, arising out of government policies and privatization receipts, and will be discussed later. Similar arguments may be made regarding investment spending, in that, while interest rates reflecting the opportunity cost of capital are of considerable importance, many businesses focus on other factors. The *expected yield* on the investment is especially crucial to an investment decision. Certain investments will be seen as strategically necessary, irrespective of interest rates, while others may take account of government incentives.

While it is clear that sharply increased interest rates in the late 1980s affected investment spending, especially among firms that were over-borrowed, it took a series of sharp increases over a period of time before the effects were widely felt.

Change in the circular flow

As shown above, both saving and investment behaviour responds to changes in income levels. It was this recognition that allowed John Maynard Keynes, in his book *The General Theory* (1936), to demonstrate the possibility of an economy getting stuck in a depression. He showed that there was no inbuilt tendency for an economy to operate at high employment levels, at least in the short run. Since the short run might extend into years, as it did in the early 1930s, he concluded that governments should take action to move the economy towards levels of higher activity. 'In the long run we are dead', he concluded, underlining that waiting for market forces to work was not a realistic option.

This can be seen in Figure 16.6. From an initial equilibrium level (of income, output and

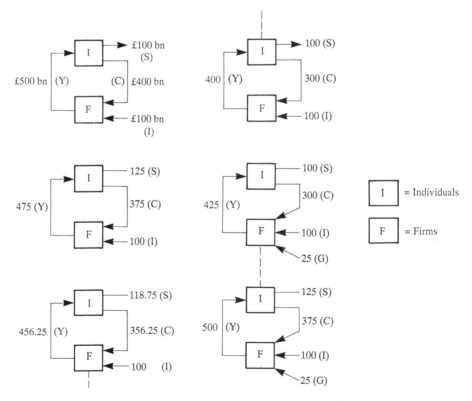

Figure 16.6 *Changes in the circular flow*

expenditure) of £500bn, suppose that individuals decide to raise the proportion they save (S) from 20 per cent of income received to 25 per cent, while investment spending (I) remains constant at £100bn. In effect consumer spending (C) falls by £25bn, but this is not compensated for by extra investment spending, as the additional savings lie idle and unborrowed in the financial institutions.

Aggregate demand (C + 1) falls from £500bn to £475bn, causing unsold stocks to accumulate. Lower spending reduces sales revenue, forcing firms to cut their output plans and demand for factor services. Only £475bn is available to be paid out for factor incomes in the next period of production.

Individuals still plan to save the same percentage of their income, but the fact that this has fallen causes total savings to fall £118.75bn. This reduces C + I below planned output of £475bn, and the process repeats itself.

This contraction in income will continue as long as savings exceed investment. However, with each contraction the amount saved falls, until a new equilibrium is reached at £400bn, with savings once again equal to investment but at an activity level 20 per cent lower in real terms.

In the short run nothing is likely to change the levels of injections or leakages. Reduced savings and rising consumer expenditure are unlikely, owing to the high level of unemployment among privately owned resources and uncertainty regarding the future. Businesses cannot be expected to raise investment, given the depressed conditions, high stock levels, and existing idle capacity. Confidence and expectations regarding the future will be subdued. It should be recognized that in the above model, investment spending was assumed to remain unchanged. In practice capital expenditure would more likely be cut, reinforcing the falling level of activity and income.

It was this reasoning, combined with a lack of faith in the ability of wages and prices to bring about a rapid adjustment, that led Keynes to argue the case of government intervention to manage aggregate demand in order to achieve the desired level of income and employment. To restore the initial position in Figure 16.6, the state would have to increase injections into the circular flow from £100bn to £125bn. This might be achieved indirectly, by providing firms with incentives or subsidies to invest more, or with more certainty by spending funds directly on various government programmes.

The injection of £25bn reverses the above process by raising aggregate demand for output. Firms respond by raising output plans and hiring additional resources, so producing a flow of extra income to individuals. Twenty-five per cent of additional income is saved but the balance is spent on extra consumption. This secondary rise in spending expands aggregate demand still further, so that national income continues to rise. It will be consumer-good industries rather than investment-good industries that benefit at this stage. So long as the amount of leakage is less than the injections, income levels will rise in the circular flow, a process that continues until the income level of £500bn is restored:

Leakages of savings (125) = investment (100) + government injections (25)

The multiplier

The original increase in government spending that brought about the expansion in output and employment was just £25bn, compared to a fourfold rise in national income from £400bn to

£500bn. This is known as the *multiplier effect,* and it is an important concept for the marketer to grasp. Formally it is defined as:

$$\text{Multiplier} = \frac{\text{income (V)}}{\text{injection (G)}} \quad \text{or} \quad \frac{1}{\text{leakage propensities (L)}}$$

In Figure 16.6 Y, the change in income (£100bn), resulted from the change in injection (G = 25):

$$\text{Multiplier} = \frac{Y}{G} = \frac{100}{25} = 4$$

The leakage propensity is the proportion of income that leaks out of the circular flow:

$$S = 25\% \text{ or } 0.25 \text{ of each £ of income, i.e.} \frac{1}{0.25} = 4.$$

$$\text{Multiplier} = \frac{1}{L} = \frac{1}{0.25} = 4$$

In practical terms the initial £25bn injection of government spending would typically take the form of contracts to renew or expand infrastructure such as roads, railways, sewers and other construction projects. Additional welfare payments would also serve the purpose of injecting extra spending into the flow.

To fulfil these extra contracts would require firms to employ additional resources. Previously unemployed, these resources, including labour, would now receive incomes that would be largely spent on consumer goods and services. Demand would rise for the output of these industries, which would in turn employ extra resources and generate more income. This would continue so long as planned spending exceeded planned output at profitable prices, providing firms with the incentive to expand production. The multiplier effect explains why only £25bn was injected initially rather than the full £100bn. A £100bn injection would have generated excessive demand, to which firms could not have responded once resources were already fully employed. The situation could only have been resolved by firms raising their prices, which in turn would bid up resource prices and incomes.

The real economy

A complex economy like Britain's is no different in principle to the one analysed above. There are additional leakages and injections to consider but the condition for stability in the circular flow remains as before, namely:

INJECTIONS = LEAKAGES

Similarly sustainable growth achievement at high employment and stable price levels would require steady expansion of injections funded by a commensurate increase in corporate and personal savings. Figure 16.7 shows the main components to be considered.

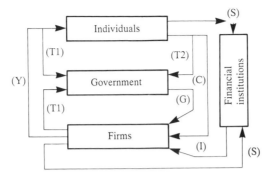

Figure 16.7 *The full model*

On the leakage side we have:

1 *Savings* – personal + corporate + central and local government.
2 *Taxes* – direct taxes (T1), such as corporation tax, income and capital taxes; and local taxes and indirect taxes (T2), such as VAT and excise duty.
(3) *Imports* – such purchases create demand for firms overseas.

On the injection side of the flow we have:

1 *Investment* – including fixed capital formation and physical increase in stocks.
2 *Government expenditure* – on goods and services as well as capital spending.
3 *Exports* – representing expenditure by foreigners on home-produced goods and services.

Stability is achieved where planned levels of:

$$S + T + M = I + G + X$$
(leakages)   (injections)

If planned injections exceed leakages, national income will tend to rise and *vice versa*. It should be noted, however, that the multiplier effect is normally quite small, owing to the size of the leakage propensities.

In the case of Britain tax payments account for 40 per cent of GDP, imports 20 per cent and savings 10 per cent. The leakage is therefore 70 per cent or 0.7 of income. The multiplier may therefore be calculated as $1/0.7 = 1.43$, meaning a £10bn investment programme will raise national income by less than £15bn in total.

A distinction may also be made between the investment multiplier and a tax multiplier. If a government decides to cut income tax payments by, say, £10bn, the multiplier effect will be smaller, because extra government investment spending creates demand for output to the full amount spent, whereas lower tax payments result in higher post-tax disposable income, which will not all be spent on output, since individuals save a proportion.

National income and expenditure, 1980–90

Marketers must not only understand the national accounts, but actively use the data to inform their grasp of the structure and workings of the economy. No market can be fully insulated from changes in its momentum and performance over time. An appreciation of the economic aggregates must be the foundation stone in any market analysis. Monitoring quarterly changes should normally suffice for most purposes, although more detailed analysis may be necessary to identify turning points in activity.

The index of GDP at factor cost (1985 = 100) recorded a rise from 1980 to 1990 of around 30 per cent as shown in the figures below:

1980	1981	1982	1983	1984	1985	1986	1987	1988	1989	1990
90.7	89.7	91.3	94.6	96.2	100	103.2	107.8	111.5	116	118.7

The period divides into two, with an actual fall in real GDP up to 1982 being succeeded by continuous and steadily accelerating growth through the rest of the decade. Manufacturing output, however, did not exceed 1979 output levels until 1987.

Expenditure on consumption is the largest and most stable element of aggregate demand on a seasonally adjusted basis. It accounts for two-thirds of GDP at market prices, and peaks in the last quarter, with the approach of Christmas. Even in recession, when national income falls, consumer spending tends to be maintained. Consumption is broken down into categories of spending in Figure 16.8.

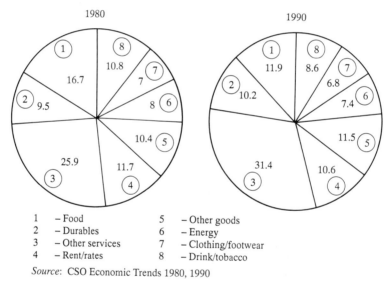

1	– Food	5	– Other goods
2	– Durables	6	– Energy
3	– Other services	7	– Clothing/footwear
4	– Rent/rates	8	– Drink/tobacco

Source: CSO Economic Trends 1980, 1990

Figure 16.8 *Share of consumer expenditure, 1980–90*

The significant changes over the decade are the declines in spending on food, drink and tobacco. Food has a low income elasticity, while tastes and taxation have moved against drink and tobacco. The rise in 'other services' reflects rising leisure expenditure.

What is not saved out of personal disposable income is by definition consumed. As can be seen in Figure 16.9, consumption as a proportion was rising through most of the 1980s, as personal savings correspondingly shrank.

Determinants of consumption and saving

As seen in Figure 16.9, consumption is primarily a function of income. Figure 16.10 represents this relationship between consumption (C) and national income (NI) and shows the following:

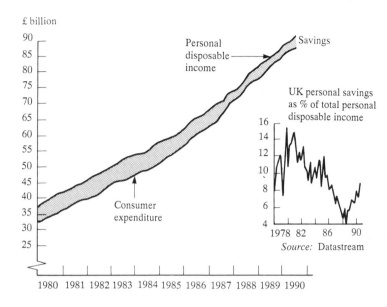

Source: CSO

Figure 16.9   *Personal income and expenditure, 1980–90*

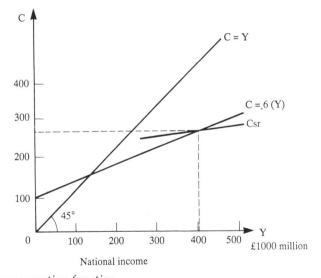

Figure 16.10   *The consumption function*

1 A 45 degree line representing all points where income is fully spent on consumption.
2 As income rises, consumption increases, but by less than the rise in income.
3 The average propensity to consume (APC) i.e. C/Y, falls as income rises.
4 Marginal propensity to consume (MPC) $\Delta C/\Delta Y$ is constant at around 0.65Y.

While this relationship has been stable over time, shorter periods can exhibit considerable variations. Marketers must recognize that rapid income growth may initially cause a smaller rise in spending than will occur in the longer term. This reflects natural caution by individuals, who may not believe the improvement of their income will be permanent. If extra income arises out of bonuses or overtime payments, this caution would seem sensible.

The permanent income hypothesis of Milton Friedman suggests that individuals base consumption decisions on their idea of a sustainable level of income over time. If the change in income is thought temporary, then they will not adjust their spending (i.e. react along the short run curve Csr, Figure 16.10). The fact that consumption is maintained in real terms during recessions also supports this theory. Households would prefer to reduce or run down savings than cut their living standards in what they judge, from past experience, is a temporary reverse.

The stability of the aggregate consumption function also disguises its complex composition. Individual saving and consumption behaviour does not remain constant over time, but change throughout the different stages of life. Expenditure is likely to exceed income during home and family formation periods, for example, financed by building societies' mortgages, and bank and hire purchase loans. Such borrowing and the consumption it finances will be influenced by availability of credit, interest rates, and tax allowances.

As children leave home and career incomes approach peak levels, the propensity to save rises sharply. The approach of retirement and established levels of ownership of consumer durables reinforce this pattern. The ageing of the population, with increasing numbers of over-40s and over-50s makes this the currently dominant phase of the family life-cycle.

Retirement sees the rundown of savings to maintain 'permanent' living standards, the effects of which should therefore impact on consumption in the early decades of the next century. The effect of mid-life property inheritance will also have a yet to be determined effect on consumption. Rising property values and share prices, at least until 1990, combined with high real interest rates, demography and inheritance, are producing a significant *wealth effect*. This may help to explain the fall in the proportion saved among wealthier households.

Since consumption is determined primarily by disposable income, changes in income tax and national insurance may be expected to affect it. However, it may be that savings are adjusted, so leaving consumption unchanged, at least in the short run. Significant changes in personal taxation have also affected the distribution of income. A redistribution of income to the rich with below-average propensity to consume depresses consumption for a given income level and *vice versa*.

Investment

This has been defined as gross domestic fixed capital formation (GDCF) plus physical changes in stocks and work in progress. It is more volatile than consumption, and an injection into the circular flow may be the source of considerable fluctuation. Distinction should be made between two components of gross capital formation:

- *Replacement investment* – replaces capital consumed or worn out in producing the annual flow of output.
- *Net investment* – is in excess of replacement investment, thereby adding to capital stock.

Both components will contribute to growth in national income. Replacement investment will usually embody improved technology, while net investment will help shape growth opportunities.

The quantity, quality and distribution of investment spending is an important determinant of economic growth. Britain has frequently been found wanting both in the proportion of

GDP invested and the rates of return obtained. Where Japan and Germany invested in bread and butter manufacturing industries, such as vehicles, electronics and machine tools, Britain tended to concentrate on high status technology, often in direct competition with America.

GDCF fell nearly 15 per cent between 1979 and 1981 in real terms, but then rose by 80 per cent from this low point to 1989. This may be seen in Table 16.1, which shows the rates of growth of the main items of investment expenditure.

Table 16.1 Components of GDCF, 1980–90

	1980	1982	1984	1986	1988	1990 (estimate)
GDCF as % of GDP	18.6	15.8	17.0	16.7	19.0	19.0
GDCF excl. dwellings as % of GDP	12.7	12.4	13.3	13.3	15.3	16.0
Private sector investment as % of GDP	12.0	12.1	12.9	13.3	16.4	16.5
Government investment as % of GDP	4.6	3.7	4.1	3.4	2.6	2.5

Source: *CS0 Blue Book.*

The 80 per cent rise in investment is put into perspective by an investment ratio that only rose noticeably when the economy was in substantial boom. The tendency of the British to invest in unproductive real estate rather than plant and machinery is shown in the one fifth of GDCF accounted for by private dwellings. A substantial change in the distribution of investment has occurred with privatization and the scaling down of state business, reducing government investments significantly. Measures to raise the after-tax return on investments also contributed, especially following the 1984 budget, which cut corporation tax rates.

Stocks and work in progress

These items fluctuate even more sharply, given their role as a buffer between the needs of production and consumer demand. This makes demand forecasting in business to business markets even more complex and critical.

The contraction in the 1979–81 recession was extremely severe, as businesses reacted to steep falls in orders and high interest rates. While stock investment recovered along with the economy, it has been subdued compared to earlier years. Firms wishing to avoid a repeat of the recession experience, combined with enhanced information technology, capability to control stock and the spread of 'just in time' (JIT) production and distribution, may account for this trend. Certainly industry does not appear to be overstocked in the current recession, with a background of high real interest rates providing the financial incentive to keep stocks as low as possible.

Accelerator

One final aspect of investment is the concept of the *accelerator*. This may be explained by the use of an example.

Suppose national income is at a stable level and the demand for vehicles is 2 million units. These are produced in the equivalent of ten factories, and annual depreciation requires one-tenth of plant and equipment to be replaced each year. Annual replacement investment is therefore the equivalent of one factory. If, as occurred in the UK car market from the mid-1980s, GDP and hence consumer spending rose by, say, 10 per cent per annum, demand would rise by 200,000 vehicles. Meeting this demand would require investment in expanded capacity equivalent to one extra factory, in addition to ongoing replacement investment of one factory. In effect investment response to the 10 per cent rise in consumer spending is a doubling of replacement investment.

In principle therefore any change in final demand for goods and services will have an accelerating effect on investment as its consequences ripple back along the supply chain. Combined with the multiplier, it forms a powerful engine for cumulative change in the level of national income, output and employment in *either* direction.

This contributes to our understanding of the economic fluctuations known as the business cycle. Just as the power of the multiplier was reduced by substantial leakages, so there are a number of qualifications to the full operation of the accelerator:

- Factories do not normally have rigid capacity limits, and there is normally a degree of flexibility in the use of equipment, allowing more or less intensive use over short periods. Vehicle manufacturers will respond to the initial rise in consumer demand by expanding along the short-run average cost curve, by operating extra shifts, working overtime or speeding up the line. The increased unit costs incurred will be preferable to committing the business to expanded capacity. This will only occur when and if the rise in demand is thought to be permanent.
- It is impossible to expand the supply of investment goods quickly. In practice orders will have to be spread over time, as suppliers allow their order books to lengthen. Imports could provide a quicker route, but this would create extra demand overseas.
- The vehicle producer could delay scrapping plant in order to meet the extra demand.

The power of the accelerator should not therefore be exaggerated. However, since the working life of consumer durables and capital equipment is variable and their purchase and replacement can be readily delayed, this provides ample scope for pendulum swings as business and consumer confidence changes.

One area where the accelerator effect can be savagely felt is in inventory. Stocks of both work in progress and finished goods form a crucial buffer between the forces of supply and demand. Since sales can seldom be predicted with accuracy, stocks must be maintained, but firms will wish to avoid overstocking, since physical and interest-rate costs will erode profitability. A trade-off will therefore be adopted.

A fall in the demand for vehicles, such as the 25 per cent decrease over the year 1990–91 in Britain, caused an accelerated contraction as dealers, unable to move their showroom stock, scaled back their purchases to well below replacement stock levels. Fortunately for the car industry and its expanded capacity, overseas sales to the rest of Europe initially remained buoyant, compensating for the severe contraction in domestic demand.

An analysis of income determination

This chapter has examined in some detail the main determinants of the level of national income. Consumption is a broadly stable function of income, but variations in leakages of taxes, imports and savings, and injections of investment, government spending and exports, can cause changes in the level of income itself.

An alternative and more formal analysis of income determination is shown in Figure 16.11. All points along the 45° line by definition represent equilibrium, where national income (Y) = national expenditure (E). At any point above this line planned expenditure exceeds income and *vice versa*.

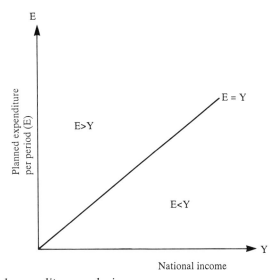

Figure 16.11   *Income and expenditure analysis*

As seen earlier in the circular flow analysis (Figure 16.6) equilibrium occurs where output produced and incomes generated in period one are balanced by expenditure in the following period. Output plans in effect are converted into actual sales, and there is every reason for firms to plan production at the same rate in the following period. Should planned expenditure prove insufficient to purchase the output, then disequilibrium exists. Firms will experience an unintended rise in stocks of finished goods equal to the shortfall of demand. Output plans will be scaled back and income levels fall continuously until planned expenditure is brought back into equality with income.

Take, for example, income level Yu in Figure 16.12, representing a disequilibrium situation with considerable unemployed resources. Planned expenditure is E_1, significantly in excess of the income level at Yu, due to a willingness to run down savings to maintain living standards. Firms will be unable to meet this demand out of production (also Yu), causing stocks to run down, but will have the encouragement to produce a higher level of output for the next period. Extra resources are employed and incomes paid out equal to Yu_2. Planned expenditure still exceeds income, however, and the process of expanding income continues until equilibrium at Yc is achieved. Given that the planned expenditure function remains unchanged, national income will stabilize at this level.

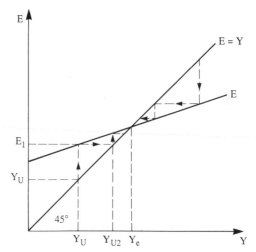

Figure 16.12   *The movement toward equilibrium*

The *expenditure function* is made up of the components of aggregate demand – C + I + G + X. In the circular flow analysis it was implicitly assumed that the injections were given and constant, whereas in practice they are positively related to income. This can be seen in Figure 16.13, which shows the composition of the expenditure function. Any one of these components can pivot upwards or downwards, thereby causing the expenditure function to shift. Were individuals to decide to consume a smaller proportion of income, the slope of the line (marginal propensity to consume) would fall to say C_2, causing expenditure to fall to E_2.

The effects of a change in expenditure may be seen in Figure 16.14. Suppose an incoming government, concerned at the high level of unemployment, decides to expand public expenditure, shifting the expenditure function from E_1 to E_2. At the initial income level Y_1 planned expenditure is now greater by the amount AB. This sets in motion a cumulative expansion in income, output and expenditure, until a new equilibrium is reached at Y_2. The

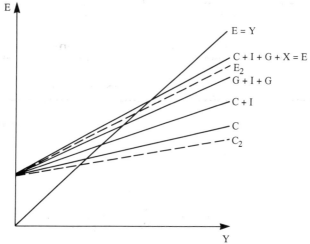

Figure 16.13   *The expenditure function*

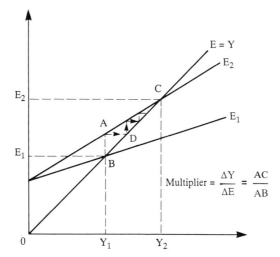

Figure 16.14 *A change in the level of income*

increase in expenditure (AB) has through the multiplier process caused a much larger rise in income (AC). The process takes a number of periods to work itself through, although much of the effect is felt in the first period or two.

Deflationary and inflationary gaps

In the analysis above it has been assumed that a change in planned expenditure is met by an equivalent change in real income and output. This is a reasonable assumption to make when an economy is deep in recession, markets are weak and resources are unemployed. In such

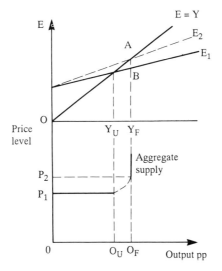

Figure 16.15 *The deflationary gap*

circumstances it is most unlikely that firms would respond to a rise in planned expenditure by raising prices. Similarly additional resources could be obtained without putting upward pressure on their cost.

However, economies are not always to be found in recession, and for much of the post-war period at least have operated at or near to full capacity working, with many critical resources often in short supply. In these circumstances a rise in national income is unlikely to represent real income. It will include the effects of rising prices as well as real income and output rises. In Figure 16.15 the initial equilibrium is at Yu. This was termed by Keynes a 'deflationary gap', since planned expenditure is insufficient to produce equilibrium at the full employment level Yf. The shortfall in expenditure is equal to AB. If the government attempts to fill the gap by raising injections to E_2, this causes prices to rise as well as output from P_1 to P_2.

Output cannot expand beyond full employment in the short run, since all resources are being used. The aggregate supply line becomes vertical at this point and any further increases in planned expenditure will create an 'inflationary gap'.

This is represented in Figure 16.16, where the demand gap CD bids up money incomes and prices, leaving no scope for real income increases. Clearly, aggregate demand needs to fall in these circumstances to E_3, if the inflationary pressure is to be removed.

The problems of unemployment and inflation as represented in Figures 16.15 and 16.16 are the subjects of the next two chapters.

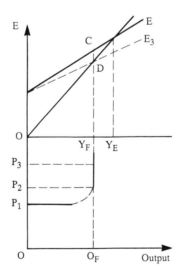

Figure 16.16   *The inflationary gap*

Summary review

This has been a difficult chapter, containing a large amount of analysis. You must take in the knowledge a step at a time, and keep reviewing your understanding as you work through the concepts discussed. While appearing very theoretical, the concepts are at the heart of macroeconomic understanding. A full appreciation of current economic events is impossible without this grasp. The following questions will help you to review the chapter content:

1 Use a circular flow diagram to analyse the causes of Britain's recession in 1990–91.

2 Savings fell sharply in the 1980s. Can you explain this and comment on the contribution that marketing activity may have made?

3 The Channel Tunnel is a £7.5 million project. What are the likely multiplier effects of the project and where will the main effects be felt?

4 If you were the Chancellor, faced with a deflationary gap but wishing to avoid taking action that might raise prices rather than output, what measures would you take and why?

17
The problem of unemployment

Aims

The aims of this chapter are as follows:

- To understand the nature of the problem of unemployment.
- To consider the accuracy of unemployment figures and their effectiveness in moderating pay pressures.
- To provide a description of short- and long-term types of unemployment.
- To distinguish between full employment, the natural rate of unemployment and what is an acceptable rate.
- To analyse the three main causes of unemployment.

Glossary

Business cycle – left to themselves economies tend to fluctuate between high and low activity rates. Actions by governments have reduced the cycle's effects, although recessions and recoveries still occur.

Comparative advantage – normally applied to trade, it suggests that individuals (and countries) should specialize in what they do best.

Deflationary policies – policies to diminish the pressure on price rises by reducing demand, using tax increases or government spending cutbacks.

Employment/Poverty trap – normally a problem for the unskilled who also have dependents. They find that tax and national insurance payments, combined with the loss of state benefits, leaves them worse off if they take up employment.

Gold standard – a monetary system where the value of each country's currency was fixed in terms of gold. Currencies were freely convertible, causing an outflow of gold if a balance of payments deficit arose.

Marginal revenue product of labour – the productivity of labour × the price obtained for that additional output.

Production possibility curve – a curve on a graph whose axis represents different types of goods, e.g. public and private sector, that could be produced by means of the available resources.

Social costs – costs imposed by actions of individuals or businesses on the rest of society.

Trade balance – the balance between visible imports and exports. Inclusion of services would produce the current balance.

Is unemployment a problem?

Unemployment in an economy is a problem for a number of different reasons:

1 Economically it indicates resources are being wasted, preventing the economy operating on its production possibility curve. It may therefore be defined as a failure of resource utilization.
2 It suggests that markets are not working fully or effectively where 2 to 3 million are unemployed.
3 The burden of benefit payments to the unemployed may cause tax increases, thereby adversely affecting incentives.
4 Employment is the major source of family income and 'spending power' in the marketplace.
5 Unlike other resources, labour and its employment may be viewed as 'special', since work is also the main source of a person's identity and status within society. Unemployment is a very negative condition, often expressed in terms of 'idleness'. Studies confirm that the experience can be very stressful, producing feelings of guilt and anxiety. Positively correlated with domestic violence, divorce and suicide, its corrosive effects on self, family and whole communities can produce large *social costs*.
6 Long-term unemployment tends to be concentrated among certain groups and areas:

(a) The young and unskilled.
(b) Ethnic groups.
(c) Inner cities and regions of structural decline.
(d) Over-50s.
(e) The disabled and disadvantaged.

7 It may discourage risk-taking and job mobility, as people worry more about their security of employment.
8 It has proved to be very resistant to easy or rapid solutions. Quick-fix policies have become discredited after producing rising inflation rates and surging imports.
9 Some managements contest the idea that unemployment is an evil. A pool of appropriately skilled workers actively searching for work allows businesses to expand output without the need to bid up wage rates. Similarly the threat of redundancies may serve to moderate wage pressure and assist management to maintain authority and discipline.

It may be questioned whether the existence of high unemployment does moderate wage claims. If, as in Figures 17.1 and 17.2, the trend of average earnings over the past decade is superimposed on the pattern of unemployment and skill shortages the answer is unclear.

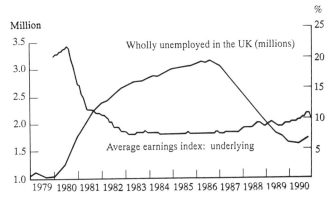

Source: Datastream

Figure 17.1   *Unemployment and average earnings 1980–90*

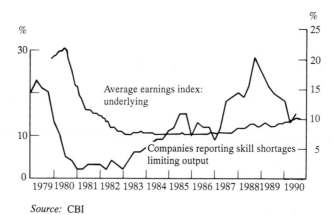

Source: CBI

Figure 17.2   *Skill shortages and average earnings*

Average earnings certainly fell sharply through to the end of 1982, as unemployment climbed to unprecedented levels. They then levelled out while unemployment continued to grow but at a reduced rate. The fact that those companies reporting skill shortages limiting output began to rise from this point may provide part of the explanation.

It may be the case that wage claims are moderated more by the fear of unemployment than the actual total itself. Unemployment rose sharply to over 2.5 million up to 1982 and earnings fell back, but as the rate of rise eased, so the threat of further redundancies receded.

It is also the case that few employers will contemplate replacing 'insiders' with unemployed 'outsiders' even at lower wage rates. They are an unknown quantity, especially the longer-term unemployed, whose skills, motivation and work discipline may have been eroded. There would also be hiring, firing and training costs if job-specific skills were required.

The jobless total

The above argument casts doubt on the idea that high unemployment in itself moderates wage inflation. If this is so, positive action will be necessary to ensure that labour markets work more effectively.

Unemployment is a flow in that there are normally a large number of movements on to and off the register in any one month. The published figures are just a monthly snapshot reflecting the net change. Despite a sharp increase in the number and proportion of long-term unemployed, as the total climbed it was not the same 3 million who were permanently unemployed.

There has been considerable debate as to the accuracy of government unemployment statistics. Critics claim there have been a number of changes to the criteria defining unemployment. All but one of these have reduced the headline total, including the 1983 switch of the unemployment count from job centres to social security benefit offices. Justified by savings arising from the introduction of computerization, an estimated quarter of a million who previously registered at job centres but who did not claim benefits were no longer counted.

Other adjustments included:

1 More exhaustive eligibility tests.
2 Changes to the timing of the count and extended disqualification periods for those not taking up the job offers.
3 Students on vacation, school-leavers over summer and males over 60 were other groups removed from the register.

Despite the government providing explanations for all these changes, it is important that official statistics provide a consistent reflection of the *problem of unemployment* 'over time', especially when policy action may be based on them.

In summary, then, it is the view of many critics that the statistics consistently understated the problem, especially in the mid-1980s. It was claimed that official figures also excluded:

- The net impact of government training and job-creation schemes.
- Discouraged workers, such as married women, not entitled to benefits.
- Those laid off or on short time.
- Those involuntarily continuing in full-time education, owing to lack of job opportunities.

A breakdown of unemployment

There are also reasons that suggest a degree of overstatement in the figures. Fraudulent claimants and malingerers, for example, should not be counted as part of the 'problem'. On the other hand, many unemployed do not take jobs, because they are caught in what is termed the *employment trap*.

Other arguments for overstatement relate to the composition of the jobless total. Unemployment is not homogeneous but arises out of different causes and circumstances, each of which may respond to very different policy approaches. It could be argued that governments should concern themselves only with *involuntary unemployment*, which occurs where the unemployed are unable to obtain work even though they are prepared to accept lower wages and conditions than similarly qualified workers in employment. In contrast, *voluntary unemployment* arises if individuals *choose* not to work, despite available jobs for which they are qualified but at wages and conditions less attractive than the option of not working. It is not an easy task, however, to distinguish which are which in the jobless total.

Other types of unemployment are more readily identified. They may be conveniently divided into short duration and long duration categories as follows.

Short-term types of unemployment

Seasonal

Most industries have a seasonal pattern of demand. While this may be very pronounced in some industries, e.g. 70 per cent of jewellery sales around Christmas, or car sales after new car registrations in January and August, it need not lead to unemployment where businesses are diversified or can manufacture for stock or export. However, many services and outdoor trades do not have this flexibility, and must lay off staff out of season.

Casual

Often unskilled and migratory, such work is prevalent in construction and agriculture. Imperfect market knowledge may easily lead to mismatching of supply and demand.

Search or frictional

Labour markets seldom work perfectly. There will always be a proportion of the unemployed with the skills to obtain work in the current job market but currently in the process of changing jobs, which may cause some voluntary unemployment in the period between leaving one job and starting another. This type of unemployment is not part of the 'problem'; indeed it tends to rise in a buoyant economy, as workers are encouraged to move because of increasing numbers of vacancies. Such mobility is to be encouraged, being a necessary part of the process by which resources are reallocated to more productive uses.

Cyclical

This unemployment arises in the downturn or recession phases of the business cycle. It is due to a temporary deficiency of aggregate demand, which forces business to reduce output and employment. The scale will depend on the severity of the downturn. Businesses often have considerable flexibility to adjust their workforces through halting overtime, reduced use of contractual labour, voluntary severance or a halt on recruitment. This explains why youth and over-50s' unemployment tends to rise in the early stages of a recession. Unemployment in the recent downturn has been felt first in service companies in the overheated South of England, although manufacturing has been increasingly affected as activity has slowed.

Long-term types of unemployment

Residual or hardcore

This refers to the lower limit of unemployment. Even where demand for labour is extremely strong, certain individuals will constitute unattractive applicants to most employers. The potential productivity of such prospects will not be viewed as sufficient to justify the wage rates on offer. This may be due to a number of possible reasons:

- Approaching retirement age does not justify induction and training expenditure.
- Mental or physical handicaps.
- Unsuitability due to lack of skills, experience, a prison record, poor English, or poor references, suggesting an 'attitude problem'.

The fact that unemployment did not fall below 1.5 million at the height of the recent boom must give cause for concern as to the current employability of such categories.

Structural

This occurs where there is a mismatch between the unemployed and available vacancies in terms of appropriate location, required skills or any other relevant dimensions. It arises from the time lags in redeploying labour, resulting from long run changes in supply and demand. Complex industrial economies based on regional, national and international specialization are bound to experience instability as changes in taste and technology bring about the rise and decline of industries, areas and occupational skills.

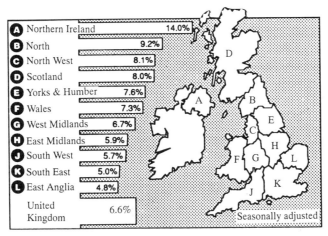

A Northern Ireland 14.0%
B North 9.2%
C North West 8.1%
D Scotland 8.0%
E Yorks & Humber 7.6%
F Wales 7.3%
G West Midlands 6.7%
H East Midlands 5.9%
J South West 5.7%
K South East 5.0%
L East Anglia 4.8%
United Kingdom 6.6%

Seasonally adjusted

Source: CSO, Department of Employment

Figure 17.3 *Regional unemployment 1990/91*

In Figure 17.3 so-called staple industries in structural decline have tended to produce higher unemployment in the 'regions' located above a line drawn from the Bristol Channel to the Wash. Transferring the redundant skills of an ageing population to a so-called high-tech sunrise industry in another part of the country is unlikely to be susceptible to short-run solution.

Technological

This form of unemployment represents the possibility of a widening imbalance of labour supply and demand as superior technology substitutes man by machine. It may affect the semi-skilled and unskilled labour force in a cumulative way as the capital stock is progressively replaced. This technological displacement is shown in Figure 17.4. Outdated

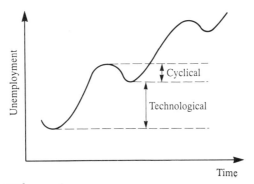

Figure 17.4 *Structural unemployment*

labour-intensive capacity will be taken out of service in the downturns, producing a ratchet effect. Deindustrialization has already allowed output to rise, with sharply reduced employment in manufacturing. Should service employment be similarly affected, a serious rise of this permanent type of unemployment could ensue.

Economists such as Professor Stonier believe it will worsen in the transition to an information society; indeed the mismatch of redundant skills in declining manufacturing and skill shortages in high technology sectors can already be observed. Market-based correction would require a fall in the real wage rate relative to the return on capital, but strong union resistance might make this difficult to achieve.

Samuel Brittan, who writes a regular column on economics in the *Financial Times*, has argued that such reasoning reflects the 'lump of labour' fallacy. If a robot can produce much more per unit of cost, then labour is likely to be displaced. However, so long as our wants exceed resources and relative scarcity prevails, the labour force will be assured of employment. It will be deployed in uses where its comparative advantage is greatest, or its comparative disadvantage is least.

Looked at historically, there has been a tendency for the number of jobs to rise broadly in line with the working population. While technical progress is perceived as the enemy of employment in the short run, clusters of product innovations are thought to have produced 50-year cycles. Associated employment creation in the recovery and boom phases of these cycles has so far prevented any tendency towards long-term stagnation.

What is full employment?

As currently defined, a zero rate is impossible, owing to the presence of frictional and hardcore unemployment. A zero rate is probably only possible in a static society, with little or no change in tastes or technology. This static attitude may have assisted the USSR in pursuing a full employment goal until its recent dismemberment.

Normally it would require perfect knowledge within the labour market, combined with attitudes and actions that were focused on the rapid adaptation and redeployment necessary to strike a balance between the redundancy arising from structural change and the new job opportunities created by it. In practice people are neither perfect nor rational, and may well be immobile or resistant to change.

The formula applied up to 1975 was defined by Lord Beveridge, the architect of Britain's post-war full-employment policy. He believed there should always be more vacant jobs than unemployed workers, and that these should be at fair wages and of such a kind and so located that the unemployed could be reasonably expected to take them. The bias was towards the worker, in the belief that unemployment was a catastrophe to be avoided at all costs – despite the weakening of employer bargaining power and skill shortages that were likely to arise.

The outcome was over 25 years of near full employment, an achievement undreamt of following levels of over 20 per cent experienced in the early 1930s. However, by 1975, with prices rising sharply and the pound under serious pressure, the policy had to be finally abandoned as one condition of a loan negotiated with the International Monetary Fund (IMF).

A natural rate?

The failure of full-employment policies arose primarily from conflict with the attainment of other goals, most notably price stability and the balance of payments. The first affected international competitiveness, while the second formed a fundamental constraint, making high employment seem sustainable only when the country grew relatively slowly.

An empirical analysis by A.W. Phillips had suggested the existence of a trade-off between inflation and unemployment. The so-called *Phillips curve* related the pressure of aggregate demand, as represented by unemployment, with the rate of change in money wages. This non-linear relation showed that as the pressure of demand increased, so too would money wages but at an accelerating rate, becoming almost vertical at very low levels of unemployment. This represents the inflationary gap situation, where wages and prices are bid up rather than increased output produced. See Figure 17.5.

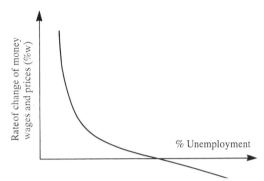

Figure 17.5   *The Phillips curve*

With labour productivity taken into account it appeared that full employment could be identified, using the Phillips curve. This was estimated at 2½ per cent for a zero inflation rate. Policy-makers, however, were not satisfied with this, and viewed the curve as a trade-off, where even lower unemployment could be bought at the expense of a given rate of inflation. In Figure 17.6 suppose that Wmax is the highest possible money wage rate increase consistent with maintaining inflation at a level that does not weaken the balance of payments. Umin would therefore represent the minimum sustainable rate of unemployment. A higher rate of wage increase would force unit costs and prices to rise faster than overseas competitors', weakening exports and encouraging import penetration. The worsening trade balance would eventually force the adoption of deflationary policies to cut aggregate demand pressure and therefore imports. Unemployment would then rise above Umin to politically undesirable levels.

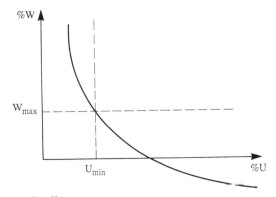

Figure 17.6   *The Phillips trade-off*

The credibility of the Phillips curve came increasingly into question when it began seriously to underpredict inflation. This suggested a shift had taken place to the right from AA to BB, as seen in Figure 17.7. If Um was maintained, the rate of wage change was now much higher at W2, causing inflation incompatible with a stable trade balance. To curtail wage rates to Wm meant that the pressure of demand had to be reduced, causing unemployment to rise to U_2. In this case full employment was inconsistent with low and stable inflation, and a trade-off was no longer possible.

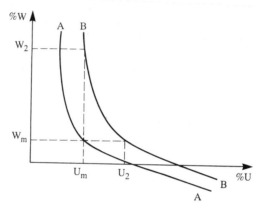

Figure 17.7   *A shift in the Phillips curve*

Milton Friedman, an American economist responsible for the development of monetarist economics, also attacked the Phillips curve trade-off. He pointed out that governments could only trade-off lower unemployment for a given rate of inflation over short periods. The original curve, he pointed out, was drawn on the assumption of *zero expectations* of inflation, yet such a policy would create them as prices began to rise. As inflation was experienced, union negotiators would feed expectations of further rises into their wage demands, in effect shifting the curve to the right as in BB (Figure 17.7). As long as the government tried to maintain the higher employment level, inflation would not only increase, it would do so at an accelerating rate as bargainers sought to anticipate the higher inflation.

To restore stability, it would not be enough to return demand pressure and unemployment to the original level, since this would merely halt the acceleration. To reduce inflation would require the economy to operate for a period with much higher unemployment than was originally the case.

The rate consistent with stable prices he termed the 'natural rate' or NAIRU (the Non Accelerating Inflation Rate of Unemployment). This concept was to exercise great influence over successive Thatcher governments.

An acceptable rate

For unemployment to rise over a million was viewed as political suicide, yet a Lib–Lab pact survived the experience in the late 1970s, while Margaret Thatcher secured re-election with unemployment well over 2 million. Despite protest marches, riots and increased crime and vandalism, the unprecedented levels appeared acceptable. A number of factors might help explain this:

- Improved state benefits encouraged the notion that, unlike in the 1930s, there was no real poverty or deprivation.
- The view that many causes, such as oil crises, were beyond the governments' direct control.
- The sharply rising prosperity of the 90 per cent of the labour force who were still in work.
- That it was the price to be paid for past inefficiency and resistance to new technology.
- That many were workshy, scroungers or working illegally in the shadow economy.
- The power of the natural unemployment rate idea, and that there were no alternative policies to the ones being pursued.
- That unions had become too greedy and powerful and had priced workers out of jobs.

The young, old and unskilled were unlikely to bring down the social and economic structure, and despite their numbers had no real lobbying power. The effects of their unemployment were more corrosive than explosive, especially for a lost generation of school-leavers who formed reluctant conscripts in a war against inflation that was not of their making.

The causes of unemployment

Given the variety of different types of unemployment, there will, by definition, be a number of contributory causes. No general agreement is possible regarding the precise causes, but three major explanations may be identified.

Workers pricing themselves out of employment

Employment is a function of the real wage, and involuntary unemployment will result if this is too high. Employers will only employ up to the point where the marginal revenue product of labour equals the real wage (see pp. 96–97). In the early 1920s, for example, it was believed that labour markets were slow to adjust, owing to the pressure of strong unions.

If, in Figure 17.8, unions set wages at W_2, then demand for labour would contract to E_2 while those wishing employment at this wage would be E_3. $E_2 - E_3$ represents the involuntary unemployment arising from overpricing of labour. Unless unions could be persuaded or forced to reduce real wage levels to W_1, then this unemployment would continue. Government efforts to achieve this led directly to the General Strike in 1926, yet despite union defeat and an across-the-board fall in wage levels, there was no increase in employment.

To understand why, one must recall the lessons of circular flow analysis, whereby incomes paid out by firms finance consumer expenditure. A general fall in wages reduces consumer income and the ability to demand goods and services. As aggregate demand falls, so firms scramble for available consumer spending by cutting prices.

The price level fell continuously throughout the 1920s and 1930s, in common with the fall in money wages. The net result was that real wages actually fell by very little and the unemployment persisted.

This process of falling prices and wages should, however, have made British goods more competitive at home and abroad. This source of stimulus to jobs did not materialize because

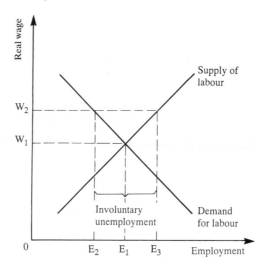

Figure 17.8 *The real wage and unemployment*

the pound was revalued when it was restored to the *gold standard* in 1925. The analogy today would be Britain's entry into the exchange rate mechanism (ERM) at a demanding value relative to the German mark. The strength of the pound then offsets any benefit from falling rates of wages and price increases promoted by recession.

Finally it should be noted that any rise in real wages relative to revenue product will put a squeeze on profitability. Falling rates of return will cause reduced investment in the domestic economy and a flow of funds towards more attractive opportunities overseas. Investment that does occur will tend to be 'process' innovation, to economize in expensive labour, rather than 'product' innovation, for future growth and employment.

Demand-deficient unemployment

As seen in the last chapter, this was the chief source of involuntary unemployment according to Keynes. A rise in savings and reduced borrowing encouraged by high interest rates has recently reduced consumer spending. Negative multipliers have been reinforced by falling confidence and investment levels. Actual falls in the volume of retail sales, despite bargain prices, reduces the revenue available to business. Desperate cuts in labour forces have been necessary, especially in the consumer-durable and leisure sectors, causing unemployment to rise to over 2.5 million by early 1992.

Market frictions

Frictions help to explain why the market does not clear with zero involuntary unemployment. Mismatching of supply may arise for a number of reasons, causing 'stickiness' in labour markets. The natural rate of unemployment is seen as reducible only if such market frictions are removed. The frictions are said to include union power and restrictive practices, imperfect knowledge of job information, immobility, minimum wage laws and state benefit payments, failure to retrain, tax disincentives, institutional rigidities, and employment discrimination.

The majority of other causes suggested to explain the presence of unemployment are variants of the above. External shocks, such as oil crises or increased competition from newly industrialized countries (NICs), will be reflected in import leakages and possible wage demands. Similarly government policies, such as monetarism, will negatively affect the circular flow. Aggregate demand may also fail to expand fast enough to absorb the rapid rise in the size of the working population. The only other significant cause would involve the accumulation over time of structural inefficiencies and low productivity which would require a shakeout when the problem was addressed.

Summary review

1 Unemployment was over 2 million in 1991–2, yet inflation was higher than our competitors'. How would you explain this?

2 Study the Department of Employment statistics in Figure 17.9. What do they suggest about the patterns of economic activity in Britain over the decade?
Obtain figures from the DoE to bring the chart up to date. Are such swings in unemployment acceptable in an affluent society such as Britain's?

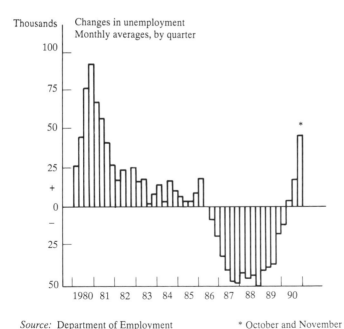

Source: Department of Employment   * October and November

Figure 17.9   *Department of Employment figures on changes in employment*

3 For each type of unemployment identified in the chapter, brainstorm possible policies to minimize its occurrence without causing higher inflation or inefficient use of resources.

18
The problem of inflation

Aims

The aims of this chapter are the following:

- To discuss the measurement of inflation and the importance of selecting the correct measure upon which to base pricing decisions.
- To consider the benefits of gently rising prices.
- To understand the destructive potential of rapid and uncertain inflation.
- To explore the main types of inflation and the various wage–price spirals that may result.
- To outline the monetarist view of inflation and relate it to the Phillips curve.

Glossary

Cost of living – measured by the retail price index as the percentage change in the average level of prices of a representative basket of goods.

Militancy – willingness to fight for pay and conditions of employment. It is influenced by union power, the cost of striking and employer resistance.

Standard of living – measured by national income at constant prices and divided by population to give per capita income.

Stock appreciation – rising prices cause the value of stocks to increase, realizing higher profits than originally anticipated.

Store of value – a function of money that allows the purchase of goods and services to be delayed by storing value in notes, coins or bank accounts.

Background

Inflation is a process of sustained and generalized rises in the average price level. It may, however, be disguised or suppressed through state subsidies or price controls, although shortages and financial deficits would still tend to reveal its presence.

Price rises were not a major economic problem so long as the rate of increase was acceptable. Inflation and measures deployed to counteract it have, however, dominated macroeconomics in recent years. At their peak prices were rising at rates approaching 25 per cent per annum, a marked contrast to the 3–4 per cent of the previous three decades. With current rates only recently well down below double figures, due mainly to the depth of the recession, it remains a problem yet to be fully solved.

Measuring inflation

There is no single or uniquely correct method of measuring price rises, since different sectors of the economy may have different rates of increase. No perfect way of aggregating them exists, and the marketer must relate the most appropriate measure to the use required. Every business, for example, will be particularly interested in price increases affecting the cost of sensitive inputs, since these will significantly determine both output prices and margins.

Index of retail prices

The monthly index of retail prices or RPI is the most widely reported measure, and comprises the total cost of a representative basket of final goods and services. All households are included, except pensioners, who are mainly dependent on state income, and the wealthiest 4 per cent. Clearly those businesses whose target population includes the 15 per cent of households that consist of retired people could be misled if they based their calculations on the RPI alone!

An index expresses data relative to a given base year value. If 1990 is made the base year, its price level will be assigned a value of 100. Base-year prices will then be divided into successive year prices and multiplied by 100 to yield a series. To translate this into an annual percentage, the following formula is used:

$$\frac{\text{Year 2 index} - \text{Year 1 index}}{\text{Year 1 index}} \times 100$$

The index is derived from the prices of around 600 items on a specific day each month, and weighted according to importance. Weights are revised annually, using sample data from the Family Expenditure Survey, to reflect changing patterns of household consumption. The main elements comprising the index are shown in Figure 18.1 in rough proportion to their weights.

Published the following month, the RPI is not seasonally adjusted. Instead it is expressed as a rate of increase on the same month a year earlier. A full understanding of the underlying trend requires study of the contribution of the various components to the aggregate outcome. In February 1991, for example, the prices of many household goods, such as footwear, actually fell, despite an RPI rise of 9 per cent. Marketers also need to recognize that the published RPI informs customers' expectations and perceptions of price changes. During times of high inflation customers often 'perceive' themselves to be worse off and there is a marked tendency to trade down – buying basic products, more inferior goods and 'value for money' promotions.

The index includes a wide cross-section of items, including housing costs, and therefore is used by governments to determine the annual increase in index-linked benefits, such as unemployment pay and tax thresholds. The index reflects changes in the cost of living or the money that must be spent to purchase a typical basket of goods consumed by a representative household.

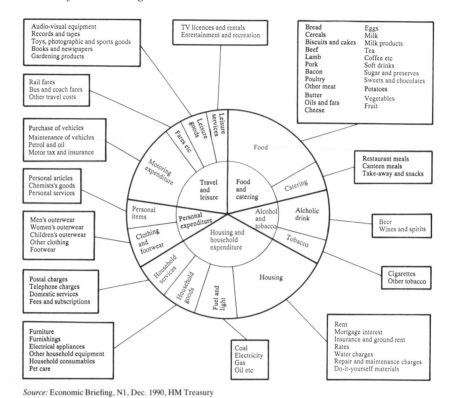

Source: Economic Briefing, N1, Dec. 1990, HM Treasury

Figure 18.1   *Composition of the RPI*

The RPI has become a matter of concern in recent years, since, unlike indexes in many other industrialized countries, it may have overstated inflation, owing to the inclusion of mortgage interest payments and the community charge. Sharp rises in these have caused the RPI to rise above the so-called 'fundamental rate of inflation'. By feeding into index-linked payments, it will also raise prices by inflating government expenditure. With the RPI making headlines in financial markets, it would be politically attractive for the government to remove these elements. The difficulty of justifying the case that mortgage payments do not reflect rises in housing costs has so far prevented this.

The tax price index (TPI)

This index measures the change in gross income required to maintain the real living standards of taxpayers on average earnings after allowing for changes in direct taxes and national insurance contributions. It was introduced by the newly elected Conservative government in 1979 to put downward pressure on wage demands as planned tax cuts were progressively introduced. Unfortunately for the government the need for tight budgets and sharp increases in national insurance actually caused the TPI to rise, eclipsing its value in depressing inflationary expectations.

GDP deflator

This measures costs and prices across the whole economy. It includes investment goods and exports, labour costs and profit margins, but not import prices.

Producer (previously wholesale) price index

The PPI measures the prices of manufactured goods for the home market as they leave the factory gate. Despite its reduced significance, price trends in manufacturing still give important signals of inflation to come in the rest of the economy. Average monthly prices are available for individual industries as well as such broad sectors as materials and fuel.

The problem and costs of inflation

Inflation assumes problem proportions when the general level of prices rises both continuously and unpredictably. However, it is far from agreed that zero or even falling prices are preferable. Prices fell between 1920 and 1934, yet this period was associated with stagnation, unemployment and widespread poverty. In comparison, the period from 1952 to 1967 was associated with historically rapid economic growth and near full employment, despite inflation averaging 3–4 per cent.

This *mild or creeping inflation* appeared a small price to pay for such performance. Its association with growth held true in many countries, and its beneficial effects included:

- A stimulus to investment, margins and profit through the effects of stock appreciation and the repayment of debt using gradually depreciating currency.
- Money illusion on behalf of workers made nominal wage payments appear more than they were in real terms. Prices changed so slowly that compensating wage claims did not occur.
- The *cost of living* was rising but the *standard of living* was rising even faster, as earnings easily outpaced prices. Varying levels of pay settlement enabled structural change to take place without any groups suffering actual pay cuts.
- Capital was raised easily, since shares formed a hedge against inflation. Money illusion over nominal interest rates also encouraged savings.

The nature of this inflation differs markedly from the image prevailing after 1967, as the costs and inefficiencies of more rapid inflation reversed the benefits outlined above. Once inflation exceeds the critical rate of around 10 per cent, it becomes a problem that negatively affects most groups within society.

Arbitrary redistribution of income

Such inflation causes as arbitrary redistribution of income, from the weak to the strong, the saver to the borrower, and from the retired to those still in full employment. People on fixed incomes suffer the greatest erosion, closely followed by those unable to keep pace with its rise, owing to weak bargaining power. Nominal interest rates, for example, failed to keep pace with prices through much of the 1970s, imposing a double penalty on pensioners.

Debtors, such as mortgage-holders and the government, benefit from the process as the real value of their debts evaporate. Inflation is in effect 'taxation without representation', as rising prices and incomes increase tax yields. Known as fiscal drag, this process literally drags previously exempt low wage earners into the tax net. Since both the above mechanisms make governments the major beneficiary from inflation, it should not be assumed that they will consistently pledge themselves to its defeat.

Breakdown of adjustment mechanisms

The *disappearance of money illusion* causes the adjustment mechanisms in the economy to break down. A fierce competitive struggle ensues between self-interested groups to maintain or improve income shares. Futile attempts to recover real income eroded by unexpected inflation only encourage further efforts to anticipate future rises, causing the problem to worsen until it is out of control. Once destroyed, an illusion will be difficult to recreate.

Money acts as a measure and a store of value, and confidence in it is crucial to the efficient operation of markets. Markets signal the relative value of goods and resources, providing the basis for efficient allocational decisions. Any distortion of these values caused by unexpected price increases will undermine this process. It is the uncertainty of price changes that is the main problem, since if inflation was a predictable 10 per cent, then all values could be indexed relative to it and allocation would not be seriously affected.

When money values can no longer be trusted, their usefulness is gone, bringing the danger of a disastrous disruption of economic life known as *hyper-inflation*. Such dramatically high levels of inflation, defined as rates in excess of 50 per cent per month, seldom last long, but the consequences of reducing them are very painful. Many hyper-inflations, as experienced in Germany in 1923 and South America during the 1980s, have their origins in political as much as economic factors.

Effect of weakening confidence

Weakening confidence in money causes movement into 'inflationary hedges' such as land, gold and fine arts. Effort and resources are therefore diverted into protecting wealth rather than creating it.

Effect on company accounting

Businesses using *historic cost accounting* standards can be misled by paper profits. When plant is due for replacement, depreciation allowances will be inadequate. A machine tool costing, say, £10,000 with an expected life of 20 years would be normally depreciated at £500 per annum. Annual inflation of 10 per cent would, however, cause such a fund to be over £50,000 short at the time of replacement.

Failure of government intervention

Attempts by governments to alleviate the symptoms of inflation through devices such as discretionary allowances, price freezes, subsidies and controls merely serve to impair the market mechanisms still further, as one control leads to the need for another. Such intervention gives the appearance a government is taking action, but only addresses the symptoms rather than underlying causes.

Problem of domestic price rises

The extent to which domestic prices rise faster than international competitors also produces problems. The gap between UK and other ERM countries is shown in Figure 18.2. If the currency is part of a fixed exchange rate mechanism such as the ERM, then a rising balance of payments deficit will force its value to the lower end of the permitted range. The government would therefore be forced to raise interest rates and deflate the economy until differential inflation was squeezed out of the system. In this respect the real problem is not the inflation itself but the economic pain suffered in squeezing it out of the system.

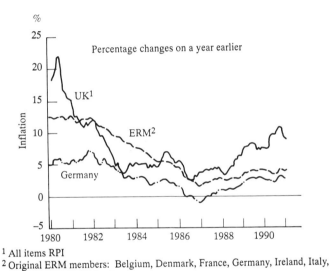

1 All items RPI
2 Original ERM members: Belgium, Denmark, France, Germany, Ireland, Italy, Luxembourg, Netherlands

Source: Budget in Brief, HM Treasury

Figure 18.2   *UK, German and ERM consumer price inflation*

   Downward flexibility in the exchange rate has also proved unable to avoid this outcome. Successive devaluations of the pound provided only short-term relief of businesses seeking to compete at home and abroad. The falling pound, which made overseas manufacturers less competitive, also made imported foods, fuels, materials and other inputs more expensive, feeding directly into domestic factory costs and wage demands. The outcome was a *wage–price–devaluation spiral*, with shortening time spans between the spirals.

The causes of inflation

Inflation is often defined in reference to its causes. 'Too much money chasing too few goods' is one such example. There is, however, little agreement as to the precise cause of the inflation

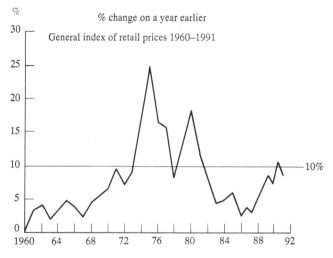

Adapted from *Department of Employment Gazette*

Figure 18.3   *The general index of retail prices, 1960–91*

shown in Figure 18.3, especially amongst economists. Three major inflation theories will be discussed below and various strands from each will then be woven into a general framework for understanding the process concerned.

Too much spending – demand pull inflation

This explanation derives from Keynsian analysis. The inflationary gap occurs when aggregate spending plans (C + I + G + X − M) exceed full employment output at current prices. The pressure of this excess demand is unable to induce extra output, so prices rise to ration out the available supply. Attempts to secure extra resources will suck in imports and bid up wage levels, fuelling further spending. If excess demand persists, a price–wage spiral will result.

As referred to in Chapter 16, A.W. Phillips had identified a stable relationship between the pressure of demand and the rate of change in money wages over the period 1861–1957. This is shown below:

Unemployment rate (per cent)	1.0	1.5	2.0	2.5	3.0	3.5	5.0
Change in money wages (per cent)	8.7	4.6	2.8	1.8	1.2	0.8	0.0

Given a trend productivity growth of 2 to 2½ per cent, zero inflation would be achieved at 2 ½ per cent unemployment. Attempts to operate the economy below this level would generate demand pull inflation. The Phillips curve predicted inflation very accurately up to 1966, but began to understate it by 4–5 per cent up to 1969, and by over 10 per cent in the early 1970s.

Cost push inflation

This occurs when price rises originate in increased factor costs without excess demand being present. It may be seen as a process resulting from owners of factors competing in an attempt to maintain or increase their real income to what proves to be unsupportable levels.

If pricing is based on a cost-plus formula, for example, higher costs will be automatically reflected in price rises as businesses struggle to maintain profit margins. Such supply-side pressures may be expected to diminish rapidly if such rises result in sharply reduced sales, output and factor employment. If, on the other hand, businesses and unions believe the government is unwilling to contemplate the consequences of resisting cost push pressure, then employers will condone inflationary settlements and pass them on in higher prices.

The government would then have to accommodate the price increases by expanding money supply and aggregate demand by the amount necessary to maintain sales at the higher price level. Any government prepared to underwrite such a wage–price spiral will ensure that little incentive will be provided for management to resist cost pressures.

The sources of cost push inflation are as follows.

Wage push

The primary engine here would be a struggle between labour and capital to achieve real shares of output that are mutually inconsistent. While desired shares can sum to over 100 per cent of the cake, actual shares cannot. Thus as unions demand and obtain higher wage settlements to raise their share, businesses restore profitability by raising prices and reducing the real value of the pay increases. This process can only be halted if one of the following occurs:

- Wage or profit expectations are adjusted.
- The government refuses to underwrite the process, so suppressing the conflict.
- Another group is forced to accept a lower share, e.g. rent receivers.
- Money illusion on the part of workers or business.

A similar struggle over shares could equally arise between different wage groups. Key wage groups achieving a wage increase justified by productivity gains may prompt *comparability* claims. If conceded, these would raise final prices, eroding the value of the rises obtained by the high productivity workers, and prompting compensating claims. A rigid wage structure provides many such linkages, and could readily support a general *wage–wage spiral*.

Profit push inflation

This arises when businesses seek to widen margins by raising output prices more than the rise in input prices. The need to rebuild profitability after its heavy erosion in the 1970s led to profit push after 1982. Input prices were low, owing to falling primary product prices and near constant unit labour costs as productivity improved sharply. Profit push contributed to inflation through most of the remaining decade.

Tax push

This occurs where wage groups have real income targets. The effect of progressive taxation and increases in tax rates is to make these unattainable, causing compensating wage claims. The switch from direct to indirect taxation, as occurred in 1979, served to raise the RPI by 3½ percentage points, while government policies to cut borrowing by reducing nationalized industry subsidies and raising council-house rents and rates have also caused above average rises in the RPI. The 1991 budget also shifted the balance of taxation by raising VAT and excises to finance a cut in the community charge.

Import push

Imports account for over a fifth of total final expenditure, so any rise in their prices will be reflected in domestic inflation after a lag. The international dimension to inflation is very important in an open economy like Britain's. Inflation is very much an international problem, with industrial nations experiencing similar patterns. The causes of this international inflation must be a large part of the explanation of British inflation, while domestic factors can be examined to explain any divergence from the average. The common factor in recent inflationary surges were oil-price shocks. This could be viewed as OPEC in a struggle to increase its share of the world cake at the expense of oil consumers. Accommodating this with an expansion in world money supply produced inflation, while eroding the real value of OPEC gains. OPEC therefore responded with a further round of price increases. These sharp and unanticipated rises had a generalized impact on other costs and prices, as energy-users found themselves unable to reduce their dependence in the short term.

Well placed in energy terms, the UK, however, fared much less well than import-dependent competitors, making further explanation necessary. The downward float of the pound in the early 1970s was one factor, since it caused import prices to rise sharply, feeding into inflation and prompting compensating wage demands.

Cost push pressures as outlined above were identified as explanations of the under-prediction of inflation after 1970. Despite unemployment rising to 1 million (4 per cent), inflation remained high, producing a condition termed *stagflation*. It was argued that this new inflation was due to union militancy, underpinned by strong membership growth. The incidence of strikes were rising, led by a new and younger breed of shop steward. Politicians too were partly to blame by stimulating faster growth expectations at election times. These proved unsupportable, especially in recession. More sophisticated media coverage made inflation more noticeable than before, while unpopular experience of decimalization and the introduction of VAT served to focus minds on real money values. Little wonder that as incomes policies lost their effectiveness, there was a dam burst of defensive wage claims.

Too much money – the monetarist explanation

Sustained inflation is always associated with monetary expansion. Such expansion in excess of the quantity required to support the full employment level of real expenditure will normally precede faster inflation. The process that links the supply of money to price rises is complex, with long and uncertain lags. The long run relationship is represented by the *quantity theory* equation of Irving Fisher:

$$MV \equiv PT$$

where: M = supply of money,   P = price level
           V = velocity of circulation of money   T = level of transactions.

This expression is known as an identity, in that the value of one side by definition equals the other. If the level of transactions is fixed at full employment, and velocity changes only slowly over time, any recourse to the printing press by the government will feed directly into the price level. Reform of the monetary system in 1971 produced an unplanned expansion in money supply that added to inflationary pressure, as did financial deregulation in the mid-1980s.

Monetarists explained the breakdown of the Phillips curve by relating the rate of change in money wages to the *expected rate of inflation*. Expectations were seen as part of an error-learning process, in that they would be adjusted to the extent they had been proved wrong in the past. The only way that the government could maintain unemployment below the natural rate was if actual inflation exceeded expected inflation, thereby reducing real wages to justify the extra jobs created.

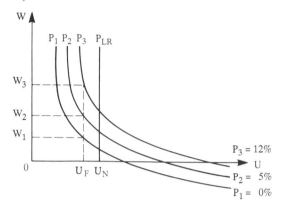

Figure 18.4 *Inflationary expectations and the Phillips curve*

Error learning meant that this could only be achieved at the expense of accelerating inflation. In Figure 18.4 any attempt to reduce unemployment to U_F by expanding the money supply causes an increase in money wages to W_1. The anticipated inflation this produces shifts the short-run Phillips curve to P_2 as expectations adjust and compensating wage demands rise to W_2. To maintain employment at U_F, money supply must again increase, and the process repeats but at an accelerating rate shown as wage rises to W_3. There is *no permanent trade-off* of a little less unemployment for a little more inflation. Instead the acceleration would be unsustainable, ending in hyper-inflation. Only with zero excess demand is a steady inflation rate possible under this theory. On this analysis, then, curing the problem, although painful, is no worse than the sickness, since inaction will only produce a worsening in the condition.

Conclusions

When inflation becomes rapid and uncertain, it creates net costs for business and society. It poses particular problems for the marketer, not least in the area of pricing. Consider the customer service problems of the German café owner in 1923, forced to raise the price of coffee while customers sat waiting for the bill. At one stage during the German hyper-inflation prices were rising at 5 per cent per hour.

Even more modest rates of 10 per cent per annum pose awkward problems for the marketer. Price changes unsettle customers. They lead to administrative costs in revising price lists; packaging has to be altered and promotional copy amended. Enhanced price awareness of customers also makes the timing and size of price changes relative to competitors much more critical.

The main sources of inflation discussed above are shown in Figure 18.5, which explains the leakages and feedback loops present in the inflationary process. The money supply provides the fuel, wage settlements the engine and expectations the reinforcement for the process.

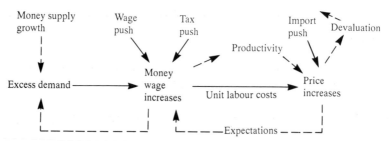

Figure 18.5   *The inflationary process*

Wages in a modern economy are not simply determined by supply and demand forces, but by collective bargaining between unions and employers' representatives. The outcome is influenced by many factors, including the progress of key bargains, wage relativities and the direction of the current wage round.

The *going rate* is an important concept in this regard, underlining the importance of inertia in the inflationary process. One writer has likened this going rate to a massive flywheel. It is mainly influenced by yesterday's inflation rate and the pressure on unions and employers to maintain comparability. Its present speed largely determines current settlements. Its momentum in the longer term, however, is determined by forces acting on the brake and engine. These are small relative to the momentum of the wheel, although sparks will fly when attempts are made to slow the pace! See Figure 18.6.

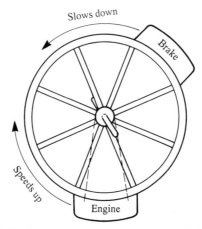

Figure 18.6   *The flywheel of inflation*

Different inflation theories will put different emphasis on what activates the engine and the braking mechanism. Keynes would point to the stage of the economic cycle, with booms driving the engine and recession the brake. Monetarists would emphasize market supply and demand forces relative to the natural rate, while cost push analysts would look at tax changes, import prices and evidence of changing militancy among work groups. Whatever explanation is favoured, the faster the flywheel turns and the more entrenched the circle of wage and price rises becomes, the more painful and difficult is the eventual adjustment.

Summary review

1 Explain why countries such as Britain have experienced increasing rates of inflation and unemployment over the past two decades, often at the same time.

2 Why might the rate of inflation for a pensioner differ from that applying to someone on average earnings?

3 Why is inflation said to produce an arbitrary redistribution of income and wealth? Consider how (a) you personally and (b) your organization has been affected over recent years.

4 Taking the idea of the flywheel, predict the course of inflation over the next 12 months. Carefully specify in numerical terms if possible the factors you consider are acting on the brake and the engine.

Section Six: Projects

1 Using your central or college library, gather the data necessary to draw up a league table of living standards for ten countries, including your own, referring to (a) the figures for the most recent year available, and (b) the figures for 10 years ago. (United Nations, OECD and EC yearbooks would be helpful here.)
Consider the following questions:

- How should living standards be measured?
- Can living standards of different countries be meaningfully compared?
- Why do the living standards of some countries grow faster than others?
- Do rising living standards force improvements in marketing, or does improved marketing force improvement in living standards?
- What price is paid for the pursuit of higher living standards?

2 The marketer must not only understand how the level of national income is measured and determined in theory but also how to collect and apply the knowledge in practice. A useful exercise to achieve this is to list the economic terms mentioned in Chapters 14 and 15 and then look up their current values.

Use the *CSO Blue Book, Economic Trends,* and *Monthly Digest* and/or the *Bank of England quarterly review* to locate these values for the various national income concepts and the circular flow components. These may be combined with the indices you have gathered for the Foundation exercise in Appendix 1 (p. 379).

3 The unemployment rate is an average calculated at a point in time. Using the resources of your local job centre and Department of Employment publications, obtain a breakdown of unemployment for your region. This should include figures, where possible, by locality, town, sex, age, skill, duration and any other characteristic you consider relevant. What do the figures tell you regarding the nature of the problem in your region? What are the main types of unemployment and why? What implications are there for a business with outlets across the region?

4 Conduct a survey based on a small representative sample of goods and services drawn from Figure 18.1.
   Ask respondents to estimate the following:

   • What is the price of the good(s) or service(s) today?
   • What was their price 12 months ago?
   • What do they expect their price(s) to be in 6 months' time?
   • Will these expectations affect their buying behaviour?

   Use the data collected to discuss the following:

   (a) The degree of money illusion in your sample population.
   (b) Whether your population has rational price expectations.
   (c) Variations in perceptions according to the type of good/service, e.g. necessity v luxury; public v private.

Section Seven
Economic management

This section will consider various policies available to the government to assist it in its management of the macroeconomic environment. Section Six raised a number of problems in the economy as a whole, including the level of national income, the rate of inflation and the degree of unemployment. This section will address what can and what cannot be done about fluctuations in the level of income, and the problem of rising price levels or under-utilized resources.

The aims of this section are as follows:

1 To study the framework of government intervention in the management of the economy.
2 To review the strengths and weaknesses of various economic policies.
3 To assess the impact of taxation and its implications for business.
4 To examine the financial system and the various sources of finance available to the firm.
5 To consider the policies available to achieve the main macroeconomic objectives of growth, employment and low inflation.

The section consists of three chapters:

Chapter 19 What can be done about national income fluctuations?
Chapter 20 The financial institutions and monetary policies
Chapter 21 What can be done about inflation and unemployment?

19

What can be done about national income fluctuations?

Aims

The aims of this chapter are:

- to find out what the various stages in effective economic management are, and to appreciate the conflicts and constraints implicit in the process.
- To understand the basis of counter-cyclical policy, and why it has proved impossible to achieve in practice.
- To review trends in public expenditure and their significance.
- To consider the principles and functions of taxation, and the implications of various taxes for business.

Glossary

Automatic stabilizers – these operate to raise injections into the circular flow as national income falls, and raise leakages when it rises. No policy decision is necessary for them to take effect.

Fine tuning – the use of fiscal and monetary policies to regulate short-term fluctuations in the economy.

National debt – comprises accumulated internal debt owed by government to nationals in the form of bills, bonds and national savings.

PAYE – pay-as-you-earn tax collection, in which payment is deducted at source by employers.

Pump priming – a term given to the injection of government spending into the circular flow. The effect of the multiplier reinforces and sustains the flow.

Rate Capping – legislation allowing the government to limit the annual rise proposed by high-spending local authorities.

Self-regulatory economy – one in which individuals pursuing their own self-interest in decisions on supply and demand produce forces resulting in equilibrium and the common good.

Background

Before the 1930s the accepted political and economic wisdom was of a self-regulating market economy that prospered through the free play of market forces. This *laissez-faire* approach meant that government intervention in industry was deemed unnecessary, other than to provide the basic framework of laws and regulations. Macroeconomics was largely ignored in the belief that the economy was self-righting around the full employment level. Supply would create its own demand. Why else would individuals and firms produce but to use the income generated to purchase the output of others?

The critical experience that upset this conventional wisdom was the 1930s depression, which brought misery and unemployment on a mass scale. Keynesian analysis showed full employment was by no means automatic in the short run, and that an unacceptably long period of time might be necessary before market adjustments to wages and prices proved effective in restoring it.

It was Keynes' advocacy of the need for government management of the economy that shaped macroeconomic policy after World War II. When unemployment showed signs of increasing, his prescription of increasing aggregate demand was applied; and when inflation or the balance of payments worsened, the rise in demand was moderated or reduced. The early success of such policies, evidenced by unemployment rates below 2 per cent, combined with only gentle inflation, gave governments added confidence to push employment and growth up as far as the trade-off with inflation would allow. This approach came to be known as counter-cyclical policy or *fine tuning*.

The policy framework

As seen in Figure 19.1, the approach taken in this chapter is to analyse the various stages in government macroeconomic management.

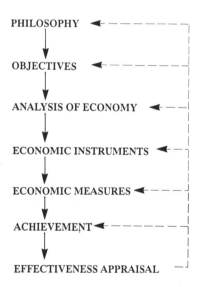

Figure 19.1   *Stages in economic management*

The Keynesian philosophy discussed above was superseded in the 1980s as the Thatcher government adopted *monetarism* and market-related *supply-side policies*. This new philosophy will be explored once Keynesian policies have been fully appraised.

Objectives have remained constant through the period, although the priority has varied. Achievement of high employment and economic growth has tended to conflict with maintenance of price stability and a balance of payments. Full employment had priority to 1975, after which inflation assumed centre stage.

Other policy goals given significance from time to time have including redistribution of income, the achievement of a balance between different regions, and environmental concerns. Difficulty was also found in their achievement, not least when price stability became the priority. Governments seeking simultaneous achievement of these goals discovered numerous constraints on their freedom to act:

- *Political constraints* – imminent by-elections, manifesto commitments.
- *Institutional constraints* – pressure from unions, the CBI, financial markets.
- *Social constraints* – public opinion and attitudes, public sense of fair play.
- *International constraints* – Agreements entered into, e.g. EC, GATT, IMF, etc.
- *Policy constraints* – economic instruments having an effect on more than one goal.

As a member of the European Community, for example, Britain would find it very difficult to introduce certain policies, such as tariffs and quotas, to deal with the balance of payments problem. The need to carry a majority in parliament also affects the timing and forcefulness of necessary measures.

In contrast to the analysis in the previous section, this chapter will focus on the main economic instruments of fiscal and monetary policies and the measures to which they give rise. Appraisal will explore the causes of progressive under-achievement of objectives, which led to the radical change in philosophy and approach under Mrs Thatcher. Attention has switched away from managing demand pressure to relaxing constraints on the supply side.

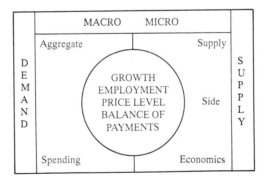

Figure 19.2 *The policy framework*

The relation between the supply and demand side of the economy and economic objectives may be seen in Figure 19.2. Just as in the wheel of retailing, it seems that government macroeconomic policy has returned full circle to reliance on market regulation. The prevailing philosophy once again supports tax cuts in preference to government expenditure on the premise that individuals spend their income more wisely than governments do. A loss of faith in governments' ability to manage aggregate demand or the money supply has produced both a sense of humility and a more pragmatic approach to economic policy.

Demand management – fiscal policy

Fiscal policies refer to government taxation and expenditure measures designed to regulate the level and composition of output. The aim of the policy in demand management terms is to achieve the pressure of aggregate demand relative to available productive capacity necessary to meet the growth and employment targets set by the Cabinet.

The means of achieving this outcome is by adjusting the tax leakages and government injection in the circular flow. The difference between government revenues and expenditure is called the *budget balance*:

Government revenue (T) = government expenditure (G) = a balanced budget.
Government revenue > government expenditure = a budget surplus
Government revenue < government expenditure = a budget deficit

Budget deficits raise aggregate demand and stimulate economic activity. Extra injections of spending will in effect *pump prime* the economy by triggering the multiplier. A budget surplus will have the opposite effect. If the Chancellor introduces a *neutral budget*, then any changes in taxes and spending will cancel each other out, with no effect on the budget balance. If extra spending is financed by borrowing rather than taxes, it is termed *deficit financing*. This creates a *public sector borrowing requirement* (PSBR), which adds to the level of any outstanding national debt.

to reduced tax revenues in recession would force it to cut spending. According to Keynes this would reduce national income still further, since reduced injections would produce a multiplied contraction in demand. To avoid this outcome Keynes argued that governments were in a position to counter the cycle by running an *unbalanced budget*.

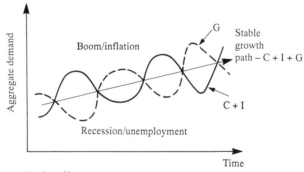

Figure 19.3   *Counter-cyclical policy*

If the solid line in Figure 19.3 represents the path of aggregate demand excluding (G), then allowing government spending (G) to follow the dotted line would counter the cycle. Deficit financing in recession and surpluses in boom would, if successfully timed, move the economy on to the stable growth path shown. It was argued that the greater stability and predictability of such a path would encourage business investment and confidence, so enabling a faster growth line (steeper) to be achieved.

Successful counter-cyclical policy may be seen in the income expenditure analysis in Figures 19.4 and 19.5. Shifting the aggregate demand line from AD_1 to AD_2 by increasing government

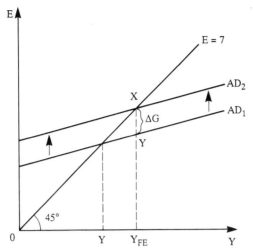

Figure 19.4 *The deflationary gap*

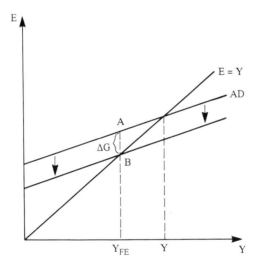

Figure 19.5 *The inflationary gap*

spending (ΔG) fills the demand gap and achieves full employment at Y_{FE}. Conversely, cutting G and running a budget surplus removes the inflationary gap.

It should be recognized that because the government expenditure multiplier is larger than the tax multiplier (part of the increased after-tax income created is saved), a net stimulus can be achieved through a balanced budget rise in both. Furthermore the final size of the budget deficit incurred in closing the deflationary gap will be significantly smaller than the initial rise. If the government expenditure multiplier ($\times$) was 1.5 and taxes account for 40 per cent of national income, then for an injection of £1,000m the net deficit is just £400m ($\Delta G - \Delta T$).

i.e.: $\Delta G = $£1,000m ($x = 1.5$) $\rightarrow \Delta Y = $£1500m ($T = 0.4$) $\rightarrow \Delta T = $£600m

Marketers should note that changes in government spending and taxation will also affect aggregate expenditure to the extent that income is redistributed from rich groups with low propensities to consume to poorer groups with high propensities or *vice versa* – thus shifting demand from luxury products that are price-elastic to more inelastic necessities.

Public expenditure in practice

Over the last decade the objective has been to hold growth of public spending at less than the rate of growth for the whole economy. An attempt was made early in the decade to reduce spending in real terms, but unplanned rises in unemployment benefit prevented this. The aim was then amended to holding spending steady in real terms. Though not succeeding fully, the rate of growth did fall from 3 to just 1 per cent per annum. When combined with a quickening rise in GDP, the share of government expenditure began to decline.

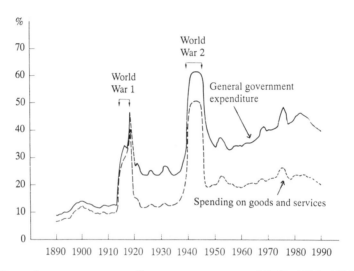

Figure 19.6   *General government expenditure as a percentage of GDP, 1890–1990*

The effect can be seen in Figure 19.6, as the share fell from 46.5 per cent to less than 40 per cent over the period. This reversed a trend of rising state activity that had spanned three decades and appeared irreversible. It was also a pattern that was duplicated in other industrial economies. Where the government share of GDP had risen on average from a quarter to nearly a half by the mid-1980s, according to OECD figures.

The marketer should always study the government's expenditure plans, published each autumn, for marked shifts in spending. With government expenditure accounting for 40 per cent of GDP, the consequences for suppliers to the various government departments of such changes may be substantial.

Real spending on social security has risen more than 40 per cent over the period shown (Figure 19.7), reflecting rising pensions as well as higher average unemployment. Defence spending initially rose strongly but is now on a declining path. This arises from the 'peace dividend' associated with the disbanding of the Warsaw pact forces and a succession of arms reduction treaties. Spending on education has marked time in real terms over the decade, owing to falling school rolls, although increasing birth rates and participation in higher education are now raising spending in this area.

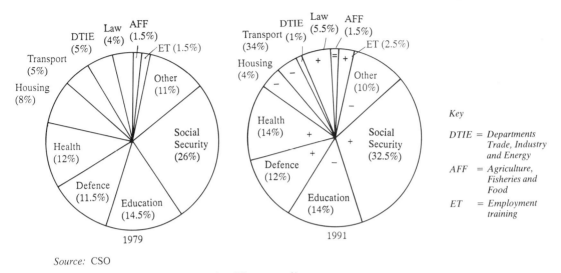

Source: CSO

Figure 19.7 *The changing patters of public expenditure*

Public sector investment in the areas of housing, transport, industry, trade and energy were cut back in real terms, while subsidies and grants were dramatically reduced. Only employment and training expenditure expanded rapidly to cope with rising unemployment.

With regard to the future it is difficult to see how the government can easily curtail spending on health, education and social security. Having squeezed most of the other sectors already, its longer-term plans to keep reducing government spending as a percentage of GDP become progressively more difficult and painful to achieve. The only alternatives will be to make GDP rise more rapidly or to privatize provision.

The budget

Major changes in fiscal policy are normally announced in the budget statement, made by the Chancellor in March or April each year. Interim budgets may also be introduced to make corrections to the economy. However, such mini-budgets, while associated with fine tuning, are seldom used today.

The budget reviews the performance of the economy and its likely prospects. Measures may be concerned with reform of the tax structure and redistribution of income and wealth, as well as the management of economic activity.

When aggregate demand was being actively managed, the budgetary process covered the following:

1 A statement of objectives.
2 Economic forecasting, using the Treasury economic model to:

(a) Determine the path of national income if policies were unchanged.
(b) Determine the required path of output to achieve the objectives set.
(c) Identify the 'gap' between (a) and (b).

3 Selecting economic instruments of the appropriate direction, strength and timing to make the correction to demand pressure required and fill the gap.
4 Implementing specific measures.
5 Monitoring effectiveness.

This process is in marked contrast to the budget of 19 March 1991, where the stated aim of fiscal policy was to balance the budget over the medium term. The Chancellor reaffirmed the government's commitment to defeating inflation and creating the conditions for sustainable growth of output and high employment. The medium-term financial strategy now provides the framework for the conduct of both monetary and fiscal policy to achieve those ends.

It was the government's belief that the use of fiscal policy for short-term demand management would destabilize the economy and damage supply-side performance. Accordingly, its aim was to achieve a budget balance in the medium term, while accepting that the PSBR would rise and fall with the cycle. Figure 19.8 reflects this position, with recent budget surpluses giving way to renewed deficits as the economy moves into recession.

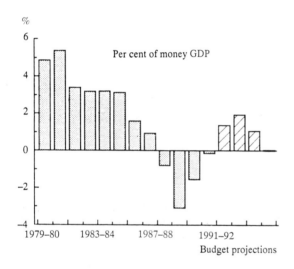

[1]Negative values indicate a public sector debt repayment

Figure 19.8   *Public sector borrowing requirement*

Criticism of demand-management policies

Attempts to fine-tune the economy along a steady high employment growth path attracted growing criticism on the following grounds:

- The economy still fluctuated in a stop–go pattern.
- The techniques of demand management were crude and inadequate to the task.
- An increasingly turbulent economic environment made forecasting unreliable.
- Policy objectives conflicted and were not pursued consistently by politicians.
- Demand-management errors actually destabilized the economy.

It was also argued that deficit financing *crowded out* private spending. The extra borrowing requirement caused interest rates to rise, choking off consumer and investment spending. Once full employment was reached, any further increase in government spending would by definition reduce private spending by an equal amount.

Keynesian demand management was underpinned by a number of the beliefs, as follows:

1 Full employment could and should be achieved.
2 Expansionary fiscal policy was the best policy instrument.
3 Growth will respond positively to higher demand pressure.
4 Excess demand did not matter overmuch.

Politicians also had a vested interest in the vote-catching potential of extra spending, as had economists in their desire for 'hands on' control of the economy.

The actual processes of managing the economy were described by Prof. Cairncross as equivalent to driving a car with all but the rear window blacked out. You can't see where you are going, you can't see where you are, you can only see where you have been!

This arises out of the various time lags that come into play:

Forecasting lags

Statistics only provide a snapshot of the economy 3 to 6 months in the past. Figures are not completely reliable, and are subject to frequent revision. This information must then be projected forward to predict the present state of the economy and its future path.

Awareness lags

It takes time to recognize unique or non-recurring events affecting relationships in the Treasury model of the economy, including the problem of predicting reactions to the policy changes themselves. These reactions depend on the state of confidence in the community, which is in turn influenced by the impact the policies are expected to have.

Execution lags

Where ignorance is very real and uncertainty inescapable, effective execution is never straightforward. Necessary action is not always politically appropriate. It may be necessary to mobilize support or judge the time is right before the decision is taken. There may also be frictions to smooth over and pressure-group compromises to be made. Political decisions are often made under pressure and in response to short-term horizons, causing lags to be under-estimated.

Impact lag

It will take time before a tax or expenditure change will impact on the circular flow. Further time will then elapse while multiplier–accelerator reactions work themselves out to produce the full effect. Depending on the measure, this could take up to 2 years.

Handle with care

The marketer must beware of the limitations of most government figures provided through the Central Statistical Office (CSO).

- Figures provided are *not* information. They require understanding and interpretation in marketing terms.
- Information is often out of date or redundant, owing to market changes.
- Figures are often published in a form that makes comparison difficult.
- Government statistics are often subject to errors and omissions in calculation.
- Figures may be subject to substantial revision later.
- Government statistics provide a general, non-company-specific picture.

Note: the 1989 financial statement and budget report confirmed that the average error in the Treasury computer model for GDP was 1 per cent, with revisions averaging 1.3 per cent. If the Treasury forecasts GDP at 3 per cent, it could lie anywhere between 2 and 4 per cent. In effect CSO publications should carry a government health warning. However, with this caution in mind, their consumption with care and moderation should give business people some understanding of the economic environment.

Given the above considerations, it is surprising that policy has not been even more inaccurate than it actually has been. The car with its windows blackened also had only a brake and accelerator, both of which took effect long after being applied. To have had any chance of stabilizing the economy, the driver would have had to apply the brakes going uphill and the accelerator going downhill!

Disillusion with fine tuning

The danger of actually destabilizing the economy may be seen in Figure 19.9. The wavy line represents the actual path of the cycle if no action is taken. The objective of counter-cyclical demand management is to move the economy on to the high employment growth path represented by the line XY.

The business manager who has experienced the difficulty of precisely measuring product demand in a rapidly changing market may have some sympathy with those trying to manage the economy.

At time period T_1 in Figure 19.9, owing to the forecasting lag, the planners only have a picture of where the economy was in time period T. It appears that the economy is accelerating into inflation, and to move the economy back on to the full employment growth path will require a deflationary package to take some of the heat out of the economic situation. After T the economy actually begins to slow and turn down under its own forces. The planners cannot know this, since prediction of the turning point is the most difficult factor of all to forecast. The Chancellor introduces the deflationary package, which causes the economy to turn down along the dotted path, as the measures progressively reinforce the natural downturn.

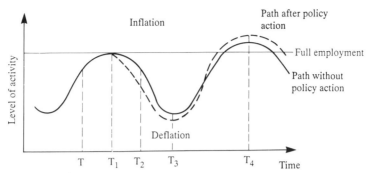

Figure 19.9 *Destabilizing the economy*

By time period T_2 the Treasury forecasters can see their error and promptly advise the Chancellor to reflate to offset the developing deflation. The natural inclination to 'wait and see' if the economy has truly turned down, combined with execution lags, means that by the time the policies begin to have an effect, the economy is already beginning to turn up again. This merely reinforces the recovery, 'shooting' the economy into an inflationary situation at T_4. Such criticisms, together with empirical evidence of destabilization, led to disillusion with fine tuning, noted in the budget section above.

The introduction of the *medium-term financial strategy* by the Conservatives ended this discretionary approach. Short- term fluctuations were now accepted as inevitable, while fiscal policy was subordinated to the use of monetary policy. *Automatic stabilizers* were to be used to reduce the degree of cyclical fluctuation. Progressive direct taxes, for example, reduce the size of the multiplier through higher leakages of spending power as the economy booms. The size and stability of government spending, especially on social security and welfare payments, also tends to limit the severity of a downturn. Such stabilizers can play a crucial role in preventing recession turning into depression.

The disillusion with fine tuning therefore produced an almost inevitable reaction in favour of macroeconomics on autopilot, based on the principles of sound money and a balanced budget.

Supply-side economics

After 1979 the emphasis shifted from managing aggregate demand as a means of promoting growth and employment to relaxing constraints on Britain's productive capacity. Shifting the aggregate demand curve to the right can only be sustained without inflation if aggregate supply is increased at the same rate. The only other alternative would be to suppress the inflation through incomes policies, and experience had clearly demonstrated the impracticability of this course of action.

Supply-side difficulties had plagued Britain with capacity problems since the 1950s. It was hoped that setting the supply side free would not only allow her to grow as fast as her competitors but also enable living standards to be boosted without causing inflation. The aim was to assist markets to work better, achieved primarily by low government expenditure and taxation. Policies included the following:

- Removal of tax distortions that hinder long-term investments in plant and equipment.
- Reform of trade unions and industrial-relations practices to raise productivity.

- Creating a keener business climate to force improved quality of investment.
- Encouragement of flexibility and mobility.
- Improvement of training and skills, owing to the failure of market forces to produce an adequate supply of trained personnel.
- Policies to encourage small firms and the activities of entrepreneurs.
- Reduction of red tape and the introduction of simplified planning procedures.
- Privatization and the injection of market forces into state-provided services.
- Abolition of foreign exchange controls.

Taxation

The budget sets out the sources of state income for the coming year. The primary concern is to raise sufficient revenue to meet government expenditure plans. Any shortfall will have to be met by borrowing, adding to the *national debt*, which as the total of all past borrowings, net of repayments, has to be financed. Interest on debt currently accounts for 10 per cent of total state expenditure.

The main objectives of taxation are:

- To raise revenue.
- To redistribute income and wealth.
- To influence the level of aggregate expenditure.
- To correct market failures by influencing expenditure patterns.

Taxes may be divided into three main types, namely taxes on income, expenditure and capital.

Note that taxation rates and levels change regularly, and the figures quoted here represent the position in 1991/92. Students using this text in preparation for examinations and assignments should ensure they quote current figures.

Taxes on income – direct taxes

These are levied on the income or earnings of an individual or organization and are the largest revenue-earners. Tax is levied on income after various reliefs and allowances have been deducted, to reach the *tax threshold*. Taxable income is currently taxed at a basic rate of 25 per cent up to the threshold of £23,700, and then at a higher rate of 40 per cent on any income earned above this level. Allowances are normally indexed automatically each year to account for inflation, causing the thresholds to rise in money terms.

The amount persons pay on an extra pound of income is termed their *marginal tax rate*, while actual tax paid as a proportion of gross income is the *effective tax rate*.

Since those on higher incomes pay a higher rate and low income earners below the threshold pay nothing at all, the tax is termed *progressive*. Its effect as income rises may be seen in Figure 19.10. In comparison, a *regressive* tax would hit the incomes of the poor proportionally harder than those of the rich.

Income taxes have become less progressive in Britain over the 1980s, as rates have fallen dramatically from an upper rate threshold of 83 per cent and a basic rate of 33 per cent. Allowances have not improved in real terms, causing lower income taxpayers to foot a larger

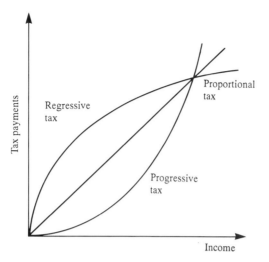

Figure 19.10 *Progressive and regressive taxes*

proportion of the total tax bill. On the other hand, the fact that top income earners are now paying a higher share despite lower rates suggests that supply-side policies may be working.

Lower marginal tax rates were introduced to increase the incentive to work and be enterprising. The *Laffer curve* suggested that government revenues would still be maintained as the incentive to extra effort produced extra taxable income. Lower tax rates were also expected to reduce the attractions of tax avoidance and discourage outright tax evasion.

The tax disincentive

Adam Smith recognized that taxation beyond a certain point would realize lower revenue. Higher excise rates applied to goods with price-elastic demand will have this effect. Arthur Laffer, an American economist, applied such thinking to the tax burden as a whole, suggesting that rates had been pushed beyond the taxable capacity of the economy, causing them to yield less than maximum revenue. His recommendation of lower taxes became part of the supply-side economic approach adopted by both Britain and America. Sharp cuts were made to higher income tax rates (the top 4 per cent) on the arguments that:

● The incentive to work harder rises with lower marginal tax rates.
● Less effort is given to tax avoidance.
● More reward is provided for enterprise among the critical managerial and entrepreneurial groups who start new businesses.

Tax cuts were expected to raise revenue (X to Y), as seen in Figure 19.11. Evidence is inconclusive, despite rising tax revenues from the top 1 per cent of income-earners. Other factors such as skill shortages and changes in payment methods have also increased incomes, and, as with any price change, there is a substitution effect as well as an income effect, encouraging the better off to consume more leisure.

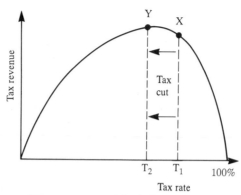

Figure 19.11   *The laffer curve*

Tax cuts for lower paid workers were largely offset by national insurance increases, while their opportunities for working harder are limited by overtime possibilities. The greatest tax disincentive affects low income earners discouraged from seeking employment because of the loss of state benefits that would result.

Indexed allowances and the lower 25 per cent rate have improved the situation for some, but many argue that a *negative income tax* system, replacing state benefits with tax credits for the poor, is the only complete solution. No agreement exists at what tax rate revenue is maximized or what the precise shape of the Laffer curve is. It may vary according to the mix of taxes and the nature of offsetting allowances and benefits. As such, its practical value in policy terms may be limited without further research being undertaken.

National insurance contributions

These are paid at a flat rate by the self-employed and proportionately up to a ceiling by both employer and employees. The entitlement to various state benefits is dependent on payment of these contributions. Rates have risen sharply from 6.75 to 9 per cent of income over the last decade and Labour pledged to remove the ceiling in their 1992 election manifesto.

Corporation tax

Levied on company profits at a rate of 25 per cent up to a threshold of £250,000. The normal rate was reduced in the 1991 budget from 35 per cent to 34 per cent in the current year. This gives Britain the lowest rate of company tax in the European Community. Allowances for plant and equipment also provide an incentive for retention and reinvestment of profits, and may reduce the effective tax rate significantly.

Petroleum revenue tax

This is of decreasing significance in revenue terms with falling oil prices and North Sea production. The tax is levied on drilling profits at a 75 per cent rate, with the objective of realizing benefits from the oil wealth for the economy as a whole.

Taxes on expenditure – indirect taxes

While revenue-raising is again the primary concern, other objectives may also be evident. For example, excise duties may be levied to discourage consumption of alcohol and tobacco. As can be seen in Figure 19.12, since 1979 the real value of taxes on beer and cigarettes has increased by nearly 60 per cent. Differential duties applied to leaded and unleaded petrol may serve to encourage the adoption of environmentally more acceptable vehicles. Customs duties may also be adopted to protect an industry from overseas competition.

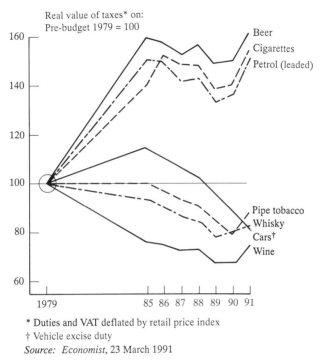

Real value of taxes* on:
Pre-budget 1979 = 100

Beer
Cigarettes
Petrol (leaded)

Pipe tobacco
Whisky
Cars†
Wine

* Duties and VAT deflated by retail price index
† Vehicle excise duty
Source: Economist, 23 March 1991

Figure 19.12 *The price of vice*

The impact of indirect taxes normally falls on producers, who then shift the tax down the supply chain by rising prices, causing the final burden to fall on the consumer. The two main forms of indirect tax are the following.

Customs and excise duties

Customs duties are levied on goods originating outside the EC but are now of limited significance in the UK, accounting for less than 1 per cent of revenue. Excises are specific taxes levied per unit of the commodity irrespective of the price. Fuel, alcohol and tobacco are the main excises, and together with car tax, betting and gaming levies, account for about 10 per cent of revenue.

Value-added tax

This is the most important tax in revenue terms. It is an *ad valorem* tax levied on the selling price of the commodity. Owing to its regressive nature, there are two rates, zero and 17.5 per cent. Basic necessities such as food, fuel, construction and transport are zero-rated. Sellers do not charge VAT for these but are able to claim back anything paid previously by their suppliers. There are other categories known as tax-exempt that are unable to do this: examples include health, education, land and financial services. The turnover threshold for VAT was raised in the 1991 budget from £25,400 to £35,000, which is expected to remove around 150,000 small businesses from VAT registration.

Other indirect taxes include stamp duties, car tax and television licences. Governments find such taxes relatively cheap to collect, since much of the administration is undertaken by traders themselves. They are difficult to evade and also attractive in that consumers are not fully aware of them. Over two-thirds of the final price of petrol, cigarettes and spirits are accounted for by tax, while in the case of cars it is a quarter.

Clearly decisions by governments to change such duties will transform the marketing task in industries affected. When VAT was raised from 8 to 15 per cent in the 1979 budget, it helped inflation to surge to 22 per cent. This was unlikely to occur after the 1991 budget, which succeeded in reducing the retail price index by 1.3 per cent, via the £140 reduction in the community charge offsetting the rise in VAT.

The tax burden

Despite significant changes to the tax structure in Britain over the last decade, it remains a burden in a number of senses:

- With current tax receipts running at 43 per cent of GDP, the burden is much less than many European countries but much more than Japan and the USA.
- The tax burden is above its level at the outset of the 1980s, since falls in income tax have been offset by sharp rises in national insurance, value-added tax and local authority rates/charges.
- The burden has been dramatically redistributed, with those up to 150 per cent of average earnings now paying a higher percentage in tax, with the poorest worst affected.
- The poorest, including pensioners, unskilled and the unemployed, have been doubly affected, since their real incomes improved little over the last decade. State benefits only rise in line with prices not average earnings.

Table 19.1   League table of tax burdens (%)

Scandinavia	60	UK	44
France	50	USA	31
Germany	45	Japan	31

The top 20 per cent have enjoyed real income rises of well over a third, compounded by sharply increased property and share values. Since 20 per cent of such marketable wealth is concentrated in the hands of the top 1 per cent, and 40 per cent in the top 5 per cent, the long-term redistributive trend (excluding pension rights) is likely to show a sharp reversal, once figures are available to confirm it.

Taxes on capital

These are levied on the owners of wealth, with the primary objective of redistribution. Capital itself is not taxed, although a wealth tax has been proposed by the Labour Party. Instead taxes are levied when capital is sold, inherited or transferred.

Capital transfer taxes

Taxes of 40 per cent are applied to assets transferred to another person above an exemption threshold. Transfers on death are exempt if under this threshold.

Capital gains taxes

These are levied when assets such as land or shares are sold at a profit. Relief is given on assets such as residences and vehicles, and a threshold below which no tax is paid applies.

Local-authority (LA) finance

LA finance is included under the heading of taxes on capital, since the community charge, which replaced the rates in 1990, is currently being phased out. The government plans to replace it by a property-based tax in 1993–4, one related to banded residence values, together with an adjustment for the number of adults in each home. Alternatives such as a local income tax or a local sales tax were ruled out as currently impracticable.

Local government has been under increasing pressure to curtail its spending in recent years. Central government therefore sought to reduce the proportion of local-government expenditure financed from the centre. The reluctance or inability of local authorities to make cuts inevitably meant increasing rate bills and charges for local services. Rate capping was introduced in the mid-1980s in an attempt to curtail excessive spending by certain councils. The community charge itself was expected to make them politically more accountable, where

Table 19.2   Local authority revenues

	1991–2 forecast	
	£bn	*Per cent*
Receipts		
Community charge, net	7.3	11.0
Non-domestic rates	14.1	21.2
Current grants	35.4	53.1
Capital grants	2.9	4.3
Other	6.9	10.4
Total receipts	66.5	100

Source: Red Book.

high spending meant higher charges, but in the event high community charges were blamed not on local authorities but on central government.

Business rates were also reformed, with the introduction of the *national uniform business rate*. The current nationwide level of 34.8p in the pound, set by the government, is applied to rateable values, which themselves have been revalued. Revenue is collected by authorities, and pooled and redistributed on a per capita basis. The reform is being phased in, since service firms and many businesses in the South and around town fringes face substantial increases in real terms, while northern manufacturing businesses gain. The rate is being increased by 10 per cent, with one in three businesses facing increases above inflation of up to a maximum of 20 per cent.

Local authorities account for nearly a quarter of all government spending. Income is raised through government grants, local tax and trading income. The reduction in poll-tax bills announced in the 1991 budget, together with the transfer of education spending to central government, means that in future only 11 per cent of total income will be raised locally, as shown in Table 19.2

Principles of taxation

The provision of central and local government goods and services, such as defence, health, education and social welfare, makes taxation inevitable. It should be clear from the above discussion that the marketer must be aware of the incidence and level of taxation on both products and target customer groups.

As you saw in Section 3, the incidence of a tax depends on the responsiveness of both supply and demand to the resulting price change. In Figure 19.3 an *ad valorem* tax such as VAT levied as a percentage of the price would shift the supply curve upwards and to the left by the amount of the tax. The new equilibrium is at P_2Q_2. While price has risen above P_1, it has not done so by the full amount of the tax, and the final incidence of the tax is shared between the customer (P_1-P_2) and the supplier P_0-P_1). The more inelastic the demand curve, the greater the share borne by the customer and *vice versa*.

The marketer must also be alert to changes, both proposed and implemented, by the Chancellor, especially at budget time, and assess their possible impact on the business. The significance may vary according to the government's objective. Raising income tax to dampen

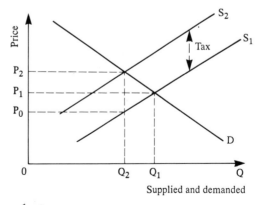

Figure 19.13   *The incidence of a tax*

demand will affect the various income groups to different degrees. Since after-tax discretionary income is being affected, this will impact more on income-elastic luxury products, especially where the rises are progressive. Alternatively, changes in VAT classification or a specific excise duty may be introduced to deter or switch demand, with serious repercussions for the producers concerned.

Since taxes are unavoidable but also electorally unwelcome, governments have an interest in making them as fair as possible. Adam Smith laid down four canons or attributes of good taxation. These principles still hold good today:

- *Equity* – a just tax should be based on the ability to pay. Progressive taxation ensures the rich not only pay more but also a larger proportion of their income.
- *Economy* – a good tax should not be costly to administer, allowing the largest possible proportion of the tax to accrue as revenue. It should be difficult to avoid, as with the rates levied on visible land and buildings. Indirect taxes meet this criteria, although they are regressive. Income and capital taxes tend to require an expensive bureaucracy, although the abolition of nine higher rate bands in favour of a single 40 per cent rate has now simplified matters.
- *Convenience* – this means that the method and frequency of payments should be convenient to the taxpayer. Income tax payable in small regular amounts through PAYE meets this requirement.
- *Certainty* – taxpayers should know their tax liability, and when and how tax should be paid. Despite efforts by the Inland Revenue to simplify procedures, income tax and VAT returns continue to pose considerable problems for many people.

Two further attributes may be added to the above.
- *Flexibility* – a modern tax system needs to be adaptable to changing circumstances. The Chancellor already has the power to alter certain taxes. The 'regulator' allows him to make a 10 per cent change in either direction on VAT rates without the need to consult parliament.
- *Neutrality* – tax changes should not distort the efficient allocation of resources.

Poll tax cannonball!

The community charge as the short-lived replacement for the rates was introduced despite its contradiction of *all* the canons of taxation:

- *Equity* – as a straightforward tax per head levied at a uniform rate irrespective of income, property or circumstances, it was heavily regressive. To the wealthy lord it represented but a fraction of total income, yet to the unskilled labourer it might have been the straw that broke the camel's back!
- *Economy* – the maintenance of an up to date register of a footloose tax base proved difficult and expensive. Introduced against Treasury advice, it had a heavy cost in lost revenue, lost votes and lost political credibility. A succession of administratively costly rebates (up to 80 per cent) were applied to half the population, yet a 1991 survey by CIFPA revealed that 4.5 million had paid nothing and 9.5 million were in arrears by over a month, out of 36 million registered. Shortfall on expected revenue forced authorities to borrow, the interest cost of which added to the problem.

- *Convenience* – it was a lump-sum tax, despite easy payment methods being available. Start up, running and administrative costs were estimated to be in excess of £1bn, while sweeteners, rebates and the VAT increase of 2.5 per cent were calculated to have cost in excess of £10.7bn.
- *Certainty* – the variety of rebates and public confusion over the charge made it anything but certain. Its objective was an equal charge for community services on all, making payers sensitive to service quality and provision. It could be argued, however, that the well off make much greater use of local services, such as education, roads, police and leisure facilities, than the poor.

Direct versus indirect taxes – a summary

A marked shift was made from direct to indirect taxes in 1979, and again in 1991, as VAT was raised from 8 to 15 to 17.5 per cent and income tax rates were cut. A cost–benefit summary of the arguments for and against is provided below in Table 19.3:

Table 19.3   Direct and indirect taxes

DIRECT TAXES

Costs	Benefits
Disincentive – to work, save, enterprise	Equitable – can be progressive
Administrative costs of changes, and needs	Flexible – relief given to various groups
Needs an Act of Parliament	Broad tax base
Tax advice industry exploits loopholes/allowances	Economy – cheap and easy to collect
Tax push inflation if target income is pursued	Convenience – deducted at source in regular amounts
Implementation lags in fiscal policy	Certainty – incidence is not transferable
	Liability and yield can be calculated
	No direct impact on inflation
	Automatic stabilizer

INDIRECT TAXES

Costs	Benefits
Regressive impact	Individual freedom – can be avoided by non-purchase
Feeds directly through to inflation	No disincentive to work
Alters relative prices and may distort consumption patterns	Incentive to save
Uncertain yield when rate changes	Discourages undesirable consumption
	Flexible – can be changed quickly
	Concealed in the final price
	Convenient to collect
	Cheap to administer

Changes in taxation bring additional problems to the marketer. Sudden and unexpected impositions of tax, as, for example, with car telephones in the 1991 budget, have a dramatic and unplanned impact on price and demand. Equally unexpected, the rise in VAT to 17.5 per cent gave firms only 2 or 3 weeks to reprint price lists, catalogues and price tickets.

Summary review

1 Why has fine tuning been discredited? Do the various lags that were identified apply to marketing forecasts and policy implementation?

2 Determine the economic effects of the changes that have taken place in the tax system during the last decade on:
  - the propensity to save,
  - the demand for luxury cars,
  - the demand for tax accountants.

3 Every spring the budget raises large amounts of money, and each autumn public expenditure plans are announced to spend large amounts of money. On each occasion analyse how the measures adopted impact on the business sector and its constituent companies.

4 Disregarding the canons of taxation, the government has rejected the idea of a local sales tax and a local income tax. Why? What alternative to the current local taxation system would you suggest and why?

20
The financial institutions and monetary policies

Aims

The aims of this chapter are as follows:

- To trace the considerable changes that have taken place in the financial sector over recent years.
- To examine the operation of the retail banks and other financial institutions.
- To assess the short-, medium- and long-term sources of finance available to business.
- To detail the current functions of the Bank of England, and the measures presently relied on to ensure monetary control.
- To examine the meaning of monetarism and the medium-term financial strategy, and to assess their effectiveness.

Glossary

Accepting houses – merchant banks that sign commercial bills, accepting them for repayment. This guarantees repayment on maturity.

Cash flow – the movement of money receipts and payments in and out of a business.

Certificates of deposit – negotiable instruments issued by banks receiving loans from other banks. They state the principal and interest repayable at given dates.

Corset – a form of special deposit where retail banks place a stipulated percentage of their liquid assets in the Central Bank as their deposits grow.

Current or sight account – an account from which a withdrawal is payable on sight or demand.

Deposit or time account – an account from which a withdrawal is payable only on giving stipulated notice.

Discount market – comprises eight discount houses that specialise in discounting (buying) bills close to maturity, using funds borrowed from the retail banks.

Finance houses – businesses mainly engaged in hire-purchase finance.

Gilt-edged securities – fixed interest securities issued by the government and traded on the Stock Exchange. They are considered safe stock, since it is very unlikely that the government would fail to honour its debts.

Liquid assets – those with 3 months or less to maturity or repayment.

Provisions – amounts set aside in a bank's balance sheet to provide reserves in the event of a bad debt.

Special deposits – introduced in 1960, they required retail banks to deposit a specified fraction of their total deposits with the Bank of England to prevent over-expansion of credit.

The retail banking sector

The origins of today's high street banks may be traced back to seventeenth-century goldsmiths. Customers making deposits for safekeeping began to use their paper receipts to finance transactions rather than go to the inconvenience of withdrawing the gold. The astute goldsmiths realized they could use these idle deposits to support interest-bearing loans, often to many times the value of the gold they held in their vaults. Since only a small proportion of the 'notes' they issued were normally presented for payment, a prudent reserve was sufficient to maintain public confidence in their ability to settle on demand.

Retail or clearing banks no longer have the right to issue notes, but undertake the same basic function – attracting funds from depositors and using them to make loans to individuals or business borrowers through a branch network. Services traditionally provided by retail banks such as Barclays, Lloyds and TSB include the following:

1 Current (or sight) and deposit (or time) accounts.
2 Cheques and cheque clearing.
3 Overdrafts and personal loans.
4 Safekeeping of valuables.
5 Standing orders, credit transfers and direct debit.
6 Currency transactions.
7 Financial advice, trustee services and customer references.

Changes to legislation in the financial sector have removed previous barriers, allowing building societies and other financial institutions to enter the banking market. The increased competition has helped to shift financial-service providers from a product- to a market-oriented approach to their business. The results of this can be seen in the considerable innovation that has taken place over the last decade, transforming the provision of many of the above services:

- Interest is now paid on current as well as deposit accounts, reflecting building-society competition (offering instant access accounts) and increased customer awareness of uneconomic, idle bank balances. The distinction between accounts is rapidly disappearing, especially as banks have ceased even to levy bank charges on transactions.
- Cheque guarantee, cash and credit cards have revolutionized payment methods. Electronic funds transfer (EFT) is progressively replacing paper-based transactions.
- Automated teller machines are often preferred for their convenience, total access and privacy.
- Euro-cheques and credit cards have provided greater flexibility for the traveller.
- Competitive pressures and the need to spread the overheads of expensive branch networks have led to the development of complementary financial services. These include mortgage finance, managed unit trusts, share dealing and pensions advice, all with the aim of providing a *'one stop' financial service* to customers.

Retail banks must seek to balance conflicting requirements. As profit-making organizations, they require to make loans at high rates of return, yet such rates can only be realized by accepting risk and lending on a long term basis:

CASH/BALANCES AT BANK OF ENGLAND	← ———— Liquidity ← ———— ———— → Rate of return ———— →	LONG TERM LOANS

As illustrated above, liquidity and rates of return tend to be inversely related. Cash, for example, is completely liquid but offers no return. Depositors require ready access to their funds, forcing banks to retain cash or near cash assets to meet likely withdrawals. Such action is prudent, given the huge amount of short-notice or instant-access deposits. With banks forced to pay interest to attract deposits, cash represents lost money not just dead money. Returns increase on longer-term loans but at the cost of increasing illiquidity and risk. The large provisions made recently by certain banks for bad debts show how real this risk can become in a recession.

Liquid assets include notes, coins, balances at the Bank of England, plus loans to the discount and inter-bank markets. Eligible bills, which the Bank of England will purchase through the discount market in order to remedy cash shortfalls, are also included. Collectively such assets represent as much as 25 per cent of total bank assets.

The balance is primarily composed of advances to the private sector. Traditionally such loans were made to firms rather than to individuals, but the borrowing boom in the 1980s saw this position reversed. A loan credits a customer account with the full amount upon which interest is charged, whereas an overdraft is an agreed credit limit attracting interest only on the amount overdrawn. Interest is fixed in relation to the bank's base rate, with the nature of the loan and the status of the borrower determining the margin charged. A change in base rates normally moves the whole structure of rates in parallel.

Retail bankers know their depositors will not all try to withdraw their funds on the same day, given that confidence in the bank's ability to provide cash on demand is rock solid. Suppose a 25 per cent reserve of liquidity is maintained by 'Single Bank plc' to meet such demands. If a new deposit of £1,000 is made, this will support advances credited to loan accounts not of £1,000 but of £4,000. The balance sheet will show this as follows:

SINGLE BANK PLC
Assets
Cash   £1,000
Advances   £4,000   £5,000

Liabilities
Initial deposit   £1,000
Created deposits (loans)   £4,000   £5,000

The above assumes that loans made will be redeposited in the bank. However, in a competitive banking system many of these deposits will be in rival banks, causing a net outflow of cash from Single Bank plc. This would force it to maintain a higher liquid assets ratio than it would have originally.

In practice it is more likely that all banks will create credit as new deposits are received, producing a similar outcome to the Single Bank plc situation. If there are four major clearing banks and all receive a new deposit of £1,000 and create £4,000 in new loans or overdrafts, on average one quarter will be redeposited in each bank. After cheque clearance, each should achieve the Single Bank plc balance sheet position. Things will probably not work as smoothly as this, and a somewhat higher cash ratio might have to be maintained.

Other banks and money markets

Certain markets have already been briefly mentioned. The first three discussed below, together with local authorities and inter-company markets collectively, form the *parallel* or *secondary* markets. Bank of England supervision of these has been very flexible, allowing their rapid growth.

Discount market

It borrows money at call or short notice from retail banks with surplus funds, and invests in assets that are close to maturity.

London money market

It combines the activities of retail banks, discount houses and the Bank of England, and provides short and medium-term finance.

Inter-bank market

It consists of all types of banks operating in the UK. Participants may deposit surplus funds with other banks for periods of up to 5 years. Alternatively, certificates of deposit are issued by a recipient bank.

Wholesale markets

Around 600 wholesale banks operate in the UK. They deal in large deposits that are not usually withdrawable on demand. Cash reserves are much lower than retail banks' and can be supplemented by inter-bank loans if necessary.

Merchant banks

These are primarily wholesale banks, although they still continue their original role of 'accepting' commercial bills, enabling exporters to obtain payment for goods in advance of actual settlement by the importer should they require it. Their role in business has evolved into the provision of overseas and financial services. They supply a diverse range of banking services, handle new share issues on behalf of clients, and provide consultancy on mergers and acquisitions. Established relations with corporate clients are forged in these ways, making their financial advice often crucial to the making or defending of a takeover bid.

Euro-currency markets

Overseas banks operating in London have increased rapidly in recent years. The presence of American and especially Japanese banks, whose deposits rival the collective strength of UK retail banks, reflects both the growth of Euro-currency markets centred on London and financial deregulation. The market operates with funds denominated in a currency different to that of the country in which they are deposited. Oil-exporting countries or multinationals place such funds on short-term deposit, which the bank then lends in the market. Deregulation has also attracted internationally mobile money to London, a trend accelerated by electronic fund transfer on a global basis.

Non-bank financial institutions

The importance of the insurance companies, pension funds, building societies, and unit and investment trusts that make up this group is their collective assets, which exceed those of the retail banks.

Building societies

The 1986 Building Societies Act transformed their role from specialist providers of long-term mortgage finance to the provision of more general banking and investment services. While still focused on home loans, secured on property, they can now use up to 5 per cent of their assets to make unsecured loans and other investments. They have lost no time diversifying, not only into conveyancing, valuations and estate agencies, which complement mortgage activities, but also into other financial services, such as pensions and life assurance. A Building Society Commission supervises their activities, including a minimum requirement for adequate reserve capital of 3.75 per cent of deposits.

Increased competition for retail savings has seen the demise of the cosy interest-rate cartel that operated before the legislation was passed. Mortgage business is under attack from both retail and overseas banks. The latter do not have the branch network overheads, and are active in the larger loan segment of the market. Societies are responding by restructuring through merger, as shown by their number more than halving since 1980. The number of branches peaked at nearly 7,000 in the late 1980s and is now falling back. Advances though have continued to rise strongly, despite competition, rising over fivefold in money terms during the decade. This was only possible, however, with borrowing from the wholesale markets. Other restructuring has included the Abbey National's conversion in 1989 from non-profit-making, mutual status to a public limited company.

Life insurance companies

These receive regular payments from policy-holders over a specified period, after which a lump sum will be dispensed, often 'with profits'. Premature death will trigger payment of the lump sum to specified beneficiaries.

Pension funds

In return for regular contributions during one's working life the accumulated fund provides income security for the duration of retirement. Both individuals and companies may contribute to the fund, although the self-employed must arrange personal pensions. The massive assets of pension and insurance funds are held in equities, gilts and property, and as such have a significant impact on those markets.

Unit and investment trusts

These mobilize the savings of individuals by providing participation in a diversified portfolio of shares and other assets. This gives a reduced risk, which is unavailable to the individual investor in equities with limited funds.

The capital markets

Both companies and governments have recourse to these markets when they require medium- or long-term finance. The international stock exchange comprises a *new issue* market, where companies can arrange for new securities to be offered, and a *secondary* market, where existing securities are bought and sold. The latter is nearly ten times as large as the former. Shares or equities normally carry voting rights and a value set by market forces, whereas stocks comprise fixed interest bearing gilts or company debentures redeemable at a specified date. Despite attractive privatization issues, individuals hold a decreasing proportion of shares, preferring instead less risky investment in pensions or unit trusts.

Raising finance on the Stock Exchange is expensive for all but the larger companies, since a prospectus containing a comprehensive financial listing must be provided and the advice of a merchant bank or issuing house obtained. Cheaper alternatives include a 'public placing' with a few institutions, or quotation on the Unlisted Securities Market. Existing shareholders may also be offered 'rights issues', providing the right to buy additional shares if desired; all that is required in this case is a circular to shareholders making them the offer.

The London exchange has been increasingly overshadowed by Tokyo and New York. Deregulation of the Stock Exchange, or the 'big bang', was introduced in 1986 to improve its competitive position relative to New York, which had already been deregulated, operated electronic trading and offered cheaper commissions. The Act ended fixed commission rates, distinctions between jobbers (independent market makers) and brokers (of stocks on commission for clients) and the block on takeover of Stock Exchange firms. A real time information system, known as the Stock Exchange automated quotations (SEAQ) was also introduced, virtually ending face to face transactions on the 'floor' of the Exchange. Computer trading was widely blamed for the severity of the October 1987 crash, as price falls triggered automatic 'sell' orders which reinforced the downward spiral.

Summary of business sources of finance

Finance is required to lubricate business operations. Fixed and working capital is necessary, with different sources of finance appropriate to each need. Long-term capital would normally finance the acquisition of fixed assets, whereas short-term finance is more appropriate for day to day needs.

A business will wish to maintain a balance between equity capital and other forms of long-term finance. The ratio between the two is known as gearing. Too high a ratio may cause problems in meeting the required fixed interest repayments if profits fall. Most companies therefore allow a margin of safety to meet likely variations in profits.

Short-term finance (under 1 year)

Net profits

Retained profits are a valuable source of working capital over which the business has direct control. Ploughed-back profits have always been the primary source of expansion for most firms. As the difference between total revenue and total cost, however, their size cannot be guaranteed in changing trading circumstances.

Bank overdrafts

These are normally used to cover variations in cash flow due to seasonal or unanticipated factors.

Trade credit

An increase in creditors or reduction in debtor liabilities will both provide finance for the business. Faster invoicing and reduced settlement periods will therefore enhance cash flow, but at the possible expense of customer service and competitiveness in credit terms.

Factoring

Small and medium-sized firms are very vulnerable to delayed payments by large companies, especially in times of recession. The adverse effects of this on cash flow and working capital may force an otherwise efficient firm into liquidation. Factoring provides a solution by advancing cash against credit sales. This realizes immediate liquidity for the business, reduces the risk of bad debts and allows administrative savings to be achieved.

Invoice discounting

Here the business is still responsible for collection and bad debts but receives payments of up to 75 per cent of invoice value immediately, and the balance, less a discount, on final payment. The cost of both the above, however, is often considerably more than the interest rate charged on bank advances.

Medium-term finance (1–5 years)

Bank advances

Banks provide loans to businesses over a variety of time horizons and repayment conditions. The government has encouraged banks to make medium-term loans to new and smaller companies with a loan guarantee scheme introduced in 1981.

Leasing

Apart from highly specialized plant and equipment, productive assets, including vehicles, office equipment and machine tools may now be leased. The business makes regular payments to the lessor in exchange for the use of equipment. Retail and merchant banks as well as finance houses are active in this area. For the business such arrangements prevent any drain on cash reserves, with rent being paid out of revenue created by the use of the asset. Where design and technology are improving rapidly, it also removes the risk of buying potentially obsolete equipment.

Hire purchase

This is similar to the above, in that the cost of acquiring assets may be spread over the medium term. A down payment is normally required, with the balance, including a fixed interest charge, being repaid monthly. Assets become the property of the business when the final payment is made. Although expensive in comparison to overdrafts, this form of finance is often suitable for smaller businesses, since no form of collateral security is required.

Long-term finance (over 5 years)

Share capital

A firm may raise new capital by issuing either shares or debentures. The former include ordinary and preference shares, while the latter are effectively loans, normally secured on company assets and upon which interest is guaranteed, even if the business makes little or no profit. Default would, however, allow holders to appoint a receiver, removing control of the business from the shareholders. Issuing shares, on the other hand, is an expensive business, and a merchant bank would normally be appointed to provide specialist advice. Its evaluation of the options may be seen in Table 20.1.

Mortgages

These are important in the purchase of land and buildings by commercial and industrial companies. Institutional investors are normally prepared to lend up to two-thirds of the purchase price of the property, normally repayable in regular payments over a 25-year period, using the asset as security.

Sale and lease-back

Considerable potential finance may often be found within the balance sheet. Certain assets may be surplus to current operational requirements, and reorganization may allow for their disposal. Owned assets may alternatively be sold and leased back for up to 100 years. Many companies make use of third-party contractors, as, for example, in the management of the distribution function. Companies such as TNT and NFC will buy existing vehicle fleets and facilities, and operate the whole function in return for a negotiated annual contract charge. The main drawback for business is the loss of title to the asset, which might appreciate over the period of the lease, c.g. property until recently. Repayments also add to the gearing ratio of the business.

Table 20.1   Evaluation of equity options

Options	Size of business	Cost/returns	Method
Issue by prospectus	Large	Very expensive	Prospectus published, inviting application
Issue by tender	Large	Uncertain but possible premium	Subscribe for shares at/ above specified minimum price
Rights issue	Large/medium	Cheaper but depresses share price	New shares offered in proportion to existing shareholdings
Offer for sale	Medium	Certain but lower price	Sell shares to issuing house, which then sells them at a higher price
Private placings	Small/medium	Poor marketability makes expensive	Issuing house places with institutions
Public placings	Small/medium	Very expensive	As above, but 25 per cent must be made available to the public

Euro-bond market

This competitive form of borrowing is becoming more popular with home and foreign companies alike. The bonds form longer term financial instruments for companies with access to the Euro-currency markets.

Venture capital

This is increasingly available to finance the needs of high-growth, high-technology companies without the size or track record to command risk finance from other sources. Venture capitalists often provide both finance and management expertise to assist the business. Investors in Industry (or 3i) is the best known of many organizations providing such services. It is owned by the Bank of England and a consortium of commercial banks. Such investment is extremely long-term and risky. Venture capitalists will hold a portfolio of investments, of which at least two out of every ten will fail, and only two or three at most will turn out to be runaway successes.

Government finance

Department of Trade and Industry (DTI) and government subsidies were scaled back substantially during the 1980s, reducing external finance for the nationalized industries while expanding it in other areas.

Government support for science, technology, research and development projects are intended to raise the efficiency and competitiveness of industry. The emphasis is on the successful innovation of technical advances into commercial reality. Since R & D is normally a risky process, with benefits extending beyond the innovating business itself, support is thought necessary to secure the nationally desirable level of investment.

Regional incentives were available under the current policy, which was introduced in 1984. Development areas qualified for regional development grants, while intermediate areas qualified for selective assistance only. Development grants were automatic and paid at 15 per cent of eligible capital expenditure, subject to a cost ceiling per job created. These are now being phased out, with all aid being discretionary in future. The Scottish and Welsh development agencies also provide loans and guarantees, as well as a wide range of advisory services to business.

Local support is provided through *enterprise zones and freeports*. Tax advantages include exemptions from business rates, and there are simplified planning procedures and other administrative requirements.

Regional policy also operates as part of the expanding structural fund of the European Community (EC). Aid is now being directed towards approved projects in regions of industrial decay, declining rural areas, and others with long-term and youth unemployment problems. The scale of Britain's recent deindustrialization should attract a significant proportion of these funds given that community regulations are complied with.

It is often claimed that government support is necessary because of the failure of capital markets to finance expensive and risky projects. The provision of private finance for the Channel Tunnel and North Sea oilfields appears to refute this, however, and the lack of support elsewhere may in fact be due to its judgement that only inadequate returns would arise from such projects.

Summary review

1 The availability of funds is often the constraint that prevents firms from expanding to take advantage of potential economies of scale and evolving market opportunities. Review the sources of finance in the light of Chapter 7.

2 What is the meaning of credit creation and the credit creation multiplier? Is it possible for any one retail bank to create money?

3 What is (a) a bank, and (b) a financial institution?

4 How would you suggest an established computer software company with a £20m turnover and a high debt to equity ratio raises further funding of £5m to develop a new range?

Financial control and the Bank of England

Established in 1694 and nationalized in 1946, the Bank of England has long performed the functions of a central bank and implementor of the government's monetary policies. Despite a residue of private customers, it is essentially non-profit-making, acting in the national interest by providing leadership within the framework of rules and good practice it prescribes for other financial institutions. Its main functions and corresponding objectives embrace the following:

1 *Sole issuer of notes* and coins in England and Wales, with the objective of meeting demand.
2 *Banker to central government departments*, financing their working balances to minimize debt and interest payments, in the most efficient manner.
3 *Banker to the banking system.* All retail banks maintain operational balances at the Bank of England for clearing purposes with other banks and public sector agencies. They may be required on occasion to maintain *special deposits* when the Bank of England wishes to reduce their liquidity. The Bank of England's role gives it control of the system.
4 *Exchange rate management and currency reserves.* The abolition of exchange controls has reduced this role.
   Entry into the ERM requires the Bank to buy or sell sterling to maintain its value within the bands set. It maintains accounts with overseas central banks and liaises with them closely. Many overseas countries still hold their sterling balances in the Bank of England.
5 *Advice to the government.* The bank conducts research, monitors and forecasts key financial indicators, and advises on any changes in policy or controls it deems necessary. It is the Chancellor, acting through the Treasury who is ultimately responsible. The Bank, however, works closely with the Treasury and has considerable discretion on a day to day basis.
6 *Supervision of the financial system.* Maintaining confidence in a complex, technologically sophisticated and internationally competitive financial system is a crucial requirement. Achieving the balance between fair play and competitive flexibility requires constant evolution in the rules of the game. The Banking Act of 1987 now supervises banks in a uniform manner. Requirements are evolving and cover such matters as prudential reserves, bad-debt provision, proper accounting procedures and proposed bank mergers. The Bank of England's role is regulatory.
7 *Implementation of monetary policy.* This policy affects either the price or the availability of money and credit. The measures of implementation are part of the armoury the government can draw on to pursue its objectives, but control lies with the Bank of England.

Open market operations

As manager of the national debt, the Bank is continuously engaged in buying and selling government gilt-edged securities. This process evens out the variable flow of receipts and payments between the public and private sector. Since the sale of gilts brings corresponding payments to the Bank, it is in a position to drain away deposits held by the retail banks, forcing them to restrict loans and advances. Conversely, redeeming gilts will inject extra deposits into the banking system. Such operations will also affect gilt prices and hence interest rates. These operations are important, although until recently public sector surpluses have reduced the volume of gilt sales.

Funding

This process converts short-term, high-interest debt into longer- dated securities. Retail banks hold Treasury bills and other government stock with less than a year to maturity as part of their liquid assets. Reduced quantities may therefore force them to curtail advances. Treasury bill issues, however, had also fallen to very low levels now reversed by the return to budget deficits.

Liquidity ratio controls

These were formerly of great importance in the control of bank lending. Individual banks are now expected to maintain what they themselves consider to be prudent levels of liquidity. They must, however, operate procedures for monitoring these levels that the central bank may scrutinize. Non-retail banks also face formal regulation covering their ability to manage reserves. Since 1981 the remaining cash ratio requirement for most banks is the holding of 0.5 per cent of eligible liabilities in non-interest-bearing cash balances at the Bank. These 'free' funds provide the income to finance the central bank functions. Liquidity ratio controls have not been used since 1982.

Lender of the last resort

Discount houses perform an important role in maintaining liquidity in the financial system. Should retail banks find they need additional cash to settle accounts, they know they can demand their money at 'call'. Surplus cash, on the other hand, may be readily invested to earn interest. Heavy net cash demands from the banks would force the discount houses to raise short-term interest rates in order to attract extra funds, and *vice versa*. To avoid such volatility and smooth the flow of funds, the Bank of England will normally intervene to buy the bills at going interest rates when cash is short, or sell bills if there is excess cash to soak up.

Interest rates

Currently the primary instrument of monetary policy employed by the government is interest rates, although the overriding factor in setting them is the need to meet ERM obligations. If the Bank wishes to change interest rates in a particular direction, it will vary the rate at which it will offer to buy or sell bills, in effect indicating to the market its views as to the appropriate level. If necessary it can, through open market operations, create the conditions that force the discount houses to use it as the lender of last resort. Starved of cash, they are forced to pay the higher interest rate, and restore their profit margins by passing on the increase. This higher rate then affects interest rates throughout the market.

The Bank normally leaves rates to be determined by the market, but intervenes when appropriate to give a clear signal of its intentions. Entry into the ERM has now made interest-rate management crucial to the maintenance of the value of the pound.

Quantitative controls

Physical measures to limit lending have been used extensively in the past. Directives to limit lending to particular groups such as property developers and personal borrowers while exempting small businesses and exporters have also been employed. Such rationing of credit, while effective for short periods, tended to encourage evasion. The development of secondary financial markets undermined controls such as the 'corset' in the 1970s. Quantitative controls are no longer used.

Monetarism and the medium-term financial strategy (MTFS)

Monetary policy took second place to fiscal policy during the period of Keynesian fine tuning. However, as accelerating inflation brought disillusion with the Phillips curve trade-off, so monetarism was introduced to rein back aggregate demand and restore control over prices. The Thatcherite doctrine of reduced state intervention in the activities of business shifted the policy focus towards the financial framework.

The task of raising output and employment was seen as secondary to inflation control, and was left to supply-side economic policies. The control of inflation was seen as primary because:

- The allocative function of relative prices would be restored.
- Competitiveness would be improved.
- Interest rates would fall, providing the main stimulus to increased investment and economic recovery, thus creating the conditions for sustained growth.
- Any associated business failures would be transitional, and serve to weed out accumulated inefficiency.
- It would force employers to resist unrealistic pay claims and pursue productivity improvements.

Summary of the MTFS

1 *Aim* – A stable non-inflationary environment.
2 *Method*
   (a) Control of the money supply, using MTFS as the regulator.
   (b) Supply-side policies to stimulate growth and employment.
3 *Means*
   (a) Declining targets of £M3 over a 4–5-year time scale.
   (b) Dampen wage–price inflationary expectations.
   (c) Use of interest rates and debt funding, not direct controls.
   (d) Tight fiscal policy to reduce the PSBR through reduced government spending.
   (e) A floating exchange rate, which deflated the economy as the pound rose (import prices fell).

The MTFS was revolutionary when first introduced. It signalled the end of fine tuning, it being argued that highly active and discretionary fiscal policies risked damaging the economy by misleading investors and consumers. The medium-term objective of a balanced budget would provide a clear and simple discipline for keeping public debt factor under control.

Monetarist philosophy

Monetarism was based on the belief, as expressed by Friedman, that 'inflation is always and everywhere a monetary phenomenon'. The rate of monetary growth was viewed as a powerful influence on the rate of inflation in the medium term. As argued earlier, any stimulus below the natural rate would achieve only a short-term and temporary effect on growth and employment, maintainable only at the cost of accelerating inflation.

It was recognized that any slowing of monetary growth would inevitably reduce output and employment until inflation responded to treatment. The speed of the adjustment, and therefore the cost in jobs, depended on how fast inflationary expectations and wage demands responded. It was hoped that the speed of this adjustment process could be raised by setting credible medium-term targets for reduced monetary growth and then sticking to them.

Friedman argued that the first and most important lesson that history teaches about monetary policy is the need to prevent money itself becoming a major source of disturbance. Since erratic changes in monetary growth were seen as creating potent forces for disequilibrium, the aim should be to stabilize the growth of money supply in line with the growth of transactions demand in the economy.

Monetary policy instruments operate with a long and often variable time lag. They affect the financial system in either price (interest and exchange rates) or quantity (of money and credit availability) terms. These in turn influence real economic decisions through the *transmission mechanism*. This either impacts directly on prices through the quantity of money formula (according to monetarists) or indirectly through interest rates (according to Keynesians).

The problems of monetarist control

Monetarists assumed that the precise money supply could be determined by policy-makers. In practice it proved difficult to identify the quantity of money for which targets could be set, leading one observer to label monetarism 'the uncontrollable in the pursuit of the indefinable'.

The main measures to be targeted are as follows:

- £M0 = notes + coin in circulation + operational balances at the Bank of England.
- £M1 = notes + coin + private sector sight bank deposits.
- £M3 = M1 + private sector time deposits + certificates of deposit.
- £M4 = M3 + net building-society deposits.

Deregulation and increasing financial sophistication, however, had made assets more liquid. The above measures tended to understate their growth, so that in practice monetary targets proved impossible to attain and their role was de-emphasized after 1981. M3, for example, was planned to rise by around 40 per cent over the first 4 years of the MTFS. In fact it rose by nearer 70 per cent and was phased out in 1985. Only M0, which represents the transactions demand for money, is still targeted, with a range between 0 and 4 per cent for 1991–2.

Monetary control was loose relative to fiscal policy over the 1980s, as seen in Figure 20.1.

Broad money (M4) grew strongly, despite the falling path of inflation. The closer correspondence of M0 perhaps explains its retention as a target. The fact that money does matter, however, was clearly demonstrated in the credit boom of the late 1980s. The strong growth in incomes, combined with an explosion of personal credit, which more than tripled over the decade, provided the motive power for expansion. Savings slumped from 14 per cent of personal income to as low as 4 per cent, as excess monetary growth was translated into:

- A house price boom.
- A share price boom.

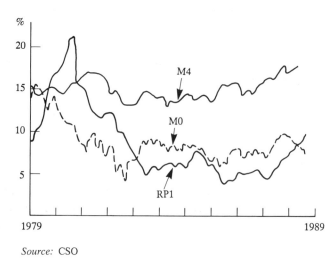

Source: CSO

Figure 20.1   *Broad and narrow money targets and the RPI, 1979–89*

- A consumer durables spending boom.
- An overseas investment boom, adding £100bn to net assets.

Financial market liberalization, associated with the ending of the 'corset' restrictions on bank lending in 1980, and the onset of vigorous competition between retail banks and the building societies, underpinned this credit boom. Individuals borrowed on the strength of windfall property gains, or 'traded up', causing their liabilities for mortgages, bank loans and credit card debts to double as a percentage of pre-tax incomes. Interest rates, which had been managed to maintain a competitive exchange rate, were forced into a belated correction, rising by 5 per cent in just one year.

Entry into the ERM may be viewed as a reaction to this loss of control. Commitment to an exchange rate target provides credibility for the government's anti-inflation stance. Exchange rate stability requires monetary stability, since policy must be co-ordinated to other currencies, especially the German mark. Any relaxation of interest rates, unjustified by falling inflation, would put downward pressure on sterling and undermine stability.

The inevitable consequence is that the trade sector once again bears the brunt of adjustment, as in 1979, when manufacturing output fell by 18 per cent in real terms and an unexpected million was added to the jobless total.

The debate on how to ensure stability has therefore come full circle. If monetary control does not provide the answer, what is to be done? Experience suggests that simple rules to guide policy do not work sufficiently well in periods of turbulent change. Both fiscal and monetary targets have been found wanting, forcing politicians to use their discretion. Current policy reflects a learning from experience in its blend of interest rate control, on the one hand, and a relaxation of public expenditure limits, on the other. A budget deficit to cushion the recession provides a degree of stabilization, and should allow investment in vitally needed infrastructure renewal to at least moderate the rise in the long-term unemployed.

Summary review

1 What are the main changes in recent years to the methods by which the Bank of England controls retail banks?

2 Interest rate is the essential instrument of monetary control. How does the Bank exercise control?

3 Why has it proved so difficult to control the money supply?

4 Why is a medium-term strategy thought to be better for business than short-term intervention to manage the economy by means of tax and expenditure changes?

21
What can be done about inflation and unemployment?

Aims

The aims of this chapter are as follows:

- To understand the importance of a credible anti-inflation policy if unnecessary unemployment is to be avoided.
- To draw conclusions regarding the effective control of inflation.
- To distinguish alternative approaches to deal with the problem of unemployment.
- To assess the effectiveness of current policies towards the unemployed.
- To analyse the sources of economic growth and one approach to its achievement.

Glossary

Adjustment mechanism – this refers to the links between the money supply and changes in prices. If money growth is controlled, this will reduce spending, either directly, or by raising interest rates.

Capital output ratio – the amount of capital stock required to produce national income.

Golden triangle – the area within lines connecting Birmingham, Milan and Cologne.

Lifetime hours – number of years worked × number of weeks per year × number of hours per week.

Organizational slack – arises where businesses with market power earn acceptable rather than maximum profits. The excess cost is reflected in unnecessary staffing and other forms of expenditure.

Secular stagnation – predicted by Marx as market economies experienced a succession of crises based on the declining profitability of industry.

Sunrise sectors – high technology industries with considerable growth potential, e.g. electronics, biotechnology and IT.

Wage drift – the tendency for earnings to exceed wage rates. The differences arise from overtime, bonuses or other payments above agreed rates.

Background

Inflation is at root a monetary phenomenon. People worry about money when they don't have enough, especially when prices are rising. Governments worry when there is too much of it, fearing inflation. In fact any inflation not accompanied by a corresponding rise in the money supply will be starved of fuel. The shortage of money causes interest rates to rise, choking off aggregate demand and closing the inflationary gap.

The solution appears obvious – prevent any rise in the money supply and the adjustment mechanism will do the rest. This monetarist prescription fails to answer certain questions, however:

- How fast should adjustment take place?
- Can the money supply be accurately controlled?
- Is the political cost of adjustment in terms of unemployment and reduced output acceptable?
- Is there a less painful adjustment process?
- Need inflation be squeezed out completely?

If the problem is to break inflationary expectations that rest on the belief that the government will continue to accommodate higher wages and prices by expanding demand, then the government must convince wage- and price-setters that it will no longer underwrite inflation. Inflationary expectations would rationally then stop dead in their tracks without any loss of output or jobs. The medium-term financial strategy introduced by the Conservatives in 1979 gave notice of its intention to squeeze out inflation by progressively tightening monetary and fiscal policy. In the event inflation fell, but at a massive cost in jobs and manufactured output.

The credibility of anti-inflationary policy

After years of high spending and borrowing by governments it was thought that a U-turn would be made before the promised cuts took effect. The hard lessons learnt when this did not happen should lend more conviction to current pledges by government to purge the economy of inflation. What is important therefore is the credibility of the government's anti-inflation stance. This explains the government's current commitment to the ERM. Transfer of the power to print money to a constitutionally independent central bank with a tradition of financial rectitude, as in Germany, might convince price-setters that the government is serious about controlling inflation.

Membership of the ERM ties the government's hands on monetary policy. Until inflation is brought under control, interest rates must be kept high to prevent the pound falling through the bottom of its permitted range. Entry should therefore have applied a short, sharp shock to inflationary expectations, enabling a reduction in actual inflation to occur without the pain of deep recession. The reality of sharply rising job losses, however, suggests this has not occurred. The explanation may be that ERM entry lacked credibility, owing to the government's failure to convince observers that a devaluation was definitely out of the question.

A largely discredited approach for painlessly rupturing inflating expectations is a *prices and incomes policy*. The attractive pay-offs available if all parties play to the rules of the game would unfortunately require an ideal world. Such policies implied interference with efficient market forces and an admission that governments were unable to tackle the root causes of the problem. An argument may, however, be made for temporary controls placed alongside a government pledge to remove excess demand. Even when action taken to stop printing money, cut government spending and raise taxes convinces wage- and price-setters that inflation will be removed it will not be rational for any one group to act first to halt increases until they are certain other groups have done so.

The aim is to reduce pay pressure for a given level of unemployment. Unfortunately those who demand and obtain excessive wage rises are seldom those who are punished by the resulting unemployment. Similarly self-interest places maximum value on achieving a high pay rise when everyone else receives a low one. However, this is likely to lead to a scramble for pay at the expense of both lower inflation and higher employment. Since the alternative of mutual restraint requires mutual guarantees and enforceable sanctions to ensure fair play, a case may be made for a temporary but universal wage and price freeze.

Sharp shock or gradualism?

Another important question is whether inflation responds best and with least cost in lost jobs and output to a short, sharp shock or more gradual treatment. Latin American hyper-inflation has been tamed by combining a fiscal squeeze, monetary reform and various controls. Bolivia reduced its inflation from 20,000 per cent to zero in weeks during 1985, using such methods. However, curing hyper-inflation where the currency has already been largely rejected is a different proposition to eradicating high but relatively stable inflation that society has learnt to live with.

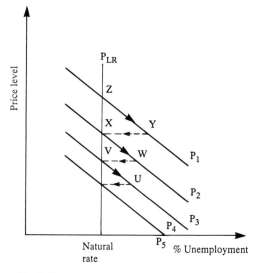

Figure 21.1   *The breaking of inflationary expectations*

It has been argued that to break inflationary expectations requires a reduction in demand pressure, represented by a move along the short-run Phillips curve from, say, point Z to point Y in Figure 21.1. Once this has forced price- and wage-setters to adjust their behaviour to reduced inflationary expectations, activity and employment can rise to point X, the natural rate. Further deflation to point W will continue this process of reducing inflationary expectations, although less unemployment may be required if lessons have been learnt from the earlier experience. However, the lower inflation is pressed, the more resistant public and political opposition is likely to become.

It has already been argued that gentle inflation can have a stimulating effect on the economy, whereas a long period of above NAIRU rates might undermine work skills and attitudes, shifting the long-run curve to the right. The uncertainties of predicting the natural rate in practice have led to a questioning of its usefulness in policy terms. On the other hand, living with inflation rather than acting to reduce it gradually may create a base level for future price surges.

The above discussion suggests the following guidelines regarding the effective control of inflation:

- Control monetary growth in broad terms as a long-term policy, and avoid destabilizing swings in its rate of growth.
- Adhere to announced spending plans and resist any temptation to fine tune the economy.
- Maintain a margin of spare capacity, consistent with the natural unemployment rate.
- Maintain supply-side policy initiatives, to stimulate aggregate supply and reduce the natural rate.
- Index transfer payments to protect weak bargaining groups.
- Make monetary discipline independent of governmental discretionary influence.

The margin of safety

This was suggested by F.W. Paish in the 1960s. He argued that while such a margin would produce higher rates of unemployment in the short run, it would avoid the dangers of an overheated economy and accelerating inflation. The logic of the natural rate of unemployment idea and acknowledged inability of governments to fine tune demand suggests this approach might produce a better average outcome over time.

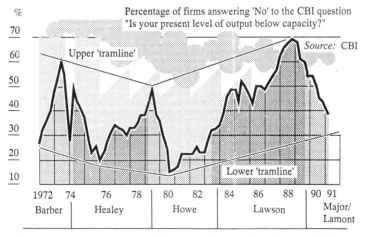

Figure 21.2   *Capacity utilization. Source FT, 31 Jan. 1991*

The tramlines in Figure 21.2 connect the upper and lower points of the economic cycle. If politicians could lower their sights and maintain a safety margin of capacity, then the peak of inflation and troughs of unemployment might be avoided.

What is clear is that inflation not only damages industrial competitiveness when it is increasing but also when it is brought under control. Government commitment to halting inflation causes uncertainty as to which specific policies will be used. Higher interest rates and the consequent rise in the exchange rate will adversely affect long-term plans for research, product development, investment and process innovation. The need for recurrent policy initiatives against inflation should be avoided at all costs; a stop–go cycle in inflation and its control would be the worst of both worlds for Britain's international competitiveness.

Finally it may be noted that if election outcomes are studied, there is considerable advantage in controlling inflation. No government that has significantly increased prices while in office has ever been re-elected. In contrast, those that have adopted price control as a major priority have usually proved victorious.

Summary review

1 Why is inflation so difficult to cure?

2 Draw up a balance sheet of positive and negative effects arising out of a determined effort by government to eliminate inflation completely.

3 How would you criticize the gradualist approach to reducing inflation?

Policy approaches for unemployment

A number of possible approaches to getting an economy back to work can be identified. It must be remembered, however, that Britain is an open economy, reliant on trade, and international considerations will frequently constrain its freedom of action in this respect.

Conservative policy approaches might be said to have progressed from helping the unemployed:

- to helping the unemployed to help themselves,
- to helping business to help the unemployed, and
- to helping to train workers without jobs to fill jobs without workers.

It must be recognized that in the process there were well over 2 million net new jobs created in the period 1985–90. Whether this was a result of creative accounting, creative incentives or creative policies is, however, a matter of some debate.

From the analysis of causes in Chapter 17, policies may be divided logically into those that:

- Stimulate the demand for labour directly.
- Reduce the number of job-seekers.
- Improve the matching of the unemployed to available jobs.
- Share out the available work.
- Increase domestic employment at the expense of foreigners.

Each type of unemployment may also require a tailored policy approach.

Job creation

Policies to generate more jobs must meet the criteria of sustainability. Real jobs are not protected by hidden subsidies or made possible only with extra demand pressure, leading to higher price rises than overseas competitors. Unemployment will only fall if the growth in national output exceeds the growth of the labour force and output per worker. With the latter two factors both growing strongly, output has to rise even faster.

Counter-cyclical policies

Keynesian analysis has defined the framework for producing sustainable growth in income and employment. Unfortunately the techniques to forecast and fine tune aggregate demand within the necessary margins of error and safety have so far proved inadequate. A Keynesian stimulus may still be used when substantial unemployment exists, especially where pressing capital expenditure programmes with low import content are the chosen means, e.g. sewer replacement, civil engineering, road improvements, etc. Such policies would 'prime pump' the economy, producing multiplier and accelerator reactions resulting in a cumulative expansion of aggregate demand and jobs in the rest of the economy.

Attempts to raise output to a fully employed level have, however, been found to carry many dangers:

- Is there spare capacity for industry to respond with?
- Won't employers and unions bid up wages and use higher demand to justify price and profit rises?
- Will extra state expenditure 'crowd out' private sector spending?
- As higher incomes are spent, won't imports be sucked in, with no matching rise in exports?
- Will business believe the stimulus to be sustainable and therefore invest, or will it merely work plant more intensively and raise prices?

Prices and incomes policy v pricing workers out of jobs

The tendency for wages and prices to rise as higher employment and output are achieved chokes off the sustainability of further growth. It is not surprising therefore that prices and incomes policies were suggested as means of relaxing this constraint to higher employment. If, as in Figure 21.3 the Phillips curve could be converted into a horizontal wage norm at

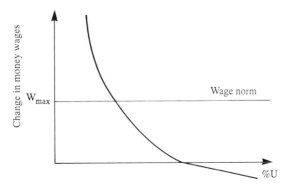

Figure 21.3 *The wage norm and Phillips curve*

W_{max}, then full employment would be achieved without inflation. Everyone would gain, since demand could be expanded to ensure maximum resources are employed. While attractive in principle, this overriding of the market mechanism has proved ineffectual in practice.

The interests of powerful groups whose labour was in very high demand were not served by the norm and they sought to evade it. Skill shortages also caused employers to circumvent the norm in order to recruit, retain and motivate their workforces. Various bonuses and fringe benefits were the chosen means of rewarding extra effort and productivity; this had the effect of breaking the norm and producing 'wage drift'.

The norm operated as a price ceiling (Figure 21.4), preventing adjustment to the market clearing wage W_e. In effect it created excess demand for labour at the wage norm, acting like a lid placed on a boiling pan. It held down wage pressure in the short term but eventually led to a compensating pay explosion.

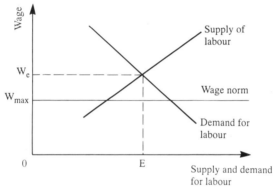

Figure 21.4   *Microeconomic effects of a norm*

The longer the norm remained in effect, the greater the allocational inefficiencies it created. Attempts to make the policy more flexible included exceptional increases for such reasons as higher productivity, low pay and labour shortages. Any union negotiators worth their salt were able to argue a special case, using such criteria.

Subsidies v pricing workers out of jobs

Temporary employment or recruitment subsidies and youth employment programmes have been used to alleviate certain hardcore types of unemployment. Reducing the real cost of labour to employers without reducing real wages to workers might be justified as a means of relief in hard times. The net cost may be low when savings in unemployment benefit are taken into account, especially when recipients would be otherwise very unlikely to obtain work. As such, they could be used as a stopgap measure until more constructive policies were developed.

The main criticism is that such supports would merely delay inevitable adjustment to structural change. They would be costly to administer and susceptible to abuse. They would tend to be maintained as a permanent subsidy of in effect *artificial jobs*, which might only serve to displace jobs elsewhere in the economy.

However, if the long-term unemployed are excluded from the labour market and exert little pressure on pay levels, then a strong case can be made for their retraining and redeployment. Active labour market policies of the type deployed in Sweden have been geared to this end. Training and mobility subsidies are linked to careful job matching, while benefits are withdrawn from those not taking up the opportunities on offer. Retraining focused on skill shortage areas has the added benefit of reducing pay pressures as businesses seek to expand.

Industrial growth policy v structural and technological unemployment

A succession of post-war governments attempted to nurture new growth industries as an antidote to structural decline. Efforts focused on identification of so-called 'sunrise sectors' in the early growth stage of their life-cycle. Injections of government funding for research and development would take place, supported by initial government contracts.

While support for innovation is acknowledged to be the means of avoiding secular stagnation, the problem lies with the identification of 'winning' technologies and their timely and effective exploitation. Given the very patchy record of commercial success by governments in this respect, e.g. Concorde, advanced gas-cooled reactors, many have concluded that their role should be less actively interventionist, and they should concentrate instead on creating the right climate for structural and technological change. The state is well placed for encouraging fundamental change in attitudes and institutions, not least in the sphere of education and training. Britain has proved adept in the realm of basic research, invention and creative ideas, but less than impressive in their successful application.

It should be noticed that supply-side policies designed to raise labour productivity are part of this approach to job creation. Productivity growth is the source of real income improvement and competitiveness. Growth in output per person means businesses earn more profit, or can afford to pay more without increasing prices. Lower wage costs per unit of output therefore allow faster growth for a given inflation rate.

In the short run any measure that results in improved organization and methods or process innovation will tend to displace labour. A dramatic pruning of the UK manufacturing base in the early 1980s was proof of this, as years of accumulated inefficiency and organizational slack were extinguished by exposure to intense competition and cost pressure. The pay-off in terms of strong productivity growth and sharply improved competitiveness helped to alleviate the balance of payments constraints; and underpinned a sustained expansion in investment and jobs without immediately boosting imports and widening the trade deficit.

Such improvement, however, takes time and ultimately depends on the initiatives of private business. It is by necessity a continuous process, which will be neutralized if other countries succeed in raising productivity and competitiveness at a faster rate.

Policies to reduce the supply of labour

Such policies can be regarded as crisis responses to politically unacceptable levels of unemployment. Unless there is a latent desire on behalf of workers voluntarily to reduce their lifetime hours worked, they must be regarded as devices to share the pain of unemployment more equitably across society.

An increased school-leaving age, higher participation rates in higher education and retraining sabbaticals constitute the more constructive means of reducing job-seekers. A permanently higher proportion of the working age population in some form of training provides a once and for all reduction, and should raise skill and educational levels into the bargain. This assumes that educational standards are enhanced through a linkage of provision to the needs of future employers.

Increased holidays, fewer hours, job-sharing and early retirement seek to reduce lifetime hours worked through the sharing out of available work. Eliminating overtime is often seen as one means of achieving this objective, for employers would have to take on extra staff. However, despite high rates of overtime, especially in manufacturing, its elimination would pose problems:

- It would be difficult to group hours into full-time jobs, since the need fluctuates with variation in sales.
- Overtime provides instant flexibility to ease short-term bottlenecks.
- It often comprises essential work to be done outside normal hours, e.g. maintenance.
- It provides a cushion against demand falls, which might otherwise force redundancy of core workers.
- It would be difficult to recruit unemployed people with necessary skills in many cases, and would call for extra induction and training courses from employers.

Despite their superficial attractiveness and fairness such measures should be treated with extreme caution. In a growing economy the choice between more income or fewer hours is acceptable, but not in a depressed economy, where less work or early retirement must mean less income. If this were not the case, then employers would be faced with higher wage costs. Whether this led to higher prices or lower profits, it would damage competitiveness, the incentive to invest and long-term job prospects. This would be avoided if productivity rose sufficiently to compensate for the lost hours, but no new job opportunities would then be created. Finally, such policies might be very difficult to reverse once a recovery took place.

Policies to improve labour market efficiencies v short-term unemployment

Markets in general and labour markets in particular do not work at all perfectly, owing to failures of one kind or another. If these failures could be overcome, a quicker and more accurate matching of supply and demand for labour could take place. Active labour market policies mentioned above are employed extensively in Scandinavia, and are claimed to have resulted in unemployment rates of 2 per cent or less.

The various frictions and the policies to help overcome them are detailed below.

Imperfect knowledge

The lack of accurate and up to date knowledge of job requirements and labour availabilities applies equally to businesses and individuals. Such information is not freely or easily available and must be largely provided by the state through, for example:

1 A public employment service to facilitate matching via a national network of job centres linked by computer. Many private agencies also perform this role in the more lucrative sectors, such as computer programmers and secretarial staff.
2 Vocational and career guidance to match aptitudes to jobs.

3 Improved forecasting of future skill requirements. This should underpin manpower planning by individual businesses. Success in managing sustainable economic growth without recurrent or severe cyclical fluctuations would, however, contribute most to effective business planning.

Immobility of labour

Real time information systems showing vacancies across the regions is needed. Immobility of labour can also be combated by specific policies to assist mobility, e.g. travel warrants, and assistance with housing and removals, resettlement allowances, etc.

Inappropriate skills

Retraining would form a rational investment for many of the unemployed, but there may be unacceptable risks and costs. Initiatives by the state in employment training will therefore be necessary to realize a socially efficient level of provision. The new Technical and Education Councils (TECs) have sought to ensure that business needs and priorities are fully reflected in the programmes provided.

Heterogeneous needs

It is assumed that labour is homogeneous in perfect competition theory; in practice, however, this is far from the truth, with numerous disadvantaged groups contributing to hardcore unemployment. Special measures to promote employment among groups such as the disabled or ethnic minorities in inner cities are therefore economically justifiable.

Note that statutory encouragement to employ the handicapped already exists, as do laws outlawing discrimination.

Transport costs

Although significantly scaled back in the 1980s, regional policies partly financed by the European Community have stimulated employment in the North of Britain. Distance from the main markets and the south-east, and the so-called *golden triangle of Europe*, produces a competitive disadvantage.

A variety of regional investment grants, training subsidies, rent and rate rebates, and other sweeteners have lured many footloose multinationals into these regions, regenerating the local economies. Local authorities and development agencies have become very professional in promoting the attractiveness of their areas. State investment in roads and other infrastructure has also assisted in the process of revival.

Freedom of entry and exit

There are many impediments to the unrestricted operation of labour markets. Despite legislation, bias in recruitment extends in many directions, by age, sex, class, race and religion, to name just a few. Barriers to employment and mobility are often maintained by professional associations, trade unions or just custom and practice. Concerns over dilution of skills, e.g. teachers, demarcations, wage differentials, and job security serve to limit the freedom of movement. Efforts designed to weaken the power of vested interests that protect jobs, however, have to balance achievement of freer access with the need to ensure that service and performance standards are maintained.

Rationality

Mention has already been made of those caught in the poverty or employment trap. Taking employment would leave them worse off. Restructuring tax and benefit payments to remove these disincentives could transform the situation.

Conclusions

While policies to deal with all the types of unemployment that have been distinguished exist, a serious question mark hangs over their long-term effectiveness. It serves no real purpose if unemployment is reduced in the short term, only for the problem to magnify in the long term. Any policies proposed must also be financed by taxation or borrowing, thereby affecting incentives or increasing inflationary pressures.

Unemployment reduced below its natural rate cannot be sustained, yet there is no agreement as to what that rate is. Some of the policies above are in any case intended to reduce the natural rate itself, especially those designed to improve labour market efficiency. The situation experienced in 1990, when extreme skill shortages coincided with national unemployment of 1.6 million, seemed to allow scope for significant improvement, yet inflation was also over 10 per cent. This suggested a natural rate of close to 7 per cent, well above the unemployment rate then prevailing in the South-east.

The fact that deepening recession and mounting job losses in early 1991 had done little to moderate pay settlements or unit costs provided ample proof of *wage rigidities*. The CBI believes that industry cannot afford unit labour costs to grow above 2 per cent per annum inside the ERM. Yet with productivity actually declining, unit labour costs were running at 12.5 per cent, their highest level since 1981 (Figure 21.5). With sterling values pegged by the ERM, a squeeze on trade-sensitive manufacturing employment seemed inevitable.

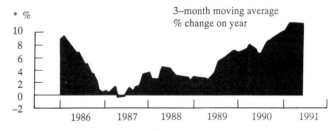

Source: CSO, Department of Employment

Figure 21.5 *Manufacturing unit labour costs*

Figure 21.6 indicates the disparity between British and European wage levels. The failure of wages to respond quickly to rising unemployment is the perennial weakness of the British labour market. Government reforms may have succeeded in making wage relativities more flexible, but not the average level. In 1980 earnings peaked during the second quarter of the recession, whereas in 1991 there was still no convincing evidence of this until after the third quarter of negative growth.

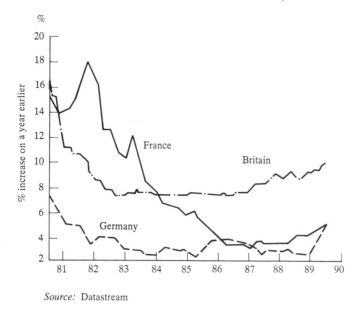

Source: Datastream

Figure 21.6 *Wage trends in Britain, France and Germany*

Businesses have preferred to respond to contraction by cutting investment and employment. Unemployment had risen to over 2.5 million by early 1992 and looked set to rise towards 3 million by the year end, with the government appearing no further forward than it was a decade ago.

The UK's entry into the ERM is now seen as the macroeconomic policy that will deliver stability and low inflation without the need for deep government-induced recessions of the type Britain has now experienced twice in a decade.

Surviving a recession

Britain was officially in recession in mid-February 1991 after production had fallen by 1.2 per cent and 0.9 per cent in consecutive quarters. A humorous Yorkshire definition pinpoints its arrival at the moment when even the customers who have no intention of paying stop giving you orders! Its effects, however, are anything but humorous on the worst affected sectors, such as construction, vehicles and retailing.

The ability of British industry to withstand this recession should, however, be better than 10 years ago, given the restructuring that has taken place although the following points make clear this is not always the case:

- The manufacturing sector is now much less significant, and foreign ownership has increased to around one-fifth of the total. Many foreign plants are central to European strategies, and are not likely to be at risk.
- A cushion of improved profitability now exists, although financial deregulation has encouraged corporate indebtedness to grow. The privatized monopolies are especially well placed to increase investment.

- Smaller companies' share of manufacturing, output and employment has risen. Although flexible, they are also more dependant on borrowing and the domestic market, so for many recession will be the first real test of their management in depth.
- The trend is towards smaller manufacturing plants, with the proportion of the workforce employed in plants over 1,500 falling from one-third to one-fifth.
- Privatization of major employers, such as BT, has made their reaction to the recession very different to that of 1980. Their continued transformation into more commercial businesses may combine with falling demand to force large job cuts.
- Substantial improvement in manufacturing productivity and investment has increased international competitiveness, but rapid inflation is eroding it.
- The recession has severely undermined recent progress towards restoring Britain's manufacturing base. Fixed capital expenditure per employee was still 30 per cent below that of European competitors, and only two-fifths of Japanese levels, before falling sharply with recession. Fixed investment trends are shown in Figure 21.7.

UK manufacturing industry

Total gross fixed investment, seasonally adjusted at 1985 prices (£m)

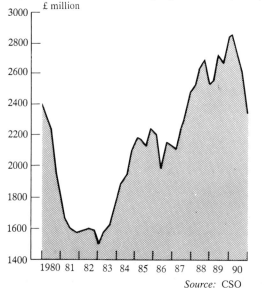

Source: CSO

Figure 21.7 *UK manufacturing industry*

- Recession lays bare management deficiencies previously masked by high growth. A broad range of measures designed to cut costs and expenditures must be flexibly introduced. Customers must still be carefully nurtured however, if their loss to eager competitors is to be avoided.

The nature of the growth process

The determination of national income based on a balance of injection and leakages in the circular flow is a short-run and static analysis. Investment is viewed as producing fluctuations in income and employment around a given capacity, rather than raising the potential capacity itself.

This dynamic process is termed *economic growth*, and has the effect of shifting out the production possibility curve (Figure 21.8) from aa to bb. Such growth must be distinguished from that arising out of increased utilization of existing capacity as occurs in the movement from x to y. Without real growth the combination of public and marketable goods shown at z is unattainable. In principle there are two main ways of achieving this.

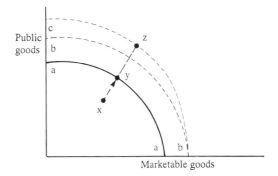

Figure 21.8   *Production possibility curve (PPC)*

Increased resources

New resources are seldom free, and investment is normally required to locate, develop and utilize them. Additional workers have to be raised, oil wells drilled; factories built and equipment installed. Extra resources will transform production possibilities for all goods, producing a parallel outward shift of the PPC (aa to bb in Figure 21.8).

New methods and technology

Improvement in the productivity of resources arises out of new products, technologies and methodologies. These are achieved through investment of resources in research and development. Since most advances tend to be specific to particular resources or industries, the PPC will pivot from bb to bc (Figure 21.8). This might represent improved productivity in the health service through the development of new preventive drugs. The higher investment required to facilitate both of the outward movements described above must, however, be financed. This would normally mean a sacrifice of current consumption and living standards.

The British economy

Economic growth as an expansion of real GDP is often expressed in per capita terms to allow for population increase. Although economic growth does not necessarily lead to economic progress, it has characterized the economic history of the industrialized world for the best part of two centuries. Adam Smith, entitling his work *An inquiry into the nature and causes of the wealth of nations*, clearly viewed the process as of prime concern. It remains today a central preoccupation for most politicians whose election promises have frequently fuelled over-optimistic expectations. Its political attraction lies in its ability to make all constituents better off and electorally well disposed.

Britain has been repeatedly criticized for her comparatively poor growth performance. All too often she has been placed bottom of the annual growth league, allowing once poorer countries, such as Germany, France, Japan and Italy, to overhaul and outpace her in the post-war period.

There are no firm conclusions on the causes of economic growth or why international growth rates differ. E.F. Denison isolated sixteen separate factors and attempted to measure their relative significance in the period 1950–62, yet was unable to explain over half the differential growth between Britain and West Germany.

The causes of growth have to do with the quantity, quality and distribution of resources, as follows:

- *Increase in the quantity of factors* – growth in labour force, activity rates, hours, migration, investment per employee.
- *Augmenting the quality of factors* – technological improvements, human capital and knowledge, reduced capital/output ratio.
- *Size of the market* – to allow full economies of scale.
- *Structural factors* – redistribution of resources from low to high productivity sectors, e.g. agriculture to industry; mobility of labour and capital.
- *Management of the economy* – to ensure operation on the PPC.

International growth rates will differ to the extent the above factors vary. Britain, for example, has shown a much greater preference for consumption than Germany and Japan, where high savings ratios support higher investment rates. A preference for prestigious R & D and difficulty in providing technical training have added to Britain's weaknesses.

The size of the market is less of a constraint, with entry into the EC and moves towards the Single European Market. The Japanese, however, already possess a large and relatively well-protected market, which provides them with a springboard for overseas sales. It is the competitiveness as much as the size of the market that is important. British firms are comparatively large in Europe yet not always efficient, perhaps reflecting over-concentration and monopoly power.

Michael Porter, in *Competitive advantage of nations*, argues that industries should be constantly stimulated and challenged through strong competitive measures. In contrast, successive governments have either neglected or cocooned British business. They have acted as midwife to a series of mergers and amalgamations to produce *national champions* to defend British industrial interests. The futility of such efforts may be measured by the fate of the TV, vehicle and mainframe computer industries.

Japan, in contrast, boasts a structure blending government initiative in the form of the Ministry of International Trade and Industry (MITI) with fiercely competitive markets possessing too many rather than too few combatants. This stimulates creative dynamism rather than barriers to entry and change.

The failure of economic management to allow Britain to operate on the PPC may also be compared to the success of Japan and Germany, where emphasis on tight money and limited state expenditure helped to produce low inflation and low taxation. These fed into a virtuous circle of self-sustaining growth and high employment.

The substantial residual

Growth differences between countries are thought to arise from qualitative influences rooted in culture and the social structure as much as economics. Factors relevant to Britain might include:

- Custom and practice at work.
- Attitudes resistant to change.
- Class divisions producing us versus them attitudes.
- Elitist education system.
- Outmoded institutions inappropriate to modern needs.
- Emphasis on pure research and low status for industry.
- Lack of professional status and qualifications in management.

Such factors were central to an understanding of the *British disease*. Restrictive practices produced lamentable productivity comparisons with our competitors in the 1960s and 1970s. Examples of overmanning, time-wasting, and the sabotage of technical change abounded. Management at times appeared fatalistically to accept the situation, lacking both the right or the will to manage.

Britain's success in two wars had left its institutions intact. For example, the static class-bound education system seemed more geared to producing administrators for a disappearing empire than engineers for a high technology revolution. There was little scientific tradition in the schools or universities, in contrast to Germany, where all managers and foremen possessed a minimum 2-year grounding in science and technology.

People respond to the stimulus and challenge of economic growth, its opportunities and its expanded horizons. There is a world of difference between a country making progress and one firmly stuck in a rut, and between a business exploiting advances at the frontiers of knowledge and one presiding over technology decades old.

Summary and conclusions

The 1980s saw a halting of Britain's comparative decline, as successive Conservative governments promoted redeployment of the nation's limited pool of resources into more productive uses. A radical shake-up of industrial structures was central to restoring competitiveness and promoting growth in national income. The instrument of change was the injection of market forces and sharply increased domestic competition. The government's role in the process was to control inflation and create a dynamic and challenging business environment through supply-side policies.

Attention shifted to improving tax incentives, reducing subsidies and deregulating markets. Despite initial recession and a hard pruning of the manufacturing base, the survivors emerged leaner and fitter to enjoy an unparalleled period of rising sales and profitability.

This approach fits well with Porter's view that a nation's living standards are crucially determined by its capacity to innovate and upgrade itself. This underpins productivity growth and is the means by which a country achieves sustainable advantage. Figure 21.9 represents the determinants of this capacity. The ability of a country to achieve and maintain global leadership in various industries depends on them. A challenging environment is a crucial condition for the emergence of such industries. National cultures and institutions will also influence the sectors that are likely to flourish.

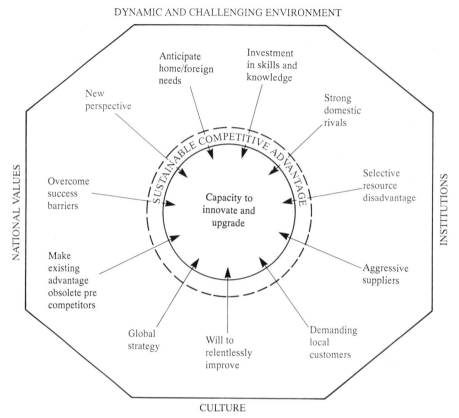

Figure 21.9   *Sources of competitive advantage*

The critical factors, however, are industry-specific and require that a combination of circumstances are met. Strong domestic rivalry is necessary, often within a geographically concentrated area, e.g whisky distilleries in Scotland. This provides the spur for sustained innovation. Strong and aggressive suppliers will also play a complementary part in constantly upgrading performance, as will discerning and demanding clients. Marks & Spencer maintains continuing pressure on its suppliers, pointing the way to future needs. Resources too must be progressively upgraded and any disadvantages compensated for. Sustained competitive advantage requires specialized assets and specific knowledge, which are not easily imitated.

The business also needs the foresight to upgrade and improve its operations, even where this results in making a current advantage obsolete. Imitation by competitors will achieve this in time anyway, so it is better if the business forms a moving target through continuous innovation. Porter sees the overcoming of organizational resistance to change formed by current success in the marketplace as one of the most difficult of the developmental processes.

The successful outcomes of the above forces are industry clusters contributing positively to a country's national income growth. This can be seen in the camera and audio industries of Japan, pharmaceuticals and banking in Switzerland, and chemicals in Germany. The coming decade should demonstrate if the economic revival of the 1980s will prove short-lived or underpin a 1990s rebirth of world leadership clusters in the British economy.

Postscript – the limit to growth

One development likely to limit growth significantly is rising environmental concern. Worries ranging from product safety and urban congestion to the greenhouse effect and acid rain imply a need for increasing regulation and standards. Climatic and atmospheric changes, desertification, toxic waste, coastal degradation and many others can be traced to shortsighted pursuit of economic gain.

Such concerns are not new, but strengthened as the world economy boomed. Oil crises, recession and rising unemployment had caused them to subside in the 1970s. They raise the question whether economic growth is truly sustainable. Green parties are anti-growth and anti-competition, viewing the intense international rivalry favoured by Porter as the main engine of eventual global catastrophe. Porter's response would acknowledge that dealing with the externalities of the growth process is a difficult challenge for market forces, but governments should agree to enforce strict environmental standards in order to channel competition into conservation of the quality of life.

The force of innovation can work equally effectively in pursuit of environmental good. Concern over finite resources, for example, was confounded by the incentive to conserve and substitute as oil prices rose. The result has been a weakening of oil prices and demand throughout the 1980s.

The power of market-based approaches must not therefore be under-estimated. They include the following:

- Pollution charges.
- Tradeable permits, licences or quotas.
- Consumer taxes and differential duties.
- Recycling credits.

The alternative is regulatory standards or outright prohibition, which have the advantage of certainty but may be administratively costly. The international nature of pollution makes intergovernmental accords, such as the 1987 Montreal protocol on CFC production and the EC agreement on North Sea dumping, vital.

Despite rising environmental costs, the forces for continued growth are strong, not least from businesses wishing for expansion, political parties wishing for election and individuals

---

Summary review

1 Compare the characteristics of a company that is expanding to one that is standing still or in a decline.

2 In the light of this chapter and also Chapter 11 on the effects of Thatcherism, consider the extent to which the factors accounting the British disease have been overcome.

3 Can you identify potential industry clusters which may give Britain sustained competitive advantage?

4 How does the marketing approach of your organization take account of environmental concerns? Where is there scope for improvement that can be justified on economic grounds?

wishing for happiness. People's wants are not fully satisfied, and they desire the rising living standards that economic growth allows. The marketer must work towards a reconciliation of these conflicting demands and ensure the fundamental relationship between economic action and environmental consequence is recognized and accounted for by all the relevant decision-makers in their organizations.

Section Seven: Projects/Exercises

1 You have been appointed by a local authority development agency in an area of high regional unemployment to co-ordinate a campaign to market 'appropriate finance' to business through the local Chamber of Commerce and Industry. Thoroughly research the appropriateness of different sources for different business circumstances and make recommendations.

2 Study the full text of the Chancellor's budget statement and the detailed press comment the following day in the quality financial papers. Then:

(a) Summarize the current economic priorities and the strategy for the years ahead.
(b) Identify any changes in the policy stance.
(c) Assess the impact of the main measures announced on your organization.
(d) What actions, in marketing and other terms, should be taken (i) in the short term, and (ii) in the longer term?
(e) What is the budget balance and how will this impact on income, output, employment and prices?

3 Undertake a SWOT analysis on the British economy. Strengths and weaknesses should be identified in broad terms and divided into physical, social and cultural characteristics. Opportunities and threats should be at the macroeconomic level, although points relevant to particular sectors or broad industries may be considered.

   In the light of your analysis make recommendations for appropriate strategic action to be taken by (a) a large business, and (b) a present or future government.

4 The mounting problem of household waste is of increasing concern to individuals, local authorities and central government. Collection and disposal are increasingly expensive, and pressure is mounting for action to be taken. Since much of the waste arises out of the packaging policies of manufacturing companies, the implications are considerable.

(a) Provide examples of the type of waste in question.
(b) Assess alternative approaches to dealing with the problem.
(c) What would be the repercussions of an outright ban on plastic containers?
(d) What scope exists for encouraging recycling?
   It is practical? How would you market it to (a) householders, and (b) the packaging industry?

Section Eight
International economic relations

There are few managers in Britain today who can be isolated from dealings with overseas customers, suppliers or competitors. Britain is termed an 'open economy', because of the scale of its import and export activities. The degree of openness is actually increasing with the evolution of the European Community. With both imports and exports currently accounting for around a third of GDP, and capital flows of gigantic proportions, it is clear that the external economy will impact significantly on the domestic economy that we have so far discussed.

The aims of this section are as follows:

1 To examine the economic significance of international trade.
2 To explain the determination of exchange rates and the operation of the ERM.
3 To outline the balance of payments and its effect as a constraint on policy.
4 To consider the business implications of the Single European Market.
5 To assess the case for attracting multinationals to Britain.
6 To understand the importance of GATT and efforts to reverse the tide of rising protectionism.
7 To consider the plight of less developed countries and their interdependence with the world economy.

Chapter 22 will discuss the basis of international trade and the factors affecting its growth and development. The balance of payments accounts will be considered, together with the determination of the exchange rate. Its significance as a policy instrument will be developed alongside current government policy designed to achieve a trade-off between domestic and external policy objectives. Successive chapters then will deal with wider developments in the world economy with particular attention being given to:

Chapter 23 *The European Community and the single European market*
Chapter 24 *The multinationals*
Chapter 25 *GATT and protectionism*
Chapter 26 *Third World Debt*

22
International trade and payments

Aims

The aims of this chapter are as follows:

- To understand the importance of international marketing.
- To identify the gains from trade and the factors that inhibit it.
- To gain an appreciation of exchange rates and the exchange rate mechanism.
- To analyse the various components of the balance of payments and how it acts as a constraint on economic policy.

Glossary

Bilateral trade – trade between two countries only.

Bretton Woods system – a system of international monetary control established by the UK, USA and Canada in 1944.

Comparative advantage – where one country is able to produce tradeable goods and services more efficiently than another.

Dirty floating – where exchange rates are supposed to be determined freely by demand for and supply of the currency, but the government intervenes covertly to influence its value.

Dumping – when goods are being sold abroad by an exporter below cost or at prices lower than those charged in the home market.

Fundamental disequilibrium – a balance of payments deficit arising from a disparity between the officially maintained exchange rate and what would be a realistic value.

Less developed country – one where economic development is not sufficiently advanced to allow internal generation of funds necessary to finance self-sustaining industrialization.

Multilateral trade – each country trades with many others and accepts a surplus or deficit on its balance of payments with each, while seeking to balance its position overall.

Multinational – simultaneous manufacture of goods and services in several different countries.

International marketing

Trade between nations has existed for centuries. Early merchants amassed fortunes exchanging locally produced goods for the often exotic and unusual produce of far away lands. These early foundations have progressed into a complex trading network, which the marketer must analyse and understand if a business is to prosper through international trade. While the basic principles that underpin the gains from trade remain the same, in practice international marketing has become increasingly complex. The demands imposed in satisfying customers from different cultures and with different languages and expectations are compounded by the existence of frontiers, different legal frameworks and self-interested intervention by governments. Since the competitiveness of nations is crucial to their living standards and rates of economic growth, it is not surprising that trade between them is seldom completely free.

Theorists such as Porter argue that businesses must increasingly compete in a global marketplace on a multinational scale if they are to achieve sustainable competitive advantage. Such businesses are not primarily exporters, since they simultaneously manufacture and market in many countries. However, the situation in the majority of industries falls short of this degree of internationalization of marketing. Instead firms will be ranging along a spectrum, with true multinationals at one end and small businesses with little or no overseas trade at the other. In between lie businesses that export a relatively small proportion of their turnover, primarily through sales agents, as well as those with more active and strategically co-ordinated international marketing initiatives. The latter will have made the crucial adjustments in attitude and focus necessary to adapt their marketing mix to one appropriate to the market concerned.

Specialization and the gains from international trade

It is by no means clear to the lay person that gain is associated with foreign trade. Often the natural reaction of consumers is that buying home-produced goods is for the best. This feeling that it is 'the right thing to do' is reinforced by concern for jobs and a wish to avoid dependence on foreign imports.

Such a bias, however, ignores the potential benefits of trade to be realized through the concept of *comparative advantage*. Since human, material and technical resources are not evenly distributed around the world economy, the cost of producing different goods and services will vary. These cost differences are the basis for mutually advantageous international trade and specialization, providing a major potential source of rising living standards and economic growth. Countries, like individuals, can specialize in what they do best, and exchange their surpluses for those of others.

The theory of comparative advantage or the gains from trade derived out of the work of D. Ricardo and J.S. Mill. They wrote at a time when the UK was exporting the product of its workshops to the world at large in exchange for food and raw materials. They viewed international trade as leading to 'more efficient employment of the productive forces of the world'.

This conclusion stemmed from the diversity of conditions and resources existing in different countries. The UK, for example, owing to its technical expertise and a skilled workforce, can produce chemicals and pharmaceuticals more cheaply than West Africa. However, by virtue of the climate, the latter has an *absolute cost advantage* in producing commodities such as cocoa. It is therefore in their mutual interest to trade. It can also be demonstrated that trade may be mutually advantageous even where one country has a comparative advantage, in that it can produce every commodity more cheaply than the other.

This may be seen by considering the brain surgeon who is also an excellent mechanic and administrator. This fortunate individual has a comparative advantage in surgery and should leave car repairs and paperwork to others with less rare skills. Similarly the marketing director creates more value by determining sales strategy than in making the actual sales calls.

A country should therefore specialize not in what it is absolutely best at producing but what it is relatively best at. Ricardo illustrated the advantages of specialization and free trade by considering the exchange of wine and cloth between the UK and Portugal. The same principle applies, whether it be to a rich or to a poor country, or to primary or manufactured goods.

Suppose Firstworld has a working population of 10m and Thirdworld 20m. In Firstworld a day's labour produces either 20 units of food or 18 manufactured goods, whereas Thirdworld only realizes 10 units of food or 4 manufactured goods. Firstworld has an absolute advantage in the production of both, but if trade does not take place, they must divide resources between the two.

Figure 22.1 shows the production possibilities for Thirdworld along AP and Firstworld along AR. The slope shows the opportunity cost of food in terms of manufactured goods in domestic trade.

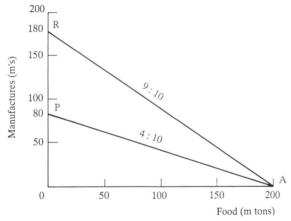

Figure 22.1 *Production possibilities between First and Third World*

If trade were to take place, 10 units of food in Thirdworld would exchange for 9 units of manufactures in Firstworld rather than the 4 obtained in domestic trade. From Firstworld's point of view it could obtain 10 units of food at a cost of just 4 units of manufactures rather than the 9 required in domestic trade. Thus, despite an absolute advantage in both, it pays Firstworld to specialize in the commodity in which it has the greatest comparative advantage or is relatively most efficient at, and trade the surplus for food in which Thirdworld specializes.

Without comparative advantage there is no specialization and reallocation of resources within the two countries that will increase world production. With specialization there is additional benefit to be reaped through economies of scale by virtue of the enlarged market. This would especially advantage economies with only small domestic markets. Indeed as cumulative output rises, advantage should also be gained from the experience curve effect.

Trade then is beneficial whenever there is a difference in the opportunity cost ratio between two countries. The resulting international trade ratio lies between the two domestic ratios and would be determined by the forces of supply and demand. The above example, based on two countries, is termed *bilateral trade*, whereas in practice trade is normally *multilateral*. This greatly extends the scope and flexibility of trade, binding countries together into a world trade system.

While it is clear from the example above that the potential advantages of specialization and trade are substantial, in practice the benefits are modified by a number of considerations. Trade will only be advantageous, for example, if transport costs do not offset the gains from specialization. Trade in heavy or bulky low-value goods will be discouraged in favour of compact high-value products.

Other barriers to international trade include frontier controls, language and differing cultures, as reflected, for example, in the technical and safety standards required of products. Different national currencies and the possibility of unexpected changes in their value also create uncertainty that may inhibit trade. The fact that government policies themselves may be framed deliberately to alter the flow of trade adds to this uncertainty.

In the case above, for example, while in the long run everyone benefits from trade, in the short and medium term Firstworld agriculture would contract, with resulting unemployment, partly offsetting the benefit to consumers of cheaper food prices. Many traditional UK industries, for example, have suffered decline in recent years at the hands of cheaper Far Eastern suppliers.

Its relevance in Thirdworld may also be modified by a desire to industrialize, leading to infant industry protection by means of tariffs and quotas. Such action may also be justified in Firstworld by a desire to avoid dependence on imports in strategic industries, especially if it is suspected that 'dumping' is taking place. Customs duties also raise valuable revenues and may assist in correcting payments deficits. They may also serve as useful bargaining counters in trade negotiations such as the current GATT round.

It may be concluded that the current pattern of trade does not fully reflect the potential of comparative advantage. Politics and the reality of protectionism have served to modify its application.

The terms of trade

The gains from specialization and trade must be shared between the participants. How much each country gains depends on the terms of trade. They reflect the amount of domestically produced goods that must be exchanged to obtain a given quantity of imports. In effect it is the relation between export and import prices defined by the following index:

$$\text{Terms of trade (index)} = \frac{\text{Index of export prices}}{\text{Index of import prices}} \times 100$$

An index is used to allow different goods to be weighted according to their importance in trade. Should export prices rise relative to import prices, then a favourable movement in the terms of trade is said to occur; but a rise in import prices relative to export prices is an unfavourable movement, requiring increased exports to purchase a given quantity of now more expensive imports.

Any factor affecting the conditions of supply and demand for imports and exports will influence the terms of trade. Primary products are particularly volatile, as seen most dramatically in the pattern of oil prices. Boom conditions tend to improve the terms of trade sharply for primary producers, while recessions cause deterioration.

The exchange rate

Most international trade does not consist of exchanging goods direct for other goods (known as counter trade), but rather goods are paid for by currency. For trade to take place it is therefore necessary to determine an exchange rate, which is the price of one currency in terms of another. Trade will only take place if the exchange rate allows imports to be purchased more cheaply than home-produced goods. However, a country will wish to set its exchange rate at the correct level. If it is set too high or over-valued, imports will exceed exports, producing a deficit on trade. Import prices in terms of domestic currency will fall, putting downward pressure on inflation. If set too low, the exchange rate will be under-valued, thereby stimulating exports, and producing a trade surplus. Higher import prices, however, will tend to stimulate inflationary pressures.

Governments have traditionally taken an interest in the exchange rate, often manipulating it in order to gain trade advantage. At one extreme they may allow markets to operate freely, taking no action that would influence the exchange rate. At the other extreme they may prevent any movement at all by either buying or selling the currency as conditions change. In between there are a mix of policy stances, combining varying degrees of freedom with managed adjustment and intervention.

The value of a currency is often an emotive subject, and supposed 'weakness' has led many governments to spend considerable sums in supporting often unrealistic rates. After 1973, however, many countries, including Britain, experimented in flexible or so-called floating rates. The free play of market forces became the main determinant, although governments still reserved the right to 'manage' the rate if it showed signs of moving outside broad limits. This approach is known as managed flexibility or dirty floating.

The exchange rate is the price at which one currency exchanges for another in the foreign exchange market. In Figure 22.2 supply and demand are in equilibrium at an exchange rate of £1 to 3Dm or 1Dm to 33p. Demand for pounds represents German requirements for sterling to purchase either goods and services from Britain or direct assets. The supply of pounds to the market represents British requirements for marks to purchase German exports. Any shift of the demand curve out or the supply curve in will cause the exchange rate to rise – known as

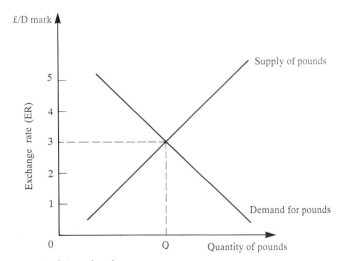

Figure 22.2 *Exchange rate determination*

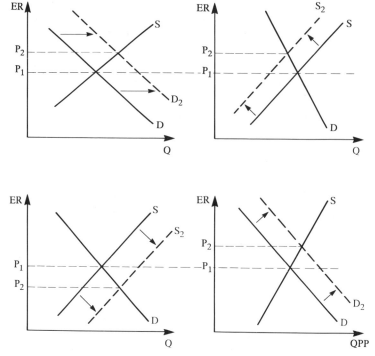

Figure 22.3   *Exchange rates and changing market conditions*

an *appreciation*. On the other hand, a shift of the demand curve in or a shift of the supply curve out causes the pound to depreciate, as the Deutschmark becomes more expensive. See Figure 22.3.

In practice changes in supply and demand conditions may shift in offsetting directions, making analysis complex and prediction of exchange rate movements hazardous. Factors other than demand for imports and exports influence the rate. For example, Britain's inflation is still above European competitors', tending to reduce demand for more expensive British goods relative to cheaper European alternatives. This shifts the demand curve in and the supply curve out, depressing the price of sterling.

Relatively high interest rates may prevent this depreciation, as inward capital flows for investment or speculation maintains the demand for pounds. In the longer term, however, the benefits are less certain, owing to the damaging disincentive effects of such rates on home investment.

One concept of interest here is the Purchasing Power Parity (PPP) theory, developed by Cassells in the 1920s. This seeks to explain the fundamental exchange rate value by reference to the goods two currencies can buy in their respective countries. If an identical basket of goods may be bought for £1,000 in Britain and 3000Dm in Germany, then the exchange rate should logically be determined at £1 = 3Dm. If prices then rise 50 per cent faster over the decade in Britain than in Germany, the PPP theory would predict an exchange rate of £1 = 2Dm. In practice, however, not all goods enter trade, and transport costs have to be accounted for. A variety of other factors also influence the exchange rate in the short term, including the underlying state of the economy concerned, the balance of payments position, and the government's view regarding the 'right' exchange rate.

Confidence is also a crucial consideration in the determination of exchange rates. International businesses require currency to finance their trade and overseas investment needs. An adverse movement in rates before an overseas transaction is completed can easily convert a profitable contract into loss. Such companies therefore protect themselves against this exchange risk by 'buying forward' on their currency requirements. They agree to purchase the foreign currency at an agreed price and date in the future. Future rates are very much dependent on confidence, not least in the government's policy towards the economy in general and the balance of payments in particular.

The exchange rate mechanism (ERM)

Over the post-war period there have been a succession of international exchange rate approaches, including the Bretton Wood system up to 1971, when currencies were pegged to the dollar, and managed floating, which succeeded it. The ERM based around the Deutschmark is a key component of the European Monetary System, which aims to achieve monetary stability in the European community. This system also envisages a wider role for the European currency unit (ECU), and arrangements for central bank credit-swops and closer co-ordination of economic and monetary policy. Currencies are maintained within agreed bands against one another, with the aim of creating exchange rate stability. The ERM was established in 1979. Britain only became a full member in 1990.

Each ERM currency has a central rate against each of the other currencies: for example, the sterling Deutschmark rate is £1 to 2.95Dm. Changes in these central rates can only be made by agreement. The ECU is a 'basket' of all EC currencies, combining a weighted amount of each according to relative economic importance (see Table 22.1). Seven of the nine member

Table 22.1   The ECU's composition

Currency	Weight* (%)
Belgian/Luxembourg franc	8.1
French franc	19.3
Lira	9.7
Guilder	9.6
Deutschmark	30.4
Danish krone	2.5
Irish punt	1.1
Peseta	5.2
Drachma	0.7
Pound sterling	12.6
Escudo	0.8
	100.0

* Weights based on exchange rates on 30.10.90.

currencies fluctuate within 2.25 per cent margins above or below the central rate in one 'narrow band', while Britain and Spain occupy a band of 6 per cent either way. With Britain moving back to a fixed exchange rate system after a period of floating rates, it is useful to consider the arguments for and against the two systems.

The case for the ERM and fixed exchange rates

Certainty

Business can be certain of the future value of the currency, removing the exchange risk in overseas transactions. Consider a £1 million transaction negotiated at current exchange rates with a German company, which offers a profit on completion of 10 per cent. This satisfactory return could be transformed into a 10 per cent loss with a fall in the rate from 1–3 to 1–2.4Dm. The need for forward exchange contracts under floating rates adds to costs and does not remove the uncertainty. Fixed rates should therefore encourage long-term trade and investment. Currency stability worked well for a long period after World War II, stimulating considerable expansion in world trade.

Anti-inflation

A falling exchange rate raises import prices. More expensive foods and materials feed back on to factory prices, and may prompt compensating wage demands.

Devaluation discredited

Devaluation is a cut in the value of a fixed exchange rate normally forced on a country by an adverse trade balance. The intention is to stimulate exports by making them cheaper in foreign currency terms, and discourage imports as they become dearer. As mentioned above, however, the benefit may be short-lived. The trade balance in any case actually worsens initially, since dearer but necessary imports have their effect before any stimulus to extra exports works through. This produces what is known as the J curve effect (Figure 22.4) as the trade balance gets worse before it gets better.

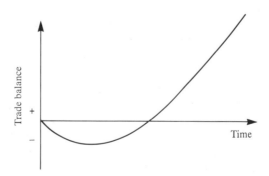

Figure 22.4   *The J curve*

Improvement also requires that the trade elasticities are positive. The Marshall Lerner conditions require that the sum of the import and export elasticities must add up to greater than unity for devaluation to work. (To understand this, refer to the discussion of elasticity and the revenue effects of a price change in Section 2, p. 57). Experience of devaluation and depreciation suggests this is so, since Britain produces a similar mix of goods and services as its main trade competitors, allowing scope for substitution as home prices become relatively cheaper. If, however, the elasticity value is not much greater than unity, adjustment will be slow.

Automatic stabilization

Fixed exchange rate systems operate to correct imbalance automatically. As seen above, downward pressure on the rate triggers the need for a rise in interest rates and an associated tightening of monetary policies. Higher interest rates will, on the one hand, encourage short-term currency inflows to relieve exchange rate pressure, but will also dampen demand and inflation. Imports will fall, correcting the deficit on the balance of payments.

The reverse process occurs in response to upward pressure on the rate. In effect the rate of growth a country can sustain will be controlled by its ability to manage inflation successfully. Any attempt to push growth and employment beyond this rate will prove unsustainable in the long run.

Since the ERM is tied to the Deutschmark, which is in turn controlled by a strong central bank with an historic aversion to inflation, this should stabilize the system at low inflation rates.

Trade relations

Manipulation of exchange rates for national economic advantage disrupts trade. So called 'beggar my neighbour' policies in the early 1930s contributed to world trade falling to a third of its 1929 level. Attempts to export unemployment by cutting exchange rates for competitive advantage led to retaliation and greatly increased business uncertainty.

Speculation

Correctly set fixed exchange rates remove speculative activity, whereas day to day changes in exchange rates may be reinforced by such behaviour. International banking has made money much more mobile now that short-term flows can be instantly transferred from currency to currency electronically. Many multinationals and foreign governments hold such funds in the London markets. Termed 'hot money', these funds can generate a crisis at the hint of a currency depreciation.

Influenced by short term factors, including confidence, some movements can be self-fulfilling, as the belief that a currency will fall causes funds to flow out, confirming the belief. In such situations speculators cannot lose, but their activity destabilizes the basis of business transactions.

Any system that serves to increase the degree of certainty for international transactions will ensure that the marketer has one less variable to worry about. However, a weather eye must constantly be maintained on Britain's status within the system to guard against unwelcome surprises that might disrupt the market plan.

The case for floating rates

Automatic correction

Whereas the ERM removes imbalance by changing the domestic activity level, floating rates work through the currency value. A balance of payments disequilibrium should be rectified by an offsetting movement in the exchange rate. A surplus would cause appreciation in the exchange rate, making imports cheaper and exports more expensive. Both Japan and Germany have seen their large trade surpluses shrink in this way recently.

Policy flexibility

Fixed exchange rates require unpleasant deflation to bring about adjustment. Floating exchange rates may provide a less painful alternative in terms of lost growth and unemployment. In effect extra resources are switched into exports and import displacement at the expense of domestic consumption. However, activity levels are maintained. Correcting a trade deficit by reducing aggregate demand across the board is criticized as unnecessary overkill.

Adjustability

Continuous day-to-day adjustments are to be preferred to occasional but disruptive currency realignments, which are often taken to signify national humiliation. The greater the degree of turbulence and change in the world economy, the more the need for flexible adjustment. Fixed exchange rates presume fixed supply and demand relationships, which are difficult to reconcile with experience. A country may quickly find itself in a fundamental disequilibrium, and fixed rates will only delay an adjustment.

Market valuation

Fixed exchange rates are set by politicians, not by market forces. An over-valued currency, for example, will create problems for business in remaining competitive. A shakeout, as occurred in British manufacturing in the years 1979–81, may be the result. Floating rates should prevent such problems.

Anti-inflation

A floating rate should limit the transmission of inflation through trade. The exchange rate would rise in the low inflation country, thereby reducing the cost of imports and countering the effect of their otherwise inflationary impact. Under fixed exchange rates the full effect is imported. Unfortunately national authorities may seek to prevent the inflation arising from trade surpluses by correspondingly reducing the money supply, thus preventing correction of the deficits and surpluses taking place.

Lower reserves

Floating rate adjustment means that reserves are largely unnecessary and can be re-deployed to finance trade.

Absence of exchange controls

Such controls were abolished in 1979 as inconsistent with free currency markets. They are frequently applied to justify often wildly unrealistic exchange rates, as is the case in many Eastern European countries. It may be noted that, in a regime of floating exchange rates, trade-weighted indices are used to measure a currency's performance against others. ERM currencies, for example, are weighted according to their importance in trade. The effective *exchange rate* is a weighted average representing the share of trade conducted in each currency. This rate fell for sterling almost continuously throughout the 1980s.

The balance of payments

This is a systematic annual account of all transactions between the residents of one country, which includes individuals, businesses and government, and the rest of the world. It includes any item giving rise to the purchase or sale of foreign currencies. Credit items generate an inflow of currency, while debit items, representing the purchase of overseas goods and services, create an outflow. The balance of payments always balances, since domestic purchases of foreign currencies to finance transactions must equal what foreigners are prepared to sell. However, particular components of the accounts may be in imbalance and require correction.

The balance on current account

This records all international transactions in goods and services and is made up of two main parts, visible and invisible trade figures.

Visible trade

Figures published monthly refer to the import and export of goods and constitute the *balance of trade*. Britain has seldom had a surplus on this account, since deficits on imports of foods, fuels, materials and semi-manufactures usually more than outweigh the surplus on manufactured trade. Peak production and export of North Sea oil transformed the balance of trade into surplus in the early 1980s, but this was progressively found to be at the expense of manufactures. The rising exchange rate and high interest rates forced a sharp contraction as imports grew rapidly. Despite some recovery the deficit at the end of the 1980s was £18bn.

Table 22.2 reveals changes in the composition of visible trade over two decades. This reflects the relative decline of manufacturing, especially such industries as textiles and vehicles, and the rise of oil.

The geographical distribution of UK trade in Figure 22.5 reflects the dramatic rise in both imports and exports with EC partners, a trend that should continue with the Single European

Table 22.2   Distribution by category of trade (percentage of total)

Category	1970		1980		1990	
	Export	Import	Export	Import	Export	Import
Food	6.2	22.6	6.8	12.2	6.8	9.9
Materials	3.2	13.7	3.1	7.4	2.2	4.9
Fuels	2.2	8.3	13.6	14.2	8.1	6.2
Semi-manufactured	34.4	29.2	29.6	27.3	21.4	17.9
Finished manufactured	50.2	24.6	44.0	36.3	61.5	61.1

Source: CSO Monthly Digest of Statistics.

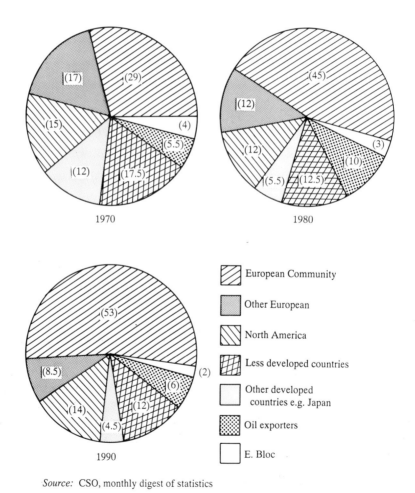

Source: CSO, monthly digest of statistics

Figure 22.5   *Geographical distribution of UK trade*

Market. The increasing proportion of trade with developed countries reflects a move into higher value-added production and weakening links with less developed countries.

Invisible trade

Figures for this item include the sale and purchase of services. Most notable are financial services, such as banking and insurance, in which Britain has a very large net balance. Invisible trade has historically produced a surplus and is therefore of considerable importance in offsetting any deficit recorded on visible trade. Visible and invisible trade figures combine to produce the *current balance of payments*. This may be seen in Figure 22.6, where, but for the contribution of services, the balance would have been in extremely serious deficit.

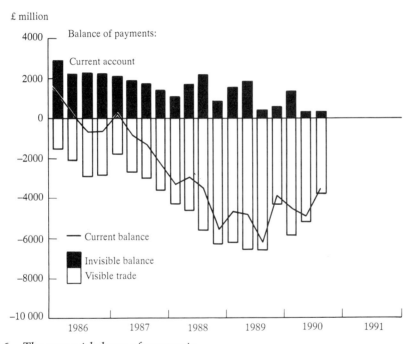

Figure 22.6   *The current balance of payments*

Other service categories include travel and tourism, where successful marketing of Britain's heritage has frequently produced surpluses in recent years. However, air tragedies, terrorism, wars, and adverse exchange rate movements often produce consequences to confound the best laid of marketing plans and push the account into deficit. The opening of the Channel tunnel may be expected to introduce a new dimension to travel and tourism after 1993. Shipping and civil aviation are in deficit, unlike 'other services', which include the earnings of consultants, construction companies, education and entertainment.

The other main items are as follows:

- *Interest, profit and dividends*   as a trading nation Britain has invested heavily overseas in the form of loans, direct investment, and acquisitions, and this accelerated with the ending of exchange controls in 1979. While adding to the demand for foreign currency in the year the investment is made, a subsequent flow of returns will be recorded as invisible receipts. Due to the scale of Britain's net overseas investment, these make a very substantial contribution to the credit side of the balance.

- *Government expenditure* – this is required to finance a worldwide network of embassies and trade missions, as well as any military presence, as in Germany or the Gulf.
- *Transfers* – these include remittances by foreign workers or those receiving pensions abroad. The main transfer for Britain, however, is the net contribution to the EC budget.

The capital account

This is concerned with the movement of long- and short-term capital between countries, and includes:

- Overseas investments in/by Britain – known as direct investment.
- Government loans to/from overseas countries.
- Overseas borrowing and loans by UK and foreign banks – known as portfolio investment.

Overseas investment by British firms has risen sharply since exchange controls were removed. This has been on a scale to mirror the size of the current deficit in the late 1980s. However, the development of Euro-currency markets has also made London the location for 'hot money', which responds to differential interest rates and currency value expectations. This is a source of potential instability whenever sterling's future exchange value is in doubt. Some have argued that successive governments have placated the financial markets through support of the sterling value to the competitive disadvantage of manufacturing industry.

The balancing item

The trade accounts are notorious for errors and inaccuracies in the data. As such, they are frequently subject to revision and outstanding discrepancies must be balanced by an appropriate adjustment. The balancing item rose considerably in size in the late 1980s, reflecting increasingly deregulated and sophisticated international capital markets.

The balance for official financing

The probability of current and capital accounts exactly balancing out is very low. The resulting surplus/deficit on the total currency flows must therefore be financed. Deficits mean that more has been spent than received from overseas and must be balanced by an outflow of currency and *vice versa*. This might be achieved by either drawing on official reserves or increasing foreign indebtedness by borrowing foreign currency, through arrangements with central banks abroad. In the last resort an approach may be made to the International Monetary Fund (IMF), as occurred in Britain in the mid-1970s. The balance for official financing is the balance referred to in the term 'balance of payments'.

Types of imbalance

The balance of payments always balances through official financing of any deficit or surplus. In the long run, however, a continued current deficit is unsustainable, since reserves would deplete and foreigners would become progressively less and less willing to lend. Final recourse to the IMF would result in conditional loans, requiring governments to act to eliminate the deficit. Similarly an ever-accumulating surplus would confer little benefit on the country unless spent or invested.

All countries cannot be in surplus at the same time, since one country's surplus is another country's deficit. Balance must eventually be achieved, but in the short term a deficit should not necessarily give rise to concern. If countries incur a deficit to finance productive investment that generates exports or import-saving, then it becomes self-financing and equilibrium will be restored. Measures to deal with the short-term deficit include raising interest rates to encourage capital inflows, borrowing and running down reserves. Problems arise when the deficit is persistent, resulting in what is known as *fundamental disequilibrium*.

A fundamental deficit requires radical action if persistent currency outflow is to be stemmed. The correct action depends on its size, cause, and the exchange rate policy being pursued by the government. The state of the domestic economy will also be relevant, with appropriate action being influenced by the current rates of unemployment and inflation. For example, if the root of the problem is excessive price inflation, which is reducing exports and stimulating imports, then policies to stimulate productivity rather than devalue the currency might be more appropriate.

There are two cures.

Expenditure reduction cure

Restrictive fiscal and monetary policies are used to solve the deficit by deflating aggregate demand. Falling consumer and investment spending reduces import demands, and resources will be released for transfer into export activity. Reduced demand pressure should also reduce domestic inflation relative to that of competitors, providing business with a price advantage. Firms will be encouraged to respond to the depressed domestic market conditions by seeking export opportunities to maintain production volume.

Such policies are more effective when competitors are not suffering depressed economic conditions themselves. Otherwise the cost in high unemployment and lost output growth may be significant.

Britain's obligations under GATT and the Treaty of Rome, especially now that Britain has joined the ERM, means her freedom of action to use the alterative of expenditure switching measures is limited.

Expenditure switching cure

This means transferring expenditure and resources from imports to home-produced goods and services. Expenditure reduction may be necessary to create the capacity to allow such policies to work. Measures include various forms of protection, including tariffs, quotas, embargoes and subsidies. Non-tariff barriers may also be raised to discriminate in favour of home producers. Border controls and health and safety regulations are examples of such barriers, as are measures designed to foster nationalism in buying preferences. Public sector procurement policies also discriminate in favour of home producers. The various forms of protectionism will be discussed later, as will currency depreciation.

Switching measures have been criticized for dealing with the symptoms rather than the causes of imbalances. As discussed earlier, devaluation does not always provide a permanent solution if inflation increases to erode the price advantage gained. Furthermore there is a real cost to living standards in paying more for essential imports. The 14 per cent devaluation that occurred in 1967 meant that export volume and value had to rise by more than 14 per cent just to maintain revenue in foreign currency terms.

Deficits must therefore be diagnosed with care. With fundamental deficits there are no simple or painless solutions. It may require considerable time and a combination of measures before balance is restored.

The balance of payments constraint

Throughout the post-war period attempts by successive governments to achieve faster economic growth have come up against this constraint. The balance of payments is a problem when receipts of foreign currency are too small or unstable to enable a country to achieve its objectives. These might include maintenance of a military and diplomatic presence in the world, financing overseas investment and foreign aid, or repayment of debt. If the average current account surplus is insufficient to meet these requirements without recourse to trade restrictions or less than full employment output, then a constraint exists. Its effect can be represented schematically, as in Figure 22.7.

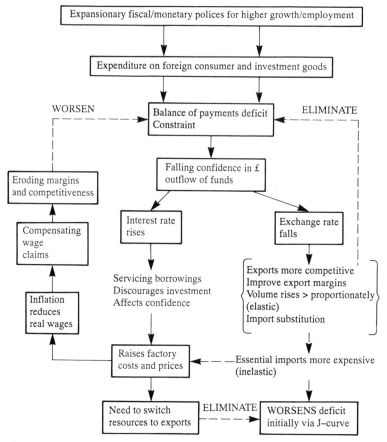

Figure 22.7 *Balance of payments constraint*

Demand-side promoted dashes for faster growth were prompted by a desire to achieve a virtuous circle, where higher output produced the extra exports or import substitution to overcome the deficit. Instead, spiralling imports tended to produce a run on the pound, forcing the government to put the brakes on further expansion and devalue the pound. This helped produce the characteristic stop–go pattern of activity.

Business was often criticized for not investing sufficiently in export capability, preferring to earn higher margins than stimulate extra export volume. Unions were criticized for seeking compensating wage increases despite the fact that real wages are reduced by higher import prices. Consumers were criticized for preferring to buy foreign goods even after devaluation had made them more expensive. Non-price factors, such as poor quality and poor customer service, were cited as reasons for this negative consumer reaction. Whatever the explanation, the balance of payments remains the fundamental constraint on domestic expansion. Economic growth can only be justified if it is consistent with competitiveness, low inflation and international confidence in the pound.

Britain's balance of payments

The visible trade surplus (see Table 22.3) in 1980–2 reflected a rising contribution of North Sea oil. The oil surplus, which peaked at £8bn in 1985 was not sufficient to prevent a deteriorating balance from 1983 onwards. The severe damage done to the manufacturing base in the recession helped to produce a rising volume of imports, which grew at twice the rate of exports from 1982 on. Many manufactures were simply no longer producing in Britain.

Table 22.3   The current balance (£bn)

Year	Visible balance	Invisible balance	Current balance
1980	1,357	1,487	2,843
1981	3,252	3,496	6,748
1982	1,910	2,741	4,649
1983	−1,537	5,325	3,787
1984	−5,336	7,168	1,832
1985	−3,345	6,095	2,750
1986	−9,484	9,420	−65
1987	−11,224	6,907	−4317
1988	−21,077	5,744	−15,333
1989	−23,998	4,217	−19,781
1990	−17,911	1,867	−16,044

Source: CSO

Invisibles performed strongly up until 1986, but then began to weaken at the same time as oil prices collapsed, producing a big rise in the current account deficit. The halving of oil prices in 1986 and demise of sterling as a petro-currency were not, however, associated with an equivalent recovery in manufacturing exports. Only with deepening recession in 1991 did the current balance begin to improve sharply, as imports slowed.

It must be noted once more how suspect the data has become. On a worldwide basis in 1987, for example, there were $45bn of exports unaccounted for. This arose mainly out of the difficulties in accurately recording invisibles and capital flows. While it would be speculative to suggest the extent to which Britain's own exports are understated, the recent size of the balancing item gives cause for concern:

Balancing item	1980	1985	1987	1988	1989
£m	873	6,294	11,025	11,338	12,283

International competitiveness

Problems with comparing data and the difficulty of accounting for non-price factors makes judgement of relative national performance very difficult. The marketer must be aware that available measures focus almost exclusively on cost and price competitiveness in manufactured goods. Figure 22.8 shows the movement in unit costs, export prices and profitability over recent years. In comparison to the sharp deterioration that occurred in the

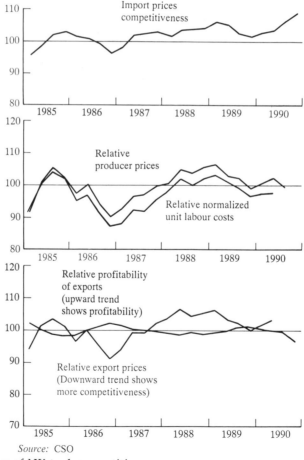

Source: CSO

Figure 22.8   *Measures of UK trade competitiveness*

1970s, the 1980s saw a decade of relative stability and improving export profitability. This was against a background of decline in the effective exchange rate and a resumption of rising costs and prices towards the end of the period. Given Britain's entry into the ERM, continued wage pressure and falling productivity growth, her profitability must be projected as weakening into the foreseeable future. The sharp deterioration in import price competitiveness in 1990 certainly appears to support this conclusion.

Summary

- A healthy balance of payments provides the freedom to pursue other policy objectives.
- A deficit may be temporary, arising out of borrowing to finance capital investment, or it may be fundamental, due to structural change in the economy.
- A deficit may also be due to mismanagement of the macroeconomy when excess demand draws in imports to fill the gap.
- A deficit represents suppressed inflation.
- A fall in the exchange rate to correct a deficit tends to be inflationary. With imports accounting for a third of expenditure, the associated rise in their prices will be significant, especially when compensating wage demands are triggered.
- The only alternative is slower growth. Relatively high interest rates necessary to attract foreign funds to finance the deficit will depress spending on imports. An interest premium must be paid to foreigners for holding sterling, given the risk of exchange rate depreciation.
- A marked turnaround from deficit to surplus without currency depreciation is seldom achieved without rising unemployment and falling output. Japan's flexible adjustment to successive oil shocks is the only recent exception.
- Conservative policy currently rules out both import controls and currency depreciation.

338   *Economic Theory and Marketing Practice*

Summary review

1 The following table measures output per unit of factor input in three alternative cases:

	Case 1 A	Case 1 B	Case 2 A	Case 2 B	Case 3 A	Case 3 B
Britain	60	15	60	30	60	45
Germany	90	45	90	45	90	45

 (a) Will benefits from trade arise in these three cases?
 (b) If benefit does arise, in what product should each country specialize and why?
 (c) Suggest reasons why a country might not wish to take full advantage of specialization and trade.

2 Will membership of the ERM be good for you, good for business and good for Britain?

3 What was the visible trade deficit at the end of the 1980s? In the light of Britain's GDP is this a matter of great concern? Can you explain the declining invisible trade balance?

4 Should only international marketers pay attention to fluctuations in the exchange rate and balance of payments?

5 Research the outcome of the Uruguay round of GATT trade talks to discover the implications for:
 (a) trade in services,
 (b) trade in farm products,
 (c) trade in basic manufactures.
What is the likely impact on world trade in general and the Third World in particular?

23
The European Community and Single European Market (SEM)

Aims

The aims of this chapter are as follows:

- To discuss the benefits associated with customs unions.
- To understand the forces leading to the Single European Act.
- To appreciate the philosophy of the single market and progress towards its achievement.
- To consider the implications for British business.

Glossary

Benelux – Belgium, Netherlands and Luxembourg.

Common agricultural policy – a policy agreed by member states to fix target prices for agricultural output. Variable import levies ensure that non-member's supplies never enter below an agreed threshold price. The Commission buys up surpluses if prices fall to agreed intervention levels. It also pays out a variety of general and export subsidies.

Common external tariff – identical tariffs applied to all members' imports from outside the customs union.

Customs union – an area within which trade may be conducted freely between members. A common external tariff is applied to imports.

EFTA – European Free Trade Area, comprising Norway, Sweden, Iceland, Austria and Switzerland.

European Commission – controls the workings of the EC through commissioners appointed for 4-year terms by the unanimous agreement of member governments. It proposes policies to the Council of Ministers and implements the decisions made.

Introduction

The European Community (EC) is a customs union. Free trade areas such as EFTA also abolish internal customs and tariffs, but do not agree to a common external tariff (CET), preferring instead to set individual duties on non-members' imports. The Caribbean Economic Community (CARICOM) and Association of South East Asian Nations (ASEAN pact) are other examples of such arrangements.

Formed in 1957 under the Treaty of Rome, the Common Market originally had six members – France, West Germany, Italy and the Benelux three. Britain acceded in 1973, with Eire and

Denmark, after two earlier attempts had been blocked by France. Greece (1981), Spain and Portugal (1986) have now joined to form the twelve.

The benefits of customs unions flow from the arguments for free trade outlined in Chapter 11, and greater opportunities for specialization and trade have certainly resulted. Free trade allows *trade creation*, as some goods and services are imported from other members in preference to being produced domestically. This improves resource allocation and provides scope for greater economies of scale.

Trade diversion also occurs, as the common external tariff causes countries to discriminate in favour of member imports, even though non-member pre-CET costs of production may be lower. After Britain's entry, cheaper New Zealand butter and Caribbean sugar were displaced in this way by more expensive Community supplies. Despite the higher prices, trade-creating effects appear to have outweighed the diversion effects, but to the cost of many non-member nations.

Other benefits include the stimulus of competition provided by the free market. Britain saw entry as one route towards improving its own comparative growth rate by association with the faster- growing Community. Despite a fall in Community-wide economic performance to the mid-1980s, a degree of catching up has occurred, assisted by Britain's booming economy in the late 1980s.

The creation of the EC was designed to achieve much more than enhanced trade. It consolidated a process of unifying links between previously warring nations. The political aim was to create a stable framework of relations, which included:

- A common agricultural policy (CAP).
- Harmonization of tax structures.
- Free movement of people and capital.
- Technological co-operation.
- Social and regional funds.
- Progress towards monetary union.
- Progress towards political union.

From Britain's point of view it is difficult even in hindsight to judge the consequences of entry. While perceptions have improved, the EC has often been viewed in Britain as a massive but distant bureaucracy, interfering with national sovereignty. Overpaid politicians in Luxembourg, Strasbourg and Brussels are seen as wrangling over butter mountains and budget contributions. Successes in industrial co-operation, such as ARIANE (space) AIRBUS (aircraft) and ESPRIT (computers), seem to be the exception rather than the rule.

One area of continued concern is the Community budget. As a large importer of food and materials from non-member countries and therefore subject to the CET, Britain's contribution was out of proportion to its economic size. This was compounded by the Commission's inability to control Community spending, especially the two-thirds of the budget going to agriculture. Britain's small but efficient farm sector obtained receipts far less than the contributions made. A determined stand by the prime minister resulted in a 66 per cent contribution rebate on the difference between VAT payments and Community receipts. Britain remains a net contributor to the budget but at a much reduced percentage of GDP (Figure 23.1).

The Community has continued to experience budgetary problems, arising out of excessive farm supports. Budget contributions were raised to 1.2 per cent of GDP in 1988, derived from CET revenue and 1.4 per cent of VAT receipts. However, despite binding controls on farm spending, the amount devoted to the farm sector continues to grow, as seen in Figure 23.2.

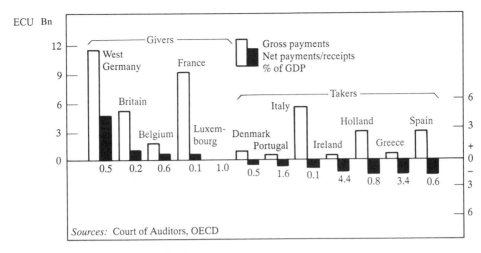

Figure 23.1 *All about give and take*

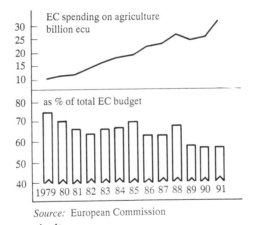

Source: European Commission

Figure 23.2 *EC spending on agriculture*

Background to 1992 and the Single European Market

During the 1980s there was concern that Europe was being eclipsed by a resurgent America and the mounting challenge from the Far East. In 1970 the EC had a GDP equal to that of the USA and double that of the ten major Pacific economies. By 1984 GDP had fallen to 93 per cent of the USA's, while the pacific ten's had risen to two-thirds the GDP of the EC.

It appeared that the world centre of gravity was shifting from the Atlantic to the Pacific rim. Economic vitality in North America was increasingly to be found on the western seaboard, notably California, rather than in the declining industrial areas of the east. Japan set the pace on the other half of the rim for the newly industrializing economies, such as Korea, Hong Kong, Taiwan, Singapore and the Philippines. Any reawakening of China would also offer a vast potential market.

The EC was faced with an erosion of technological leadership, and with high levels of persistent unemployment. Europe, for example, accounted for 30 per cent of world information technology spending but just 10 per cent of its production. Tax regimes to support generous expenditure levels were rising yet the necessary flexibility for achieving successful change and innovation was lost in an overwhelming concern for job security. Unless new momentum could be injected, it was feared that Europe's decline would become terminal. Its institutions seemed incapable of making decisions, while government intervention and bureaucracy grew ever larger.

The potential solution was the Single European Act, initiated in 1985 and taking effect in 1987. The approach adopted was consistent with the developing trends towards deregulation and liberalization in many member countries. To make it effective, qualified majority voting was adopted on all non-fiscal matters within the Community. A qualified majority required 54 out of a total of 75 votes (Britain had 10) to be cast in favour of a proposal. Members now found it more advantageous to negotiate an outcome acceptable to themselves than risk being outvoted on an unsatisfactory proposal. Every agreed directive on the road towards the SEM does, however, imply a loss of sovereignty to Brussels on the part of the member states.

Single European Market – the philosophy

The SEM was a response to the rise of the countries of the Pacific rim and the trend towards global markets. If European firms were to close the high-technology trade deficit, they had to achieve a sustainable competitive advantage. Full deregulation of the EC market and release of competitive forces was seen as the means of revitalizing its mature industrial base.

European markets were still very fragmented, preventing economies of scale being realized in production, research, development and marketing. The SEM required the removal of the physical, technical and fiscal barriers that sustained this fragmentation. These changes were to be fully implemented by the end of 1992.

1 *National standards and regulations* – the lack of a community standard meant twelve different products had to be developed to meet national specifications. This added to development costs and time delays in innovation, while failing to provide the production volumes to allow international competitiveness.
2 *Administrative barriers* – excessive paperwork associated with the distribution and sale of goods and services across frontiers.
3 *Actual physical frontier delays* – add to cost and journey times, hinder just-in-time distribution and deter corporate restructuring.
4 *Public procurement* – purchases by public agencies account for a significant proportion of GDP, yet the vast majority are supplied by domestic producers. Governments pay the price in higher contract prices, owing to the lack of competitive bidding. Businesses are unable to exploit competitive advantages and realize economies. National pride preserves the existence of domestic champions across the range of procurement rather than encouraging specialization and trade between members.
5 *Regulations on transport.*
6 *Community laws.*
7 *Capital market restrictions.*
8 *Fiscal barriers* – excises and VAT diverge significantly across the Community. Britain's VAT has been brought into line with the EC average (France and Italy 19 per cent, Germany 14 per cent), but excises on beer are ten times German and twenty times French levels, for example. Compliance with different tax regimes again adds to business costs.

The Commission is currently in the process of securing agreement to a timetable of 279 directives planned to remove the above and realize the single market. By early 1991, 158 had been passed, although only 21 had been fully incorporated by the twelve member states. Italy has proved the slowest in this process, while Britain had the best record.

Detailed technical specification will be left to a standardization body known as CEN, and British standards, such as BS5750, will secure approval with this body. The mutual recognition directive of 1983 also means that any new national regulations must be notified to CEN and may be frozen for up to a year.

1992 – Implications for business

The huge pan-European market of 320m relatively affluent consumers gives considerable opportunities for domestic companies. Those currently supplying profitable niches in national markets have the prospect of lucrative returns in a single Community-wide market. There are also threats, however, for those who fail to prepare for more intense competition. Protected home markets will be exposed, and prices and margins will fall. Only those firms that take the initiative in production and marketing will achieve the extra volumes necessary to offset this erosion of profit.

A checklist of preparations for 1992 might include the following:

- Undertake a strategic review of current operations in the light of single-market opportunities.
- Appoint a top level executive with responsibilities for 1992 to provide focus and leadership.
- Undertake thorough market research within the EC.
- Establish contacts with potential customers, suppliers, competitors, etc.
- Consider attendance at European trade fairs and exhibitions.
- Reorganize the business to recognize the EC dimension.
- Consider licensing agreements, co-operative or joint ventures, acquisitions or mergers, whether national or community- based.
- Introduce in-house training, including languages and national culture.
- Appoint sales agents or consider opening a sales office.
- Plan restructuring to take account of the SEM, regarding location of manufacturing and distribution facilities as the focus shifts from national to regional markets.

Success in European markets will require a very different and more demanding marketing mix than that for domestic operations. Design and implementation of market research surveys or an advertising promotion will be made more difficult by linguistic and cultural differences. Product changes will be less important than effective product positioning and image. Packaging and labelling will also need adjustment to cover legal, linguistic and cultural requirements.

Pricing, as already noted, is complicated by exchange rate movements and distribution costs. Available strategies divide into:

1 Price skimming – especially suited to innovative and speciality products.
2 Penetration price – though risky if exchange rates worsen.
3 Market-based strategies – imposed by competitors where the scope for differentiation is limited.

The ability to reduce costs is a major source of opportunity. Common standards and procedures, simpler administration and faster logistics should all save time and reduce costs. Major savings are expected from the rationalization of product ranges, scale economics and restructuring. Reduced development costs, combined with a huge single market, should encourage innovation, produce more rapid diffusion of new products and accelerate life-cycles. This would enhance the role of the marketing function and provide a springboard for more effective global marketing. Low barriers to entry and vigorous competition should provide the best environment for promoting costly high-tech innovation, and allow European firms to recover some of their lost market share.

Threats from intensified competition may also be identified. These may originate in competitors from outside the EC but be well adapted to large unified markets. State-owned monopolies using subsidized finance may also compete across boundaries, while low wage countries should be expected to fight fiercely for enhanced market share.

A corporate decision to go for the single market will be expensive if it is to be done properly, and must be carefully considered. It may be taken in order to facilitate growth or as the best means of achieving the volume of sales necessary to support innovation and scale economies. Alternatively, overseas sales may allow falling unit costs and provide a contribution to overheads. Where the domestic market has matured or competition has become increasingly severe, then single-market opportunities may provide the means for extending the product's life-cycle. Building a long term presence in Europe should also provide a counterweight to depressed market conditions at home and *vice versa*. Exposure to overseas competition will also introduce new standards of quality and performance, against which the firm may be judged and can strive to improve.

Entry to the SEM should be decided on profitability relative to risk. Research on political, economic, social and technological factors should be studied carefully in this assessment. Systems must be reorganized to meet the new demands, as must the people taking part. Their attitudes will be crucial to the quality of customer service provided, making the provision of appropriate training vitally important. Success requires an understanding of culture which is difficult to achieve, since it is largely unwritten and unspoken. It requires a knowledge of religion, morality, class and status, not to mention etiquette and humour, all of which vary widely between regions.

Overseas agents or distributors are usually nationals in the markets concerned. Normally paid on commission, their role is to identify potential customers and provide representation on the ground. They may assist the company to bridge the cultural gap outlined above, making the quality of the partnership with them crucial to success. They require appropriate reward and field support, however, if they are to operate effectively.

Transition to the single market will also bring its problems. Some argue that directives will not be fully implemented until the turn of the century. Delay in dismantling barriers or lack of full-hearted commitment will bring the possibilities of double standards, evasion and continued protection. Businesses will also have to learn to deal with the Community regulators, who will be enforcing the new single-market system.

Only a robust and positive response to the opportunities and threats will produce benefits for EC firms. Governments must represent national business interests in Brussels and provide support in the form of advice and information. However, the hard decisions will remain for business, allowing no easy options in adjustment to the SEM. Retraining, redeployment and restructuring appear inevitable if a successful adjustment is to take place.

1992 – projected impact on the economy

The Cecchini report of the European Commission suggested an addition to GDP of around 5–6 per cent accruing in a number of steps. Initial gains from removal of physical and trade barriers would be relatively small (0.25 per cent) compared to technical and other barriers (2.2 per cent). Medium term gains from the economies of scale were expected to add 2 per cent and increased competition a further 1.6 per cent. The impact arises from a combination of supply-side shocks, dynamic efficiencies, a psychological stimulus and various macroeconomic impacts.

Inflation was expected to fall by over 5 per cent, owing to increased competition and greater cost efficiency. Employment in net terms was also expected to rise by over 2 million through the dynamics of faster growth, but with particular sectors losing through restructuring and specialization. Public finances would improve through savings on procurement and boosted tax revenues from faster growth.

The liberalization of financial services was expected to bring particular gains to Britain. Protected markets in Spain, Italy, France and Germany were expected to see substantial price falls (25 to 30 per cent) through increased competition.

One unresolved issue is the size of the CET after 1992. Certain industries and countries wish to raise it and protect the internal market for themselves, whereas others, including Britain, wish to see it fall to stimulate world trade and reduce consumer prices.

After 1992 the domestic market for British firms will be in effect the SEM, and marketers must work towards changing the mindset of their organizations towards this new reality. The stability in exchange rate values provided by the ERM, combined with further progress towards monetary union and fiscal harmonization, should make competing in Hamburg no different to competing in Huddersfield.

Uncertainty will still exist for international markets outside the Community, since exchange rates, such as those for the dollar and the yen, will continue to fluctuate. One response is to view the world as a global marketplace, and deploy resources and marketing effort to optimize activities on this basis.

Conclusion

The SEM may be a belated reaction to Europe's changed circumstances, but it does provide an opportunity for revitalization. Although 1992 has for business become an overworked slogan, it does offer a vision for the future, and to the extent that business responds through restructuring and investment, it should become a self-fulfilling prophecy. However, should the initiative lose momentum or the opportunity be grasped by American or Japanese business, then the eventual payoff will not be forthcoming.

Summary review

1 Why was the 1992 initiative necessary when there was already a Common Market?

2 What evidence is there that British companies have made or are making the investments to ensure the SEM becomes a self- fulfilling prophesy?

3 Is the SEM approach consistent with:
    (a) Thatcherism (Chapter 11)
    (b) Porter's analysis (Chapter 11)?

24
The multinationals

Aims

The aim of this chapter is to consider the following questions:

- What is a multinational (MNC)?
- What is the significance of multinational business in Europe?
- Why should an exporter go multinational?
- Where should Britain encourage Japanese multinationals to locate?
- How can the global power of multinationals be harnessed?

Glossary

Capitalization – the value of a company as measured by the value of its entire issued capital, i.e. stock market price × issued shares = market capitalization.

Enterprise zones – these offer rate-free occupation of premises, simplification of planning procedures and enhanced capital allowances for taxation purposes on investment in industrial and commercial building.

European content requirements – to be considered a European product and able to access the SEM without attracting CET; foreign subsidiaries must ensure that a specified content percentage is made up of European components, thus preventing a multinational merely shipping parts to be assembled by a 'screwdriver' plant in the community.

Footloose – a term often applying to multinational subsidiaries that have no fixed preference in terms of location, but will respond to the most attractive package on offer.

Freeports – there are three of these in operation in the UK, where goods may be stored or processed duty free for re-export to destinations outside the European Community. They offer simplified customs procedures and economies of scale from the physical concentration of facilities, and potential for improved marketing and presentation.

Global marketing – the successful marketing of products with minimal physical or image differentiation in most countries of the world.

Greenfield site – location in a purpose-designed facility, providing maximum scope for achieving optimum layout of equipment and flow of production.

Market concentration – the percentage of total output or sales accounted for by the five largest firms in the industry.

transfer prices – prices applied to the internal transfer of components, sub-assemblies and finished products between MNC subsidiaries in different countries. Pricing items expensively when shipping to countries with high tax regimes will raise costs and reduce profits, so minimizing tax liabilities and *vice versa*.

Introduction

A multinational has been described in many ways by many different writers. A synthesis would suggest a true multinational has the following characteristics:

- Simultaneous production of goods and services in several different countries.
- An integrated system of distribution and marketing that ignores frontiers.
- A cluster of companies of different nationality bonded by common ownership and management.
- Global strategy that draws from a common pool of human and financial resources.

The scope of the definition is important, since one that included any company owning an overseas subsidiary, however small, would encompass thousands, whereas the concept of a multinational being organized on a global rather than a national perspective would restrict the count considerably.

The country that contains the headquarters of the MNC houses the *parent company* while the location of the subsidiary is in the *host country*. The development of truly global multinationals had to wait upon the communications revolution of the last two decades. Information technology was required if far-flung subsidiaries were to be managed in a strategically integrated manner. It is the technology of the jet, the satellite, the television and the computer that makes the global marketplace the final and increasingly accessible frontier for business.

Cultural convergence has already seen the development of global brands, ranging from Shell to Chanel and Levi's to the Hilton. Global companies can take advantage of business opportunities wherever they arise. They can utilize capital markets throughout the world and draw on an international pool of labour. They also benefit from their freedom to establish production facilities where resources can be most efficiently and effectively deployed.

Britain has a tradition of direct investment across national boundaries. The establishment of overseas subsidiaries, combined with acquisition of foreign corporate assets, has given it a significance second only to the USA in terms of multinationals. The global turnover of Britain's five largest multinationals is equivalent to over one third of her GDP, well over double the equivalent percentage for Japan, the USA, France and Germany.

Multinationals have grown dramatically since the 1950s to form complex and successful examples of international business co-operation. A list combining countries by GDP and multinationals by sales turnover results in over forty of the top 100 being companies. Oil majors such as Exxon and Shell have turnovers well in excess of countries such as Austria and Norway.

Multinational subsidiaries form a network that links the countries of the world in economic if not in political terms. The opening of a MacDonalds in Moscow or a Coca Cola bottling plant in China are isolated threads in a strengthening web of mutually advantageous relationships that make an important contribution to the maintenance of world peace.

Multinationals in Europe

The reader will no doubt be familiar with household names such as ICI, BP and BAT, but less so with European companies such as SKF, BASF and ABB. Table 24.1 shows the top European companies, ranked by capitalization, including those mentioned above.

Table 24.1 Extract from the FT European top 500

Rank 1990	Rank 1989	Company	Country	Sector	Capitalization ($bn)	Turnover ($bn)	Employment (000s)
1	1	Royal Dutch Steel	N/UK	Oil	68.5	89	135
2	3	British Telecom	UK	Telecoms	32	21	248
3	2	BP	UK	Oil	29	51	120
4	11	Allianz	Germ.	Ins.	27	n/a	43
5	9	Daimler Benz	Germ.	Auto	23	45	368
6	4	Unilever	N/UK	Food	23	37	296
7	10	Siemens	Germ.	Elec.	23	36	365
8	5	Nestles	Swi.	Food	22	34	197
9	16	Deutschbank	Germ.	Bank	21	n/a	57
10	7	Glaxo	UK	Drugs	21	4	28
13	8	BAT	UK	Cong.	17	31	312
16	23	ABB	Swe./Swi.	Elec.	15	21	190
19	13	ICI	UK	Chem.	14	23	134
40	26	BASF	Germ.	Chem.	9	28	137
150	140	SKF	Swe.	Mach.	3	4	50

Source: FT 11/1/91.

N = Netherlands; Swi. = Swiss; Swe. = Sweden; Ins. = Insurance; Cong. = conglomerate.

Turnover and employment measures are also included, but these criteria show a very different rank order. Fluctuating fortunes on the stock exchange cause much larger changes to take place in rankings based on capitalization than those based on turnover. UK companies dominate Table 24.1, although German multinationals are rising fast in significance.

Multinationals tend to predominate in certain sectors, such as oil, vehicles, information technology, chemicals and electrical engineering, although the significance of financial services may also be seen in Table 24.1. The most visible features of multinational companies are their size and concentration in high-technology and rapidly expanding sectors. Foreign firms already control one-fifth of British manufacturing, while proportions in other countries vary from well under 5 per cent in Japan to over 50 per cent in Canada.

In Britain, American multinationals are long established, accounting nearly two-thirds of all foreign subsidiaries. IBM (UK), for example, is located in Greenock, employing over 10,000 in a plant that outproduced ICL before the latter was taken over recently by Fujitsu. Eighty per cent of components are bought from over 400 British-based suppliers, providing much of the nourishment for the development of the Scottish electronics industry in Silicon Glen. IBM's global set-up is shown in Figure 24.1.

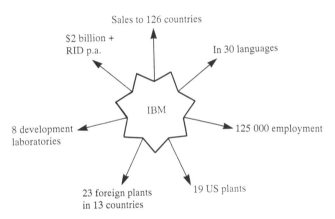

Figure 24.1 *IBM's operations worldwide*

More recently European and more visibly Japanese MNCs have established bases in Britain. Why should companies such as Sony, Nissan and Toyota choose to locate here? Japan's overseas direct investment has accelerated in recent years to a point where it rivals Britain for second place. Japan originally located subsidiaries in its immediate sphere of influence in East Asia. While factories in Japan exploited their comparative advantage in sophisticated consumer products, the basic assembly operations went multinational to exploit the cheaper labour in Far Eastern countries. In 1986 44 per cent of Japan's overseas consumer electronic plants were in Asia, with only 18 per cent in Europe (UK – 6 per cent) and 16 per cent in North America.

Most Japanese investment in Europe up to 1986 was in financial services. Investment has increased recently, with the impending arrival of the SEM, with Britain accounting over 40 per cent of the total, mainly in the form of greenfield developments. The Japanese do not normally favour takeovers of existing companies, although Fujitsu's £743m acquisition of ICL proves an exception.

Why the Japanese go multinational

The following arguments summarize the main considerations:

1 *Avoidance of tariff barriers* – the enviable success of the Japanese in exporting vehicles, cameras, consumer electronics and so forth produced a rapidly rising trade surplus, on the one hand, and increasingly vocal opposition, on the other. The result was voluntary export restraints negotiated under duress of the threat of denied access to the emerging SEM.
2 *European government pressure* – to set up plants and therefore reduce imports from Japan.
3 *Demonstration effects* – when one Japanese company locates in Europe, it puts pressures on others to follow suit or risk losing competitive advantage. The success of pioneer plants in achieving higher productivity also overcame Japanese concern about European workforces. If exports are the first wave and overseas assembly plants the second wave, it may well be that a third wave of Japanese component producers will increasingly follow their customers as they migrate abroad. Nippondenso, Japan's largest vehicle components maker, is already building a £65m plant at Telford.
4 *A rising yen* – this made it progressively cheaper to manufacture abroad than to ship exports. Relatively cheap labour costs in parts of Europe and generous government incentives reinforced this.
5 *Access to markets* – physical presence is often the only means of breaking into certain markets, especially the public procurement market. The firm on the spot has the ability to respond more effectively in marketing and distribution terms to local needs. Local plants promote familiarity with Japanese products and confidence in their ability to provide customer after-care.

The attractiveness of the UK as a Japanese base

The strategic choice of the UK for the lion's share of Japanese investment in Europe may be explained by the following factors:

Britain's membership of the EC

This provides access to the single market, given that the European content requirements are met.

Language

English is Japan's second language, as well as being the business language of the world. It covers an estimated 80 per cent of all computer programs and is used by most multinational companies.

Incentives

Britain now possesses an extremely favourable climate for business. Red tape has been reduced and corporation taxes (Figure 24.2) are among the lowest in the industrialized world. Political stability is also important, as is the warm welcome extended by the government and local authorities in attempting to secure the inward investment. Such attitudes are in marked

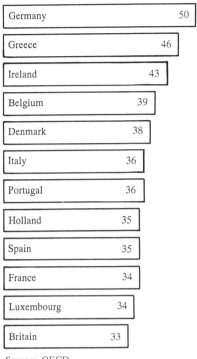

Germany   50
Greece   46
Ireland   43
Belgium   39
Denmark   38
Italy   36
Portugal   36
Holland   35
Spain   35
France   34
Luxembourg   34
Britain   33

Source: OECD

Figure 24.2 *Company tax rates*

contrast to those found in the USA and many other European countries. Rivalry between different regions to attract Japanese companies has produced a very professional approach, making maximum use of available regional and EC incentives. Nissan, for example, received grants making up almost 25 per cent of their initial investment.

Infrastructure

Britain is a compact country possessing integrated transport and communications. Ports offer cheap and easy access to other EC markets. Its well developed capital markets make for efficient financing, and it also possesses a pool of skills at relatively low wages.

Consumer markets

Britain often forms the strongest market for the Japanese companies that locate in Europe. High ownership of consumer durables and vehicles, plus a willingness to pioneer new product offerings, make the market an ideal base. The efficient distribution system also provides for rapid diffusion of products into the marketplace.

Union flexibility

New attitudes under Thatcherism and the pressure of high unemployment in regional areas has prompted many unions to sign single union agreements and no-strike deals.

Multinationals can be powerful engines of change and progress. They improve international division of labour, and support the development of a global market. Some might even argue that they are an effective counterbalance to the power of the unions and governments. From Britain's point of view, if she does not attract them, they will almost certainly locate elsewhere in the EC to her competitive disadvantage.

Nissan Motor Manufacturing (UK) Ltd

Nissan's association with Britain started in 1952, when it produced Austin cars under licence in Japan.

Despite a false start in 1982, production began in 1987 with 24,000 vehicles. At £600m it was the largest single Japanese direct investment in Europe. Facilities included a paint shop, final and body assembly, with press shop, injection moulding and engine assembly added later.

Teeside was selected as its export terminal, and shipments to nine continental countries began in 1988. By 1991 these accounted for over 80 per cent of production, as local content rose to move them 80 per cent. The Washington site now includes three test tracks and ample space for expansion. There are plans to produce 100,000 vehicles by 1991 and 200,000 by 1993, as the workforce rises to 3,500.

Of over 120 EC suppliers appointed, nearly 100 are British. By 1991 80 per cent had located in the North-east, including joint ventures such as Ikeda Hoover (seats) and TI Nihon (exhausts). All bar Nissan's financial director are British, as is the young workforce. It is a single status plant where accommodation is open plan and a loose decision-making structure based on wide consultation is used. A single union agreement with the AUEW is combined with an elected company council.

Productivity is reported to be extremely high (40+ vehicles per man year), double that in other British plants and equivalent to performance in some Japanese plants.

The case against active encouragement

Despite the strength of the economic arguments outlined above, there are a number of considerations that must give governments pause for thought before opening their doors to multinationals:

- The cost of the package necessary to attract and retain them may be substantial. Multinationals are in a position to play one state off against another in order to maximize inducements obtained. It could also be argued that this unfairly subsidizes the multinational to the disadvantage of domestic firms. The new entrant obtains the benefit of a greenfield site designed to the production needs of the 1990s at a subsidized price, while existing firms must compete in established but often outdated plants.

  Governments may also be forced to compromise their policies under threat of multinationals ceasing investment or even moving their operation elsewhere.
- Multinational decisions are more likely to respond to global imperatives and profit than domestic priorities. There is a danger of becoming over-dependent on foreign firms in key sectors of the economy. The so-called *branch factory* economy has been cited as a risk of such

dependence, since it may be these that are vulnerable to closure in the event of a world recession. It is also argued that multinationals locate *screwdriver* (assembly) plants in preference to high-technology research and development facilities. The latest design, products and processes are developed and marketed initially in Japan, allowing the parent company to retain the edge.

- Multinationals are flexible, being able to switch output investment and exports on a global basis. Through *transfer pricing* they can manipulate costs and profits in different subsidiaries so as to minimize their tax liabilities.
- To the extent the new entry causes domestic producers to merge, the degree of market concentration in the industry will rise.
- The fact that multinationals are so large suggests they possess an unequal power compared to many unions and governments. This is often argued to be the case in less developed countries, where they have often been viewed as exploitive.
- Multinationals are also criticized for contributing towards a progressive loss of national identity and culture. This criticism is particularly levelled against American multinationals, which have gone furthest towards global product marketing.
- Problems of multiple jurisdiction may arise where the parent government imposes policies that apply not only to its home companies but also to their subsidiaries abroad. US high-technology trade embargoes on the USSR have been examples of this.

Policies to control the multinationals

In order to secure the benefits but avoid the dangers and costs of MNCs, governments have tried to regulate their activities. To counter the power of the multinationals requires collaboration and exchange of information between governments to prevent them being played off against one another. Codes of practice have been developed by the OECD and EC, for example, but these have seldom been enforced to any great effect.

EC directives governing the size of incentive packages, content requirements and progressive harmonization of legal, fiscal and other policies should, however, remove much of the incentive to switch resources across frontiers.

Less developed countries often encourage or insist on joint ventures with national companies, while local content requirements and employment of nationals in the strategic management of the subsidiaries are often useful in reducing tensions. In some cases governments have countered the risk of dependency on MNC's by encouraging domestic competitors. Industries in the vehicle, aerospace and computer fields have been restructured with state encouragement in order to realize scale economies and counteract the market power of multinationals.

Governments also use the various methods of regulation that check the activities of any large organization. These include monopoly and fair-trading legislation, standards and requirements of various types. If regulation is too strict, however, investment may be frightened away, with a possible reduction in prosperity. If instead a selective and flexible approach based on mutual understanding of needs is used, then benefits to all concerned may result.

Conclusion

The scale and importance of the multinationals is bound to make them controversial. From one perspective they are powerful engines of change and progress, and may be viewed as efficient, flexible and the latest stage in the evolution of large-scale business. They form the most effective means devised so far of organizing business on a world scale. From another perspective they are criticized as being exploitive, especially of poor countries. The tendency of British multinationals to invest more overseas is attacked, for depriving domestic industry of much needed investment, and exporting jobs.

While accused of forcing concessions from governments, MNCs in a host country are also concerned for their image. They often transfer superior home standards to their overseas plants, paying relatively high wages and providing excellent training and welfare. Their relatively high profile may also cause them to take greater account of social responsibilities than domestic firms.

Whatever the balance of the arguments may be, multinationals will continue to represent an increasing influence on international marketing activities. Chapter 25 will focus on one possible threat to the fortunes of the MNCs in the shape of protectionism and its implications for world trade liberalization.

Summary review

1 What adjectives would you associate with the term multinational? How many American, European and Japanese MNCs can you think of in:
    (a) Vehicles.
    (b) Consumer electronics.
    (c) Banking.

2 What considerations led Nissan to locate in the North-east, whereas Toyota has located in the Midlands?

3 Do foreign multinationals herald the revival or demise of British manufacturing industry?

25
GATT and protectionism

Aims

The aims of this chapter are as follows:

- To outline the scope of the General Agreement on Tariffs and Trade (GATT).
- To describe the main forms of trade protection used by governments, and examine their economic effects.
- To discuss the case for and against the use of protection.
- To examine the potential appeal of protection.

Glossary

Bilateral trade agreements – negotiations between two countries only. Much of the trade with Eastern bloc countries remains on this basis.

Countertrade – is a form of barter trade between firms or governments. For example, one country might import machinery but make payment with a quantity of oil or coal. It has increased in situations where a country's trade 'credit' is suspect.

Export credit guarantees – insurance provided by government, giving cover for major risks in exporting.

Most favoured nation – this requires any GATT member offering a tariff reduction to one country to offer reciprocal arrangements to all other members.

Reciprocity – this requires that a country provides a tariff reduction comparable in value to that introduced by a trading partner.

GATT

The General Agreement on Tariffs and Trade was signed just after World War 2 as one part of a new international economic order designed to avoid a return to the protectionism that had blighted the 1930s. Accounting for over four-fifths of world trade and with membership currently around 100, it aims:

1 To eliminate existing trade barriers.
2 To deter the formation of new ones.
3 To work towards the elimination of all forms of trade discrimination.

Less developed countries are not expected to fully reciprocate the tariff reductions of richer countries and are granted a generalized system of preferences. Their obligations are, however, expected to increase as they successfully develop their economies.

Originally applied primarily to manufacturing trade, negotiations have been extended in the latest Uruguay round to cover services and agriculture. The key principle in GATT's operational effectiveness is the equality of treatment implied in the *most favoured nation* clause. Similarly if after the required consultation a tariff is raised against one member, it must be raised against them all. This discourages members from taking such actions, since it would greatly increase the risk of retaliation. Such principles also provide member governments with support against their own domestic vested interests, which might otherwise seek privileged protection.

Regular discussions take place between members with a view to achieving concerted progress towards further liberalization of trade. The Tokyo round, completed in 1984, achieved a tariff reduction of around one-third among industrial countries but against a background of creeping non-tariff protection.

The current Uruguay round is the eighth and possibly the most ambitious initiative. These negotiations should have been concluded by the end of 1990, but broke down over American demands for deeper cuts in EC agricultural support than the 30 per cent on offer. While talks have resumed, a considerable gulf appears to separate the various trade interests being represented. The USA is also seeking to achieve full reciprocity, meaning balanced access in specific product sectors. This is directed against Japan, who, it is claimed, prevents equal access to many of its markets. Britain and the EC, for example, have threatened to prevent Japanese access to financial service markets unless access on an equal footing in Japan is allowed.

The forces of protectionism

Despite more liberal trade practices, inspired by GATT, all governments restrict free trade to some degree. The three main methods or barriers to trade are the following.

Tariffs or duties

These are either specific (lump sum tax per unit) or *ad valorem* (percentage of selling price) taxes, which have the effect of raising import prices relative to domestic prices. Revenue is earned but the effect can be inflationary. Tariffs are usually selectively targeted on sectors where domestic producers are most vulnerable to competition.

Import quotas

These form an upper limit on the quantity or value of imports allowed per time period. One example of quotas would be those established under the multi-fibre agreement in textiles. A number of European countries also have voluntary export restraint agreements with the Japanese vehicle exporters. The Italians have a voluntary quota limiting vehicle imports to just 3,000 per year. The spread of restraints such as these are attempts to evade GATT rules, and often carry official sanctions to encourage compliance. One special form of zero quota is an *embargo*, as applied until recently to most South African exports.

Non-tariff barriers

These include all other means of restricting trade, and have formed a growing category since the early 1970s. There are a variety of possibilities, including:

1 Specific standards or requirements on quality, environment or safety.
2 Tax advantages or subsidies to domestic producers, e.g. export credit guarantees.
3 Exchange controls to regulate capital flows.
4 Public sector procurement policies discriminating in favour of domestic firms.
5 HM Customs and other administrative requirements.

The economic effects of a tariff are the same as for an indirect tax (Figure 25.1), shifting the supply curve from S_1 to S_2. The quantity imported falls to OQ_2 while domestic prices rise to OP_2. A quota of OQ_2 makes the supply curve vertical at that point with an identical effect on price. However, while a tariff yields the shaded area in tax revenue, a quota confers the benefit onto foreign suppliers. This may be avoided if the government is able to auction the quota to the highest bidder. Any improvements in cost-efficiency will shift the supply curve down, causing higher imports but lower prices under the tariff regime. No such benefit would be felt with quotas, since quantity remains fixed at OQ_2. Non-tariff barriers act to shift demand curves for imports in to the left causing quantity to fall but not the price.

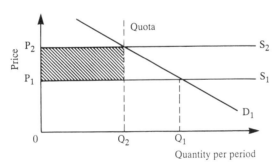

Figure 25.1 *The effects of a tariff and a quota*

The case for protectionism

Although a number of points may be made under this heading they vary in the degree to which they hold true:

- Protection allows the achievement of other objectives, such as a *balanced industrial structure*, which avoids the dangers of over-specialization and dependence on overseas suppliers. Support given to defence and other strategic industries, such as computers and the common agricultural policy, are good examples of such protection.
- *Infant industry protection* to allow newly established sectors time to build resources, achieve economies and move down the experience curve is a frequently used justification. Lack of initial comparative advantage may be remedied in this way, although concern centres on whether such infants ever grow to independent maturity. When governments identify

sectors for such encouragement, there is doubt expressed as to their ability to pick winners effectively. It may also be argued that it is the very exposure to full international competition that forces the efficiency and innovation necessary to achieve a sustainable advantage in the long run. Exposure to open competition while still protecting the industry might be better achieved by way of a subsidy that avoids raising prices but forces the home producers to market on a progressively more equal footing. Unfortunately for a less developed country subsidies need to be financed by politically unpopular taxes, whereas the less efficient tariffs raise revenue at the expense of importers and the consumers.

Similar arguments to the above have been made to allow temporary protection for mature industries in order to restructure after being overtaken by superior technology. The revival of the Italian motorcycle industry would be a case in point.

- The *revenue* from tariffs or improvement in terms of trade may make protection beneficial for one country even if all others lose. The danger of inviting damaging retaliation may however be significant.
- Protection also offers temporary relief from an *adverse balance of payments*. Co-operation of trading partners would, however, be necessary if retaliation was to be avoided.

An argument often put forward in favour of protection is to defend home producers against *cheap foreign labour*. This runs counter to the comparative advantage principle, and would deprive consumers of the benefit of buying from the cheapest source. It would also protect inefficient local producers and tend to depress domestic wage levels to lower standards in these countries. Tariff protection may safeguard jobs but at the expense of higher prices and a frozen industrial structure. Retraining and redeployment to higher value added activity is a better route to improving living standards in the long run.

Similar arguments are made in respect to the *dumping* of goods by foreign firms at below cost or with unfair export subsidies. Domestic consumers clearly gain in both cases, but if the intent is to destroy local industry and create import dependence as the prelude to raising prices in the longer term, then protection may well be justified. GATT's anti-dumping code allows penalties to be imposed where deliberate under-pricing causes material damage to domestic producers.

The case against import controls

The key arguments against control may be summarized as follows:

- It invites retaliation and the possibility of trade war in which all parties suffer a contraction in activity.
- It may divert competition into one's own export markets.
- It destroys the benefits of free trade.
- It insulates industry from the need to change.
- It increases the power of business and union interest groups.
- It raises domestic prices and reduces consumer choice.
- Once established, it breeds dependence and is difficult to abolish.
- If believed to be temporary, it will not encourage investment in import substitution.
- It will conflict with international obligations to GATT, the EC and IMF.
- If the objective is to switch demand to the domestic economy, this is better achieved by a monetary or fiscal stimulus.

The effects of protectionism

Research has shown that protectionism yields greater costs than benefits in both the long term and the short term. Circular flow analysis shows that a reduction in exports caused by protectionism will, other things being equal, cause national income to fall. The multiplier contraction in national income will in turn reduce a country's ability to import from other countries, setting up a chain reaction. The country that initiates the protection may succeed in protecting jobs in the threatened sector but ultimately loses jobs generally across the export industries. Despite the logic of this analysis, protectionism still occurs, since:

1 Jobs are obviously saved once the protection is applied.
2 Such jobs tend to be visible and protected by vocal political lobbies of business, unions and local political representatives.
3 Jobs lost will be widely spread across other countries' export industries.
4 Jobs lost in domestic export industries are more diffused and unorganized.
5 Consumers who lose through higher prices and reduced choice are also less effective as a lobby unless particularly dependent on the product in question.
6 The affected country may not allow national income to fall but would rather finance the balance of payments deficit that will result. This may prove inflationary.

Any moves towards protectionism threaten the multilateral trade system promoted by GATT. GATT has limited influence, with adverse publicity for offending countries its only real sanction.

The main threats currently include:

- The growth of non-tariff barriers.
- A rise in trade-diverting bilateral deals, e.g. between the USA and Canada.
- Countertrade deals.
- An increase in anti-dumping actions.

Anti-dumping actions have been taken against a number of high technology Japanese products in Europe on the argument of preserving capability in the technology. This has been seen by some as part of the foundation stones to the construction of a 'fortress Europe'.

Summary review

1 Can you explain why the forces of protectionism are said to be increasing?

2 Taking your industry or one you are familiar with, identify efforts made by businesses or their associations to obtain or maintain protection from foreign competition.

3 Make a convincing case to the European Commission justifying the dismantling of CAP protection. How could you implement your ideas to make them more acceptable to community farmers?

26
Third World debt

Aims

- To compare the economy in 1990 with that in 1980.
- To examine the origins and consequences of the debt crisis.
- To recognize the interdependence of the world economy by considering trade in the circular flow.
- To review developed country responses to the problems of the Third World.
- To describe the functions of important international agencies.

Glossary

Conspicuous consumption – government or consumer buyer behaviour where utility is derived from impressing others by purchasing ostentatious goods. Presidential palaces and executive jets may be purchased ahead of real development projects.

Debt exposure – the ratio of outstanding loans to a bank's equity capital.

Flight capital – is invested by less developed country nationals in overseas assets. It arises over fears that capital invested domestically may either earn very low returns or be appropriated by the state.

Rescheduling – is where a borrower, unable to meet the original terms, renegotiates the duration and repayment pattern on a loan.

Secondary market – any market in which debt sales are transacted outside the recognized or primary market.

Tied aid – is aid granted to one country by another on the proviso that it will be spent only in the lender nation.

Background to the world economy

The world economy in 1980 closely resembled the position in 1990. Oil price rises, associated with the Gulf War, reached record heights in real terms, adding a twist to the spiral of inflation. The decision by American and British governments to control this inflation by means of monetary and fiscal policy induced global recession and sharply rising levels of unemployment.

Business and public reaction to the mounting jobless increased protectionist pressures on government. As interest rates rose and business confidence fell, it was Third World countries that were the worst affected. Having sustained their development programmes with recycled borrowings from the western banking system in the mid-seventies, they now found themselves in a classic debt crisis. Recession reduced their export revenues, on the one hand, as developed countries curtailed demand for commodities, while higher interest rates sharply raised debt repayments, making it difficult for them to make ends meet.

Despite the gloomy beginnings, the 1980s saw oil prices, inflation and unemployment fall, producing the longest period of sustained expansion for many years. This was made possible by the severity of the initial recession, combined with a renaissance in free market economics. A rolling back in the importance of the state, combined with progressive privatization, deregulation and liberalization in the major economies, sustained business confidence. This change in mood was reflected most stunningly in the liberalization of the planned economies in Eastern Europe.

By 1990 the long boom was over in Britain and America, as real interest rates rose to cope with the overheating economies. Another Gulf crisis was pending, triggering stock-market collapses at the end of the year. The Third World debt situation had become a persistent problem, producing a growing gap between North and South.

There were also tensions arising out of chronic trade and payments imbalances, most notably between Britain and America on the one hand and Japan and Germany on the other. Increased protectionism remained a real threat as America searched for solutions to its sizeable deficit. Concern for the longer term environmental threats, arising from global warming, were also beginning seriously to exercise world consciousness.

North v South

With the well-fed and well-educated North (or developed countries) accounting for four-fifths of global income and energy consumption but with just one quarter of world population, the distinctions are clear. Figure 26.1 shows the north's share of gross world product (excluding USSR and Comecon) actually increasing from 65 to 72 per cent between 1975 and 1987. Progress was made by the South in manufactured trade, however, as GATT figures (see Figure 26.2) registered a doubling in their share over the period 1973–87.

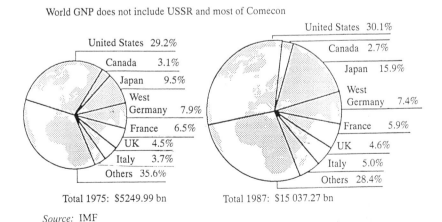

World GNP does not include USSR and most of Comecon

United States 29.2%
Canada   3.1%
Japan   9.5%
West
Germany   7.9%
France   6.5%
UK   4.5%
Italy   3.7%
Others   35.6%

Total 1975: $5249.99 bn

United States 30.1%
Canada   2.7%
Japan   15.9%
West
Germany   7.4%
France   5.9%
UK   4.6%
Italy   5.0%
Others   28.4%

Total 1987: $15 037.27 bn

Source: IMF

Figure 26.1 *Gross world product*

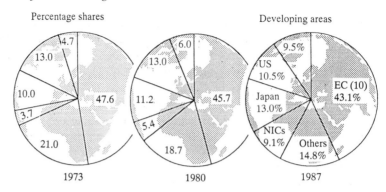

Figure 26.2 *World manufacturing trade*

Dealing with Third World debt

The scale of outstanding debt has continued to rise in real terms, as seen in Figure 26.3. The debt figures for oil exporters is accounted for by oil prices, which fell continuously from 1980 to 1988. The trend in real commodity prices was also downwards until 1987, when the boom in developed economies eventual brought a recovery.

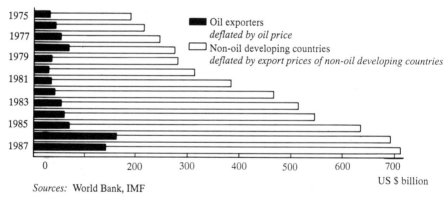

Sources: World Bank, IMF

Figure 26.3 *Real debt*

The debt crisis came to a head in 1982, when Mexico, second only to Brazil amongst the debt heavyweights, was unable to service its $100bn debt. The exposure of the world's 100 largest banks in Latin American loans alone was 125 per cent of their equity. Had widespread default occurred, many would have been technically bankrupt, including the four major British retail banks. In the event the debt was successfully rescheduled, but only at the expense of hobbling the economic growth prospects of the debtors into the foreseeable future. Debtors were obliged to submit to IMF adjustment programmes as the price of obtaining further funding, yet new credit extended by western banks to assist the necessary development of these countries has all but dried up. They were understandably wary about lending more good money after bad. The result has been a reversal of the flow of funds in the world economy, with a net outflow from South to North of $120bn in the 5 years to 1990.

Normally there would be a positive flow of long-term development finance from North to South as a vital ingredient in their economic progress. Such loans would be officially sponsored through government agencies and make sound economic sense. They would finance purchases of equipment and technical assistance from developed countries, stimulating trade flows and world growth.

Western banks have now made reserve provisions to cover a large part of their Third World debt exposure, making a collapse in the international financial system now unlikely. The issue is still of vital international concern, however, owing to the prolonged austerity being suffered by the debtor countries. Many are fragile democracies susceptible to social and political unrest arising out of their depressed conditions.

The threat of the debt may be seen by considering the scale of world trade flows in Figure 26.4. In circular flow analysis terms any interruption in these flows would have serious implications for world income, output and employment. The size of the flows between the EC and less developed countries is particularly noticeable and attention will be focused on that. The importance of North America's trade with the rest of the world, and especially with Asian and Pacific economies, should also be noted. Its attitude towards protection is clearly of crucial importance to the maintenance of these flows.

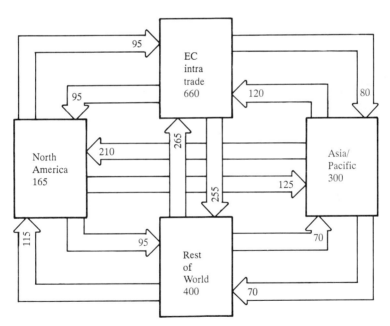

Figure 26.4   *World trade flows ($ Bn)*

The flows of expenditure support real income, output and jobs (Figure 26.5), with net injections boosting growth. For less developed countries this should be in the form of developmental finance from more prosperous countries, usually in long-term loans and short-term credits to finance trade. Direct investment by multinationals would also inject extra finance.

Despite a UN resolution for aid to rise from 0.7 per cent to 1 per cent of GDP, limited progress has so far been made. The majority of rich countries provide less than 0.5 per cent, with only Scandinavian countries approaching the target.

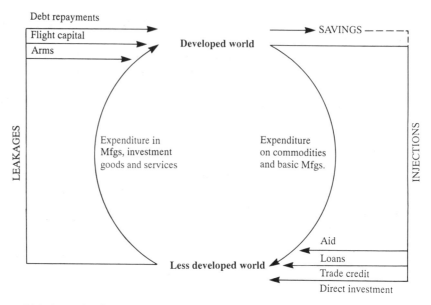

Figure 26.5   *Global circular flow analysis*

On the leakage side, debt repayments have already been mentioned as exceeding capital inflows by a large margin. Flight capital also contributes to the debt problem, with up to 45 per cent of the total debt outstanding thought to be held in balances in western banks. The shortage of development capital is compounded when expenditure is on conspicuous consumption and arms sales. Such spending is unlikely to produce self-sustained take-off into industrial development.

Critical responses required

The current state of Third World debt produces a number of dangers:

- *Of creeping default* – much of the outstanding debt already realizes just a fraction of its full value in secondary markets. Sovereign state defaults in the 1930s occurred long after the initial crisis and may do so again.
- *Of recession and creeping protectionism* – as tariff and non-tariff barriers are introduced by debtors and creditors alike, the circular flow becomes constricted, risking a cumulative contraction.
- *Of hobbling Third World growth* – by requiring them to take the full burden of adjustment.

Taking the EC as an example, the possible responses to the crisis may be divided into the following.

Action to raise revenue flows to the debtors

1 The most positive contribution the EC could make would be the achievement of sustained economic growth. This would raise demand for their materials, fuels and manufactures, generating revenue for repayment of debt interest and principal.

2 Trade preferences for debtors would also generate revenue, and the EC operates such a system primarily with former colonies.
3 A progressive dismantling of quotas on sensitive manufactures such as textiles would allow repayment in the only way possible for debtors, by selling creditor nations exports.
4 Stabilizing the earnings on primary products, which tend to fluctuate in a volatile manner. The EC operates limited schemes to help achieve this, known as 'Stabex and Minex'.
5 Provision of export credits.

Action to alleviate the debt burden

1 Lower interest rates would have a major impact on debt repayments.
2 A lower dollar exchange rate would also help, since many debts are designated in this currency, as are primary product prices.
3 An increase in bank lending would help to reverse the flow of funds.
4 Restructuring, with debt write-offs, would also reduce the burden. The difficulty here lies in who pays the bill. Western governments have resisted bailing out either the debtors or the banks, since it would not penalize them for having made doubtful loans in the first place. A bad precedent would be set, with taxpayers left to carry the cost.
5 Increase lending through official channels.

International Institutions

The institutions established to achieve increased official lending include the following.

The International Monetary Fund (IMF)

Founded in 1945, with a membership of nearly 150 countries, its main role is the achievement of exchange rate stability. Resources provided by member nations are lent to countries experiencing deficits. Borrowing is normally for 3 to 5 years, conditional on agreement to a programme of macroeconomic adjustment policies.

Countries with temporary balance of payments problems have turned increasingly to bank borrowing to avoid submitting to IMF conditions, forcing it to transform its role. It has therefore established a facility that provides loans to less developed debtors unable to borrow at normal commercial rates. Around sixty of the world's poorest countries are now eligible for virtually interest-free loans, but they are expected to introduce IMF restructuring programmes in return.

The World Bank

This was established alongside the IMF to encourage long-term capital investment in member countries. Loans are made at market rates, almost invariably to less developed countries. It encourages participative ventures with private financial institutions and provides technical expertise as well as the funds subscribed to it by member governments. It has two affiliated organizations:

1 The *International Finance Corporation*, which aims to channel aid to less developed countries without the need for guarantees. Funds are obtained from a variety of private sources, including subscriptions.

2 The *International Development Association* provides very low interest loans for specific LDC projects that cannot obtain commercial funding. These normally involve very long term infrastructure investments.

The European Investment Bank

This was established by the Treaty of Rome to fund projects that benefited less developed regions of the community or required finance by a number of member countries. Since 1980, a proportion of these loans have been made to signatories of the Lomé Convention between the EC and developing countries.

In summary the economic development of Third World debtors depends largely on policy-makers in the industrial countries. Only they have the resources to deal with the problem. Sustained growth in the industrial countries, combined with a strong rise in the volume of world trade, would constitute a better antidote to debt than any number of recovery plans. In the absence of increased capital flows or default, the only way the debtors can meet their obligations is through trade surpluses. Against the background of renewed recession it is an open question as to whether creditors will allow this to happen and run the corresponding deficit on their balance of payments.

Summary review

1 Assess the prospects for another long boom in the 1990s. Will less developed countries participate in the process?

2 What evidence can you find to suggest that critical responses to deal with Third World debt and under-development are being made?

3 How would British business be affected if Brazil defaulted on its debts?

Section Eight: Projects and exercises

1 Having completed the macroeconomic part of the text, turn to the foundation exercise you undertook at the start of your studies (see p. 146 and Appendix 1), and

(a) Find current values for all of the indices listed.

(b) Now work through each pair of values and on the basis of your macroeconomic knowledge suggest why the values have risen, fallen or stayed the same.

(c) Complete the third column, which requires you to forecast the value of the indices in 6 months' time and 1 year's time. Justify your prediction in the box provided.

(d) In the light of your predictions make recommendations for your chosen organisation to undertake in:

(i) the short term,

(ii) the medium term.

2 You have been given responsibility to compile a report for senior management on the statistical and other market research information currently available to assist potential exporters to the European Community. Your report should cover as wide a variety of sources as possible and assess their value. Clearly identify the limitations of the available information.

3 Formulate a marketing strategy to meet the challenge of the Single European Market for *one* of the following:

(a) A consumer goods supplier.

(b) A capital goods producer.

(c) A financial services provider.

It might be helpful to consider this in the context of an actual company, e.g. the Halifax Building Society. Think about how its strategies might vary with different markets. Identify the economic advantages to be gained. What are the economic risks?

4 In the light of the following article from the *Financial Times* management page, summarize the economic characteristics of a business likely to be accepted as a Toyota supplier.

How Toyota filters its component suppliers

John Griffiths *reports on the Japanese car maker's exhaustive search in the UK*

Toyota, Japan's largest car maker, is in the very last stages of whittling down to 150, from 2,000, the would-be suppliers of prototype components to its £700m UK car plant now under construction in Derbyshire.

Toyota would be desperately vulnerable to any shortcomings in its parts suppliers. It buys in 75 per cent of the value of its cars, compared with only around one half for European vehicle makers.

Yet far from 'importing' tried-and-trusted Japanese suppliers, Toyota insists that when all its Derby suppliers are disclosed they will include only a handful of Japanese companies. The vast majority, it says, will be based in the UK and continental Europe.

The disclosure by Lucas Industries on Monday that it is to supply prototype brakes, batteries and wiring harnesses to the Derby project provides yet further proof that Toyota is paying more than lip service to maximizing 'local' (EC, not just UK) content, insist Bryan Jackson, a Toyota Motor Manufacturing UK director, and Jim Robinson, its parts procurement manager who has overseen the selection process.

The point was underlined by managing director Yukihisa Hirano at a Welsh Development Agency conference last month when he talked of 'misperceptions' about the so-called Japanese 'transplants'.

'Toyota has never asked any Japanese companies to set up in Europe,' Hirano declared. 'Among the companies from whom we have ordered prototype parts only a few are Japanese, and they were established in Europe before we made our decision to manufacture here.'

The list has been drawn up on the basis that the companies' technological abilities, investments in research and development, plant, equipment and other resources are of a standard that should allow long-term partnerships to develop with Toyota.

And while Hirano stresses that 'there is a great deal of work ahead,' his senior management maintains that there appear to be no insuperable problems over quality standards or the prices Toyota is prepared to pay for its parts. The prototype parts supply winners, who also stand to gain the overwhelming majority of full production orders for components when the assembly line at the 280-acre site starts rolling towards its 200,000 cars annually next year, will not formally be listed until two months' time.

But they include British engineering group GKN, Pilkington Glass subsidiary Triplex, Pirelli, the Italian tyres and cables group which has a subsidiary at Burton-on-Trent and instrumentation group VDO.

The process by which Toyota has arrived at its supplier list should be assimilated by any European supplier seeking a share of Japanese 'transplant' business, which is expected to continue expanding in Europe throughout the next decade.

Even though the first car will not come off the line at Burnaston, Derbyshire, until December 1992, the selection process is already three years old. It began in early 1989, with Toyota's European administrative office in Brussels compiling initial data on 2,000 potential suppliers.

At this initial stage, 'we had open doors', recalls Jackson. 'Lots of companies came to talk to us off their own bat; some applied through contact with the SMMT (the UK's Society of Motor Manufacturers and Traders), some through chambers of commerce, and so on. There were too many to see individually so we checked their reputations, resources, customer bases, and so on, and there were some we could disregard straight away.'

A little closer scrutiny left Toyota quickly able to whittle down the number in which it was seriously interested to 400 – already fewer than half the number of direct suppliers to most European vehicle makers.

Even this partial selection process serves to highlight one of the key differences between Japanese and European component supply structures. In the former, few but large 'first tier' suppliers account for more than 60 per cent of the total added-value of a vehicle, with thousands of small 'second tier' companies supplying the big component companies like Nippondenso. In Europe the number of direct suppliers is greater and they are more highly specialised.

Both British-born Toyota men, with long backgrounds

in the indigenous European industry, say that from what they have experienced of the thinking behind the Japanese system, it has clear-cut advantages over the old European ways. 'It's rather difficult to have a relationship with 1,000 suppliers,' observes Jackson. 'It's much better to have fewer, who are more closely involved.'

Closer involvement in Toyota's case has meant shortlisted companies being asked to quote for entire product groups, not individual components, 'to give them a larger, more worthwhile chunk of the business,' says Jackson.

At the 400-candidate stage, the selection process became much more painstaking. Over a period of 10 months a number of multi-disciplinary Toyota teams assessed capabilities according to four key criteria:

• management capability and attitude;
• production and manufacturing facilities, and level of investment in technology;
• quality control systems and philosophy;
• research and development capability.

This stage of weeding out reduced the 400 to 250, who were then asked to submit firm costs 'to give us a feel for price competition'. All were then deemed acceptable in terms of their potential to meet quality and price standards.

The first prototype parts orders were issued as far back as last October, and the stream of components is already flowing fast, with most expected to have been received by Toyota by the end of this month. The orders cover a sufficient breadth of components to take prototypes up to the 80 per cent 'local' content, although this is not scheduled to be reached in terms of commercial production until early 1995. Toyota fully expects to hit the 60 per cent level within 6 months of start-up, however.

The awarding of prototype contracts means, if anything, an intensification of contacts between Toyota and its would-be production suppliers. Toyota is continuing to

give a series of presentations to all of them to reinforce awareness of its expectations.

A total of eight such meetings have been held already and another series will be held as the project moves from prototype stage to the awarding of production parts contracts. 'It's a physical demonstration that being a supplier to Toyota is going to be different,' stresses Jackson. 'You start to change your mind set. One of our philosophies is to motivate – people are capable of doing much more than is usually required of them, and we ask them to demonstrate it.'

The process, Robinson claims, is a two-way street, with Toyota not necessarily seeking to impose Japanese methods by diktat. As one small example, Japanese and European manufacturers differ in the way gearshifts are usually made. But, says Robinson, it is clearly not cost-effective for a European factory to throw away large investments already made, 'so that supplier will be left to cope just as long as the product meets Toyota's standards.'

Suppliers have been left in no doubt what those standards are – they are showered with *pro formas* which minutely detail what has been discussed and understood between supplier and vehicle maker.

For most suppliers, it was a wholly alien approach and many grumbled in the early stages that there was far too much paperwork. 'But then they came to realise that this way every eventuality gets covered. No-one has to interpret anything, because it's all there in black and white.'

Subsequently, says Jackson, 'they have been very impressed by the thoroughness.' Toyota is, as yet, reticent about claiming that widespread attitude changes might be taking place – 'you can never be sure what goes on behind locked doors,' says Jackson. 'But some have been very enthusiastic about making the investments needed, and they seem to expect that Toyota will make a lot of demands, particularly about quality. The ones that I've

seen are all getting very much caught up in the process.'

The 1,850 unsuccessful would-be suppliers are being encouraged not to think they are permanently excluded. 'We've had lots of replies to our 'Dear John' letters at least thanking us for fairness and thoroughness of the selection process,' says Robinson. Adds Jackson: 'Those who failed have still got to be treated with respect. It is totally wrong for many of them to think we might have been saying they're not up to scratch – inherently within these organisations there is a lot of capability.'

Nor should they think they are excluded from Toyota business for good, he stresses. A widespread belief that Japanese vehicle companies form links for life with suppliers on a single-sourcing basing is wholly erroneous, he declares.

As for long-term relationships, they required continually to be earned, Jackson stresses.

Throughout, Jackson emphasises Toyota's need for partnership with suppliers rather than the adversarial relationship between vehicle makers and their suppliers so common in Europe.

To that end, Toyota has set up technology 'help' teams. 'If a supplier has difficulty understanding what we want, or how to go about it, we really want to go out and explain our production systems to them. That might sound patronising but it's not intended to be . . . the idea really is to give assistance rather than check on what's been done.'

At a personal level, Jackson and Robinson acknowledge some – not severe – culture shock. Within the European industry, says Jackson, he was used to instant decisions, involving little detail. 'It was 10 minutes to make the decision, 10 to implement it and three months to correct it. In Toyota there's three months' discussions, 10 minutes to approve it and no time correcting it.'

There is, he says, a simple way to adjust – 'you just hang your ego on the coathook with your coat.'

Section Nine
Study guidance

Aims

The aims of this concluding section of the book are as follows:

- To provide guidance on further reading to enable the marketer and business student to keep abreast of economic developments.
- To provide guidance on the practical use of this book to assist the marketer and business student in their day to day work.
- To provide guidance on examination and assessment techniques.

Further reading

Economics has been described as the 'study of people in the every day business of life'. It is therefore subject to continuous and in some areas accelerating change. In order to keep a finger on the pulse of this economic change, the business student must keep abreast of events.

Change may occur in tastes, methods or technology. Equally markets may be in the process of restructuring as products and industries mature along their life-cycles. Change may also be political, as governments legislate or policies are altered, perhaps in deference to international events or even the European Parliament rather than our own. Whatever the source of these economic developments, marketers must adjust their analysis of the situation accordingly.

Fortunately most of the concepts we have dealt with in this text are constant in their business relevance. It is a grasp of such crucial concepts as utility and opportunity cost, the margin and the multiplier, which are central to an understanding of the subject and its practical application to business.

We have taken every effort to ensure the illustrative material in this book is as up to date as possible, but by definition time marches on and the currency of the statistics will fade. It is therefore important that you develop the habit of constant updating and renewal, testing out your understanding against the backcloth of unfolding events and perhaps developing and justifying a theory or two of your own to explain them.

The following sources are suggested as possibilities rather than a necessity for study. The perceptive study of economics must be selective in order to prevent information overload. It is important to develop the skill of scanning newspapers rather than reading them from cover to cover, i.e. turning the pages of a quality newspaper *each* morning and registering the article captions or headings. Only those of obvious interest to the aspects of markets, consumers or the economy that concern you need actually be read in detail. If you find after reading a paragraph that it is not of interest, then move on. On finding something relevant, summarize the information on an index card and file it under an appropriate heading.

In some organizations a designated executive is given the responsibility to perform such scanning and collate relevant items for circulation to busy executives. Scanning over an extended period of time provides an important perspective on change as events unfold, develop and eventually fade away into the background. Since newspapers are limited in space, they must constantly make judgements on what is important to include and what is not. Each story has its opportunity cost, and at the margin an article printed means a number of others left out. The changing content of the quality press is therefore a leading indicator of change in the economy, and should be blended with other marketing information and forecasts to assist the business in recognizing threats and opportunities.

Sources

1 *Quality press*
   (a) *Financial Times.*
   (b) *The Times, Guardian, Independent.*
   (c) *Sunday Times, Observer.*
   (d) Good local newspaper.
2 *Other media*
   (a) Television.
   (b) Radio 4 'Today' programme or 'PM'.
   (c) Scan listings for interesting documentaries, political interviews, in-depth current affairs.
3 *Journals/periodicals*
   (a) *The Economist.*
   (b) *Bank Review* articles.
   (c) *Social Trends* (latest edition).
   (d) Economic summaries and forecasts (ask at one of the big four retail banks).
   (e) Marketing research reprints.
4 CIM Marketing Success datasheets to complement your textbook.

Textbooks can never be as up to date as the above sources of information, despite frequent revisions. However, they do have the advantage of considered reflection across a breadth of economic developments. They bring order and structure to an otherwise confusing multitude of facts and figures. As with quality newspapers, they should again be used selectively. The business student should always turn first to the contents page or the index rather than the main text or page 1.

This text should be treated as a manual or handbook for understanding, and should not necessarily be approached in a mechanical chapter by chapter approach. Supplementary texts, as suggested below, should be read in parts as and when required. Students often benefit from reading an additional text on a given topic in order to obtain a different viewpoint or perspective, and double the chances of achieving full understanding.

You should acquire the habit of searching out information for yourself. One of the macroeconomic projects suggested that you produce an information booklet that might include a variety of texts relating to topics dealt with in this book. Online bibliographical search procedures are now available at most libraries, and can quickly and easily assist you in locating further information on the topic or coursework you are working on. Do not forget the CIM library and information service, with its 4,500 titles on marketing-related subjects. Information is the lifeblood of business organizations, but it must be accessed effectively through such a medium.

Supplementary reading

The following are traditional economic textbooks that will provide more detailed analysis, should this be required. The first seven cover equivalent level; and latest editions should be read where possible.

Brownless, C. *Economics.* Letts
Buckley, M.W. *Structure of Business.* Pitman
Harvey, D. *Modern Economics.* Macmillan
Harvey, D. *Modern Economics (Study Guide and Workbook).* Macmillan
Lipsey, R.G. and Harbury, C. *First Principles of Economics.* Weidenfeld & Nicolson
Livesey, E. *Economics.* Butterworth-Heinemann
Pass, C. *Dictionary of Economics.* Collins

The following four books are higher level:

Begg, D., Fisher S. and Dornbush, R. *Economics.* McGraw-Hill
Curwen, P. (ed), *Understanding the UK Economy.* Macmillan
Lipsey, R.G. *Positive Economics.* Weidenfeld & Nicolson.
Watkins. S.T. *Economics of the Brand.* McGraw-Hill

One objective throughout this text has been to demonstrate the relevance of economics to marketing. The microeconomic approach has adopted the marketing mix as its framework for considering the contribution of economics to successful marketing. In effect the marketing toolbox as seen in the figure overleaf has been complemented with an economics toolbox providing a necessary additional perspective. Combining these tools of analysis provides the means to address the needs of the market much more effectively than could ever be achieved individually.

Examinations and assessment

Achieving success in an economics examination is an understandable goal for all students of the subject. However, as with the driving test, a pass is only a certificate of basic competence, not a passport to trouble-free marketing. An understanding of the subject and the development of an *economic way of thinking* is much more important, and will serve you well

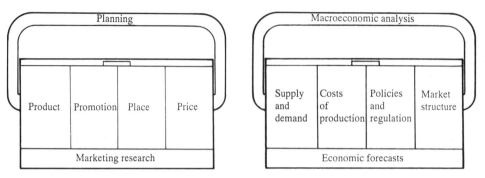

The marketing and economic toolbox

throughout your career once they are acquired. However, the test has still to be passed, and as is often the case, technique is a crucial complement to your knowledge of the subject.

The syllabus of the CIM economics for marketing course has already been redesigned with relevance and practical application in mind. This text has similarly been written with such developments in mind, although it is equally useful to business students on any course with a significant marketing component.

Studying for an examination may be likened to any business or marketing problem. One must consider the following:

1 *Objective(s)*
   (a) To pass first time.
   (b) To obtain a credit or distinction.
2 *Strategy*
   (a) Which questions to answer.
   (b) Generalize v specialize.
   (c) How to deploy your time.
3 *Information gathering*
   Preparation, reading and revision.
4 *Plan*
   Demonstrate understanding through application of knowledge.
5 *Implementation*
   (a) Efficient use of time. (b) Efficient distribution of time.
6 *Structure*
   Introduction, definition, content, conclusion.
7 *Necessary inputs*
   (a) Time.
   (b) Hard work.
   (c) Understanding.
   (d) Experience.
   (e) Brevity.
   (f) Relevance.
   (g) Professionalism.

Preparations for the examination

These begin right at the outset of the course and there are seldom any shortcuts. You must acquaint yourself with the following.

Course syllabus

This is your map, signposting the route to success. Relate to it throughout the course and ensure you cover its requirements.

Reading material

A basic course text is a crucial investment in your career prospects. Supplement it with a quality daily newspaper.

Coursework

Always undertake coursework that is set and maintain comprehensive notes you can understand and relate to the syllabus. Undertake the summary reviews included in this text and some of the projects, especially those keeping you abreast of economic developments.

Revision

This should be an ongoing process to monitor progress and understanding. Under no circumstances must it be left until the last minute. It should be planned and executed like any business task. Sufficient resources (of time) should be deployed to achieve the objective efficiently. Different people have different rhythms and capabilities in this respect, but whatever is most effective for you, do build in a margin of safety. The unexpected business trip or domestic crisis must be allowed for.

Methodology

You should always make your revision effective. It is said that we learn best 'by doing', so rather than reading your course notes or textbook (so-called passive learning), consider the following action learning techniques:

- Make your own set of notes, blending lectures, texts and other sources.
- Summarize key points on prompt cards.
- Think of at least three applications or examples for each concept or topic. If you learn something, then use it; the understanding will then be fixed in your mind.
- Produce key word plans for possible questions then compare them to the model answers. *Learn from your mistakes.*
- Ensure you know the current state of the economy and values for the main economic indices.
- Practice one or two answers under time constraints.
- Identify areas of the syllabus where topics appear fairly consistently and prepare these. Do not attempt to learn a model answer, since questions will seldom arise with the emphasis you prepared for.

- It is sometimes suggested that on the night before an examination you carefully read through your notes immediately before going to sleep. The information should then be retained in your short-term memory through the following day. Do not be tempted to burn the midnight oil, however, since you must be relaxed and alert for the examination itself.
- Always revise more topics than you are likely to need to ensure you have a reserve to meet unforeseen contingencies.

Examination conditions

Check the venue, date, number of papers, their duration, the number of questions to answer, any compulsory questions, sections etc.

Past examination papers

These provide some of the above information, together with a feel for the type and style of questions to expect. Ensure, however, that the chief examiner has not changed or the syllabus been amended in the meantime.

Examiners' reports

These are complied as a summary of examination performance for the year in question. They should be read in conjunction with questions set, and examined for any pointers or emphasis. They provide vital insight into what is considered important to achieving a successful outcome. Examiners must operate within the rules laid down by the Institute and the scope of the syllabus. Read these reports carefully, since they tell you how both to pass and fail the examination. The lack of basic examination techniques on the behalf of many candidates is a constantly recurring theme.

Model answers

These are drawn up by chief examiners and provide in-depth guidance on how to approach questions. They can be obtained from the CIM on application.

The examination itself

If you arrive ill-prepared, late and tired for a business meeting with customers, we can readily predict the likely outcome. So it is with an examination, where being well-prepared, well ahead of time and clear-headed is equally likely to pay dividends. Remember that margin of safety. Try to settle your nerves by recognizing that they are a natural human reaction to a potentially stressful situation. Nerves in moderation heighten our senses by raising the flow of adrenalin through our bodies. As such, they are healthy and should be harnessed towards positive action. Only in excess are they undesirable, and a few slow deep breaths should be taken at any sign of panic.

On the assumption that you turn up at the correct venue on the correct day and at the right time, and that you have prepared and possess an understanding of the subject matter, then the critical requirement becomes the deployment of your knowledge to its best effect. Knowing your subject is one thing; translating it into examination success is another. Certain critical skills must be developed and a number of golden rules observed.

- *Watch the time* – this is a scarce resource and must be allocated efficiently both within and between questions. Your time should be divided fairly evenly between the number of questions and in ratio to the marks awarded per element.
- Try and *apply the equimarginal principle*, and ensure that the last few minutes applied to each question yields the same return. You should not find yourself in a position whereby spending a little less time on one question (perhaps the banker you hoped would come up and know lots and lots about) and a little more on another (usually the last question or a part of a question that you don't feel confident about) could have improved your marks.
- Beware the *law of diminishing returns*, since the more you write on any one question, the more difficult it becomes to earn additional marks. Even negative returns may eventually result. As you address a question, define the terms, provide some background, and make relevant points in answer to it, so the marks will be accruing relatively quickly. If you focus effectively on the question, a pass mark should be readily achievable. However, as you continue to develop your answer further, it becomes progressively more difficult to obtain those extra marks. Indeed if you begin to digress or contradict yourself, so undermining the impression created initially, you may begin to lose marks.
- *Allocate time efficiently* within the question as well. Questions often break down into two, three or more recognizable parts. If you only focus on, say, two out of three, devoting just a line or two to the latter, then your maximum possible mark is only 66 per cent.

Read the question very carefully

This sounds obvious and is obvious, but many candidates apparently fail to do the obvious. In confronting a question paper you have some strategic and tactical choices to make:

1 Which questions do I choose?
2 In which order do I undertake them?
3 How much time do I spend on each?
4 How do I plan to approach each question?
5 What knowledge do I include, and what do I omit?

The time devoted to thought and planning, as in most business decisions, is a crucial determinant of performance. The majority of time in an examination is actually nothing more than implementation, i.e. translating your solution to the question/problem into a form the examiner can understand and judge.

In a time-constrained and stressful situation there is a powerful temptation to start writing as soon as possible, especially if those about you already appear to be writing furiously themselves. This must be resisted if you wish to produce well-considered, logically structured and relevant answers to a choice of questions that produce maximum returns:

- Read and re-read the exam paper and any instructions very carefully. Note the mark allocations!
- Screen the available choice of questions to identify those that appear 'possibles' on the basis of your knowledge, interest and initial grasp of what is required.
- Focus on each 'possible' question and identify the *key* words. *What is the main subject of the question?* A question might, for example, mention economies of scale but the main focus is market structure. *What is the question asking you do to?* Compare, contrast, discuss, suggest, evaluate – all these words will require a different approach, using the knowledge at your

command. *Are there any special instructions?* 'Choose two of the following', 'using diagrams', and 'briefly mention', for example, are instructions that should be followed.

- Consider whether you grasp the meaning of the question and have sufficient knowledge to address all its parts.
- Select your questions in rank order of ability to answer them fully and effectively, not on the amount you can write supplementary to them.
- Remember the importance of first impressions, and do your best question first and your second best last.
- For each question chosen prepare a *brief* trigger word plan, using one word if possible to summarize each idea for incorporation into the answer. Order the points to form a logical structure. A plan is important to achieving structure and ensuring you don't omit ideas you thought of initially when you come to the point for their inclusion.
- Stick to the question posed. There is a great temptation, when you have done some revision, to demonstrate your knowledge irrespective of the fact that the relevant question has not come up on the paper. Candidates often have an uncanny ability to introduce inappropriate diagrams and analysis in the most unlikely places. This is not a productive tactic, however, and should be avoided. So:

1 Don't manipulate a question into one you hoped would come up but didn't.
2 Do relate what you write to the actual question posed, and keep referring back to it.
3 Don't hope to spot actual questions, so be prepared to be flexible and adapt your knowledge to the situation, just as you would do in business.
4 Avoid the 'shot blast' approach of writing down all and everything you can think of that might have some remote connection to the question on the assumption that some of it will be right. The examiner is familiar with this approach and will penalize the tactic.
5 Be relevant, focus on the question and don't waffle because you do not have time.
6 Structure your answers.

An essay should have a definite structure

First comes the *introduction*, which provides the setting or context of the question. It should define the subject of the question and the main terms used. It should provide relevant data or statistics if required. It should signpost the structure of the essay and the approach to be taken.

A *centre section* addresses all parts and requirements of the question in a logical reasoned style and is well related to it.

Summary and conclusions should be balanced and considered, following logically from the points previously made. They should be judged in reference to the requirements laid down in the question.

If you are asked to provide a brief report, then the format will differ from the essay, being more businesslike in preparation and presentation. It should be impersonal, clear, concise and correct; and well laid out with justifications. The format would normally include the following:

- Title page.
- Summary.
- Contents.
- Introduction.
- Findings.

- Conclusions.
- Recommendations.

Be sure and write in a clean and legible manner. Set it out clearly and break up the text. In economics examinations candidates would normally be expected to use diagrams to assist them in their explanation of economic concepts and their application. While diagrams can be extremely useful in this respect, they should only be used if:

1 They can be drawn correctly.
2 They can be labelled correctly.
3 They are relevant to the question posed.

Nothing exposes ignorance in economics so obviously as an incorrectly drawn relationship. You should understand economic diagrams *not* learn them, and only use them if you are sure they will contribute to an understanding of the question concerned.

You should also seek to introduce examples and realism into your answers. These should enhance and illustrate the substantive points you wish to make and not be a substitute for them. You should use statistics, evidence, reasoning and references to justify your arguments. Economics is a positive science with testable theories where stating 'I believe' something to be the case is simply not sufficient. Questions posed in examination papers increasingly require candidates to demonstrate their knowledge through application rather than merely regurgitating theory.

An examination is required to judge that you have attained the standards set by the Institute or Examination Board. Examiners are not your opponents but are there to help guarantee standards of competence and quality in your chosen profession. They will not want you to fail, so make their task easier by meeting the standard set first time. You should approach the examination as you would any demanding business situation, with professionalism. The examination signifies the culmination of a year or more of hard work, and you should ensure your preparations and performance accurately convey your understanding of the subject and a capacity for logical exposition. The rules below provide a final tongue in cheek summary of the many serious points made above.

HOW TO FAIL YOUR EXAMS: 22 GOLDEN RULES

1 **Play it by ear.** No need to plan for an examination.
2 **Don't revise.** If you don't know it, revision is a waste of time. If you do know it, why bother with revision?
3 **Aim to just pass.** No wasted effort.
4 **Don't learn exam technique.** Exams are bad enough without learning technique as well!
5 **Do not anticipate questions.** You may be wrong and have just wasted time.
6 **Don't read previous papers or examiners' reports.** It is just not cool.
7 **Just do the first five questions.** They're all as bad anyway.
8 **Don't worry about the actual question.** It's more interesting to write what you want, and showing the examiner you know the subject is what it is all about.
9 **Ignore the instructions.** They only put you off.
10 **Don't check the time.** You could write a few more words instead.

11 **Never check answers**. There will only be a few minor errors.
12 **Always start with an introduction and end with a summary**. That way you can forget about the middle.
13 **Never write a report**. That will only prevent you following rule 14.
14 **If in doubt, waffle**. The examiner will probably think you know what you're talking about.
15 **Write illegibly, especially the words that really matter**. The examiner will give you the benefit of the doubt.
16 **Do not structure multi-part answers**. Let the examiner guess which part belongs where. It's his job after all.
17 **Do the second part of a two part paper first**. It shows initiative, makes you stand out from the crowd.
18 **Arrive late and leave early**. It impresses one's friends, and what's a few minutes anyway?
19 **Be disorganized**. You can always get a pen from the invigilator.
20 **Have a little drink just before the exam**. It helps you relax, and one must not be over-stressed.
21 **Don't bother with question numbers**. It will be obvious which question you are answering.
22 **Include a note to the examiner wishing him or her a Happy Christmas and to explain how pressured you have been**. Examiners are human, and a bit of flattery never goes amiss.

Acknowledgements to David Pearson

Issue 2, *Marketing Success, Hints & Tips/2.*

Appendix 1
Foundation exercise

Indices	A Start of course	End of course	End of 6 months	End of 1 year	Justification
1 Growth of GDP					
2 Unemployment rate (%) Unemployment total Vacancies (000s)					
3 Retail price index (%) Average earnings (%) Interest rate (%)					
4 Balance of trade Current balance Exchange rate ($) Reserves (£m)					
5 Money Mo PSBR Productivity rate Number of strikes					
6 Tax as % of GDP Govt spendings = % GDP					

Recommendations

1 Short term

2 Medium term

Index